Palgrave Studies in Economic History

Series Editor
Kent Deng, London School of Economics, London, UK

Palgrave Studies in Economic History is designed to illuminate and enrich our understanding of economies and economic phenomena of the past. The series covers a vast range of topics including financial history, labour history, development economics, commercialisation, urbanisation, industrialisation, modernisation, globalisation, and changes in world economic orders.

Orsi Husz

Bankminded

Banks as Intimate Agents of Everyday Life in Welfare State Sweden

Orsi Husz
Department of History of Science
and Ideas
Uppsala University
Uppsala, Sweden

ISSN 2662-6497   ISSN 2662-6500 (electronic)
Palgrave Studies in Economic History
ISBN 978-3-031-77652-6   ISBN 978-3-031-77653-3 (eBook)
https://doi.org/10.1007/978-3-031-77653-3

This work was supported by Riksbankens Jubileumsfond

© The Editor(s) (if applicable) and The Author(s) 2025. This book is an open access publication.

Open Access This book is licensed under the terms of the Creative Commons Attribution 4.0 International License (http://creativecommons.org/licenses/by/4.0/), which permits use, sharing, adaptation, distribution and reproduction in any medium or format, as long as you give appropriate credit to the original author(s) and the source, provide a link to the Creative Commons license and indicate if changes were made.
The images or other third party material in this book are included in the book's Creative Commons license, unless indicated otherwise in a credit line to the material. If material is not included in the book's Creative Commons license and your intended use is not permitted by statutory regulation or exceeds the permitted use, you will need to obtain permission directly from the copyright holder.
The use of general descriptive names, registered names, trademarks, service marks, etc. in this publication does not imply, even in the absence of a specific statement, that such names are exempt from the relevant protective laws and regulations and therefore free for general use.
The publisher, the authors and the editors are safe to assume that the advice and information in this book are believed to be true and accurate at the date of publication. Neither the publisher nor the authors or the editors give a warranty, expressed or implied, with respect to the material contained herein or for any errors or omissions that may have been made. The publisher remains neutral with regard to jurisdictional claims in published maps and institutional affiliations.

Cover illustration: The Swedish board game Finans (Finance) by Alga, 1950s. Used with the permission of Alga/Brio

This Palgrave Macmillan imprint is published by the registered company Springer Nature Switzerland AG
The registered company address is: Gewerbestrasse 11, 6330 Cham, Switzerland

If disposing of this product, please recycle the paper.

Acknowledgements

Writing a book is an academic journey. It takes a long time, requires the support of others, has both unexpected and planned stops, and often leads to a destination somewhat different than the one originally envisaged. I set out with the idea for this book for almost eight years ago at the Department of Economic History at Uppsala University, among business historians and historians of finance. Several research projects and a pandemic later I completed the book at the Department of History of Science and Ideas (also at Uppsala), among historians of culture, technology, science and political thought. Along the way I encountered economic sociologists and economic anthropologists, media historians and economic geographers at conferences, workshops and seminars, and while working on edited volumes. Although the culture of economic life has always been my main interest as a historian, navigating between different academic traditions has enriched my thinking and shaped my work on this book. I have learned a great deal from discussing ideas and drafts with these colleagues, and have tried to combine insights from different disciplines.

It would be an impossible task to list all the names, but I am particularly indebted to a number of groups and individuals. Jenny Andersson, Frans Lundgren and Nikolas Glover have read the entire manuscript, or large parts of it, and gave me most valuable feedback. I am immensely grateful for their generosity and help. Klara Arnberg, Oskar Broberg, David Larsson Heidenblad, Elin Åström Rudberg and Helena Bergman have all read and commented on key chapters—often on short notice—during the hectic last few months when I was finishing the manuscript. Thank you all for your wise advice and support!

In parallel with my work on the studies that make up this book, I have worked on other research projects with Klara Arnberg, Nikolas Glover, David Larsson Heidenblad and Elin Åström Rudberg, and am about to start a joint project with Oskar Broberg. I have learnt a lot, and these collaborations have both developed and challenged my ideas, making me a better historian and better equipped to complete this book. Thank you, you are the best of colleagues and friends!

For the last four years I have been part of the Neoliberalism in the Nordics research programme, an international project group led by Jenny Andersson. Thank you, Jenny, for inviting me to participate, and thank you to all my excellent colleagues, Niklas Olsen, Klaus Petersen, Jeppe Nevers, Johan Strang, Chris Howell, Nikolas Glover, David Larsson Heidenblad, Elin Åström Rudberg, Erik Bengtsson, Cecilie Bjerre, Urban Lundberg and other participants in the programme's workshops, for broadening my views and deepening my insights into the Nordics as well as the political, economic and social changes of the late twentieth century.

I would like to thank my former economic historian colleagues—all of them, but especially Lars Fälting, Nikolas Glover, Ylva Hasselberg, Fredrik Sandgren, Tom Petersson, Ingemar Petersson and the late Mats Morell, for their help at an earlier stage of my work on this book. Thanks are also due to my wonderful current colleagues at the Department of History of Science and Ideas for the uniquely inspiring and welcoming research environment there.

Kungliga biblioteket (KB, the Swedish National Library) has been an important informal academic milieu for me for years. It has offered effortless but exciting transdisciplinary conversations and a network of colleagues from different universities and departments. Special thanks to Per Lundin for our discussions about history, research and academic life over the years.

There have also been some important international stops along the way. I am grateful to international colleagues for inviting me to give talks and participate in specialised workshops. Sabine Effosse convened a series of workshops on consumer credit, finance and women which were most inspiring; Sabine was also my host during a research stay in Paris. Jeanne Lazarus, with colleagues Joe Deville, José Ossandón and Mariana Luzzi, organised an important series of mini-conferences at

SASE on *Domesticating financial economies*, and Zsuzsanna Vargha and Léna Pellandini-Simányi put together a workshop and edited a special issue on *Debt trails*. Alicia Yates brought together a group of historians working on issues of *Intimacy and economic life*—raising new questions and opening up new perspectives. In these and other contexts, I have also benefited from discussions with Mary Poovey, Liz McFall, Turo-Kimmo Lehtonen, Akos Rona-Tas, Jan Logemann, Susana Martinez Rodriguez, Bernardo Batiz-Lazo, Maria Rosaria de la Rosa, Andrew Popp, and more recently, Amy Edwards and James Taylor. Thanks also to Craig Robertson for a long and inspiring conversation about the history of identity documents in Boston in 2018.

The Centre for Business History (Centrum för Näringslivshistoria) in Stockholm, which houses many of the business archives I have used in this and other projects, has always been a welcoming place. Their helpful archivists have facilitated my work with the source material; I am especially grateful to Jessica Wahlén for her help with the images in this book.

I would also like to thank Gunilla Cronholm, Jan Kuuse and Kent Olsson for sharing their memories of the 1970s with me.

Thanks also go to Judith Rinker Öhman for her excellent last-minute help with the English language editing and to my patient and competent commissioning editor Ellie Duncan.

I have received generous financial support from Riksbankens Jubileumsfond (grant SAB17-0166) for my work on this book. One chapter was written as part of another RJ-funded research project, the Neoliberalism in the Nordics programme (grant M19-0231), and another chapter is the result of a research project funded by the Swedish Research Council (grant 2017-01342). The book's publication has been made possible by substantial funding from Riksbankens Jubileumsfond, as well as contributions from Karinfonden and Sten Lindroths fond.

My good friend, Helena Bergman, and our endless conversations during our weekend walks and breakfasts kept my spirits up when I despaired that this book project might never be finished. And I could not have completed this book without the encouragement and unwavering support in matters both large and small that I have received from my companion in life, András Simon.

Praise for *Bankminded*

"*Bankminded* is one of those rare scholarly accomplishments that opens up an entirely new perspective on what it took to transform an important financial institution into something closer to a vital social infrastructure. In this book, Husz unravels how exactly 'the banking mindset' took hold of everyday life, both domesticating finance and financing domestication."
— Liz McFall, *Professor in the Sociology of Markets, University of Edinburgh*

"Financial institutions are a crucial aspect of modern life. Engagingly written and meticulously researched, *Bankminded* illuminates how banks and banking became integral facets of everyday life and consumption in Sweden. Challenging overly simplistic narratives of recent neoliberal financialization, Husz demonstrates the longer history and complex cultural negotiations behind the rise of checking accounts, credit cards and bank IDs since the 1950s. The Swedish case offers a surprising story of early mass-banking involving not only banks and card companies, but also unions, consumer cooperatives and the Swedish welfare state. Still, the insights on banking practices and consumer identities gained from Husz' empirically rich and theoretically sophisticated account transcend national history. *Bankminded* will be essential reading for scholars on modern banking and financial history internationally."
—Jan Logemann, *Ass. Prof. in Economic History, Göttingen*

"As a preeminent scholar on the financialization of everyday life, Orsi Husz offers a masterful history of how banks became essential members of Swedish households. She intricately links the 'bankification' of the Swedes to the development of the welfare state, shedding light on profound shifts in cultural norms around class, gender, money, credit, and identification technologies since the 1950s. With remarkable depth, Husz reveals how banking strategies have woven themselves into Sweden's economic, social, and political fabric, reshaping the nation's landscape in the latter half of the 20th century."

—Jeanne Lazarus, *Research Director CNRS, SciencePo, Paris*

"In her compelling new book, historian Orsi Husz explores the process of the 'bankification' of everyday life in one nation: Sweden, typically held as an exemplar of later twentieth-century welfarism and social democracy. Conceptually original, analytically sharp, and creatively researched, Husz's study follows multiple threads to reveal the far-reaching but almost unnoticed penetration of banks and 'bankmindedness' into ordinary daily life, unpicking 'the history of the marketisation of domestic money and the domestication of market money.' It is a tale of almost queasy 'unrequested intimacy'. Across five principal chapters, Husz traces the changes wrought across the dimensions of class, gender, morality, ideology, and identity.

Husz shows just how early this process began; not in the 1980s and 1990s, but in the 1950s and 1960s. This finding upends the literature and provides historians, sociologists, anthropologists new concepts, a new language, and a new set of questions for exploring how these processes unfolded elsewhere. Other countries that have undergone similar processes deserve studies as rich as this one. *Bankminded* will, I am sure, open powerful and fruitful new vistas in the study of everyday or intimate economic lives."

—Andrew Popp, *Professor of History, Copenhagen Business School*

Contents

1	The Bankification of Everyday Life: Introduction	1
2	Welcome to the Banking Age: Redefining the Social Class of Money	29
3	Making Finance Familiar: Gender and the Domestication of Banks	61
4	Launching the Credit Card: New Moralities of Credit and Payment	89
5	Rewriting the History and Future of Consumer Credit: Ideological Change as a Marketing Strategy	125
6	The Financialisation of Identity	165
7	Conclusion	197
Notes		209
Bibliography		267
Index		289

About the Author

Orsi Husz is a Professor of the History of Science and Ideas at Uppsala University, Sweden.

Her works have explored areas of the cultural history of everyday economic life in the twentieth century such as mass consumer culture, popular investment, consumer credit, household budgets, use of banking services and financial identification practices. Her recent publications include 'The Birth of the Finance Consumer: Feminists, Bankers and the Re-Gendering of Finance in Mid-Twentieth-Century Sweden', *Contemporary European History* and 'Wage Earners, Taxpayers or Everyman Capitalists? The Making of a Mutual Fund Culture in Sweden' (with D. Larsson Heidenblad and E. Åström Rudberg), in *Nordic Neoliberalisms*, ed. by J. Andersson and C. Howell (2025).

Abbreviations

AB	Aktiebolag, Joint Stock Company
ABF	Arbetarnas Bildningsförbund, the Workers' Educational Association
ANT	Actor-Network Theory
ATM	Automated Teller Machine, Cash Dispenser
CEO	Chief Executive Officer
CFN	Centrum för Näringslivshistoria, Centre for Business History
DIY	Do-It-Yourself (shop)
Eurofinas	The European Federation of Finance House Associations
FBA	Fredrika Bremer Association
ISO	International Organisation for Standardisation
KF	Kooperativa Förbundet, the Consumer Cooperative Union
LO	Landsorganisationen, the Swedish Trade Union Confederation
NK	Nordiska Kompaniet (a large department store in Stockholm, founded in 1902)
PR	Public Relations
SAF	Svenska Arbetsgivareföreningen, Swedish Employers' Confederation
SAP	Sveriges Socialdemokratiska Arbetareparti, the Swedish Social Democratic Workers' Party
SEB	Skandinaviska Enskilda Banken
SIBOL	Samarbete för Integrerat Betalningssystem Online, Cooperation for an Integrated Online Payment System
SIFO	Svenska Institutet för Opinionsundersökningar, Swedish Institute for Opinion Research
SNS	Studieförbundet Näringsliv och Samhälle, the Centre for Business and Policy Studies

SOU	Statens Offentliga Utredningar, Swedish Government Official Reports
STS	Science, Technology and Society Studies
UC	Upplysningscentralen

List of Figures

Fig. 2.1	Bank bus by Skandinaviska Banken, *Din Bank*, 1–2 (1956)	35
Fig. 2.2	Drive-in bank in Stockholm, around 1960	36
Fig. 2.3	Number of cheque accounts for wages and salaries, 1956–1970	38
Fig. 2.4	Photograph used for advertising cheque accounts for wages at Sundsvallsbanken, late 1960s	46
Fig. 3.1	'It's your responsibility', advert for the child benefit account at Handelsbanken, *Svenska Dagbladet*, 27 January 1948	65
Fig. 3.2	Fashion show in the bank at the conference Mrs World's Economic Affairs, *Din Bank*, 3 (1956)	70
Fig. 3.3	Budget consultant Gunnel Petre at a Golden Everyday event, *Arbetet*, 14 October 1965	80
Fig. 4.1	Outstanding credit card debt with Swedish card companies 1968–1978 (SEK, millions)	98
Fig. 4.2	'Köpkort inspires confidence, the Köpkort card boosts your confidence', advertising leaflet, early 1960s	104
Fig. 4.3	Mentions of the words *kreditkort* (credit card); *kontokort* (account card); and *köpkort* (purchase card) in four major Swedish newspapers, 1955–2016	115
Fig. 4.4	'Christmas on credit', front page illustration in *Köpmannen*, 18 December 1978	118

Fig. 4.5	'In the shadow of the Savings Banks' Card, all the other cards become small', full-page advertisement for the savings banks' combined credit and ATM card, *Köpmannen*, 21 April 1980	120
Fig. 5.1	'He bet on new cards—got 200 million in the pot', portrait of Erik Elinder in *Veckans affärer*, 27 January 1977	131
Fig. 5.2	Illustration for theme section 'Leva på lån' ('Living on credit') in the daily newspaper *Svenska Dagbladet*, 14 August 1979	162
Fig. 6.1	Posters announcing that the bank now issues identity cards, 1963, Uplands bank, Uppsala	172
Fig. 6.2	Cheque fraud reported to the police, 1960–1974	176
Fig. 6.3	The new plastic bank ID card as depicted in the commercial banks' information campaign, *Dagens Nyheter*, 13 November 1972	181
Fig. 6.4	'Wherever we are! Cheque + ID card = Money', poster by Kreditbanken, early 1970s	182
Fig. 6.5	The SIBOL system for online payments, 1971	189

List of Tables

Table 4.1	Credit card accounts in Sweden, 1971–1979	97
Table 4.2	European bank credit cards, 1968	100
Table 4.3	The card companies Köpkort and InterConto compared	113
Table 6.1	Production of cards by AB ID-kort (ID Card Ltd), thousands	180

CHAPTER 1

The Bankification of Everyday Life: Introduction

Financial services and products are everywhere to be found. In most societies today, it is nearly impossible to manage daily life without a bank account. Financial institutions are involved in many aspects of life and in the allocation of almost every penny we earn, spend, borrow, invest or transfer to one another. In Sweden, a digital *BankID*, issued by a consortium of banks, is necessary for most online actions, including non-financial ones. Whether we like it or not, we have a close everyday relationship with our banks, so close and so banal that few of us reflect on it. This unrequested intimacy lies 'beneath the horizon of cultural visibility', to borrow an expression from the literary scholar and historian of financial life Mary Poovey.[1] The closeness and vulnerability it entails are only visible when the system fails to work. How this intimate relationship developed in the first place—the ideas, attitudes, habits and moralities it challenged and reshaped, the new forms of knowledge and language it gave rise to and the everyday infrastructure it brought about—is the topic of this book.

Bankminded tells the story of how banks and banking services became an integral part of people's daily lives. It unpacks the history of the marketisation of domestic money and the domestication of market money. The setting is post-war Sweden, a welfare state mainly described as de-commodifying and de-marketising many economic aspects of social and private life. Pensions to ensure financial security in old age, compensation for higher costs and lost income for parents with young children, savings and loans for education: all examples of policies that made private saving and borrowing in the market less necessary. Still, at the same time and sometimes interconnected with the burgeoning social security system, Swedes were early to become users of the financial services and products available in an emerging consumer finance market. Financial habits changed, as did people's relationship with financial institutions. How did it happen?

In 1968, a report from the marketing department of one of Sweden's largest commercial banks, Handelsbanken, concluded that recently introduced financial services, such as cheque accounts for wages, credit cards, investment funds, payment services and diversified loans, had ushered in a new era and created a new 'intimate' connection to customers: 'The fact that the bank is involved in the allocation of the consumer's every penny, and that it provides advice on investment decisions, or on buying and rebuilding a home, etc., undeniably generates a very intimate relationship between bank and customer'.[2] This had not been the case only a decade earlier. As the century progressed, the 'intimate relationship' of everyday finance grew ever closer.

Bankminded explores the challenges this transition entailed in 1960s and 1970s Sweden. It observes several cultural boundaries that had to be crossed to naturalise the new role of financial institutions like banks and credit card companies. This is a story about *class*, and how workers in social democratic Sweden started using cheque accounts in commercial banks, something that had been open to only the most privileged before. It is a story about *gender*, and why banks and finance were redefined in a more 'feminine', domestic frame. It is about *morality* and the attempts to destigmatise consumer credit when credit cards were introduced, and how moralities of debt were rearranged in everyday practice. It is an account of how *ideologies* were negotiated along the way, and how neoliberal ideas about consumers and credit could permeate everyday financial practices in a Nordic welfare regime, which was often thought of as immune to such ideas. And, lastly, it is a story about the new financialised *identities* that were reinforced by the practical management of identity documents and transactional data in society. Although these themes are interconnected, each of them will be the topic of a separate chapter.

A common thread running through all the chapters is financial know-how, the mundane knowledge that ordinary people should learn about money—and the stuff they were supposed to 'unlearn'—and from whom. Bankers reckoned that people needed to develop a new mindset, and become more 'bankminded'.³ In the late 1950s and 1960s, the word bankminded—usually uttered in English rather than *banksinnad*, its Swedish equivalent—was a favoured expression among bank officials who were working with a new and quickly broadening clientele. And that is exactly what this book examines: how were ordinary Swedes made more bankminded, and what did this mean?

My focus is on key financial aspects of everyday life in Sweden, a rich country with an economy that was not as badly affected by the Second World War as was the case in other European countries. Social democratic governments were in power from 1932 to 2006, except for centre-conservative and conservative interludes from 1976 to 1982 and 1991 to 1994. My period of study is from the late 1950s to the early 1980s, an era of general prosperity, neutrality and welfare politics, with an emphasis on 'strong society' implemented by a growing public sector, but without the nationalisation of private businesses. Nevertheless, the banking world was worried about nationalisation, as was evident in the political debates about the concentration of power in the economy in the late 1960s and about economic democracy in the 1970s. The conventional narrative about the mixed economy of post-war Sweden includes a strictly regulated financial market, and a radical shift in the mid-1980s with financial deregulation followed by a globalisation of the financial sector and a broader marketisation of the welfare services in subsequent decades.

Bankminded argues that even before the 1980s there was a shift at the micro-level, in ordinary people's financial practices. A personal financial turn, this shift must be understood not merely as a political-economic reorientation or a change in the history of the financial services industry, but also as a profound sociocultural transformation. Starting in the late 1950s, every household in Sweden (and eventually in most of the Western world) began handling its money through formal financial institutions, mostly banks. This included everything from daily purchases and payments to loans, savings and investments. Another claim is that, contrary to contemporaneous statements, the welfare state with all its financial regulations was a 'condition of possibility' for this change to occur relatively early in Sweden.⁴

How, then, was people's 'intimate relationship' with banks established? How did financial institutions and the public resolve cultural problems of class, gender, moral values, ideology and identity that this transition posed? The question is not merely how ordinary households were financialised, or rather bankified, but also how banking and financial services were domesticated.

Bankminded is interested in the point at which cultural history and financial history intersect. By writing banking and personal finance into the cultural and social history of the Swedish welfare state it becomes plain that, just as the social engineering endeavours of the post-war welfare society aimed to reshape the lives of Swedish families, banks and financial institutions also set about reshaping people's financial habits and mindsets. By lowering the gaze and looking at ordinary people's money rather than high finance and the broad sweep of economy, I offer a new cultural history of finance and also, crucially, a new chronology of the profound financial changes of the late twentieth century, typically interpreted by economic historians as institutional changes in the aftermath of the deregulation of financial markets in the late 1980s. I propose the concept 'bankification of everyday life' as an overarching term to describe a major cultural-economic change that occurred between the late 1950s and early 1980s in Sweden and which resulted in a new mindset and new mundane financial practices reinforcing the constant presence of banking services in ordinary people's lives.

FINANCIALISATION AND BANKIFICATION OF EVERYDAY LIFE

One way to make sense of the new role of banking in society is to see it in relation to another—interconnected—process, the financialisation of daily life. Randy Martin's 2002 book with the same title opened up a rich vein in the wider studies of financialisation. The penetration of a new financial logic into the lives of ordinary people has since attracted considerable scholarly interest, creating a new sub-field, albeit often focused on Anglo-American settings.[5]

The general term 'financialisation' has been used by social scientists to describe how global financial markets, financial institutions, financial practices and financial thinking increasingly came to dominate society, business and politics, and by extension also everyday life. According to the standard epochal narrative in the literature, the process of financialisation unfolded in the late 1970s and gained strength in the 1980s and 1990s. Financialisation has been interpreted as an integral part of the greater market orientation of society, almost invariably paired with the neoliberal turn in the Western world. While the overall concept of financialisation has been criticised for becoming a buzzword, its everyday life angle nevertheless retains considerable analytical potential, especially for empirically based cultural-historical studies of economic life.[6]

The financialisation of everyday life consists of several overlapping mechanisms: first, financial businesses capitalising on more and more aspects of everyday life; second, households' money increasingly being drawn into extended financial markets, and thus bearing financial risks; and third, on a discursive level, more and more aspects of everyday life being described in financial terms. The financialisation of everyday life is often exemplified by the popularisation of investing in stocks, investment choices for pension funds, or the increase in and normalisation of both consumer credit and housing mortgages in recent decades. Financialisation, the research claims, bred new thinking about the money of the household. Buying a home became an investment, and consumer credit was understood as simply an allocation of the family's financial assets, including future income.[7] This scholarship builds on theories of governmentality and performativity, inspired by Foucauldian and STS (Science, Technology and Society) studies of finance, and posits that new financial products and services created a novel mindset and self-understanding; in effect, new financial subjectivities. Scholars have emphasised, for example, the conduct-shaping effects of credit scores and how the situation of people managing their own creditworthiness creates self-surveilling subjects. Another example is how the choices available for pension fund investments individualise responsibility and turn people into calculating investors.[8] There is also scholarship on educational ventures that accompanied the launch of new financial services and products. A novel body of knowledge, a new language used to mediate it and the way people were addressed and asked to think like capitalists reinforced their new financial identities.[9]

There are some problems with the theory of everyday financialisation, however. One is its favoured chronology, which presupposes a causal linearity between the financialisation of the global economy, seen as the initial stage, and the financialisation of everyday life as a resulting effect. But the changes in how ordinary people thought about and handled their money were more deep-rooted and multifaceted than the financialisation literature suggests. As this book will show for Sweden, the financial transformation that scholars documented in the 1980s and 1990s was preceded and facilitated by changes at the micro- and meso-levels—and these were practical, cultural and moral changes rather than structural or political.

The financialisation of everyday life is predicated on bankification; or, as French economic sociologists call it, the 'bancarisation' of society, a concept rarely used in scholarship in English.[10] But the economic sociologist Jeanne Lazarus warns us not to confuse financialisation with bancarisation, as the latter simply means that households' money is increasingly incorporated into the banking system and that basically all households or individuals have a bank account. France, for example, Lazarus claims, became a 'bancarised' society already in the late 1960s and early 1970s, but it would be decades before it was financialised.[11]

In this book, I propose a new term, bankification, to underscore a new analytical focus on how banks made inroads into the spheres of mundane life, as opposed to simply saying that an increasing number of people had a bank connection. Bankification of everyday life thus emphasises the cultural rather than the economic and political aspects of the change. Nevertheless, I agree that the process is to be distinguished—at least analytically—from financialisation, even when both speak to everyday life, and even though bankification is necessary for a financialised everyday life. In Sweden, as in France, bankification began before financialisation, while in some societies, for example in post-communist countries, the two processes were closely intertwined.

The Swedish population was incorporated into the banking system early by international standards, even earlier than the French. By this I do not mean that many Swedish families had *savings accounts* already in the late nineteenth and early twentieth centuries, which is however important as a pre-history of the mid-late twentieth century's bankification.[12] Rather, I argue that Sweden became a highly bankified society in the 1960s and 1970s, when almost all the money people owned, earned or borrowed, and an increasing part of what they spent—*not only their savings*—was channelled through formal financial institutions. But where Lazarus speaks of a definancialised 'bancarisation' in France, I argue for a prefinancialised bankification in Sweden, at least regarding the mindset, moral reorganisation and micro-infrastructures of personal finance. Not all new financial products introduced in the 1960s and 1970s involved risk, but some did, and the marketing of the new banking services used a new vocabulary of domestic finance as part of an extended market. It also implied, and often explicitly advocated, a new type of financial thinking. The new financial products launched in the late 1950s and early 1960s, such as credit cards, cheque accounts for wages and mutual fund accounts, were vehicles of an emerging new morality of credit and investment, and paved the way for later changes in terms of a financialised everyday life.

The two processes were more simultaneous in Britain, where the banks' turn to a mass public was delayed until the late 1970s (see further in Chapter 2) and coincided with a neoliberal shift in government and with what is typically regarded as the era of financialisation.[13] In Eastern Europe, commercial retail banking was new after 1989, introducing at the same time both simple current accounts for salaries and advanced investment and credit products.[14] While bankification is possible without financialisation (as is claimed in the French case), it is difficult to imagine the financialisation of everyday life without bankification. The fact that the two processes happened more simultaneously in some places, such as Britain and (for other reasons) post-socialist Eastern Europe, obscures the view and makes it difficult to distinguish between the two.

This leads to another problem with the financialisation of daily life approach, which is the field's Anglo-American bias. The financialisation of everyday life played out differently depending on the national and cultural setting. Sweden is an interesting case, rarely discussed in the international literature. The dominant historical narrative about post-war Sweden is one of the financial regulations, a statist protective consumer policy and ingrained hostile attitudes towards consumer credit. The leftist popular movements of the late 1960s and 1970s, with their criticism of consumerism, commercialism and especially financial capitalism, are also an organic part of this mainstream narrative.[15] But at the same time Sweden is described as an early adopter of new computer and information technologies as well as financial technologies, and had a surprisingly high rate of consumer credit already in the early 1960s—not compared to the United States, perhaps, but certainly in a European context.[16] The bankification approach helps to reconcile these two stories.

Domestication and Relational Work

Accounts of the financialisation of everyday life tend to omit an important factor: financial products, whether per se or with normative messages about how they should be used, are rarely enough to change how people think. What was needed for a new financial mindset to take hold was an array of adjustments, negotiations and anchoring effects that reshaped people's attitudes and practices, and often reframed the idea of personal finance itself as well as financial devices.

'It takes time to adjust the human soul to the most drastic novelties', Sven Å. Cason, the CEO of a Swedish credit card company, commented in 1968, rather poetically, about his company's marketing strategies, while also pointing out that the Swedish context was different from the American one and required other interpretations of the use of credit.[17] A few years later Erik Elinder, the owner of another card company, commissioned surveys on how to change people's 'micro-thinking' about consumer credit. With a lifetime of professional experience in advertising, he complained in a dramatic tone about the 'biggest psychological conundrum' in his entire career: 'It's beyond my comprehension that you can stand on street corners and hand out money without anyone wanting to take it. ... I find myself banging my head against stone walls wherever I turn'.[18] He meant that despite high inflation, considerable advertising efforts, rather favourable offers and what he saw as obvious economic benefits for households, the Swedish public were reluctant to use credit cards. Of course, Cason, Elinder and their colleagues had their strategies. The companies engaged in intricate marketing work to change consumers' mindsets, attitudes, values and practices, as well as the cultural image of cheques, credit cards and investment accounts. And not just the image. Financial products and services were in turn reshaped in the process—they were domesticated while the households were bankified.

Domestication is one of my analytical concepts in this book. It has been used by scholars of media and technology to describe the cultural practices and meaning-making by which technology is appropriated and made familiar by everyday users and becomes anchored in the mundane routines of life. In this process, people, practices, devices, technologies and the cultural meanings attached to them can be reshaped.[19] This book argues that a domestication of finance in Sweden had begun in the late 1950s—and intensified in the 1960s and 1970s—decades before the conventional chronology of financialisation. The concept of the domestication of finance has rarely been used in *historical* studies of economic life. The economic sociologists Pellandini-Simányi, Hammer and Vargha explore the domestication of finance through a study of home mortgages in post-communist Hungary. Instead of simply bringing about a new way of financial thinking among ordinary men and women and reorganising relationships as financial ones, mortgages were reinterpreted and appropriated to existing family relationships and mundane rationalities. When choosing a mortgage, advice from friends and state subsidies (familiar terrain in Eastern Europe) counted for more than banking counsel, interest rates and actual financial calculations. The important insight here is that creating financial—and bankminded—subjects is not a straightforward process of 'education' or a performative result of the workings of financial devices. It involves negotiations, an entanglement with the mundane, with family life, with specific national contexts; and it often entails, as in the Swedish case, a hybridisation of subject positions such as wage earner and bank customer.[20]

In a theoretical overview of recent research, the economic anthropologist José Ossandon and colleagues highlight a range of cultural operations—for instance educating, attaching or infrastructuring—that are used to create a relationship between households and finance. These are variations of what they call the oikonomisation of financial economies, from the Greek *oikos* for the household, the family and its property. Whether households, individuals or financial institutions, all can engage in these operations. Oikonomisation, they argue, differs from everyday financialisation because it unpacks both sides of the same process; not only how the everyday practices of the household change, but also how financial instruments are changed when used in everyday life.[21]

In my reading, oikonomisation is close to the domestication of finance, and also to my other overarching analytical concept, 'relational work', which was originally proposed by the economic sociologist Viviana Zelizer for the study of economic life. By relational work, Zelizer means the effort ordinary people put into matching and linking the things that are perceived to belong to the realm of the economy/market with what are seen as parts of other value spheres, such as love, family or intimacy. These different spheres have often been regarded by both historical actors and many social scientists as 'hostile worlds'. Instead, Zelizer argues for what she calls a 'connected lives' approach, to best understand what people do in practice—making connections between the economy and the lifeworlds built on other values. In doing so, she writes, they are 'carrying on cultural symbolic work'.[22]

My focus is on the financial institutions (banks and credit card companies) and the relational work they conducted to reshape and reinterpret financial products and practices so that they could connect more easily with ordinary families' lifeworlds. Admittedly, public relations (PR) is by definition a form of relational work, and in many ways my study explores how financial companies marketed their services to households by building what they hoped would be lasting relationships.²³ Professional PR activities, as well as marketing and active advertising, were new features in the 1950s Swedish banking world, and the banks' marketing and advertising efforts greatly intensified in subsequent decades (see Chapters 2 and 3). While banking traditionally built on highly particular relationships of trust with clients—businesses as well as individuals—the new era brought contacts with a much broader client base and required new methods. Expertise in marketing and PR were exactly the skills the financial institutions needed, and it was probably not a coincidence that for example Sven Å. Cason, the CEO of Köpkort, the bank-owned and dominant credit card company in the 1960s, had a background in marketing. The same is true of Erik Elinder, the owner and executive leader of Köpkort's main competitor, InterConto. Another leading marketing expert, Eric Lindström, who published some of the earliest books on PR in Swedish, became one of the directors of Handelsbanken, the largest commercial bank in the 1960s with a strong profile among ordinary households. Studying the material from early banking campaigns and not only the ads but also the preparations, discussions and negotiations behind marketing and PR activities reveals the problems the banks detected—for example concerning class, gender, morality, ideology and identity—and how they wanted to handle them. As for the public's relational work, in the absence of direct sources it can be studied in reactions ventilated in the general media and through the lens of how marketing experts perceived it and wanted to influence it.

Banks, Regulations and the Financial System in Sweden

Twentieth-century Swedish banking history has been written as business history and financial history rather than cultural history.²⁴ A shift in perspective therefore brings new insights. For example, regarding the post-war era, a comprehensive volume on Swedish business history claims that '[i]n sharp contrast to later periods, especially the one from the 1980s on, the financial innovations in the banking sector were also very few. Traditional depositing and lending to the public and companies was, and remained, the banks' core business during this time'.²⁵ This might be true if by financial innovation we mean, for instance, the new derivative instruments introduced in the later 1980s; however, if we lower our gaze to the simple financial products offered to ordinary people, this claim could hardly be further from the truth. In the 1960s and 1970s, a range of new financial products were widely adopted, from credit cards, ATM cards and special cheque-based salary and wage accounts to combination products for savings and loans. In fact, it was a personal finance revolution of sorts—and it happened before the 1980s.

Histories of individual commercial banking companies do discuss the turn to a broader clientele and the growth of retail banking in the 1960s, as shown for example by the strong expansion of the banks' branch networks. Savings bank histories, in turn, depict the 1960s and 1970s as decades of institutional change with the savings banks transitioning from 'savings propaganda to banking business'. The period is described as one during which words like competition (with the commercial banks), selling, marketing and customers (as opposed to savers) entered the everyday vernacular of savings banks' employees.[26] Payroll payments are mentioned in banking histories but their cultural significance is not analysed, while other things considered in this book—such as credit cards, the marketing efforts and financial products targeted at women, or the bank's role in issuing ID documents—are missing.[27]

In the 1950s, the Swedish banking system was still divided by function and target group. Commercial banks (*affärsbanker*) served the business community and were linked to it financially and by personal networks. The savings banks (*sparbanker*) and the Post Office Savings Bank (Postsparbanken) took care of ordinary people's money, or more specifically the savings of the working class and a wider middle class, turning small savers' deposits into risk-free loans for basically the same group. The commercial banks were larger and organised as joint-stock companies that could take greater risks. The savings banks were small organisations and operated as foundations without direct owners, and therefore had more difficulty borrowing and raising risk capital for investments. The Post Office Savings Bank (from 1960 the Post Office Bank, Postbanken) was owned by the state, which also owned a commercial bank, Sveriges Kreditbank, founded in 1951, an important player in the market.[28] There were also rural banks (*jordbrukskassor*), operated by organisations with the needs of the agricultural sector in mind. Each bank category was governed by its own special regulations and was tasked with certain specific obligations in the financial system.[29]

A cultural divide emerged along organisational boundary lines. The savings banks were seen as parts of their local communities as well as being under the umbrella of a strong popular movement, such as the labour movement or the consumer cooperative movement. Savings banks also had a good relationship with the blue-collar trade unions.[30] By contrast, the commercial banks were associated with 'big finance, capitalism and the concentration of power'.[31] The cultural divide outlived the legal and regulatory differences in organisational form, which were gradually lifted between the mid-1950s and late 1960s. So, in the late 1960s and throughout 1970s, the commercial banks struggled with their image when marketing basic financial products, such as household budget accounts, to a broader population. Their branch organisation, the Bankers' Association (Svenska Bankföreningen, founded in 1910), often discussed goodwill campaigns to overcome the public's reluctance to deal with commercial banks. An advertising consultant hired by the Bankers' Association in 1968 came up with the radical approach that the commercial banks should cease their joint goodwill campaigns, and preferably completely stop acting together publicly in order to 'eradicate the collective term *commercial banks*'. Only then would the plain concept of a 'bank' stand a chance of truly becoming something mundane and ordinary.[32] While this might have improved the banks' image with ordinary people, it was difficult to implement when it came to politics. Especially in their dealings with the government and the *Riksbank* (Sweden's Central Bank), commercial banks were prone to act collectively, through the Bankers' Association.

As mentioned above, the period between the 1950s and mid-1980s saw a series of governments use regulations to exert influence on the banking sector. After the Second World War, the welfare state's ambition was to direct the commercial banks' investment capital into housing (the building sector) and to large-scale energy investment rather than private industry. The government controlled the capital flow on the Swedish market through the Riksbank and channelled it into chosen socioeconomic goals. Interest rates were set centrally. Liquidity quotas (from 1952) regulated the banks' lending relative to their liquid assets, and loan caps applied, which severely restricted their ability to provide loans to industry and households alike. The powers of the Bank Inspection Board (Bankinspektionen, founded in 1907) were increased. The representatives of the private commercial banks often complained about banking regulations, but historians note that this period offered considerable stability and helped to restore public trust in banks and the financial system after the crises of the interwar period.[33]

Regulations, motivated largely by the building of a welfare state, meant that commercial banks had to acquire new deposits to be able to cater to industry's need for financing. The small deposits of the general public became increasingly attractive and the banks looked to ordinary wage earners and their families as an important new customer category, especially as wages were rising and general welfare was growing (Chapters 2 and 3).[34] In addition, the regulation of consumer credit, part of the generally protective consumer policy of the welfare state, paradoxically facilitated the spread of credit cards, which constituted a new form of consumer credit not yet included in the regulatory legislation (Chapters 4 and 5).

Banking historians often mention how the savings banks wanted to break into the commercial banks' customer segment, the corporate market, but the opposite was also true. The commercial banks hoped to attract clientele from the savings banks, and competed for the money of the many small households.[35] Although the regulations remained, the difference between these two kinds of banks was about to successively disappear, both in legislation and in practice, starting with the Savings Banks Act of 1955, which made it possible for the savings banks to offer other types of bank accounts besides savings accounts. Mergers were made easier, and the system of different rules for interest rates at different types of banks was abolished. Savings banks and commercial banks could therefore compete for the same clientele, and by 1969, all legal demarcations between credit institutions had been removed.[36]

The competition in the banking market for household deposits and corporate clients alike led to bank mergers (especially among savings banks), but also to an increase in the number of branch offices. The commercial banks considerably expanded their network of branches. While constant in the period between 1930 and 1950, the number of commercial bank branches rose from 1,000 to 1,700 between 1950 and 1971. The number of bank accounts at commercial banks increased threefold between 1945 and 1971 to 6 million (as the population grew from approximately 6.7 to 8 million).[37]

Thus, state regulation of lending and a robust welfare state intent on investing in housing infrastructure and social policy contributed, indirectly, to Sweden's early bankification and the early development of mass retail banking. Bankification, in turn, as I will show, helped popularise consumer credit, a new financial rationality and later a mass investment culture, all of which would eventually—after the policy changes and global economic transformation of the 1980s and 1990s—feed into a financialised daily life.

Explaining the Financialisation of Everyday Life in Sweden

In this book, I argue that the bankification approach helps to understand how the financialisation of everyday life in the late twentieth century was linked to the sociocultural setting of the post-war welfare state. Swedish studies of financialisation are few, and their main narrative tends to follow the international accounts: as financial markets became more internationalised, new technology made transactions quicker just as a new political-economic ideology gained momentum in the 1970s and 1980s, and Western countries started to relax the regulation of their financial markets. Deregulations in Reagan's America and Thatcher's Britain changed the rules for international flows of capital, forcing other countries to follow suit. The Swedish government long resisted, even though influential voices within the Riksbank demanded deregulation. It ultimately came in the mid-1980s when first the interest rate regulation and liquidity quotas were removed and, finally, the so-called November Revolution in 1985 lifted the loan cap so that banks could increase their lending without centrally set limits. This, along with the introduction of new financial theories, led to a profound reorganisation of the stock market with the launch of new financial derivative instruments, a boom in the housing market, and an increase in mortgages.[38]

Swedish studies of financialisation often take as their starting point the deregulation of financial markets in the mid-1980s, while the cultural-historical entanglement of the process is frequently neglected or seen as secondary. The editors of a volume specifically on the financialisation of everyday life in Sweden distinguish between two phases: first financialisation on the institutional level (starting in the 1980s) and second, a financial 'deepening' when ordinary people's lifeworlds were transformed by far greater access to finance-related products such as bank loans, credit cards, fund savings and capital insurance. This cultural deepening, they write, was further enabled by the market-engineering efforts of banks and financial institutions to foster individual responsibility and a risk-taking entrepreneurial spirit.[39] *Bankminded* lays out just how much earlier such efforts began, and shows that it is reasonable to assume in many respects that they facilitated the changes of the 1980s and 1990s.

Views on the cultural anchoring of everyday financialisation in Sweden vary in the scarce existing research, but the 1999 pension reform, which was partly based on individual investment choices, is often taken as a case in point. Alexis Stenfors, an economist, has claimed that Swedish financialisation was late, but rapid. The market turn induced by the policy changes in the 1980s quickly had an impact on the everyday level: 'The pension reform is a telling example of how risk management and financial literacy has penetrated the daily life of Swedes'.[40] He goes on to ask how such a radical turn to financialisation could be accepted without considerable popular (or political) resistance. Drawing on the work of the historians Henrik Berggren and Lars Trädgårdh, he explains it with reference to a centuries-long tradition of Swedish individualism and pragmatism, alongside a high level of general education, which he claims predated and co-existed with the collectivist ideals imbued by decades of social democratic government. Therefore, for Stenfors, instead of being a paradoxical or unlikely case Sweden is 'the ideal country for financialisation'.[41] In contrast, political scientist Claes Belfrage has argued that the Swedish pension reform might have been designed as a highly risk-privatising model by European standards but in practice it met with, if not public resistance, at least dissent and uncertainty. He suggests that in studying financialisation and the new subjectivities it creates one must also consider competing discourses, meanings and practices.[42] Nevertheless, neither Belfrage nor Stenfors has explored these competing (or reinforcing) meanings. While both authors' focus is on the period around 2000, their historicisation is simplified, one looking back at centuries of an almost mythic characterisation of Swedishness and the other implying a dichotomous picture split by a 'risk shift' between the Swedish social democratic 'people's home' (*folkhemmet*) and a new financialised, marketised society.[43]

Against these explanations, this book offers an in-depth analysis of the cultural-economic changes in the decades preceding the 1980s. The bankification of everyday life, when banks successively inserted themselves into areas such as the workplace, the family, the popular movements and the spaces of consumption, entailed a domestication of finance. An extensive micro-infrastructure of everyday finance sprung up. Education in financial matters was largely taken over by banks and other players in the financial services market. People started to learn a new way of financial thinking and also to unlearn older taken-for-granted truths. As new financial products took hold in the period from the late 1950s to the early 1980s, they were also redefined morally and ideologically. Much of this cultural change took place before the deregulations and the shift in government policy, and indeed in part as a side effect of the regulatory policies.

It could even be argued that the consolidation of the welfare state was a condition of possibility for the early Swedish bankification process. Regulatory policies drove the banks to look for new ways to attract deposits, and with the increasing incomes and the universal pension system, ordinary people had more money. The workers/wage earners became the main target for the banks interest. Various social payments had to be administered as well, which led to the launch of new diversified products, one of the earliest being the 'child benefit account' (*barnbidragskonto*, see Chapter 3). Bankification went hand in hand with an increasing focus on personal finances: informational and educational material on how to handle one's money was often produced by banks, insurance companies and other financial businesses, as will be shown. Yet, while the domestication of finance in Sweden appears to be something of an unintended consequence of the welfare state policies, and, as I will show, was embedded in a welfare statist everyday culture, there was another side to the story.

THE POLITICS OF PERSONAL FINANCE

The personal financial revolution administered by the banks required people to be financially literate, to use a modern expression, and therefore involved an apparatus of financial education. People had to learn how to use cheques or how to manage their bank accounts, but also had to unlearn what they had once thought true about commercial banks or consumer credit. It is hardly surprising, then, that financial industries' marketing often came in the guise of education in financial matters.

Financial guidance was also a vehicle for political and ideological struggle. Consumer education was well developed in Sweden, managed by either government agencies or the consumer cooperative movement. Finance was seldom a topic, however, with the exception of warnings against buying on credit. The savings banks were engaged in campaigns to encourage thrift among the public, including schoolchildren, but other than that, financial education for ordinary people and families was rare before the 1950s.[44]

One of these rare undertakings, Sweden's first personal financial advice service, the Taxpayers' Budget Bureau (Skattebetalarnas Budgetbyrå), was launched in 1927 by the Taxpayers' Association (*Skattebetalarnas Förening*). This organisation had been founded in 1921 by financial capitalist Marcus Wallenberg and other Swedish business and industry leaders with the explicit aim of creating broad middle-class support for non-socialist policies. It criticised state spending, heavy bureaucracy and high taxes, and its anti-socialist agenda was further accentuated after the Second World War. The personal finance advice, which the Budget Bureau offered in pamphlets, books and the Association's monthly magazine as well as through individual counselling, was hands-on and often directed at women and families. It emphasised building up capital instead of simply being thrifty, stressed the importance of financial self-reliance and suggested conceptualising the family as an enterprise, at least when it came to finances. Eventually, it provided 'tax-planning' advice as well. The Budget Bureau's activities and the guidance it offered promoted entrepreneurial attitudes and financial thinking based on the idea of individual responsibility and financial independence. Mainly, it was a popularisation of anti-socialist ideology by means of shaping everyday financial behaviour.[45]

Two similar financial education initiatives were launched in the late 1940s, when organised Swedish business set out to mobilise against what it saw as the threat of an increasingly planned economy.[46] Both initiatives were financed by the Enterprise Fund (Näringslivets fond, est. 1940), which was the main Swedish hub for the pro-market opinion-shaping activities of the business sector. One was the Bureau for Economic Information (Byrån för Ekonomisk Information, 1944–1962), which produced propaganda material with seemingly objective economic information, and the other was an educational venture called Our Economy (Kursverksamheten Vår Ekonomi, 1947), which offered courses and educational packages for study circles. While neither of them reached a large public, their aims reveal that financial literacy education had a political agenda. The business historian Rikard Westerberg quotes a proponent of the Our Economy initiative, who called it 'a resistance movement' of a non-political nature that would disseminate economic knowledge among the workers, while other voices in the Enterprise Fund instead wanted to spell out its political ambitions and argued for educational courses more openly in line with a conservative, 'non-socialist view'. Indeed, the courses offered by Our Economy were criticised in some parts of the press for being 'badly masked propaganda against the planned economy' or a 'business leaders' correspondence school'.[47] At the same time, the Enterprise Fund also supported the Taxpayers' Association and its similar initiatives.[48]

Starting in the late 1960s, the channels for personal finance information multiplied. The commercial banks' and savings banks' ventures were complemented by the activities of new organisations, often linked to banks and organised business interests—for example, the Shareholders' Association, founded in 1966, or the Stock Promotion Foundation, founded in 1976. At the same time, a new popular finance journalism also emerged.[49] Key individuals associated with such channels appear in the chapters of this book. For example, Handelsbanken hired the head of the Taxpayers' Association's Budget Office, Gunnel Petre, for one of the bank's major campaigns, and then offered her a permanent position (Chapter 3). Another example is the credit card entrepreneur Erik Elinder (Chapters 4 and 5), who was on the board of both the Taxpayers' Association and the Stock Promotion Foundation. Thus, it is important to bear in mind the implicit politics of the field of personal finance, even though I would not suggest the existence of a large-scale plot or conspiracy. Many of those keen to promote new personal financial practices and thinking were more interested in the practical details of their own field of expertise than in the big political picture.

A Cultural History of Economic Life

As William Sewell notes, economic historians tend to neglect *economic life*—people's everyday engagement in processes conventionally perceived as economic—instead focusing on the 'the economy' as such. Although there are admittedly rich cultural and social histories of consumption, retail, production and business life, this neglect is even more true for the study of mundane *financial* life.[50] Meanwhile, the last two decades have seen a growing interest in the culture of economic life in disciplines outside history, such as economic sociology, economic anthropology and economic geography. An entire research field grew strong under the name cultural economy.[51] Finance is especially well represented in this field and connected ones, even though an interest in high finance dominates over the mundane low finance.

The field of *historical* studies of the culture of personal finance is expanding, especially in regard to two topics: consumer credit and the rise of a mass investment culture. Historians of credit cultures have introduced personal finance as an important theme in the study of consumerism and working-class life, or in business history and media history, showing that the history of consumer debt is also one of shifting moralities, which reveal how political and economic changes play out in practice.[52] The destigmatisation of and various justifications for consumer credit were also important ingredients in the bankification of everyday life in Sweden, as I show in the chapters on the launch and consolidation of credit cards (Chapters 4 and 5).

Historical research on popular participation in the stock market, for example, has explored the emergence of an 'equity culture' in early twentieth-century America, where an ethos of shareholder democracy became something of a defining characteristic of the nation's political culture.[53] Historian Amy Edwards has recently shown that, in Britain, not only Thatcherite politics but also media, popular culture and the marketing activities of finance institutions helped to create new financial attitudes, practices and expectations in daily life, in a process that started before the 1980s. In contrast to the American studies, she singles out the creation not of the investor citizen but of the investor shopper.[54] Here I will concentrate on an earlier version of the financial consumer, the bank customer, who was invited into the bank—the 'financial department store'—to choose among a range of products, from current accounts with chequebooks and so-called savings-loan accounts to credit cards and mutual fund investments.

In addition to the line from the bankification to the financialisation of everyday life, another common thread in this book's chapters connects to the history of monetary forms and transactions. Historicising technologies of money—such as coins, paper notes, cheques, budget sheets, credit cards and, more recently, digital currencies—makes visible that these are also moral technologies, imbued with ideology as well as class and gender differences.[55] The story of bankification is also the story of burgeoning dreams and the first steps towards a cashless society, and the financial and commercial surveillance that comes with it. It is a history of banking technology and how new financial products became links that connected people into a new informational, rather than transactional, system.[56] Money has been described by scholars such as Keith Hart, and more recently Rachel O'Dwyer, as an 'instrument of collective memory', something that keeps record of the relationships we enter into. In another scholarly context, ID documents and practices of identity verification have been analysed as 'the memory of the state'.[57] The Swedish case unveils that the process of bankification brought about a convergence of money and identity. The bank-issued ID cards cemented the new financial subject positions and have become, both in their former plastic form and in their present digital shape, a powerful symbol of a bankified identity and a bankified daily life.

In an essay on the cultural economy research field, Liz McFall and Melinda Cooper ask 'what it means to think about the economy through, and with culture'. They point out that the study of the cultural in economic life has often been operationalised through dimensions or synonyms of culture such as narratives, rhetoric and discourses—assumed not only to describe but also to construct the economic—or through theoretical concepts, such as device, assemblage, attachment and performativity, which emphasise the practical, material character of economic life and explore interactions between people and markets or financial organisations.[58] I take a similar approach in this book. I would contend, though, that the constant refinement of the theoretical toolkit—a typical tendency in the field—imposes limitations on the empirical ambitions of cultural studies of the economy. Historians are often empiricists. Although analytical concepts such as domestication, relational work, financial subjects and devices are important tools for my analysis and translate the empirical findings in my historical cases into the vernacular of the cultural-economic research field, it is the actual archival and historical evidence which is key to my understanding of how the practices and meanings of everyday finance have changed.

READING BANK ARCHIVES AGAINST THE GRAIN

The empirical chapters in this book all deal with different cases of relational work involved in the domestication of banks, financial products and services. The cases have been selected to allow an analysis of what Marieke de Goede calls 'moments of openness', when changing practices or new devices were not yet naturalised, their place, role and cultural connotations not yet fixed, in order to see how contemporary actors made sense of them; which negotiations and compromises were undertaken to deal with dissent or resistance.[59] Looking back in time, it is possible to unveil the processes and cultural technologies by which cheque accounts, credit cards or bank-issued ID cards were made mundane. This approach uncovers important pieces of a history that did not become part of the dominant narrative while historicising those pieces that did.

The main actors are banks and credit card companies (often owned or financed by banks). My interest is not their large-scale business operations but rather how they tried to reshape cultural and moral attitudes among the general public in order to create a market. I study material from some of the most important Swedish actors, such as the Bankers' Association and the two largest commercial banks of the time, Handelsbanken and Skandinaviska Banken, both of which were pioneering the commercial banks' turn to a broad public. Skandinaviska Banken merged with the third-largest bank, Stockholms Enskilda Bank (which had a more upper-class and business profile), in 1972 and formed S-E-Banken. The credit card companies that I study (Köpkort and InterConto) were also the largest in Sweden in the 1970s, but much smaller in size than the big commercial banks, which owned Köpkort jointly.

I build on extensive archival research, working with sources that allow a close reading and thick descriptions. For the credit card companies, I studied previously unexplored archival material, while the bank archives are well known to historians of business and finance, although they are typically used for other questions. For Chapter 5, I also used the archives of the Swedish Consumer Cooperative Union (Kooperativa Förbundet, KF).

Working with corporate archives poses two challenges for a cultural historian. The first is that the kind of material that one is especially interested in has rarely been preserved, for example correspondence with individual customers. Marketing and PR departments kept their documentation, but seldom the hands-on records of interactions with ordinary customers. Archival sorting bias is inevitable, regardless of the collection. As the archival scholar Terry Cook writes, 'The major act of historical interpretation occurs not when historians open boxes but when archivists fill the boxes, by implication destroying the 98 per cent of records that do not make it into those or any other archival boxes'.[60] Unsurprisingly, the archives of commercial banks are awash with material on their most important corporate clients or the company's overall business policy, as well as documentation of undertakings with the Riksbank, the government or business partners. Unlike mainstream business or financial historians, I often find the most relevant material in boxes labelled 'Miscellaneous', or among misplaced folders that might have escaped earlier weeding processes. For example, some of the rich material on the financial study courses for women (Chapter 3) was buried in boxes of newspaper cuttings.

Another challenge is the chaotic abundance one encounters when working with uncatalogued and unordered archival collections, as in the archive of the bank-owned credit card company Köpkort and the personal papers of the marketing man and credit card entrepreneur Erik Elinder. The sense of proximity to the historical actors is rewarding, as is the richness of mundane materials. However, making sense of and bringing some kind of order to such collections without losing track of the very same mundane details the historian wants to grasp is hard and time-consuming to the point of despair. Deep-diving into the messy written residues of the past, and through them not only observing practices, attitudes and ideas but also trying to understand the internal logic of the same documentation bears a clear similarity to an ethnographic field study. This ethnographic gaze becomes especially prominent in the case studies of Chapters 3 and 5.

To complement the archival sources, press material from the daily papers and more specialised weekly and monthly periodicals was extensively used, as was the Ephemera Collection in the National Library of Sweden (Kungliga biblioteket), which has unpublished printed matter from private corporations.

The Outline of the Book

Bankminded tells the story of how banking, finance and financial products became part of everyday life well before financial deregulation and the credit boom of the 1980s. It charts how citizens of the welfare state became financial subjects and how the banks entered different spaces of ordinary life. I call this the bankification of everyday life and argue that it was a silent personal financial revolution that changed practices, attitudes and ideas; indeed, it aimed to change people's minds about banks, money, credit, payments and savings. This was an important shift, without which the financialisation process of subsequent decades or the history of Sweden in the 1960s and 1970s is difficult to understand. It depended on politics and technological change, of course; but, as I will show, it also reshaped everyday financial culture.

In retrospect it might seem a self-evident and effortless transition, but it was not an easy shift. Cultural, moral, ideological boundaries had to be crossed, blurred or erased and considerable relational work was required to domesticate cheque accounts, credit cards and other financial products, making the general public familiar with a new mindset, new habits and whole new micro-infrastructure of everyday finance.

The book is structured along such cultural boundaries and the challenges they presented, with each chapter exploring how one of these challenges was handled. Banks and credit card companies conducted relational work (often in response to the public's relational work), and in the process banking, finance and credit were redefined in terms of *class* (Chapter 2), *gender* (Chapter 3), *morality* (Chapter 4), *ideology* (Chapter 5) and *identity* (Chapter 6). The banks took on new tasks and made inroads into a range of—for them—new areas that were highly relevant in the lives of ordinary Swedes: the *workplace* (Chapter 2), the *family* (Chapter 3), *consumption* (Chapter 4), *popular movements* (Chapter 5) and *government authorities* (Chapter 6).

Chapter 2, 'Welcome to the banking age: Redefining the social class of money', centres on class and delves into the case of the so-called cheque accounts for wages reform, which was where the bankification of everyday life started. In the late 1950s, Swedish commercial banks began to offer payroll services; until then the payment of wages and salaries had typically been administered by the workplace. Current accounts with chequebooks were now opened for both white- and blue-collar employees, which not only blurred the boundaries of the class-based financial system but also profoundly changed both banking practices and practices of personal finance. Cheques, once reserved for the privileged, were now a new device for ordinary people. Swedish wage earners were turned into bank customers, and the commercial banks became retail companies selling a wide range of products to a broad public. Still, this chapter suggests that one should be wary of overemphasising the importance of individual self-governing financial subjects as depicted in Foucauldian studies. Making and controlling new financial subjects in Sweden, at least in the first phase, was made possible by cultural tools and discourses rooted in a more directly disciplinary, hierarchical value system impregnated by class (as defined by production rather than consumption). Not least, the collective affiliations of large groups of wage earners proved to be instrumental. The new everyday users of financial products were created in a back-and-forth movement between the older subject positions and the models imagined for the new ones.

While the focus of Chapter 2 is class and its scene the workplace, in Chapter 3, 'Making finance familiar: Gender and the domestication of banks', I look at banks' involvement in family life through the prism of gender, domesticity and another key subject category: women. I analyse bank campaigns directed at women, especially a large-scale, recurring campaign for housewives by Handelsbanken in the 1960s. These events can be read as performances of the marketisation of domestic money and of the domestication of banking services. I argue that by playing on emotions, family life, consumerism and, literally, everydayness, the campaigns mobilised femininity to domesticate a new financial mindset—for women and men alike. The bank presented itself as a 'department store of finances'. Older financial devices, such as the traditional budget sheets, were reinvented and popularised along with cleverly packaged and diversified types of bank accounts, mutual funds and equity investments. As the bank claimed a new role in the management of the family budget, topics such as housekeeping money and financial equality between spouses were discussed in the same context as investing in stocks. Female financial experts played a leading role in these campaigns, and the banks created for them a new expert position: that of the personal finance advisor for ordinary people, otherwise known as 'budget consultant' or 'family economics advisor'. This field of expertise was nearly unknown earlier, certainly at commercial banks.

Focusing on the changing mundane moralities of debt, Chapter 4, 'Launching the credit card: New moralities of credit and payment', deals with the destigmatisation and moral reframing of consumer credit by means of the credit card. In Sweden, the early adoption of new banking and computer technologies was combined with strongly negative general attitudes towards credit for everyday consumption. Although introduced early (1959) and inspired by the American example, Swedish credit cards had to be reconceptualised, reshaped and renamed before they won acceptance. Marketers exploited the non-credit properties of the card in order to blur the boundaries between credit and cash payments. The card itself was turned into a device for *de-vicing*—destigmatising—consumer credit. By looking at the technical and cultural arrangements built into the card, I unpack the workings of three de-vicing strategies used by card issuers to overcome moral resistance: the credit card as (1) a 'certificate of trust', like a membership card; (2) modern money; and (3) a device for financial planning. All three strategies were meant to embed credit cards into the rhythm of the everyday as well as into the cultural, moral values of the Swedish welfare state. Simultaneously, the very same conceptualisations facilitated changing those values and with them everyday financial practices. This was also a domestication process, in the sense that it created a Swedish version of the credit card. Credit cards are otherwise often portrayed in the literature as typically American, and their international history mainly involves the two dominant card schemes Visa and MasterCard, which were introduced in Sweden in 1978 and 1979, respectively—by which time Swedish cards had been around for twenty years.

From renegotiations of the meaning of consumer credit on an individual and material level, Chapter 5, 'Rewriting the history and future of consumer credit: Ideological change as a marketing strategy', moves on to the societal level. Its focus is on ideological boundary work and the everyday politics of consumer credit. I explore the story of the card company InterConto and its energetic owner Erik Elinder, who in the 1970s actively worked to reshape dominant ideological views on credit in society in general and in the labour and consumer movements in particular. Elinder wanted to rewrite the conventional history of everyday credit with the help of university-based economic historians and other academics, as he reimagined the future of the plastic card. By looking at its work in redrawing ideological boundaries, this chapter also brings into the picture another stakeholder, the Consumer Cooperative Union (Kooperativa Förbundet, KF, founded in 1899), which had shops across the country and nearly 40 percent of all Swedish households as members. Long the leading opponent of the use of consumer credit, with its representatives fiercely critical of credit cards, the Consumer Cooperative Union decided in the late 1970s to launch its own card system. This ideological U-turn was contested, however. To anchor it throughout the broad layers of the cooperative movement, the well-established educational infrastructure of this large popular movement was mobilised. The outcome was not only the launch of a cooperative card but also a symbolic consecration of the use of consumer credit in general.

Chapter 6, 'The financialisation of identity', explores the pre-digital history of Sweden's digital BankID system and explains how banks, as early as the 1960s, started issuing identity documents, a task historically associated with state authorities. In addition to changing everyday identification practices, this process created a link between identification and personal finances or, in more abstract terms, identity and money. The chapter reconnects to Chapter 2 and the cheque accounts for wages reform which generated a need for identification documents. It also builds on Chapter 4, pointing out the similarities between credit cards and the bank-issued plastic ID cards. Plastic money and plastic identities converged when financial ID documents were issued to virtually every citizen. The focus on the bankification process thus reveals a *plastic regime of identification* between the paper-based regime and the digital regime, portrayed in the history of ID documents. The question of knowledge is key in this case as well, but is turned upside down, with the focus shifting from what the new financial subjects were supposed to know to what the market could know about them. As wage earners, housewives, savers, consumers and consumer cooperators were all becoming bank clients, cheque account holders, investors, credit card owners and debtors, nascent computerisation in combination with new financial devices gave rise to dreams about the profitability of the 'intimate' financial relationship that emerged.

In Chapter 7, the Conclusion, I summarise and contextualise my findings on the bankification of everyday life, arguing that it was related to but historically distinct from the financialisation of everyday life. Bankification entailed a radical personal financial transformation, and a change in the mundane culture of money, but as such it went almost unnoticed in the research literature. The shift occurred early in Sweden, with its solid banking system and speedy adoption of new technologies. Paradoxically, the strong welfare state and its regulations on the financial system facilitated the bankification process. At the same time, the inculcation of a new type of financial thinking into the population to make them more bankminded—rather than merely thrifty—sat well with both the immediate interests of the financial industry and the larger political ambitions of organised business. The bankification of everyday life, deeply embedded in a post-war welfare statist cultural context but pointing forward to the financialised everyday culture of the late twentieth century. is a missing link that reveals the intricate historical connections between the two.

Open Access This chapter is licensed under the terms of the Creative Commons Attribution 4.0 International License (http://creativecommons.org/licenses/by/4.0/), which permits use, sharing, adaptation, distribution and reproduction in any medium or format, as long as you give appropriate credit to the original author(s) and the source, provide a link to the Creative Commons license and indicate if changes were made.

The images or other third party material in this chapter are included in the chapter's Creative Commons license, unless indicated otherwise in a credit line to the material. If material is not included in the chapter's Creative Commons license and your intended use is not permitted by statutory regulation or exceeds the permitted use, you will need to obtain permission directly from the copyright holder.

CHAPTER 2

Welcome to the Banking Age: Redefining the Social Class of Money

'Today we live in the banking age, welcome!' Kreditbanken's quarterly newsletter in 1968 addressed a large group of customers: those with newly opened cheque accounts for their wages or salaries.[1] About 200,000 Swedes fell into this category and received the newsletter specifically aimed at them, while about another million held similar accounts at other banks in the late 1960s.

From the late 1950s to the early 1970s, a personal finance revolution took place in Sweden. Although its fundamental significance went largely unnoticed as such, it changed how ordinary people handled their money and how banks envisioned their clientele. It also paved the way for further important changes in the 1980s, as new practices in everyday finance received a boost from the deregulation of the credit market. The spark for this process came in the late 1950s, when Swedish commercial banks began offering payroll services to employers by opening current accounts with chequebooks first for white-collar employees and soon blue-collar workers as well. Within a decade, Swedish wage earners had turned into bank customers, and commercial banks—formerly solemn institutions serving business and the very rich—had become retail companies selling a wide range of products to a broad public. A Swedish banker, recalling the transition, said that 'we moved people's wallets over to bank accounts'.[2]

This chapter is about that move. The cheque accounts for wages reform is key to understanding the bankification process and the later practical implementation of the financialisation of everyday life in Sweden. I will explain why this new micro-infrastructure was important in economic life: how it introduced new ways of handling money, and with that a new mindset. I will also show how a wage-earner identity came to be instrumental when new financial practices were domesticated. This case also illustrates that the welfare state, with its rising wages, social security payments and credit regulations, was a key factor in the early Swedish bankification of everyday life.[3]

The number of bank accounts in commercial banks went up by about 85 percent between 1960 and 1968. With the savings banks and the Post Office Bank (*Postbanken*) included—institutions where traditional savings accounts dominated—the total increase amounted to a more moderate 32 percent.[4] The change was even more clearly reflected in the number of bank transactions, which multiplied dramatically. One of the largest commercial banks, Handelsbanken, reported a three-and-a-half times increase in yearly bank transactions in the ten years between 1958 and 1967. A further 35 percent increase was noted for the subsequent three years between 1967 and 1970, and the bank's leadership explained the changes by the introduction of cheque accounts for wages.[5] By 1968, only an estimated 13–15 percent of the adult population had no bank account, and the recruitment of new customers was ongoing.[6] Compared to the rest of Europe, Sweden was a highly bankified society. In France, the proportions were the reverse, with only 17 percent of the adult population having a bank account in 1967 (although this would soon rapidly change), and in Britain almost 40 percent of the population had no bank account as late as 1974.[7] Sweden offers an interesting case, being one of the earliest examples of bankification in Europe with a mass enrolment of both private and state enterprise workforces.

Why and how did this 'move of wallets' to bank accounts occur, and what cultural changes did it entail? The cheque account for wages challenged deep-rooted values and attitudes, many of which related to class. In this chapter, I investigate how the challenges were handled by looking at the marketing strategies and discourses used by the banks, but also how they were interpreted, adopted and sometimes obstructed by the public. And indeed, who were 'the public' and how were they addressed and controlled? Which subject positions took shape in the contacts between banks and their new clients? How did people make sense of cheques and cheque accounts?[8]

Financial Subjects and Subjective Finances

The concept of financial subjects, as developed in Foucauldian studies of financial life, is operative in my study. Often associated with the neoliberal era, it refers to an assembly of subject positions created in the process by which banks, insurance and credit companies or, more broadly, policy programmes address the population. The financialisation of everyday life is typically analysed as a process that targets individuals (albeit in large numbers), not collective bodies. The new financial subject is then often depicted as an investor, borrower or consumer rather than a wage earner. These categories are at their most powerful when they seem self-evident and 'natural', and so create self-regulating subjects.[9] Control in financial spaces is therefore often interpreted from a governmentality perspective as a vehicle of socialisation, a 'conduct of the conduct', which is done from a distance. It is depersonalised, but targets the individual.[10]

I argue in this chapter, partly in contrast to the above, that the making and control of new financial subjects in Sweden was instead possible because of technologies and discourses rooted in a more traditional (disciplinary and hierarchical) value system deeply permeated by class (even paternalism) and collectively defined identities. A wage-earner identity—the quintessential subject category of the Swedish welfare state—rather than a finance consumer or investor identity, proved to be instrumental in the initial phase of the bankification of everyday life. The new financial subjects were created just as much with the help of the old identities as with the models imagined for the new ones.

While using the notion of financial subjects as an analytical concept, albeit critically, I also draw on a rather different body of scholarship, which instead emphasises the importance of subjective finances—the subjective and culturally entangled uses of money. Here I follow the direction set by Viviana Zelizer's seminal work on the multiple cultural meanings of money.[11] For example, a cheque account was long perceived as a sign of higher class, desirable to some and obnoxious to others. Paying by cheque—or later by credit card—had a different meaning for people than paying in cash, even if it was the same amount. Cash and cheques have been, in Zelizerian terms, different 'monies'; but in addition to its form, the cultural meanings also depend on the source of the money, its intended use, and of course the specific historical and social setting. A Zelizerian approach to the cultural meanings and practices of money compensates for the limitations of the governmentality perspective, which neglects the 'relational work', such as negotiations, compromises and back-and-forth movements between alternative rationalities.

I use the word 'class' in a deliberately flexible way. I see class when the historical agents refer directly to a group's position in production (for example, factory workers, wage earners, officials or salaried employees), when socially and culturally defined groupings are only suggested and circumscribed ('a new category of clients') or when a survey or statistics differentiate between cheque users according to their education, employment or income. This lets me unpack how the historical uses of class categorisation shifted in practice along with changes in people's financial habits.[12]

COMMERCIAL BANKS AND A BROADER CLIENTELE

The Swedish financial system was segregated, as Chapter 1 explained. The small, locally based savings banks served the broader populace, offering mainly savings accounts, while the commercial banks catered for business, industry and well-to-do individuals from the upper classes. In 1941–1942, Handelsbanken's management were already discussing the possibility of expanding the bank's services into new fields attracting 'workers and common people', meaning people who traditionally were savings banks' clientele. A circular letter to its branches asked for the local bank managers' views. While many were cautiously positive, just as many bank branches signalled their scepticism. The Uppsala branch, for instance, declared that services to this kind of clientele were 'not worth the candle', and word came from the town of Kalmar that it would 'not be worth it even from an advertising perspective' as the bank would 'not get much joy in the future' from such financially weak groups.[13]

A 1949 Gallup poll showed that even among the social elite, *current* accounts were rare and only 61 percent of upper- and middle-class households had money in a bank at all; and even so, most of them used the savings banks. Strikingly, Skandinaviska Banken, the bank that had commissioned the Gallup poll to get feedback on their advertising and public relations, did not even bother to sample and survey the social group officially categorised as 'working class' (which made up 55 percent of the population). Thus, only people from the remaining two social categories, labelled 'middle class' and 'well-to-do people', were included in the poll.[14]

The lack of interest in ordinary people's money was about to change. Banking legislation had historically distinguished between the different types of banks, but from the late 1950s the judicial separation was successively removed and banks started competing for the same clientele. The savings banks became more interested in the business sector, and commercial banks set out to acquire customers among ordinary households.[15] Competition for small deposits soon turned fierce, as the savings banks already had a good grip on the broader public with their coordinated, powerful savings propaganda, developed since the interwar period. While their savings campaigns targeted the young with free piggy banks and a well-known children's magazine distributed free in schools, they also had the moral upper hand among most of the adult population.[16]

There were multiple reasons for the commercial banks' new interest in the money of ordinary households. They desperately needed to increase their deposits because of the credit regulations that tied the limits of the banks' lending to liquidity quotas, at the same time as much of their financing was being steered by the Riksbank towards the needs of the building sector, especially housing construction. 'At the commercial banks we were fully aware that the only way to increase volume, the only way to meet the borrowing needs of companies, was to go to the private market with collection boxes, even if that had to cost something', a former banker said in a 2008 documentation project. This was the oft-repeated explanation in the historical sources as well.[17]

Levelling incomes and the rising standards of the working class in welfare society were also mentioned as contributory factors, by both the historical actors and bank historians.[18] The period I study was one of major welfare reforms. A large-scale social security system was set up in Sweden based on universal rather than means-tested benefits. A child benefit for all families was introduced in the late 1940s, general sickness insurance in 1955 and a general supplementary pension (Allmän tilläggspension, ATP) in 1960, with the first payments in 1962. University education was democratised with the new student grant and loan system introduced in 1965.[19] These and other reforms reduced the social and economic gaps in Swedish society and, which is my point here, also influenced households' financial habits. They introduced a range of novel 'payments' (originally by postal order and sometimes in cash from the cashier at the local welfare office). These social incomes had to be transferred, administered and calculated. And although wages and salaries were the main part of the households' money, banks also became interested in the various social payments and in time would offer financial services, usually specialised accounts, tailored to these different 'monies', to which I will return later.[20] The commodification of banking services, often in the shape of diversified accounts for savings in combination with possible loans, was also a way to handle a common fear in the banking world that the general pension reform would adversely affect people's willingness to save long term.[21]

Banks had begun to reshape their advertising- and sales-related activities in the late 1940s, and in the 1950s the typical 'advertising departments' became 'marketing departments', conducting market surveys and adopting modern advertising techniques. The idea of PR reached the banking world in the 1950s. In 1957, Handelsbanken hired one of Sweden's leading PR experts, Eric Lindström, the author of several early books on public relations, to lead the bank's Acquisitions Department, which was then renamed the Markets Department (Marknadsavdelningen). Lindström is said to have introduced 'active market thinking', and under his lead Handelsbanken launched several major PR campaigns. Although he moved up the management ladder in 1963, the bank's marketing continued to develop, and the Markets Department was reorganised into specialised sections and subgroups for sales planning, sales promotion, product development and market research.[22] The eager interest in PR and new marketing techniques, typical of other banks as well, culminated in the 1960s. Among the many examples, Skandinaviska Banken introduced mobile bank buses and drive-in banks in larger cities, in addition to more traditional ventures such as spectacular window displays (Figs. 2.1 and 2.2).[23] The number of bank branches also increased between the mid-1950s and the late 1970s, despite the number of banks falling due to mergers.[24]

Cheque Accounts for Wages and Salaries

The most important measure that banks took to attract small deposits was the introduction of cheque accounts for wages and salaries, or, as it was labelled in a contemporaneous English translation, 'the wages-by-cheque-system'.[25] However, this was not achieved by popular marketing campaigns but rather through negotiations with employers and the

Fig. 2.1 Bank bus by Skandinaviska Banken, *Din Bank*, 1–2 (1956). In 1956, Skandinaviska Banken started an ambulant bank office, serving mainly employees in the industries situated in Stockholm's suburbs. Unknown photographer. Used with the permission of SEB

representatives of employees, the trade unions. Swedish banks began offering payroll services to employers in the late 1950s, meaning that the bank takes over all administration of salaries and wages. Instead of receiving cash in hand at work, employees would be paid by direct deposit to specially designed cheque accounts. First salaried employees, clerks and office workers, and later manual workers, were given their own chequebooks. The introduction was rapid—though not without conflict—because the banks redoubled their efforts and also played on their good relationship with industry. 'The cheque accounts for wages should be pushed as hard as we possibly can' was the consensus at

Fig. 2.2 Drive-in bank in Stockholm, around 1960. Centrum för Näringslivshistoria (CfN), Skandinaviska Banken. Unknown photographer. Used with the permission of SEB

an internal strategy meeting in 1962 at Handelsbanken, which recommended that local branches start with the bank's own corporate customers and enrol the workforces there.[26]

State-owned enterprises were favourable to the reform, and one of the first employers to pay salaries into cheque accounts (as early as 1956) was a municipality, the City of Kalmar, which worked with Handelsbanken.[27] In 1960, a report by the official government inquiry into 'measures for stimulating thrift' recommended that all wage earners, including state employees, be paid by direct deposit into bank accounts, preferably cheque accounts. This method was not only much cheaper compared to salaries paid in cash (administrative costs went down by 90 percent); it also, the inquiry suggested, encouraged people's propensity to save. They believed that, 'although it could not with numerical certainty be established', people would be more 'restrictive' in their everyday spending if their money were deposited in a cheque account with no need for them to carry around cash. The report also stated that banking professionals shared this belief.[28] Clearly, the interest in governing individual conduct was there from the beginning, if only to justify introducing the system. From the perspective of the country's economy, the report saw clear advantages to cheque accounts, which channelled private money into the banking system instead of it being kept at home as cash.

Private employers welcomed the possibility to offload their payrolls. Paying wages was time-consuming and expensive as it required risky cash transports, safe premises and endless hours of administrative work. At larger workplaces, several clerks were needed to handle the cash, under the eye of a supervisor. Wages were still paid weekly, but a change was on the way to payments every second week and thereafter monthly, bankers reasoned. In 1962, the Bankers' Association negotiated with representatives of the Swedish Employers' Confederation (Svenska Arbetsgivareföreningen, SAF) to go over to fortnightly wages as long as cash wages were abandoned for cheques. Employers were broadly positive, but said no to paying a fee to compensate banks for their administrative costs.[29] Eager to enrol as many new account holders as possible and to outcompete the savings banks and one another, the banks initially offered the service for free.[30]

As a result, the banks considerably increased the number of their depositors. Within ten years (1957–1966), over one million *new* cheque accounts were opened, of which 800,000 were at commercial banks, a figure that went up by another 200,000 by 1968 (Fig. 2.3). There were also accounts without chequebooks for salaries and wages, usually at the Post Office Bank and savings banks, which took on the competition with their commercial counterparts by also offering payroll services. But eventually even savings banks introduced cheque accounts, a new service for them. In 1970, the total number of salary accounts (with or without chequebooks) at savings banks was 870,000.[31] In 1974, after the merger of the Post Office Bank and Kreditbanken, payrolls administered by the former were added to the commercial bank statistics and the figures quickly doubled to about 2.2 million (without the savings banks). There were no official totals, but a cautious estimate is that in the early and mid-1970s over 3 million people's wages were paid through bank accounts. This meant the vast majority of all wage earners, in a country with a total population of 8 million and 2.77 million households.[32]

In 1966, a survey claimed that 'the issue of cheque wages [had] come to affect almost all people in society'.[33] Admittedly, savings banks in

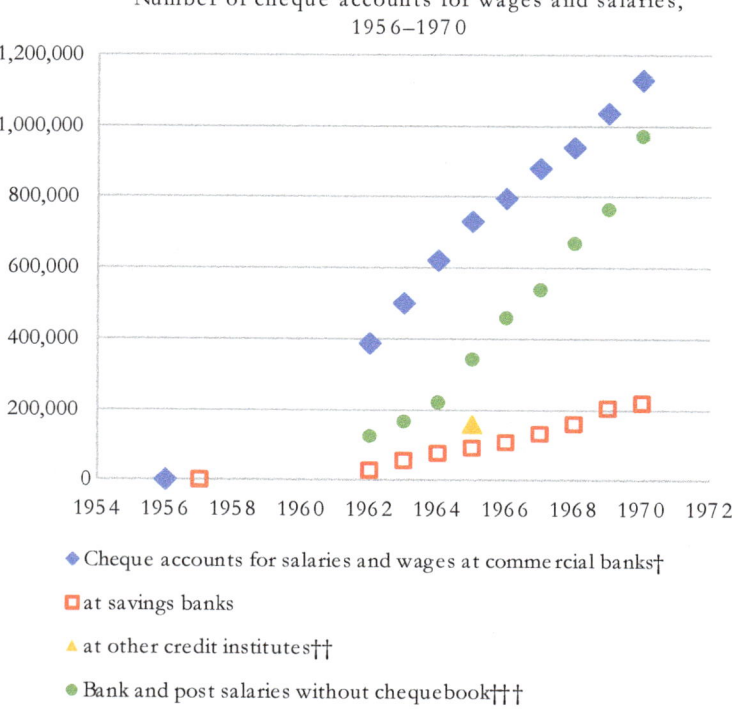

Fig. 2.3 Number of cheque accounts for wages and salaries, 1956–1970. *Source* DsFi 1971:12, Sture Lundell, *PM angående åtgärder för att motverka checkmissbruket* (Stockholm: Finansdepartementet, 1971), 8–11; CfN, Bankföreningen, F2b:6, 'Postverket och checksystemet med särskilt hänsyn till checklönen', October 1966.

† Traditional cheque accounts (177,000 in 1957) not included. †† Statistics only available for 1965. ††† Includes mainly salaries administered by savings banks and the Post Office Bank

Sweden had a traditionally strong position, with many savings accounts held by the less privileged. Economic historians even talk of a deposit market revolution as early as the late nineteenth century.[34] However, only a small fraction (about 5 percent) of the new cheque account holders had held a *current* account at a bank before.[35] Thus, large numbers of people had to learn to use a bank account for something other than saving their money.

What was unique in an international comparison was not the use of cheque accounts for wage payments per se, but the way in which they were introduced. Similar systems had been practised for some time in the United States (among other methods); however, the broad introduction of direct deposits started earlier in Sweden than in France or the United Kingdom, for example, despite cheques being more widespread in those countries in the 1950s, at least among the upper and middle classes. In France, direct deposits were introduced after a change in the banking legislation in 1966–1967, further accelerated by a shift from weekly to monthly payments after 1968.[36] In Britain, wage payments to bank accounts were delayed, partly because of the so-called Truck Acts of 1831 and subsequent legislation, which established that workers had to be paid in cash (originally instead of orders for goods valid only in the employer's shop). British trade unions resisted direct deposits so that in 1979 fully 78 percent of manual workers were still paid in cash, compared to 35 percent of non-manual workers, which was itself a high number by international standards.[37] In French and British historiography, there is no mention of collective affiliations of the kind seen in Sweden, whereby the entire workforce of a company could be given cheque accounts at the same bank overnight.[38] A 1966 report from the Swedish Bankers' Association noted that the Swedish cheque system, being 'very liberal' in international terms, led to a more rapid increase in turnover than most bankers expected, which, however, brought some 'unforeseen' practical and societal problems.[39] The early Swedish case thus offers examples of obstacles and negotiations, and is interesting both as a comparison and in its own right.

Overcoming Class Barriers

> If a customer whips out a chequebook to pay 26 kronor for some groceries, it doesn't mean you have Croesus or a nouveau riche show-off in front of you. He might well be your next-door neighbour. Several industries in the country are namely practising a new method: they deposit wages

in a cheque account and give the employee a chequebook instead of an envelope with a few hundred kronor inside.[40]

These words are taken from an article titled 'Clientele with cheques turn shop into a bank', published in 1958 in a branch magazine for grocers. Forty years later, the former director of Handelsbanken, Jan Wallander, noted in his memoirs that direct-deposit wages required 'a major mental readjustment' among unionised workers, challenging ingrained attitudes: 'Now they were given accounts at a commercial bank, one of the bourgeoisie's oppressive institutions, and they started writing cheques, something that only the upper classes did before'.[41] Many other sources, both within banking and in popular culture, confirm that a cheque account at a commercial bank had been strongly associated with the social elite, and its popularisation was a culturally controversial issue.

The commercial banks had good relationships with business leaders, but not so much with trade unions. The question of direct-deposit wages impinged on the collective bargaining agreements (*kollektivavtal*), which were the cornerstone of the Swedish model. A change in how wages were paid sometimes required formal alterations to local agreements. Regardless of the formalities, the strong Swedish trade unions often had a say when industrial companies adopted the new system. As the bank archives show, it was a challenge.[42]

The 1966 survey by the Bankers' Association said the introduction of cheque wages was often debated in workplaces, in most cases even 'vividly' so. People were far from unanimous.[43] The IFÖ factory (manufacturing ceramic and sanitary products) in the small industrial town of Bromölla in southern Sweden was among the first industrial companies to pay a couple of hundred employees in lower management by direct deposit to cheque accounts in 1956. Less than three years later, its manual workforce (1,600 people) were also given chequebooks at Skandinaviska Banken. A memo dated 10 January 1959 in the bank's archives reveals not only the practical but also the cultural and ideological obstacles to overcome. Factory workers were paid weekly, but the IFÖ management hoped to introduce monthly wages. Originally, the local savings bank had wanted to take on the payroll for the IFÖ workers, but apparently could not cope with the large number of new accounts. Judging from the wording of the memo, this class-segregated solution was self-evident to everyone involved, even though Skandinaviska Banken already handled the white-collar staff's salaries. The representative of IFÖ Industries assured Skandinaviska Banken that its workers were 'steady people, with low mobility', and if anything, would probably handle their cheque accounts 'more carefully and responsibly than the white-collar employees'. The trade union was prepared to support the direct deposits to cheque accounts if the bank offered to collect union dues by deducting them from wages. This seems to have been a controversial task for the bankers for ideological reasons, but even so they took it on ('despite objections in principle') and agreed that it would be their policy in future. The decision, the memo noted, was strongly influenced by the competition: Handelsbanken and state-owned Kreditbanken were already offering similar and other 'collective services' to trade unions in the workplaces where cheque-account wages were introduced.[44]

Class-related concerns and ideological barriers were also apparent in the discussions a few years later between the largest commercial bank, Handelsbanken, and two industrial companies in northern Sweden.[45] Handelsbanken already had a general policy about also taking on wage payments for labourers, referring (again) to the competition, the 'increasing economic importance of the working class', and the fact that the 'monthly payment of wages [could] be expected in the very near future'. However, in northern Sweden, with its strong unionist traditions, the bank faced fierce resistance from the workers. This worried the bank executives. The opposition was twofold, one of the bankers reported: the workers felt a strong, 'ideologically rooted mistrust' of commercial banks and were also suspicious of cheques and cheque accounts per se. They preferred the accounts offered by savings banks, without chequebooks. Apparently, the savings banks' chequeless salary accounts offered somewhat higher interest rates compared to the commercial banks' cheque accounts. However, the bankers pointed out, this did not actually mean more money for the workers as they would have to withdraw large sums—sometimes their entire wages—shortly after payday, while cheque accounts allowed the money to remain on deposit until it was spent. More important, as one banker put it, was the workers' 'strong ideological connection' to the savings banks; so much so that the people from Handelsbanken were banned from union meetings to discuss the payment of wages, while representatives from the local savings bank were welcomed and had the opportunity to explain the solution they were offering. Facing these difficulties, Handelsbanken's leadership discussed possible strategies for the Norrland case, and even asked themselves whether they should abandon their new policy of offering cheque accounts to blue-collar workers.[46]

It is obvious from these sources that the bank's response was rooted in judgements about the *collective* features of a large group of people, defined in traditional class terms. One of the directors argued that Handelsbanken should simply drop the idea of enrolling the workers and be content with the white-collar employees' current accounts. He feared that 'putting chequebooks in the hands of people unaccustomed to these kinds of financial techniques' would lead to an uncontrollable increase in costs; the abuse of cheque accounts on a large scale would be disastrous for the bank. But one of his colleagues responded that the northern workers would be better, more 'steady' customers than, for example, the Stockholm shop assistants working for the big chains, who were already cheque account customers. He added that the reaction of the northern workers' trade unions was understandable, considering their traditionally good contacts with the savings banks. However, it was crucial to act quickly. 'If the commercial banks did not take on the competition for the clientele in question right from the start, it would probably be completely out of their hands'. To succeed in the longer run, it was not enough to offer good products and favourable interest rates; they also had to change workers' attitudes towards commercial banks. One of those present at the 1963 discussion at Handelsbanken pointed out that it was important to think in the longer term, because the whole business of direct deposits into cheque accounts for workers was 'speculation in the future'. Rising wages, monthly payments and lower administrative costs thanks to computerisation were all in sight, as was the prospect of selling other financial products to the new account holders. The meeting decided that despite the difficulties, Handelsbanken should stick to its earlier policy and continue to enrol workers in the cheque account system.[47]

We also learn from other bank sources from the same time that measures were discussed 'to break down the ideological resistance' by the trade unions. 'The experiences of the cheque-account wages are so good that a continued investment in this form of payment can be unreservedly recommended', said one of the directors, explaining that Handelsbanken had already launched an advertising campaign in the trade union and left-wing presses, and planned to hold receptions for trade union representatives at local branches, and that even inviting them to join local bank boards was a possibility.[48]

Of course, neither workers nor bankers were homogenous in their views. Yet Handelsbanken's records, like the newspaper articles and in-house banking magazines, reveal that the introduction of cheque-account wages came with traditional, class-segregated preconceptions of society and classifications rooted in the production side of the economy. Views and attitudes on all sides—bankers, workers and employers—were challenged. The commercial banks were formerly counterparts of the companies and their management, and now the banks were exerting themselves for the chance to handle the workers' money. As a banker recalled decades later, 'The image thing was a bit difficult: the companies thought it was strange that we [the bank] were playing around in the backyard with piggy banks'.[49]

By 1968, Handelsbanken had a handy guide with instructions for how to approach the trade unions about cheque accounts for wages and the selling points to convince them. It underlined that cheque wages were key to recruiting large new groups of consumers and to selling additional financial products. Deducting union dues was part of the standard package by then, as were personal loans (on 'favourable credit terms') linked to cheque accounts. The bank also provided local trade unions with useful statistics on wages. Other 'collective services' it sometimes offered were the administration of voluntary deductions to the Wage Savings Scheme (*Lönsparandet*, a national system supported by tax benefits) and workplace savings clubs. Even so, when negotiating with the trade unions, bank representatives had to be prepared for questions about the then-topical issue of 'concentration of power' in society (*maktkoncentration*) and were instructed to defend Handelsbanken's image by stressing that it was owned by 70,000 shareholders—so no individual owned so much that they could dictate the bank's business decisions—while moving swiftly on to the wide array of services the bank offered. These ranged from financial consultancy for trade unions to individual guidance in personal finance, including stock investments and tax planning—all areas associated with the bank's older, traditionally upper-class and upper-middle-class clientele.[50] Thus, the new banking services were designed to break down the ideological and practical boundaries of class.

Capitalising on Class

Class barriers and ideological differences were there to be surmounted. Yet both the class-bound image of the cheque and class-based preconceptions about new clients seem to have been important for the initial success of the new wage payment system.

First, the prestige of cheques, as a sign of class, was used to market them as a better payment option—a 'democratisation' of a once privileged form of money. Both local and national newspapers reported about the new cheque account holders, mostly taking a positive view of the reform. For example, in 1959, the papers commented when the Volvo factory in Gothenburg started paying the wages of 1,750 employees into cheque accounts, noting that several other companies had already introduced the system. 'In other words, the democratisation of the cheque will very soon be a pleasant fact'.[51] The papers depicted the cheque wages as having been initially a 'big upheaval' but something that turned out rather well. Although the workers handled the cheques 'a bit clumsily' at first, they 'eventually learned' how to use them.[52] A chequebook—precisely because it was traditionally a status symbol—had real appeal, wrote a banking periodical: 'it gave a kind of self-confidence'.[53] This and similar statements support a Zelizerian interpretation that money can signify class not only in quantitative terms but also qualitatively.

Second, the impulse to treat new customers as a collective body (employees of a particular company) was not only important for their initial recruitment, but also for how control of the system was imagined. As I have shown, the cheque account holders were addressed and classified as a social group or category of people ('the workers', the 'shop assistants of the big chains'). In in-house magazines, the bank management kept informing their own staff about this 'new category of customers', meaning people who had never entered a commercial bank before.[54] The banks' new cheque account holders were treated differently from the old ones, even in terms of control. Before the advent of direct-deposit wages, traditional cheque accounts were normally approved after scrutiny of the *individual*. This required a written application, a credit report and a check against the banks' blacklist. When thousands of wage earners from the same workplace were enrolled, such thorough checks were impossible.[55]

The new way of thinking about control is best explained in an article published in 1956 in Skandinaviska Banken's in-house magazine, *Din*

Bank. The author, one of the younger managers, claimed that monitoring the cheque account holders was not a problem and that the risk of new clientele abusing their accounts was exaggerated. Control was, so to speak, 'built into the system': were a new customer to mismanage their account, their employer would know this and intervene. However, he continued, the mere knowledge of this was probably enough for most people to be careful with their accounts.[56] This thinking among bankers was illustrative of a common attitude towards new cheque account holders. Control was envisaged as being based on the bank clients' identities—subject positions—as employees and wage earners.

As the early press coverage shows, some banks did contact the employer when employees went into overdraft or were negligent in handling their cheque account. The Bank Inspection Board (Bankinspektionen) even had to remind all commercial banks that the section on bank secrecy in the Banking Act applied to the new cheque customers as much as the old ones.[57] Other practices, such as having the workplace's name on cheques and using the account holder's employment number as their account number, were known in the early period.[58] Thus, the cheque-account wages challenged class barriers, while the introduction of the system was accompanied by traditional views on class and a tendency to capitalise on the new customers' positions as workers and employees.

CONVENIENT MONEY: REDEFINING THE ETHOS OF THRIFT

Cheque accounts, like monthly instead of weekly wages, introduced new habits and new ways of handling money. What, though, of the everyday practices and meanings attached to cheques themselves? Cheques may have initially been promoted as a democratisation of a former upper-class privilege, but this message was problematic in practice. How were cheques reframed, what kind of money were they, and for whom? What financial thinking and practices did cheques produce, and what relational work did they entail?

The primary focus of the bank propaganda was to persuade people to use their chequebooks and not just take out all their wages as cash. At first, there were fears that those unfamiliar with cheques and current accounts would find them complicated to use. 'It was an educational matter in the long run that the bank embarked upon', read Handelsbanken's in-house magazine *Remissan*, in 1959. The goal was to make people more 'bankminded', as the magazine put it, employing this concept that included skills, knowledge and a general sense for financial matters, as well as a willingness to use bank services.[59] Therefore, an advertising apparatus was mobilised to explain the basics: cheques could be used for most payments, and there was no longer a need to carry around large sums of cash. If one wanted some change for small purchases, it could easily be arranged by rounding up the amount when writing a cheque and getting cash back from the shop. Cheques were portrayed in adverts, information leaflets and promotional films as the 'most modern, convenient and secure' method of payment, easy to use, and as protecting the user from the risk of theft (Fig. 2.4).[60] Depicting it as a substitute for cash echoed the banking industry's dream of an imminent cashless society.[61] But there was more to cheque accounts than a modern ease of living.

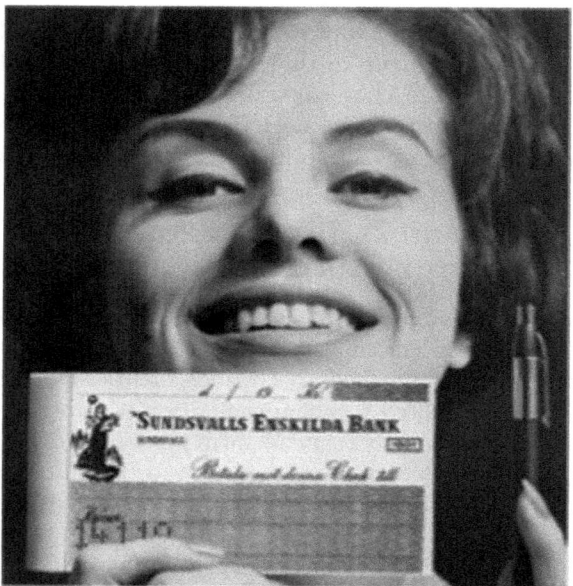

Fig. 2.4 Photograph used for advertising cheque accounts for wages at Sundsvallsbanken, late 1960s. *Photo* Norrlandsbild/Sundsvall's Museum. Used with the permission of Sundsvall's museum

The cheque account system and the chequebook itself appeared in the banks' marketing as a gateway between an older and a newer ethos of personal finance. Ethos is to be understood here not primarily as explicit norms but as a set of values manifested through practice, including both conduct and everyday materialities.[62] The older ethos included thrift, prudence, diligence and self-discipline—traits often associated in Swedish history with the ideal-typical figure of the 'conscientious worker' (*den skötsamme arbetaren*).[63] Although the newer ethos followed on smoothly from the older one, it instead embraced financial consumerism, loans and investments (often defined as savings), and also implied financial transparency within the family.

The rhetoric of the traditional ethos resulted in marketing that claimed, for example, that the cheque account system made wages 'last a little longer'. An informational leaflet declared that 'a cheque account meant higher wages': it was easier to save, and at the same time one always had money on hand. Another oft-repeated argument was that cheque-books were a good way of managing one's personal finances, as people learned to account for their money by making notes on their cheque stubs. A chequebook thus compelled its holder to keep records of their spending, and made it easier to stick to a personal budget. Monthly bank statements were a convenient means of domestic accounting and self-control—something that savings banks had been preaching for a long time.[64]

The idea that cheques were a financial device for domestic accounting also spanned the allocation of money between husband and wife. There were several options. The wife could receive the housekeeping money in the form of a few cheques made out in appropriate amounts, she could have her own chequebook and make withdrawals from her husband's account, or the family could open another account for the wife.[65] These recommendations were predicated on the traditional male-breadwinner family with a housewife. Because of the cheque wages system, whether married or not, working women—an increasingly large group in 1960s Sweden—automatically had bank accounts of their own. That said, cheque accounts were still framed as calculative devices that promoted financial transparency in the family, making secrecy about money between spouses difficult. Some of the informational material spelled out that it could be used not only for accounting but also for renegotiating the family finances. This, according to voices in the press, troubled some 'employees of an older vintage' but was welcomed by others with a more 'modern view'.[66] The new cheque accounts raised fresh questions about financial norms and practices within the family.

Both official reports and bank adverts claimed that 'having a cheque account fosters people's economic responsibility and financial thinking'.[67] However, financial thinking as such was being updated, and not only in marketing narratives but also in banking practices. Cheque accounts introduced a new financial consumerism, which was best illustrated by how banks instructed their own staff. They were now to serve a different and much broader clientele than before. Management explained the benefits of the new system: it offered 'valuable customer contacts' in addition to increased deposits. In the internal information about cheque accounts, bank staff were sometimes portrayed as advisors or educators, and sometimes as salesmen selling the bank's other products to new consumers: various types of bank accounts, traveller's cheques, savings and loans, safe-deposit boxes and share certificates.[68] Being both a salesman and an advisor was not a contradiction, as new consumers needed guidance in choosing between products in a 'financial department store'.[69] This metaphor, recurring at both Handelsbanken and Skandinaviska Banken, is one I will explore further in the next chapter.

The popular business weekly *Veckans affärer* (founded in 1965) published a long feature article in 1968 about the new bank services, explaining how banks had recently multiplied the financial products they had on offer 'by capturing the savers' dreams with various packagings', meaning that they labelled and redesigned similar types of accounts somewhat differently. The bankers in the interview confirmed that cheque accounts for wages had an important role in familiarising people with commercial banks. Once they had become customers, it was easy to introduce them to new products, most importantly to a new type of account that combined savings and loans, called savings-loan (*sparlån*).[70] The reasoning went, according to an internal document from the same year, that before the cheque accounts for wages it was common practice to organise workplace savings clubs, sometimes in collaboration with a local savings bank. Now, with the new payroll system, the savings clubs could easily be taken over and transformed into a bank service, or simply 'rationalised away', which would hopefully lead to increased savings in the cheque accounts or to a growing demand for the banks' other newly 'repackaged' savings-loan accounts.

The 'packaging' of the new banking products was sometimes done simply through the names they were given, other times also including new functions or an extra benefit. While, for example, the child benefit account (offered by most banks) was named for the source of the money and was designed to capture the monthly payments to all mothers with children under the age of 16, the Home Savings-loan and the Dream Holiday Savings-loan (at Handelsbanken) were named for the intended purpose of the savings, which after a few months of saving could be complemented with a bank loan. The account holders received various discounts on sought-after consumer goods such as TV sets, film cameras or caravans as part of specific marketing campaigns.[71] 'We are constantly striving to become more consumer-friendly', the PR expert and vice-president of Handelsbanken Eric Lindström said to the magazine *Veckans affärer*, also pointing out that 70 percent of Handelsbanken's deposits now came from households. So it was important, even in times of strict credit restrictions, to offer loans to ordinary customers. 'Lending to the public will be a growing part of the bank's operations', Lindström concluded: 'In future, we will build in more and more service [into our products]'.[72]

However, it was not only current accounts, target savings and consumer loans that were on offer. In 1968, the two largest commercial banks added another type of 'account' to their range, the Equity Investment Service (Aktietjänst), and advertised it to their new clientele along with the savings-loans. The idea was to make investing in shares easy, without eliminating the risk aspect. The account holder only had to put money in the account and the bank did everything else—for a fee—including choosing and administering stocks.[73] This differed from mutual fund saving, which had been introduced in Sweden in 1958 and popularised from 1978.[74] Rather, the Equity Investment Service set out to package share investments in the same convenient, consumer-oriented manner that worked well for other bank accounts. With its fees a bit too high, this product may not have attracted the broad public it was designed for, but it was there on display.

We can observe several things here. First, banks constructed their initial marketing of cheque accounts around a traditional ethos of thrift, which probably helped with the cultural relational work of the new bank customers. Second, this ethos—and thrift itself—was soon updated and commodified, as a wide range of new financial products were created and offered to the cheque account holders. The sociologists Turo-Kimmo Lehtonen and Mika Pantzar have pointed out that adverts for bank savings in 1950s Finland were often based on anticipatory pleasure and the lure of consumerism.[75] For the Swedish banks, the argument goes a step further: a new ethos of thrift was mobilised when consumer loans were marketed. A few years later, as will be seen in Chapters 4 and 5, this technology would be even more explicit when consumer credit was redefined as deferred savings or 'post-purchase savings'. Thus, the direct deposit reform framed cheques as a convenient form of payment and turned the cheque accounts for wages into a gateway to other 'well-packaged' financial products, which commodified not only saving but also borrowing and investing, and helped to redefine the ethos of thrift. Third, and most important for this chapter, there was a shift from the workplace to the bank as the site of personal financial activities, whether as wage payments or workplace savings clubs, thus confirming the intricate remaking of wage earners into financial consumers.

Inconvenient Money

The banks' efforts to get the influx of customers to adopt new financial habits and to turn them into competent, bankminded consumers of financial products were, however, not entirely consistent with the subject positions activated at the time of their enrolment through the mass acquisition of wage-earning groups. Some of the elements in the marketing discourse were also at odds with the prevailing financial ethos. As a result, after its optimistic beginnings the cheque system in Sweden became quite controversial.

A strong notion of money as cash—as opposed to cheques or credit—persisted in the public consciousness, making it difficult for cheques to be accepted as everyday money. Although consumer credit had been slowly increasing since the late 1950s and was taking on different forms (such as hire purchase contracts and credit cards, as discussed in Chapter 4), cash was still commonly seen as the proper medium for everyday consumption. This attitude was fuelled by the strong anti-credit norms promoted since the turn of the century by the influential Swedish Consumer Cooperative Union (Kooperativa Förbundet, KF), with its nearly 1.4 million members in the mid-1960s.[76] The cash-only policy of the cooperative shops was well established (see Chapter 5). Also considering the importance of the savings banks in Swedish society, which traditionally conveyed a similar message, one could say in a Zelizerian way that money in the bank was not thought of as money for consumption but as savings. This was initially used as an argument by both the banks and the government to justify the new system: direct deposits into the bank on payday not only meant an increase in deposits and savings but also fostered thrift among the population.[77]

In practice, however, the idea that bank money was not for daily consumption was an obstacle to the success of the cheque system among the broader public. This was revealed in the intense media debates on Saturday closing, a topic that dominates in the banks' collections of press cuttings. In 1962, Swedish commercial banks started staying closed on Saturdays during the summer months to meet the demands of the bank employees' union. Despite the general discontent ventilated in the media, in 1964 Saturday closing was extended and in 1966 it was introduced for the entire year.[78] Critics pointed out the irony of the situation: first the banks enrolled over a million Swedish wage earners and provided them with cheque accounts—whether they wanted it or not—and then shortly after decided to remain closed on the busiest shopping day of the week, and the only day when working people had time to visit a bank.[79]

Bankers complained about the 'the hysterical demand for service' aired in the media, arguing in their defence that cheques made Saturday opening unnecessary, and they encouraged account holders to pay with cheques instead of trying to cash them.[80] Despite extensive information campaigns, criticism flared up again in 1966. The cheque accounts were not at all 'convenient', the critics said; in fact, they were extremely inconvenient. It was hard to get cash, it took time to fill out the cheque and queues were growing in shops. It was not just the Saturday closing that was criticised but the whole cheque accounts for wages system, which the press described as a 'misery' and 'a ridiculous attempt to play America'.[81]

Shopkeepers complained even more loudly than the cheque account holders. Many protested at having to serve as 'Saturday banks'. Others, mainly larger retail companies, institutionalised their bank operations and opened exchange offices. For example, in 1966, the department store Ströms in Gothenburg advertised its own 'bank service'.[82] From the retailers' point of view, cash payments were preferable, not only because they saved time and avoided risks but also because they required no inspection of identity papers. Swedish banks guaranteed all cheques up to SEK 500 (approx. SEK 5,800, €530 in today's money), provided that the shop assistant checked the customer's identity. But asking for identification was considered rude and humiliating, and retailers feared it would harm their relationship with consumers. Sales assistants often preferred to take the risk and not ask. The issue was controversial and emotionally charged—and, again, it brought up the question of class. Cheques were only a 'sign of class' when they were accepted without identity documents being requested. Monitoring cheque users based on a collectively defined wage-earner identity did not work well at the shop counter (see further in Chapter 6).[83]

Clearly, cheques were inconvenient and not seen as real money, at least not by all the new cheque account holders.[84] It was considered important to have the possibility to cash a cheque at any time; therefore, the banks being closed on Saturdays was a concern. In an attitude survey conducted by the Bankers' Association in 1966, cheque users suggested that cheques should come with preprinted amounts (more like real money). In the same study, about half of the interviewees expressed that 'it was more real and honest to pay with cash'. These negative opinions about cheques, the poll shows, were more common among industrial workers and people with lower incomes from lower educational backgrounds.[85] This confirms the insight that banks had to overcome class boundaries when socialising workers into the formerly upper-middle-class practice of using cheques; or rather, the class coding of cheques and other 'bank monies' had to be changed.

FINES, FEES OR FINANCIAL EDUCATION?

The banks tried to fight the negative public opinion against Saturday closing by pointing out that people should pay by cheque. However, when the cheque account holders followed this advice and used cheques 'as if they were ready money', it led to even bigger problems, such as high bank overheads because of overdrafts, bounced cheques and higher rates of cheque fraud.[86] The costs were not limited to the banks, either; shopkeepers were also affected. The main weekly magazine of the retail trade, *Köpmannen*, complained:

> While the banks deliberately make every effort to put cheques in the hands of every Tom, Dick and Harry—without any 'aptitude tests' which, as we know, they were extremely thorough with before, when some unknown [person] wanted to open a cheque account—they put all the responsibility for the system to run smoothly on the shoulders of the shopkeepers and shop assistants.[87]

Once again, what critics saw as too broad a recruitment was raised, this time intertwined with whether the new bank customers were 'mature' enough to use cheques. How were the problems to be solved, and whose responsibility was it?

In 1965, the journal of the Bankers' Association claimed that the cheque salary system was incurring heavy losses, with every account costing the banks SEK 35–55 a year. The costs were already well known to the banking industry, and it was really a question of how to count; after all, the new customers meant profits from other services, as was often stressed in other contexts. This time, however, the commercial banks chose to highlight the costs as they wanted to introduce account charges, and lobbied for a legislative change to make the misuse of cheques, such as overdrafts and writing cheques that bounced, a criminal offence.[88] These being extremely sensitive issues, the banks failed on both points.

Banks charging fees for cheques was discussed at length in the press in 1965.[89] The discussions, as one observer put it, reflected 'a general anger' and 'a tendency for misunderstanding'. The trade unions also protested.[90] One evening paper declared that the introduction of a fee would be a 'death sentence' for the system.[91] An editorial in one of the largest daily newspapers, *Dagens Nyheter*, said the idea was simply unacceptable for wage earners:

> The idea of fees on cheque accounts is stillborn. It is the most insolent suggestion. ... Charging employees an extra fee just for getting paid for their work is something that falls by its own absurdity.[92]

The press was unanimous in its criticism. Cheques were neither the wage earners' idea nor their choice, and they had been forced to accept the new system whether they liked it or not. One commentator even urged readers to simply withdraw all their money from their bank.[93] These opinions suggest that the public, at least as mediated by the press, did not yet relate to cheques like the imagined consumers in the 'department store of finance' but rather from a subject position as wage earners and employees. Paying to access one's own wages seemed absurd. Bankers' recollections confirm this insight. 'It was impossible then, according to the banks' marketing people. Now it's a no-brainer to add such charges', said one banker in a 2007 interview about attitudes in the late 1960s.[94] The wage-earner identity category that banks had exploited to introduce cheques and recruit hundreds of thousands of new customers had backfired. Unlike the other commercial banks, state-owned Kreditbanken refused to consider charging for cheque accounts. Since this was one of the major players, and as they faced a public outcry against possible charges, the other banks hastily capitulated.[95]

Another way of dealing with the problem of profitability was to reduce the misuse of cheques, especially overdrafts. In 1964, the Bankers' Association called for an amendment to the law on cheques, seeking to make wrongful handling of cheques (whether intentional or not) a criminal offence. In 1965, a private member's bill with the same content was introduced in the Swedish Parliament. Using uncovered cheques with fraudulent intent was already punishable according to the criminal code. But overdrafts were treated as a civil wrong rather than a criminal offence, and were to be handled in a civil case between the bank and the drawer.[96] When circulated for consideration, the new proposal provoked devastating criticism against the whole cheque system that was also ventilated in the media.[97] In its comments, the Bank Inspection Board wrote that the situation with misuse and cheque fraud was not surprising when

> [E]ntirely new groups of citizens indiscriminately and without vetting were enrolled in the cheque accounts for wages system. ... [One] suddenly puts in the hands of a very broad public—young and old—a means of payment, for which they are not mature, and which can so easily be abused. What is needed is education and energetic propaganda for the right use of this new means of payment. It is therefore the responsibility of the banks themselves to steer developments in the right direction.[98]

Thus, the Bank Inspection Board recommended education—along with increased selectiveness—not criminalisation. A rather condescending tone about the new cheque account holders was combined with blame placed on the banks. The Court of Appeal of Skåne and Blekinge (in southern Sweden) was even harsher in its criticism of the banks: criminalisation was not a sound solution. The problem was not the wrongful conduct of some individuals, it said, but rather the fact that the banks had enrolled them in the first place. If the system did not work, it would be better to get rid of it altogether:

> The cheque salary system ... has been promoted because of one-sided and narrow economic considerations, without the human consequences taken into account. ... Cheque accounts were largely and without previous

screening put into the hands of people who lack the capacity to manage them.[99]

No penal measures as criminal law were introduced against cheque abuse. The authorities instead left it to the banks to take care of the problems, with intensified education and better prior screening of cheque account holders. But these were two very different strategies, the first aiming to create, through education, 'bankminded' financial consumers who had 'maturity, a sense of justice and a certain orderliness' and the other to sort out those who did not have these qualities.[100] Both strategies would address the individual rather than social groups. A return to increased selectiveness in the recruitment of account holders was not a realistic option now, in a time of 'mass-administered' cheque accounts, and when most of the population were already bank customers. The Bankers' Association sceptically reflected on the Bank Inspection Board's recommendations and doubted that it was possible to sort out in advance those employees who were not 'mature' and 'orderly' enough.[101] What remained was financial education.

Financial education was also a marketing opportunity to be exploited. A typical example of how banks tried to educate their new customers is the newsletter quoted at the beginning of the chapter. *Kontokuriren*, published by Kreditbanken between 1967 and 1971, was sent out to the approximately 200,000 cheque account holders with their account statements. Other banks also produced similar publications that combined advertising, information and financial education. *Kontokuriren* provided general information on personal finance and banking in a popular tone, as well as useful tips and ideas about how to use—fill out, sign and pay with—cheques, how to keep one's chequebook safe and how to manage the account itself. It offered advice on everyday budgeting and taxes; it discussed children's pocket money, as well as the stock exchange and how to invest in shares. The purchase of consumer durables and consumer credit were recurring topics. A Q&A column helped solve mundane financial problems, such as how to share a cheque account with family members. But the newsletter also offered a handy template for calculating credit costs, and some practical explanations of how banks assess credit applicants. There were, of course, also advertisements for the bank's various accounts, and for the credit cards of the company Köpkort, which was owned by the Swedish banks (see further in Chapter 4).[102]

This publication addressed new bankminded financial consumers—not the wage earners. It also introduced to the public, in a popular form, a few key ideas that later became dominant and are often seen as defining features of a neoliberal financialisation of everyday life. *Kontokuriren* explained that families should think about their finances in the same way as business companies do, meaning not only that they should strive for their money to 'work' and make more money, but also that they should think about consumer loans in terms of a possible good investment. The newsletter argued that 'there is nothing wrong with borrowing money'; on the contrary, consumer credit was also a way of saving one's money. It simply entailed saving after the purchase, rather than before. Households should try 'to smooth out peaks in expenditure' by using, for example, credit cards. Economists such as Milton Friedman, who introduced the concept of consumption smoothing, were not mentioned, but the idea was the same. Likewise, the emphatic phrases used in the newsletter about 'King Consumer' having a 'free choice' recall the figure of the sovereign consumer favoured by neoliberals.[103] These ideas were mediated in a jovial and banal manner, but stand out as remarkable in a society where the dominant discourse on consumers, represented by welfare state agencies and the consumer cooperative movement, was rather different, as I will explore in more detail in Chapter 5.

Turning Wage Earners into Financial Consumers

In the late 1950s, Swedish banks started a race for ordinary people's money by offering to handle the payment of wages and salaries. This chapter has explored the cultural challenges and relational work triggered by the introduction of the cheque-account wages and argued that this reform is key to understanding the bankification of everyday life. It marks the beginning of the process and reveals the challenges related to class, as well as the fact that the banks took over tasks that had previously belonged to the workplace—wage payments, collections of union fees, savings clubs—and, finally, how the cheque accounts and the banks' educational efforts concerning their use functioned as a gateway between an old personal financial ethos and a new one.

Class barriers and ideological differences had to be surmounted when commercial banks, which had formerly served businesses and the upper classes, set out to recruit a new mass public. The banks accepted collecting the trade union fees and welcomed a 'new category of customers' to their counters. The welfare state, with its financial regulations, levelling incomes, secure employments and general social payments—and not least through its key subject, the wage earner—was a condition of possibility for the reform. But it was precisely the wage earner who was to be transformed into a bank customer and consumer of finance.

I pointed out the intricate double character of the relational work that was involved. Class differences had to be overcome, but class positions and collective identifications functioned as vehicles of the bankification of everyday life: first through the collective recruitment, when the entire workforce of a company was enrolled overnight in the same bank. They became bank customers in their capacity as wage earners. Second, this group affiliation made it possible to envisage a (collective) control based on this capacity. This control was 'built in' into the system, it was claimed. While the sociologists Marion Fourcade and Kieran Healy argue that contemporary credit scoring in the United States replaced traditional categorisations in terms of class,[104] my point is that traditional conceptions of class (definitions rooted in the production side of life) were instrumental in establishing those financial services that are usually interpreted as undermining the very same traditional class-based differentiations. In contrast to the individual financial subjects depicted in studies of the financialisation of everyday life, the Swedish bankification was made possible through collective and class-based categorisations.

Class used as a means of recruitment and control on the one hand and class as something to overcome with the help of the new financial practices on the other were, however, not compatible with each other in the long run. While it was convenient to treat the new customers as a group of wage earners in order to recruit and control them, the same wage-earner identity made it impossible, for example, to introduce fees on the cheque accounts.

By looking at the cultural meanings attached to the chequebook itself, I have shown how its use was justified by references to an older, more traditional ethos of thrift, along with the simultaneous introduction of a new ethos of financial consumerism that promoted not only cheques but also loans and investments—often defined as savings or as new, updated forms of thrift. Banks were not only willing, but were also expected, to provide financial education to their new cheque customers. This further reinforced a new way of financial thinking, which, as mirrored in the banks' educational messages, included important ingredients of a neoliberal view of personal finance, such as consumer sovereignty as well as private credit as consumption smoothing and as saving after the purchase. Still, an economic ethos valuing cash purchases over cheque payments lingered even after the introduction of the cheque-account wages, as the debates about Saturday closing highlighted.

The fact that Sweden's early and successful bankification began with this reform does not mean that the cheque itself succeeded in the longer term. The cheque did not become a dominant means of payment, and by the early 1990s it had disappeared from everyday commerce. From the late 1960s, the use of cheques was gradually circumscribed by restrictions, and in the early 1970s, it even suffered a major setback when retailers declared a boycott of cheques that lasted about 18 months.[105] The solution came, already before online banking (see Chapter 6), in the shape of three plastic cards: the ATM card, the credit card and the bank-issued ID card. The first ATM opened in Uppsala in 1967, just a week after the world's first cash machine was installed by Barclays Bank in Enfield in Britain.[106] Cash dispenser machines solved the problem of Saturday closings. Also, during the cheque boycott, commercial banks, including state-owned Kreditbanken, actively encouraged their cheque account customers to register for Köpkort, a credit card developed and operated jointly by the commercial banks since 1962.[107] Note, however, that these two alternatives to the cheque—ATM cards and credit cards—although similar in material form, were loaded with opposing cultural meanings. The ATM card helped to preserve the practice of cash payments, which was deeply rooted in a traditional ethos of thrift and was historically endorsed by the strong Swedish consumer cooperative movement. The credit card (which will be further discussed in Chapters 4 and 5), on the contrary, objectified consumer credit and would soon come to be associated with reckless spending, consumer temptation and sometimes also moral degeneration. So it is interesting to observe how easy the step was from cheque accounts for wages—introduced to promote thrift—to credit cards. Last, the standardised identity card, introduced by banks in the 1960s and issued to *all* clients in the early 1970s (which is the topic of Chapter 6), individualised control and identification. The next chapter, however, will explore one of the major bank campaigns launched in the wake of the cheque wages and explain the role that gender played in the banks' newfound interest in the money of ordinary households.

Open Access This chapter is licensed under the terms of the Creative Commons Attribution 4.0 International License (http://creativecommons.org/licenses/by/4.0/), which permits use, sharing, adaptation, distribution and reproduction in any medium or format, as long as you give appropriate credit to the original author(s) and the source, provide a link to the Creative Commons license and indicate if changes were made.

The images or other third party material in this chapter are included in the chapter's Creative Commons license, unless indicated otherwise in a credit line to the material. If material is not included in the chapter's Creative Commons license and your intended use is not permitted by statutory regulation or exceeds the permitted use, you will need to obtain permission directly from the copyright holder.

CHAPTER 3

Making Finance Familiar: Gender and the Domestication of Banks

In January 1961 some 1,200 women gathered at Folkets Hus, a large working-class public community centre in central Stockholm, for a one-day conference organised by Svenska Handelsbanken, one of Sweden's largest commercial banks.[1] It was the first in a long series of similar events that went by name of Gyllene Vardag, Golden Everyday in English. The largest live banking propaganda events of the time, between 1961 and 1969 a total of 80 conferences were held across Sweden, attracting packed audiences of between 300 and 2,000 women. Altogether about 70,000 women attended the Golden Everyday conferences, which were quite spectacular and notable for their size, setting and distinguished speakers. At the same time, these events were rather mundane because of their everyday content and audience of ordinary housewives. The bank offered informative talks, a lunch, a fashion show and a folder full of conference materials. Participants received a gold-coloured bankbook with a small sum already deposited in their name. Housewives rarely had an income of their own, and this was also a group that rapidly shrank in the 1960s as an increasing number of Swedish women entered the labour market. Although the Golden Everyday events enjoyed impressive media coverage, especially in local newspapers, one may wonder why the bank chose to invest considerable sums in this campaign. What message was conveyed and why was it important? By making sense of the Golden Everyday conferences, this chapter explores why and how banking and financial services came to be embedded in everyday domestic

© The Author(s) 2025
O. Husz, *Bankminded*, Palgrave Studies in Economic History, https://doi.org/10.1007/978-3-031-77653-3_3

culture. These conferences, scrutinised in a broader historical context, reveal that gender is key to understanding the domestication of banks and the bankification of everyday life.

The large-scale Golden Everyday campaign was literally 'a performance of popular finance'. Canadian political scientist Rob Aitken proposes the term popular finance to describe financial education and promotional programmes run by government, business and non-profit organisations in twentieth-century United States.[2] These programmes, including advice, adverts and marketing materials, aimed to incorporate large groups of the population into extended financial markets, and were thus vehicles of the financialisation of everyday life. For Aitken, and for other scholars inspired by Foucauldian theory, popular finance ventures should be understood as ways to 'perform capital'. Through the new body of knowledge presented and the ways people were addressed and asked to think like capitalists, these ventures contributed to integrate the household economy into the market. Thus, popular finance, as defined by Aitken and others, created new financial identities.[3]

In this chapter I am interested in gendered aspects of the process, and more specifically in the 'relational work' carried out—by banks—to embed finance and banking in domesticity. This Zelizerian concept, as explained in Chapter 1, refers to the efforts people put into matching and connecting what is perceived as belonging to the realm of the market with what are seen as parts of spheres centred on non-economic values, such as love, family and intimacy. According to Zelizer, these different areas of social life have often been perceived as 'hostile worlds', by both historical actors and social scientists. Instead, she argues for a framework that she calls the 'connected lives' approach, as best fit for the study of what people do in practice; that is, constantly making connections between the economy and lifeworlds built on other values.[4]

I use the case of the bank conferences for women to gauge why and how representatives of financial institutions 'performed' banking and finance, and how they engaged in relational work to reconcile the bank and financial matters with domesticity and intimacy. I argue that emotions as well as references to family life and to consumer skills were used not only to popularise banking but also to *domesticate* it, to link it to the domestic world and make it feel familiar to a broad public—both women and men. Thanks to rich archival material, the Handelsbanken campaign can serve here as a lens through which connections between bankification, gender and the welfare state become visible in a focused way.[5] Before I turn to the campaign itself, the context and the prehistory need to be discussed.

Banking on Gender Equality

The fact that the banking world was long populated by men—if perhaps more in discourse and image than in actual practice—is an insight stressed by historians of different countries.[6] In Sweden, women began entering the workforce of commercial banking (mostly in lower positions) in the late nineteenth century. They were also well represented among depositors in savings banks, but not among clients of the commercial banks.[7] In the early 1950s, commercial bank adverts were dominated by images of male bankers and their male clients, or rather 'business partners'. Women, if they featured at all, were depicted as needing help or having to overcome their 'fear of banks'.[8] At the same time, in other commercial discourses women were ascribed financial agency as 'the finance ministers' of the home, a common trope that had flourished since the early twentieth century, or as 'purchase managers of the family', an idea favoured in retail adverts, especially from the 1930s to the 1950s. This implies a way of thinking in terms of two different—and clearly gendered—financial logics: one belonging to the world of the market and the other to the domestic world.[9]

International research on banks' interest in soliciting a mass female clientele often singles out the connections to women's economic rights. In France, the historian Sabine Effosse argues, the 1965 matrimonial legislation that secured women's formal economic independence and thus allowed them to open a bank account without their husband's permission, prompted the French banks to launch extensive campaigns targeting women.[10] Meanwhile, Spanish banks had seen women as a major target group for their financial services already a few years *before* the 1975 change in legislation that granted married women in Spain the right to make economic decisions without their husband's permission.[11] In the United States, many banks had had so-called women's departments since the early twentieth century, though rather than emancipating women as financial actors this solution sometimes served to reinforce the image of them as needing special attention. Another North American innovation, the feminist banks of the early 1970s, was instead the response of activists protesting against the discrimination of women in finance, which was formally resolved by the Equal Credit Opportunity Act in 1974.[12]

In Sweden, as in other Nordic countries, the legal framework was different. Swedish women were free to open bank accounts of their own long before the 1960s. The Marriage Act of 1920 (Giftermålsbalken) had already granted married women their legal majority status while widows and even unmarried women were declared legally and economically independent far earlier. The 1920 law also secured formal economic equality between husband and wife.[13] Legislation on equal pay was introduced in 1947 for those working in the public sector and in 1960 for the private sector. Lastly, in 1970 the formal financial equality of spouses was completed with the introduction of an individual taxation model.[14] Women's participation in the labour market was high, and the 1960s saw a shift from a breadwinner–homemaker family model to a dual-earner model.[15] Notwithstanding women's early formal economic independence, it was not until around 1950 that commercial banks began to target them in their marketing, and these efforts accelerated in the 1960s.

Although the legislation on women's economic rights was clearly an important factor, the international comparisons support the impression that the causal link between legislation and the banks' marketing to women was not as straightforward as it first appears.[16] Instead, the increasing representation of women in banks' marketing messages may be better explained—alongside women's growing importance in the labour market and their rising incomes—by the need to change the banks' image and actual role in society. Embedding banks and banking in domesticity was a way to meet the needs of a mass consumer society, and was not least part of the process whereby the connections between the everyday money of households and the wider financial markets were tightened. In other words, when banks turned to a female public or played on female financial agency in their marketing, it was not necessarily—or not always—a sign of female empowerment but rather a way to domesticate banking and finance.[17]

WOMEN, FAMILY AND INTIMACY IN SWEDISH BANK MARKETING

Images of intimacy and family life entered the marketing narratives of Swedish commercial banks in 1948, when several large banks ran a series of adverts targeting mothers as the recipients of the newly introduced child benefit. Handelsbanken's adverts, depicting mothers with children, were the bank's first attempts to launch an entirely new marketing strategy (Fig. 3.1).

Even before the introduction of the cheque accounts for wages in the late 1950s, commercial banks had started reorganising their marketing and discussing how to reach out with 'livelier' advertising to a much broader public.[18] Earlier bank advertising was largely a way to

Fig. 3.1 'It's your responsibility', advert for the child benefit account at Handelsbanken, *Svenska Dagbladet*, 27 January 1948. Unknown artist. Used with the permission of Handelsbanken

support certain newspapers of a preferred political affiliation, and typically depicted the bank's main building along with a short message about solidity and the bank's reserves. Although, in the 1940s, Skandinaviska Banken and Handelsbanken also produced 'real' adverts, featuring mainly male figures and emphasising the banks' productive role in Swedish industry or reassuring the public that their money was safe, the so-called support adverts dominated.[19]

A memo from 1947 about Handelsbanken's advertising strategy noted that all conventional, 'meaningless' support adverts should be discontinued and that the bank's campaigns for the coming year would be built along two lines. The first and main line involved attracting small deposits. For this purpose, the memo stated, 'an appropriate connection' could be found in the new child benefit (*barnbidrag*), introduced the same year, with payments starting in 1948.[20] The second line, called popular statistics (*populärstatistik*), was to inform the general public about Handelsbanken's broad clientele and large number of shareholders.[21] The bank's executive director called it 'the public relations of free enterprise', and it would be key to correcting the negative societal preconceptions about banks. After all, this was a time when banks feared nationalisation while the business sector was taking steps to mobilise around the idea of a market economy.[22] The intent of this second line has been noted in the historiography and would remain present in the coming years and even decades, with the banks wanting to promote free enterprise and productive risk-taking, all while tackling the criticism of finance capitalism. In this chapter, however, I am interested in the first line, which entailed attracting small deposits by softening the bank's image, and which on closer examination stands out as an essential counterpart to 'the public relations of free enterprise'.

The adverts that Handelsbanken ran suggested that mothers—with the help of the bank—use the child benefit to build up a 'starting capital' for their children. The emotionally loaded images came with a quick calculation of the size of the expected capital (Fig. 3.1). There were several reasons why the bankers found that images of mothers with children offered an 'appropriate connection' or, to follow Zelizer, that they were a 'good match' for promoting bank services. It was topical and involved actual money—the universal child benefit was newly introduced, with the first payments due in the following year. Specialised child benefit accounts were therefore the first in a series of new differentiated, commodified bank accounts, as discussed in Chapter 2.[23] A mother with her children is also a classic image of love and care, and could therefore serve to familiarise banks. However, it was not immediately obvious at the time that a commercial bank would associate itself with social welfare payments.

The key to why Handelsbanken could choose this strategy without fear of alienating its existing clients lay in the outline of the Nordic social democratic welfare regime.[24] Like other social benefits introduced later, the child benefit was individual, paid in cash (rather than in *natura* or through tax deduction) and universal, being payable to all mothers with children under 16. Importantly, it concerned all Swedish families and was not a means-tested benefit, which could have stigmatised recipients. Therefore, more than simply reflecting an ambition to recruit female customers or to absorb social welfare payments into the banking system, the launch of the child benefit adverts seem to have been a more general attempt to literally 'familiarise' the services of commercial banks.[25]

For a follow-up to its new marketing strategy, Handelsbanken hired an advertising consultant in the early 1950s. In his report, the adman stressed the importance of 'softening' the bank's image; only then would it be possible to familiarise the public with a commercial bank. This softening could be done simply by creating a more 'cosy ambience' in the bank's offices and 'lightening up the solemn atmosphere, which people associate with banks and bank premises'. He also suggested that 'it should feel as easy for a person to go into a bank as it is to enter a dairy shop'. More importantly, he pointed out that the bank should aim to reach the female audience—and, through them, ordinary families—by advertising in popular magazines and women's journals. But, he admitted, many bankers found it difficult to accept that a bank should engage in mass advertising at all.[26] The same was true of the ambition to target women as an important customer group: it was something entirely new, at least for commercial banks. There was a telling Gallup opinion poll about bank adverts, conducted for Skandinaviska Banken in 1949 (see Chapter 2)—not only was the bank uninterested in surveying the attitudes of the social group categorised as 'working class'; it also excluded women entirely, so it was only men, and higher-class men at that, who were polled.[27]

Thus, women were first targeted by commercial banks around 1950, when family life and intimacy were also beginning to make inroads into banking narratives. However, it took a while for the new discourse to be commonplace, and it was not until the 1960s that femininity and domesticity became key elements in banking campaigns.

This is the context in which the Golden Everyday conferences must be understood. Whereas workers became customers at commercial banks not by choice but through their wage deposits, their wives had to be convinced to use the bank. Female customers continued to be interesting to the banks in the 1960s, as growing numbers of women were entering the labour market and even those without an income of their own received welfare payments; not only the child benefit but also mothers' insurance (1955, 1962) and pensions (increased by the reforms of 1948 and 1959). By the 1960s, the social policies of the Swedish welfare state had made women, and especially older women, economically independent, and had strengthened the economic situation of younger women, whether they were housewives or earned their own living.[28] Women were a relevant target group because they were thought to play an important role in the management of the household finances; but also, as I argue in this chapter, because they could lend an image of familiarity and everydayness to banking. Targeting women was a way to bridge the gap between the financial world of commercial banks and the familiar world of the home, and in the process both banking and domestic financial practices changed.

WOMEN AND MONEY: EARLY FINANCIAL EDUCATION CAMPAIGNS

Handelsbanken's Golden Everyday campaign was not the first, or only, attempt by a commercial bank to directly address a female audience. In the 1950s Skandinaviska Banken organised study courses on stock investing, as well as smaller evening meetings with lectures on finance and banking for women, held in conjunction with the Fredrika Bremer Association (FBA), Sweden's oldest women's organisation.[29] Frideborg Cronsioe, one of the bank's female chief accountants—and a member of the FBA—was the driving force behind these Women and Money (Kvinnor och pengar) meetings. They were typically held at local bank branches, and attracted 20–50 participants.[30] The lectures covered a range of topics from marriage legislation to shareholding and investments, but with a special focus on new bank services such as current accounts and loans. Cronsioe argued the importance of the 'economic education' of women by referring to statistics showing that over 50 percent of shareholders in companies on the Stockholm Stock Exchange were women. She also often reminded both the bank and her female audience that over

70 percent of all women outlived their husbands. Widows, she pointed out, were a group with considerable economic power, but often had no economic knowledge. Her oft-declared mission was to make women more 'bankminded' and less governed by a 'housekeeping-money mentality'; that is, too much petty cautiousness.[31] She may even have introduced the word bankminded into the Swedish personal finance jargon as hers were the earliest mentions in the sources. By bankminded, Cronsioe meant financial skills and a willingness to use bank services—traits which in her eyes were inseparable. However, her educational message was mainly addressed to women who had some money to start with.[32]

The collaboration between Skandinaviska Banken and the FBA culminated in a Nordic conference for female capital owners in 1956: Mrs World's Economic Affairs. This three-and-a-half-day meeting gathered almost 200 participants from Sweden and the other Nordic countries, an elite group of rich or professional women. The conference included lectures and workshops, visits to Swedish export companies, a dinner banquet and a fashion show in the hall of the bank's head office. This last feature, with models using the bank counters as a runway, attracted massive media attention (Fig. 3.2).[33]

As the catwalk on the bank counter turned out to be a popular feature, some local bank branches picked up the idea. Later that year, for example, Skandinaviska Banken in Luleå in northern Sweden organised courses for teenage girls and their mothers with the headline Charm and Money (Charm och pengar) that included a fashion show, in addition to a session on how to buy clothes, a 'guess the price' competition, and of course lectures on financial matters by the branch manager and Cronsioe herself. Skandinaviska Banken was also keen to project a modern image: the press noted that the girls were served Coca-Cola, which had been introduced in Sweden only three years earlier.[34]

The 1960s Golden Everyday conferences also included a fashion show and, like the teenagers' meetings, had a more popular, consumerist character than the earlier courses for female investors. The scale was substantially larger than that of earlier bank events for women, and indeed compared to any other campaigns by commercial banks. The mix of consumer education, entertainment and hard sell would have been familiar to Swedes, though, because of the uniquely Scandinavian genre of 'housewife films' (*husmorsfilmer*), launched in the 1950s and still flourishing in the 1960s, which were shown free in cinemas across the country on weekday afternoons.[35]

Fig. 3.2 Fashion show in the bank at the conference Mrs World's Economic Affairs, *Din Bank*, 3 (1956). Unknown photographer. Used with the permission of SEB

GOLDEN EVERYDAY: SETTING THE SCENE

The very first Golden Everyday conference was a collaboration between Handelsbanken, the popular evening newspaper *Expressen* and the Housewives' Association of Stockholm (Stockholms Husmodersförbund). It turned out to be a great success. For the next ten years the bank organised subsequent events on its own, with only occasional help from local Housewives' Associations and other women's organisations in distributing invitations.

The Golden Everyday conferences did not simply reflect new conceptions of personal finance, the bank's new self-assumed task and new financial subjectivities; this was a site where they were enacted and came into being. Therefore, an in-depth study of the form (the organisation, the mix of speakers, the type of audience) and content (the message, the lecture themes, how the audience was addressed) offers valuable insights into the relational work involved in the making of the new bankminded subject.

The reasons stated for organising the event were rather prosaic. In 1960, an employee working on recruiting new clients proposed a campaign targeting women because, he argued, there was detectable interest from women's organisations. Housewives, or as they were defined by the bank, 'women whose main interests are home and family', made up a target group of about 1.5 million, which had dropped to 1.1–1.3 million by the end of the 1960s. Bankers also referred to local competition with other banks or the need to put new bank branches on a secure footing with local communities.[36] The preparatory documents show that bank representatives wanted to create a serious ('course-like') programme with 'deeper' educational content from the beginning, while the co-organisers of the first conference, the evening newspaper *Expressen*, argued for a much 'easier' programme—a couple of hours mostly addressing consumer matters, with only one short speech on finance focusing on housekeeping money.[37] The result was closer to the bank's ambition: a full-day course with longer speeches and a popular but still serious take on both consumer issues and personal finance.

The bank's reasons as communicated to the audience—for example, in the opening address at the conferences—stressed its ambition to offer 'economic education' and to help people find their way to 'financial independence'—which, the speaker admitted, also benefited the bank. The bank thus wanted to inform its audience about its new and 'wide-ranging services'. And, referring to women's role in childrearing and managing the family finances, the presenter of the programme hoped that the conference's message would spread through society 'like rings on water'.[38]

ORGANISING THE EVENT

I think the Grand Cinema took in as many as it could hold. (Västerås 1962)

A sports hall with around 1,800 people does not exactly invite intimacy. (Umeå 1963)

I never would've thought that Skellefteå could produce so many women—
over 700 had come. (Skellefteå 1963)[39]

Concert halls, large community centres, city halls, cinemas, theatres, sport stadiums and once even a church: the conferences were held in premises large enough to host audiences ranging from a few hundred in smaller towns to almost 2,000 in larger cities.[40] Everything was planned down to the smallest detail, from the invitations—sent out with the help of local women's organisations—, flower arrangements and live background music, to the conference folder filled with informational and promotional materials and often small gifts. The main concept and the programme were created centrally, but the event was organised locally. The marketing department in Stockholm sent instructions and practical tips along with the printed matter, the local bank branch receiving a long list of things to bear in mind. Representatives of women's organisations were to be invited for lunch four weeks before the event to ensure their cooperation. The speakers were hired centrally, but had to be welcomed and escorted to dinner at the house of the bank's local managing director. Their travel and hotel arrangements were also the responsibility of the local branch. The venue and the lunch for hundreds of participants had to be booked. The local press was to be invited well in advance. Extra cloakroom staff had to be hired, and under no circumstances should they forget to relabel some of the venues' toilets from gents to ladies.

All this work and more was coordinated by a new category of employee at the bank: the consultant. It was usually also the consultant who acted as emcee.[41] With their new and broader clientele some of the larger banks, among them Handelsbanken, hired new staff for day-to-day PR work. The bank consultants were engaged in the acquisition of new customer groups and in PR activities, including information, education and even home visits. The word consultant is reminiscent of the educators and advisors of government agencies, for example the 'home consultants' at the State Institute of Consumer Affairs (Statens Institut för Konsumentfrågor, aka Konsumentinstitutet), but also of today's financial consultants. They were a new category of bank professionals, shouldering a double role. Internally, they acted as PR experts, instructing and advising staff 'to create a spirit of service and a sales-friendly atmosphere'.[42] Externally, they assumed the role of personal financial advisor, with the special task of recruiting new clients. This new professional group created, managed and, first and foremost, mediated the bank's expertise in personal finance to individuals, specific groups and the general public. Handelsbanken had already hired three consultants by 1957, when cheque accounts for wages and salaries were introduced (Chapter 2). By the mid-1960s it had over 30 bank consultants, and by 1970 fully 60 people at the bank had this title.[43] They had to go through internal training in banking techniques, marketing and sales, as well as the special courses organised yearly exclusively for this professional category. It was one of Handelsbanken's first consultants who had initiated the Golden Everyday conference in 1960, but as the campaign grew in scale, along with other smaller but similar events such as shareholding courses, it required a workforce of many more bank consultants, both centrally and at larger local branches.[44]

Audience and Speakers

> A large, large hall, with many, many women. Many of them of the sweater type. (Jönköping 1961)

> The ladies were gathering from all directions. Eager little squares with bulky hats and chubby bags. Average age rather high. (Kalmar 1962)

> Good acoustics—the audience just above middle age—friendly and wifelike—they look like large items in a mail order catalogue. Mean. No, you should not be mean in this very friendly environment. (Vänersborg 1962)

> Crowded, at least 700, and a good audience—the right age, active and rather good-looking, too. (Örebro 1963)[45]

A rather high average age, very ordinary appearance and friendliness characterised the typical audiences at the Golden Everyday conferences, at least according to one of the speakers, radio celebrity Maud Reuterswärd, the constant star of the events. Extracts from her diary have been preserved in Handelsbanken's archives. Here she gives her subjective but insightful perspective on the first three years of the campaign, with over 30 conferences. We learn about the growing sense of community among the speakers. Reuterswärd and her colleagues often reflected on the art of public speaking, problems with the stage or acoustics and, most of all, the expected and received response from the audience. The comments about travel arrangements (chartered planes, trains or cars), accommodation and fees reveal that this was a group of experienced professional speakers—both experts and entertainers.

We learn a great deal about the speakers' perceptions of the audience. Through the eyes of Reutersward (and indirectly those of her colleagues), we meet crowds of women, just slightly different in every town, captured in only a few photographs otherwise. It was a very housewifely crowd; so familiar and unspectacular, they even appear a bit boring. Reutersward often noted their age; it seems that a somewhat younger audience was considered a good thing, and the speakers appreciated it when they occasionally met groups of schoolgirls. The audience clearly differed from those at the more elite, small-scale bank meetings for women in the 1950s.

It is possible to generalise even more—based on the initial definition of the target groups, the press commentaries and a survey from 1964—and characterise the audience as mainly homemakers. Most were indeed full-time housewives, though some had part-time jobs or had formerly been employed.[46] In the late 1960s, the conferences were sometimes held in the evenings so that working women could attend. The programme remained similar, if shorter, and the speeches about consumption slightly shifted focus, sometimes even touching on politicised issues such as global solidarity.[47] But the typical all-day programme throughout the 1960s was tailored to suit the homemaker group.

The Capital of the Heart

Good ambiance and a very, very good response to everything. (Piteå 1962)

A warm atmosphere and it also feels meaningful. (Visby 1963)[48]

The conference programme was carefully orchestrated, and the organisers seem to have hit on an ideal format from the beginning. Some key speakers remained throughout the period while others varied, but the content and structure were left unaltered until the late 1960s.

The day always started with a welcome address from the local bank manager, probably to raise the status of the event. The first speaker then took the stage to talk about human relationships in daily life. She emphasised 'the capital of the heart'—love, affection, generosity—and urged the audience to be as 'spendthrift' as possible with it. It was an interesting start to a conference on banking and personal finance, topics typically considered to belong to the realm of rational calculation. The speaker, Maud Reuterswärd, was a Swedish celebrity, writer and radio personality, famous for her warm informal tone and at the time the host of a popular morning show. A mother of four, she portrayed motherhood in powerful, innovative ways in her radio programmes.[49] She was always first on the conference schedule, and her speech became a constant throughout the 1960s. The hiring of a genuine celebrity for the campaign reveals the ambition to reach a wide audience. However, it was not self-evident that it would be the same person for all those years. But Reutersward's speech, urging the audience 'not to economise with love' and delivered in her warm, well-known voice, was considered central to the event because, I would argue, it worked exceptionally well for the main point: making banking services and financial matters familiar. Infusing homely affection into the world of finance and banking obviously served well to deconstruct the traditional notion that they were hostile worlds.[50]

The next couple of talks on the programme were always about consumer issues, usually home decoration and food. The speakers varied, but were typically female consumer experts from the State Institute of Consumer Affairs or sometimes consumer critics and advisors working in the media. In the latter group were well-known names such as Willy Maria Lundberg, famous for her sharp tongue and critical tone against producers and retailers of low-quality consumer products, and Lena Larsson, a renowned interior architect and media personality celebrated for her radical ideas for modern living.[51] The speeches highlighted rational and practical but still enjoyable and colourful modern consumption. The speakers talked about meals that were healthy and easy to prepare, while at the same time aesthetically appealing. They also spoke about modern aesthetics and functional design in the home. The same discourse of practical yet aesthetically pleasing consumption was echoed in the fashion show that concluded the day. A female home consultant—a consumer expert from the Consumer Institute—commented on the outfits. With its not-so-glamorous name 'Sensibly Dressed for Every Day', the fashion show expanded on the theme of everyday life and included both women's and children's clothing, with items provided by local shops.[52]

All this consumer education is remarkably familiar from histories of Swedish consumer culture in the twentieth century, and it was no doubt equally familiar to the female audiences at the Golden Everyday meetings.

By then, consumer education framing values of rationality and functionalism had a long tradition in Sweden. Previous decades had also reinforced the image of the expert housewife becoming an expert consumer.[53] As the historian of architecture Helena Mattsson has pointed out, the postwar Swedish consumer was 'already well designed', meaning that the discourses and practices of 'reasonable' or 'rational' consumption had been well established since the 1930s and 1940s.[54] Consumer guidance had been an important part of the highly influential Swedish consumer cooperative movements' activities from the early years of the century. Since the 1930s, functionalists and social reformers had strived to shape consumers through the commodity itself, by redefining the concept of quality so that it fit a mass society. During the Second World War, the government also began to engage in consumer issues. Housewives were the most targeted group, and consumer skills became an essential part of the knowledge about 'the economics of the home'.[55]

The economic sociologist Richard Swedberg has characterised American home economics as a truly 'materialistic' take on economics. Scientifically focusing on cooking, cleaning and sewing, while successful in the early twentieth century it was on the wane by the 1960s as a profession, he notes, and was severely criticised by the feminist movement.[56] In Sweden the situation was different, and despite influences from the United States, home economics did not become an academic discipline in the same way.[57] It did not even have a fixed name, but terms such as 'domestic economics' or 'the economics of the home' (*huslig ekonomi, hemmets ekonomi*) were used. When the partly state-owned Home Research Institute (Hemmens Forskningsinstitut) was founded in 1944, it also included consumer knowledge in its profile. The Institute tested a range of products (children's socks, kitchen knives, washing machines) and studied the most efficient ways of using appliances (for example by employing Taylorian time studies of doing the laundry), based on which they published recommendations and norms for rational commodities and rational behaviour for (female) consumers. The Home Research Institute often figures in the historiography of Swedish reformism as an emblematic example of its social engineering ambitions, which included the transformation of family life. In that literature, though, topics like personal finance, banking and financial knowledge are hardly ever discussed.[58]

In 1957 the focus shifted entirely to consumer knowledge when the Home Research Institute was transformed into the State Institute of Consumer Affairs, the source of the 'home consultants' who

Handelsbanken hired for the Golden Everyday conferences. Similarly, the conference folder contained several brochures published by the Consumer Institute on subjects such as laundry or frozen food, and sometimes also copies of its magazine *Råd & Rön* ('Advice & Findings'). Like its British counterpart *Which?* or the French *Que choisir?*, this publication, published since 1958, presented matter-of-fact consumer information and reported the results of quality and safety tests.

Thus, while traditional domestic skills in general might have seemed somewhat obsolete in the 1960s context, this was not the case for consumer skills in particular, although consumer education was not new. And, as the consumer lectures at the Golden Everyday conferences illustrate, in the 1960s it also became more common to add a sprinkling of glamour to a well-known consumer discourse and to emphasise not only the rational but also the emotional element in consumption.[59] The bank's reasons for including consumer speeches are not given in the sources, but the determination to establish the bank as an authority on consumer issues betrays its ambition to embrace all domestic money management, including consumer spending. This interpretation is borne out by the launch of the differentiated bank accounts for savings-loans (Chapter 2) and the narrative of the new 'intimate relationship' between the bank and its clients (Chapter 1).[60]

In any case, the consumer speeches anchored the bank's image in an already familiar discourse. Consumer skills were not only easy for a female audience to identify with but also involved economic agency and seemed highly relevant to personal finance. And not least, the speakers from the Consumer Institute—which after all was a government agency—lent legitimacy to the bank's marketing efforts, blurring the line between educating and selling.

The Bank as a Department Store

Around 1960, it was not yet self-evident that a bank would 'sell' anything, let alone to large groups of consumers such as office clerks, shop assistants, factory workers or housewives. It was only when banks started offering payroll services and hoped to sell other novel financial products to a much larger public that those responsible for internal information felt the need to explain to bank officials 'Why, how, and what we shall sell'.[61] In-house magazines pointed out that bankers needed to acquire new skills, and banks offered their staff courses in sales technique and customer service.⁶² Internal publications reveal a new emphasis on having the right 'selling attitude', which also involved the staff's attire and general appearance (including hairstyles and make-up).⁶³ In 1958, the in-house magazine of Skandinaviska Banken carried an editorial by one of the directors, titled 'Bank Services for Sale'. It started with a defence of the redefinition of banking work as selling:

> Does our work really have to do with sales? Many of us might be reluctant to even utter the word 'selling' when it comes to our daily work. A bank is surely something much finer and more dignified than a grocer's or a clothes shop? But actually, there is no significant difference.⁶⁴

This was undoubtedly a new discourse for the banking world. The same magazine launched a debate in 1962 by asking 'Are we going too far?' with the many services offered in order to attract consumers. The first contributor to the debate brought up the women's conferences as an example:

> One bank organises conferences for women and another for stock investors. ... All banks advertise cheque accounts for salaries. ... Haven't we moved too far from proper banking tasks?⁶⁵

Events like the Golden Everyday conferences were sometimes criticised by banking officials as commercial 'ballyhoos', unworthy of a serious bank. The new bank consultants were initially hired exactly because many older bank officials struggled to adjust to being proactive 'salesmen', as the former executive director of Handelsbanken Jan Wallander explains in his memoirs.⁶⁶

According to a survey conducted in three towns in 1965, the second most popular feature of the Golden Everyday conferences after Reutersward's speech was the talk given by Elsa Nygren, a female accountant, who became one of Handelsbanken's directors in 1966. Nygren was the first woman to hold this high post in a Swedish commercial bank.⁶⁷ Her speech—with the telling title 'Handelsbanken's Department Store' ('Varuhuset Handelsbanken')—was a pure 'sales talk' about all the services and financial 'goods' the bank had to offer: A commercial bank was not, as many might think, only a business partner for trade and industry. Instead, she said, most bank services were for 'us everyday people'; her inclusive 'us' is not to be missed here. She talked about travellers' cheques and foreign currency exchange. She explained the benefits of buying stocks and shares, bonds and securities. Cheque accounts had usually been brought up in the introductory talk by the local bank office manager, but Nygren also told the audience about them and the many other specialised accounts, for example the Dream Holiday account for savings and loans for travel purposes, a product conveniently launched when new legislation in 1963 increased the statutory right to paid leave from three to four weeks.[68] As one commentator wrote, 'Senior Accountant Nygren was really able to speak in favour of her product and sold the bank energetically. Who knows, we may see 1,200 new Dream Holiday accountholders in Gothenburg!'[69] The proliferation of accounts, differentiated mainly by their name, target group and purpose, as Chapter 2 explored, was typical of the period and fitted well with the department store metaphor.[70] Nygren was not the only one to invoke this analogy to explain the essence of consumer banking. In the 1960s, it featured across Handelsbanken's adverts and popular presentations, and was used by other commercial banks as well, such as when Skandinaviska Banken introduced the slogan 'Your Bank—A Department Store of Finance'.[71]

After Nygren's talk (and before the concluding fashion show), the audience were told they would receive their own Golden Everyday account, complete with a deposit of SEK 5 and a specially made golden bankbook, in yet another typical example of the differently 'packaged' banking services in the Handelsbanken 'department store'. By accepting bank accounts opened in their names, women were literally turned into bank customers.

As the bank addressed the audience with both advice from consumer experts and pure sales talks, referencing traditional consumer skills and consumer metaphors, it is safe to conclude that the typical subject position that came into being at the Golden Everyday conferences was the *financial consumer*, as opposed to the saver, investor or borrower. All these activities were indeed mentioned, but were framed as consumption. Nygren promoted shares and bonds by recommending them as appreciated gifts for youngsters: they were not only 'decorative' but also 'educational', and stocks were not only an 'enjoyable hobby' but also a way to pique children's interest in the economy and entrepreneurship, and give them 'a part of the future'.[72] Traditional bank accounts intended for savings or those for savings-loans were presented as commodities to be 'chosen' and 'purchased' by consumers.[73] Savings-loan accounts, a new

Fig. 3.3 Budget consultant Gunnel Petre at a Golden Everyday event, *Arbetet*, 14 October 1965. Unknown photographer. Discontinued newspaper

form of consumer credit (Chapter 2), were typically used for household appliances like washing machines or dishwashers. So for these accounts, housewives were a particularly interesting target group.[74] Savings-loan accounts designed for specific products were a further example of the banks' new, more 'intimate', involvement in people's everyday consumption.

Budgeting for Equal Worth—But Only After Dad's Eaten a Good Meal

The conferences thus started with love, compassion and generosity, continued with consumer skills, and ended with the bank selling its products. Two other speeches in between offered more straightforward financial education and illustrated the banks' claims to a new authority in family matters. First, a female lawyer discussed marriage legislation, prenuptial agreements and women's financial rights. She often started with the Swedish Marriage Act of 1920, which had introduced economic independence and financial equality for married women and stated that husband and wife had the right to the same economic standard of living. She then drew attention to the fact that the same law had also established that spouses had to inform each other about financial matters, for example income and expenses. The law did not, however, offer guidelines about appropriate household expenses or personal allowances for housewives or their husbands; families had to solve this on their own in their financial planning, she stressed, concluding that economic transparency was the key to a marriage without disputes and rifts.

Budgeting and accounting within the family was the topic of the next speech, the last one at the conference and the key moment of the whole event. The speech, usually called 'What Does Mother Know About Money?', introduced a concrete technical device for money management: the household budget.[75] Instructive templates for budget sheets were included in the conference folder to back up the talk. The speaker, one of the regular speakers at the conferences, was the 'budget expert' Gunnel Petre (Fig. 3.3). While she might not have been the only one with this rare professional expertise in Sweden around that time she was certainly one of few, and the most prominent.

When the Golden Everyday campaign started, Petre was the head of the Taxpayers' Association's Budget Bureau. With a membership of 60,000–80,000 in the 1960s, the Taxpayers' Association was a non-profit organisation founded in 1921 at the initiative of Sweden's most prominent industrialist and banker Marcus Wallenberg, to fight what it characterised as 'wastefulness in public expenditure'.[76] It was an attempt to mobilise broader middle-class interests for free entrepreneurship and against high taxes as well as what was seen as the costly bureaucratic machinery of the welfare state. Its Budget Bureau was established as early as 1927 to offer personal financial advice and to help individuals and families in setting up a budget. This was the first (and for a long time, the only) such service in Sweden. Its advice covered spending and allocating money within the family: the appropriate amount of housekeeping money or the cost of children and how much pocket money they should have, along with topics such as savings, taxes, investments, credit costs and insurance. The Budget Bureau's experts also published advice books, produced budget templates and advocated more informed budgeting practices for households.[77]

In the 1950s and the early 1960s, experts in household budgeting were still rare. No professional training was available in 'family finances' *(familjeekonomi)* or 'personal finance' *(privatekonomi)*—the two concepts were used interchangeably—other than the courses in the late 1950s and early 1960s for new bank consultants, which used Petre's own publications. While Frideborg Cronsioe, Petre's counterpart at Skandinaviska Banken, had professional banking experience, Petre herself had a background in journalism and experience from a couple of study tours in the United States.[78] This was a new field of knowledge, taking shape at the intersection of communication and banking.

At the bank conferences, Petre talked about how money should be allocated within the family. Husband and wife should both have insight into the family budget, she claimed. As they had the right to the same economic standards, they ought to have the same amount of 'pocket money' for their personal use. Admittedly, one of them, often the husband, might have greater needs such as work-related entertaining; however, Petre said, it was better to share equally because the same money generally signified equal worth. She also advised spouses to have their own bank accounts, and preferably an additional cheque account for daily household spending.[79] The norms and practices of personal bank accounts in Sweden were quite different to, say, those in the United Kingdom, where joint accounts were common practice, making married women a less interesting group for banks to target.[80]

Open communication about the family's budget was thus vital, according to Petre. However, feminine wiles might be needed to find the right moment. Her advice was: discuss the family finances after a good meal and combine 'cold numbers' with a 'warm attitude'.[81] This rhetoric reveals her attempt to carefully address the conventional conception of the family as an emotional sphere as opposed to the 'cold', calculative sphere of money. As Zelizer has shown, societies throughout history offer many examples of culturally specific ways in which the 'hostile worlds' of economy and intimacy could be reconciled.[82] Petre's practical suggestions to combine the 'cold numbers' with a 'warm attitude' were an important piece of the general message of the conferences (intentional or not) about reconciling emotions and finances.

Another balancing act revolved around the notion of financial independence. This concept has traditionally been a buzzword in financial education and advice literature, signalling the purpose—the ultimate goal—of all personal financial practices. At the Golden Everyday conferences, the idea was typically emphasised already in the welcome address.[83] However, placed in the context of family finances and women's money financial independence took on a gendered, emancipatory meaning. So although Petre's rhetoric and references were rooted in a traditional 'housewifely' discourse of separate gender spheres and distinctive femininity, her practical recommendations about money management pointed towards a practice informed by (financial) gender equality.[84]

Consumer credit was yet another relevant but sensitive topic that her talk touched upon. Petre's views on consumer loans were characterised as 'modern' by a banking professional of the early 1960s. A reviewer of her 1960 book, writing in a banking magazine, acknowledged that Petre looked at consumer credit in an unusually 'relaxed' and 'objective' way, 'without finger-wagging'. This was most welcome, the reviewer continued, as moralising, judgmental views and ignorance about the advantages of modern credit prevailed among those involved in financial education: modern credit, as Petre 'rightly recognised', should be understood as 'post-purchase savings' or 'future savings'. We know these ideas from the discussions triggered by the mass-introduction of cheque accounts, and they will be even more important in the case of credit cards (Chapters 4 and 5).[85] A local bank manager, however, voiced a more traditional ethos when he commented on the absence of savings and thrift from the Golden Everyday programme, wondering in a marginal note why 'this Petre, being a budget expert … did not cover it really'.[86]

Petre could not include much about her views on either savings or consumer credit in her short conference talk, but did eventually have the chance to influence Handelsbanken's main communication strategy in regard to women and families. Recruited by the bank in 1964, she left the Taxpayers' Association for a job as a 'budget consultant' at Handelsbanken. She built up an advisory service there, which started offering personal financial consultancy for a small fee. The bank published booklets on domestic topics such as 'What is Enough Housekeeping Money?', 'What Should Young People Pay at Home?' and 'How Much Do Children Cost?', edited and often written by Petre herself. But along with these and various budget templates, Petre's department also produced brochures on 'Saving in Shares' and 'Safe Asset Management'.[87]

Petre edited a follow-up brochure for the Golden Everyday campaign, running through the conference topics. Titled 'She and Handelsbanken', it was distributed to participants in 1965 and 1966. The 1966 version included an article on housekeeping money and another on stock market investments ('Want to buy some shares?'), in which she assured readers that shareholding was not only 'for the rich' and that ordinary people could also buy stocks and shares (for example by forming a shareholding club). The brochure invited people to turn to Handelsbanken for professional advice about *both* housekeeping money and equity investments, effectively blurring the lines between domestic money and market money.[88]

Thus, the campaign not only transformed the public into bank customers but also led the bank to commit itself to a new field of knowledge, which came to be known as family finances *(familjeekonomi)*. Recruiting a budget expert was clearly an important step. Similar positions were created at other commercial banks, for instance at Skandinaviska Banken, when Frideborg Cronsioe was appointed in 1961 to a newly created post with a special PR remit to provide information for families, women, and young people.[89] She had lectured on personal finance for years alongside her job as a branch manager, but in 1961 this expertise was formalised.

Until the late 1950s the experts on the domestic sphere, from the technology of housework to planning consumer expenses, were the domestic science teachers, consumer educators and home consultants who worked for various non-profit and government organisations.[90] There were negotiations—and competition—between these different agents and institutions, and sometimes commercial forces (such as department stores) also claimed expertise, but commercial banks were absent in this context.[91] Now the banks emerged as the main experts on family financial matters, which meant that both the content and the context changed. As the banks' booklets on family finances demonstrate, housekeeping money was now mentioned in the same breath as buying shares. Erasing the distinction between domestic money and market money was the main point of the banks' intervention in domesticity.[92]

In the same move, the banks also made inroads into the non-commercial spheres of domestic expertise. The commercial banks' budget experts could be hired by government or non-profit organisations, just as State Institute of Consumer Affairs staff were occasionally hired by banks. Few reflected on the fact that the personal financial thinking the banks advocated, in terms of financial independence and entrepreneurial attitudes, was built on the ideas promoted by—among others—the anti-socialist Taxpayers' Association. These were more important outcomes than the actual deposits solicited from the conference participants.

Notes from a 1969 strategy meeting at Handelsbanken reveal that its consultants were struggling to find time for the conference preparation and follow-up, as they were busy with other sales-related duties. The immediate benefits of the campaign were in doubt. Nearly 50 percent of the Golden Everyday accounts remained untouched, but local variations were significant, and it was impossible to tell whether the women had chosen to open another type of account instead. Despite the problems, however, the speakers, the public and the local branches (except for the branches in the new suburbs of Stockholm) were still positive about Golden Everyday. As local bank officials were quick to point out, such events received good coverage in the local press, which represented a considerable saving on expensive advertising.[93] The campaign was shut down in 1970, mainly due to a radical change in Handelsbanken policy, which—under its new executive director Jan Wallander—cut all its advertising and promotional activities.[94] By then, however, banking practices were already domesticated, having become familiar to a mass public who were now regularly using the bank's financial products and services.

Domesticated Banks, Emancipated Women?

The 1950s have been called the decade of the housewife in Sweden; but this period was also, one could add, the decade of the consumer expert. Gender historians of the welfare state have characterised the 1960s as a period of change, with a double-breadwinner model gradually replacing the former ideal of a breadwinner–homemaker household. The movement away from domestic work had begun in the 1950s, historians note, although this was not always mirrored in the statistics, which did not include all types of work.[95] What we know for certain is that 'gender roles' were intensely debated in the 1960s, the situation of housewives often being a case in point. Some critics, such as the liberal feminist Eva Moberg, wanted to do away with the supposedly natural connection between women and the home. Others, like Nancy Eriksson, a social democratic voice for housewives, fought instead for a higher social status for homemakers.[96]

The gender battles of the 1960s did not pass by the banks unnoticed, and the rhetoric of family finances did not remain entirely unaltered throughout the decade. The written material on personal finance shows indications of something akin to modernisation. Women were no longer treated as housewives in the last years of the decade as automatically as they had been a few years earlier. A budget template in a 1964 leaflet could still assign to the husband costs such as taxes, insurance, housing and the car, while listing household expenses such as food and 'children' under the wife's heading, with savings, holidays and healthcare sorted under 'shared' costs.[97] In 1969, an otherwise similar leaflet from Handelsbanken on 'Money in the Home' was for the first time more gender-neutral. Not only did it talk about the case of 'one of the spouses' mainly taking care of the home while the other worked, but its illustrations reinforced the impression of a more equal marriage, with both husband and wife doing the housework or sitting and calculating a budget.[98]

Yet Handelsbanken's women's conferences continued throughout the decade without substantial changes to the programme, with a persistent focus on family life, although admittedly combined with an emancipatory discourse on transparency and the equal distribution of money within the family. So why was the bank so keen to emphasise domestic values in the turbulent 1960s?

Handelsbanken's interest in housewives, and more generally in domesticity, can be explained by two factors. First, waged workers had already become bank customers due to the advent of direct deposits into cheque accounts. This left women 'whose main interest is home and family', and who according to the bank numbered over a million, as a still relevant target group in the late 1960s.[99] Second, and more importantly, there was a clear ambition to embed the bank in the practices and discourses of everyday family life. The Golden Everyday campaign was part of the larger cultural process that saw banks become *domesticated*. By recruiting housewives, banks became truly everyday institutions, almost inherent to daily life. The organisational logic of the Golden Everyday campaign, the form it took over the years and the message it conveyed all support this interpretation.

One line of thought in the literature on financialisation is that finance today intrudes into the domestic sphere because of online banking and other digital financial services. The American social scientist Randy Martin, in his book *Financialization of Daily Life*, comments on a bank advert from 1999:

> What once belonged to the workaday world beds down with leisure and domesticity. Advertised here is not only a different way to bank, but a new way of life.[100]

Martin claims that financialisation begins when money is no longer 'kept off the dinner table'. In history, though, money had almost always been on the table, as Zelizer as well as historians of economic life have shown. In other words, finance *in practice* was probably never separate from domesticity and intimacy.[101] However, if one takes Martin's words to refer to the discourses of modern banking and 'market money', he certainly has a point. And his words help to point out that what Handelsbanken called for in the 1960s was exactly that: finances should be discussed at the dinner table.

Large groups, if not the entire population, were to be familiarised with financial products and banking. To achieve this, the boundaries between high and low finance, between market money and domestic money, between money in the bank and money for daily shopping had to be, if not eradicated, then at least opened up. Establishing a connection between banking and domesticity did exactly that; and therefore, I would argue, the Golden Everyday conferences contributed to the domestication of banking services and to the spread of a new financial mindset—among both men and women.[102]

In analysing the conferences as performances of popular finance, I find that there were three main ways that helped embed banks and banking services in domesticity. First, the conferences consciously appealed to love, emotions and intimacy, showing that 'cold numbers' were perfectly compatible with warm feelings. Second, allusions to consumer skills were abundant, as were references to a well-known consumerist discourse rooted in decades of consumer education from emblematic institutions of the welfare state, such as the Consumer Institute. New bank customers might have invested, saved or borrowed, but they were still referred to as *consumers* who were supposed to choose from the 'department store of finance'. The similarities between financial products and consumer goods were stressed, along with the banks' role in both the purchase of consumer durables and daily shopping. The financial consumer who emerged in the bank campaigns was an early, homely version of the (mass) investor shopper that Amy Edwards identified in 1980s Britain, but with one foot still in the welfare state consumerist context.[103] Third, the bank stepped forward and claimed its expert knowledge in the financial matters of the family, entering a field of domestic knowledge that had previously belonged to other experts. Expertise in family finances was also taken up by other commercial banks. With this move, my study shows, banks inserted themselves between welfare state consumer experts representing the ideas and values of social democratic consumer policy, on the one hand and the kind of 'public relations of free enterprise' that the anti-socialist Taxpayers' Association stood for, with its call for financial independence, capital building and entrepreneurial thinking on the other. The banks' message combined ideas from both.

Open Access This chapter is licensed under the terms of the Creative Commons Attribution 4.0 International License (http://creativecommons.org/licenses/by/4.0/), which permits use, sharing, adaptation, distribution and reproduction in any medium or format, as long as you give appropriate credit to the original author(s) and the source, provide a link to the Creative Commons license and indicate if changes were made.

The images or other third party material in this chapter are included in the chapter's Creative Commons license, unless indicated otherwise in a credit line to the material. If material is not included in the chapter's Creative Commons license and your intended use is not permitted by statutory regulation or exceeds the permitted use, you will need to obtain permission directly from the copyright holder.

CHAPTER 4

Launching the Credit Card: New Moralities of Credit and Payment

On 22 February 1961, a public debate was held at the Stockholm School of Economics. The topic, credit cards, had been discussed in the media for months. Credit cards were new in Sweden, having been introduced only a few years before. A four-member panel was assembled. Among them was an enthusiastic representative of the credit card industry, Fredrik Lettström, the managing director of both a small credit card company (a subsidiary of Handelsbanken) and a newly established credit bureau, Kreditregister AB. He was also vice-president and soon to be president of Eurofinas, the European Federation of Finance House Associations, founded in 1959, an interest group of European consumer credit companies. Lettström argued passionately for the benefits of cards, giving consumers a new 'freedom of choice'. He was supported by the somewhat less enthusiastic head of a major shoe retailer, Åke Ström, who argued that the credit card could be a useful 'customer service'. Asked if he had any moral reservations, he said evasively: 'Morality is something at a higher level ... it's not the retailer's business to get involved'.[1] On the other side was Nils Thedin, editor of the magazine of the Consumer Cooperative Union (Kooperativa Förbundet, KF, founded in 1899), a movement which through its many members owned a great number of food shops and two department store chains, and which since the early twentieth century had been campaigning against consumer credit. He 'acted as a prosecutor', presenting a 'moral indictment of the credit card', which, he said, along with its loud advertising, could lead to misery for many.² The individual consumer's point of view was represented by Willy Maria Lundberg, a charismatic consumer journalist known for her down-to-earth manner and sharp pen, which she wielded against negligent manufacturers and dishonest advertisers.³ Lundberg was just as outspoken in her criticism of credit cards, this 'American novelty' that 'made no sense' but rather led to impulsive buying. It was obviously easier to save money first and spend it when needed than the other way round, she said. Like Thedin, she pointed out that the freedom the cards offered was fleeting, lasting only until you were in debt, after which the consumer was stuck and unfree. She also remarked on Lettström's striking information that the new credit bureau already had records with a million names. An official from the Ministry of Finance commented on the debate from the floor, mentioning that a government inquiry into consumer credit would be appointed within the fortnight. This event presented in condensed form the main arguments in the credit card controversy in Sweden and its protagonists: the banks and the financial industry, the retail trade, the cooperative movement, the media and consumers, as well as the government and academic research, the latter represented by the venue at the Stockholm School of Economics.

There are almost no historical studies on Swedish credit cards. Instead, historians have documented a strong moral criticism of consumer credit from the early years of the twentieth century. With the powerful consumer cooperative movement and the savings banks as its traditional proponents, the anti-credit discourse was reinforced by post-war social democratic ideology and regulatory consumer policy. The criticism was ideological at its core. The labour movement and the consumer cooperative movement condemned consumer credit because they believed it would 'enslave' people, both financially and politically. An indebted worker was less prone to participate in collective action such as strikes.⁴ And consumers who owed money to a 'capitalist' merchant—or worse, to their own employer, who also owned the local shop—had no power. But credit criticism was effectively translated into everyday morality, especially in the cooperative shops' ban on consumer credit and the savings banks' propaganda for thrift. An emblematic example of the latter is Sparbanken's children's magazine, *Lyckoslanten,* distributed to all schoolchildren, which from the 1920s well into the 1960s featured an iconic comic strip with a moral tale of the two young girls called Thrift (Spara) and Spendthrift (Slösa), the latter ridiculed for being reckless, untidy, covetous and irrational—and hell-bent on living beyond her means by buying on tick.⁵

According to the prevailing historiography of Swedish consumer society, the anti-credit ethos began to weaken only in the consumerist 1980s, when credit restrictions were lifted.[6] But if the spotlight is turned on the financial services industry before then, a different story unfolds: In 1962, Sweden was the first European country to introduce a nationwide credit card system, and the card market grew exponentially in the 1970s. By the 1980s, the micro-infrastructures of consumer credit were in place, and attitudes towards credit cards had changed significantly.

Clearly, the introduction of credit cards in Sweden involved a clash of moralities that took cultural relational work to resolve. How was this achieved? How did card issuers meet the challenge of creating a market for their product in the technologically friendly but culturally hostile environment of the 1960s and 1970s? This chapter pursues a twofold aim. I trace the history of the Swedish credit card market from its beginnings to the late 1970s, and analyse the strategies that credit card issuers used to reorganise moralities of debt in society while reframing and domesticating the credit card. Focusing on cards as devices in a sociocultural sense, I examine the marketing strategies of the bank-owned credit card company Köpkort AB (lit. Purchase Card Ltd., founded in 1962) and those of its predecessors and competitors.[7] Domestication in a more mundane sense was also evident in the introduction of Swedish credit cards. Swedish bankers were quick to adopt what was an American innovation, but it took time to adjust it to the specific national, cultural and political environment—by reshaping both the card and the environment itself.

From Devices to De-vicing

The moral criticism of buying and selling consumer goods on credit was so culturally ingrained in Sweden that representatives of the credit card industry in the 1960s and 1970s rarely specified what they meant when they talked about the 'moral objections' they faced. In turn, credit-critical voices in the 1960s and 1970s media often used the Swedish word *skuld*, meaning both debt and guilt, to invoke the age-old stigma about credit and loans.[8] The vices of buying and selling on credit were more often implied than spelled out, but included consumer impulsiveness, irresponsibility and overspending in addition to capitalist manipulation, exploitation and greed.

In the 1960s and 1970s the plastic card became a tool for selling, buying, lending and borrowing. But it was also an essential device for destigmatising consumer credit, having previously been a symbol of its evils. My analysis draws on two schools of thought. One is the Zelizerian tradition of exploring the interconnectedness of markets and morals.[9] Like the early life insurance industry, which, as Zelizer describes, was criticised for putting a price on human life and then gambling on it, credit card companies had to contend with a moral stigma associated with consumer debt. The specific moralities differed, however. While insurance men found themselves in the awkward position of selling 'pessimistic futures',[10] credit card issuers struggled with the problem of marketing an optimistic future, largely because of a widespread view that it was overly and irresponsibly optimistic. They dealt with the morality of the card market through what I call 'de-vicing', a concept that I borrow from the sociologist Francis Lee and the business scholar C.-F. Helgesson but use in a different way.[11] In what follows I explain in three short steps how this concept helps me to unpack the role of plastic cards in reshaping moralities and practices around consumer debt, and how it relates to the other field of research, STS (Science, Technology and Society Studies), on which my analysis builds.

The first step involves the notion of device as an analytical lens. Clearly, the credit card is a tangible device: a wallet-sized piece of plastic with the issuer's logo and sometimes an illustration, the cardholder's name and some identifying digits, and later a magnetic stripe and then a microchip. But device is also an analytical concept. Originally Foucauldian, it has been adapted by STS and ANT (Actor-Network Theory) scholars and then further developed for the study of economic life in a growing body of literature on market devices, such as trading algorithms, scoring, ranking and pricing mechanisms and their role in the practical and social construction of financial markets.[12] There are also studies on how more mundane devices shape everyday moralities in economic life; for example, how automatic queuing systems in banks have changed the morality of queuing in post-communist countries.[13] Devices can be less high-tech and have a longer history, such as the budget templates that reconfigured household accounting or the chequebooks imbued with class-based preconceptions that changed financial practices. Conceptualising credit cards as devices, even if only for 'low' finance, implies a focus on how such objects (as part of a socio-technical setup) shape—and are shaped by—culture, social life and morality.[14]

The second step is about what devices do. The sociologist Liz McFall proposed the notion of 'devising', to emphasise the workings of devices as a process rather than their technological character. Devising can with good reason be seen as relational work carried out by commercial actors who, long before the advent of relationship marketing, have tried to find what Zelizer calls 'good matches' between products and people's lives.[15] This brings to light the insight that the workings of devices are always contextual and historically contingent. Credit cards did not mean the same thing in an American context as in a Swedish one, for the rich as for the poor, or for consumer co-ops as for customers of upmarket department stores. The moralities of credit have historically depended on its forms—and its devices. In Sweden in the 1950s, for example, buying on instalment credit could still mean being imprudent and a bit greedy.[16] Using a savings-loan account, which allowed you to borrow twice as much after saving a certain amount, was a more virtuous practice. The kind of goods that were bought also influenced the cultural meanings attached to credit. Paying for groceries with a credit card was taboo until the late 1970s, as the former head of Köpkort (1969–1973), Ingvar Anderberg, recalled in an interview 40 years later. 'There was a kind of ethics in the debate back then', he said.[17]

The third step is fairly self-explanatory. In my interpretation, de-vicing refers to a particular kind of devising, in which the challenge is to turn something perceived as vicious into something virtuous, or at least morally neutral. Its advantage over other terms, such as normalisation or destigmatisation, is that it focuses on the material object itself (the card) and how its functions were created and justified. Especially as the plastic card came to play a particularly important role in Swedish bankification, even more important than the new form of consumer credit it originally mediated (see below and Chapter 6 on ATM cards, debit cards and bank-ID cards). Exploring de-vicing is helpful in understanding the domestication of the credit card in Sweden, both in the sense of a new financial device being incorporated into everyday life and in the sense of becoming part of Swedish financial culture as opposed to a foreign (American) one.

The Swedish Credit Card Market

The story of the 'invention' of the credit card in the United States, with the 1949 introduction of the Diners' Club card and the launch of the first bank credit cards through mass 'drops' (the sending of unsolicited cards) in the 1960s and early 1970s, as well as the tale of Visa and Master-Card conquering international markets, has been told many times, in both scholarly research and more popular accounts.[18] But credit cards were never exclusively American, not even in the early days.[19]

Historians and political economists have noted that Americans used credit cards and consumer credit as a substitute for social policy.[20] The situation in Sweden was different. In the post-war period, Sweden introduced not only a universal social security system (general health insurance in 1955 and general supplementary pension, ATP, in 1960) but also social loans. University education was made accessible in 1965 with student grants and a state-run student loan system open to all. Since the late 1940s the state had also offered another form of social loan, for setting up and furnishing a home. This (rather limited) credit opportunity was pushed hard in the 1960s in the adverts of furniture retailers such as Ikea, competing with commercial loans.[21] Commercial consumer credit in Sweden by no means had to serve as a substitute for welfare reforms.

In the late 1950s race for the money of ordinary households (Chapter 2), banks also gauged the idea of launching credit card schemes. All the largest commercial banks started their own companies, for example, Citykonto (CityCard, 1959) by Handelsbanken or Shoppingkonto (ShoppingCard, 1960) by Skandinaviska Banken. These small card companies (4 or 5 in 1960) had about 60–90 affiliated stores, mainly in Stockholm, and at most 10,000 account holders apiece. There was also a retailer-owned card company, Stockholms Konto-Ring AB (1959). Realising that the Swedish market was too small for so many competing players, all the bank-owned card schemes successively merged.[22] In 1962 they formed the company Köpkort AB, offering revolving credit plans across the country.

Köpkort AB became the first nationwide credit card company in Sweden, and was also the first of its kind in Europe. With the help of the Federation of Swedish Merchants (Köpmannaförbundet), the main interest organisation of non-cooperative retailers, it secured the collaboration of about 5,000 shops, to begin with.[23] The retailer-owned Stockholms Konto-Ring, was not part of the mergers and instead continued its small-scale operations until 1971, when the entrepreneur

Erik Elinder bought it and developed it into a major credit card business, ContoFöretagen (later InterConto).

Bankers were aware of the prevailing moralities of consumer credit, but believed that a cultural change was underway. Still, despite their faith in rapid growth, they were reluctant to start their card business in the banks' name. To avoid any 'bad-will', as they put it, they chose a solution with an independent (but bank-owned) company to manage their joint credit card business. This solution also exempted the new card company from banking supervision and the credit restrictions that applied to banks, at least for the time being.[24] As a freestanding firm for administering bank credit cards, jointly owned by all the major commercial banks in the country, Köpkort was internationally unique in the early 1960s. Not even California-based BankAmericard (later Visa), although much larger than its Swedish counterpart, achieved national coverage before 1966.[25]

Before the mergers, the small Swedish credit card companies engaged in intense marketing activity. Archival sources from Handelsbanken (owner of CityCard and SöderCard) and Skandinaviska Banken (owner of ShoppingCard) suggest that credit cards were advertised aggressively and even 'at the expense of profitableness' for a few hectic months in 1960–1961. A joint initiative was discussed from the start but the banks started a race for market shares, hoping to achieve a better negotiating position in any merger that might arise. In addition to advertising to the public the card companies set out to affiliate as many stores as possible, as the two endeavours were mutually dependent.[26] To tackle this problem of a two-sided market, the Swedish card companies employed various methods; one company for example hired 'a large number of ladies'—as vicarious consumers of sort—sending them to convince and recruit shopkeepers.[27]

The aggressive marketing of credit cards around 1960 triggered a backlash, sparking a heated debate (as in the opening example) with representatives of the co-op movement and others criticising consumer credit in general and credit cards in particular. A leading figure among critics and a regular in the press and on television, the cooperative leader and educator Herman Stolpe published a book arguing against consumer credit. The book even had a companion volume with course material for cooperative study circles. Stolpe warned that a new generation would blindly accept the new credit products, unaware of the 'disasters' of the late nineteenth century when workers, regularly indebted to their employer's company shops, ended up in a deplorable state of dependence. He described the credit card as the 'new usurer', thoughtlessly imported from the United States, and the 'gravedigger of welfare and prosperity'. It was expensive, it lured people into making unnecessary purchases, it eroded thrift, and it blunted people's sense of economy. Stolpe also objected to what he called misleading advertising that promoted credit cards as a rational accounting tool—to his mind, the exact opposite of what they were.[28] In general, Stolpe's attack targeted an American type of consumerism, stereotypically equated with a throwaway mentality encouraged by advertisers, which was under intense debate in the Swedish media that year.[29] For Stolpe and his peers both then and later, credit cards embodied the worst of what they saw as American mass consumer mentality. This became a well-known symbolism, and explains the Swedish card issuers' insistence in the 1960s that their card was nothing like the US credit cards.[30]

There is little statistical data on post-war consumer credit, and the estimates vary considerably. In the early 1960s charge and credit accounts (including both credit cards and traditional accounts in shops and department stores) represented only a small portion of outstanding consumer credit, no more than about 5–8 percent.[31] Since the interwar period, consumer credit—mainly as instalment buying—had been used predominantly for novel durable goods. In the 1950s and 1960s people bought cars (60 percent of total consumer loans in 1961), home appliances and television sets on credit, while smaller purchases and everyday goods were paid for in cash. When introduced, credit cards were used mainly for buying clothes, shoes and other consumer goods in the same mid-range price category. Credit limits were usually set at two months' salary, and over 75 percent of those who applied for a Köpkort card were approved. As the cards spread, they would successively outcompete other forms of consumer credit, replacing instalments as the dominant form after the mid-1970s.[32]

Köpkort dominated the card market in the 1970s as well, the number of its card accounts going from approximately 125,000 in 1969 to 350,000 in 1979. Other major players in the credit card market were ContoFöretagen/InterConto, with 320,000 cardholders by 1979, and the NK card (owned by the major department store Nordiska Kompaniet, NK, in Stockholm), with 280,000 accounts the same year (Table 4.1).[33] Cards that offered credit to corporate users rather than private individuals, so-called travel and entertainment or T&E cards, also existed in Sweden.

Table 4.1 Credit card accounts in Sweden, 1971–1979

Owner		1971	1976	1978	1979
Total number of credit card accounts in Sweden[a]		315,000	749,000	1,426,000	1,800,000
Of which at the largest companies					
Köpkort (1962)	Banks	135,000	235,000	343,000	350,000
InterConto (1971)	Erik Elinder/Rang/ Salenia	3,000	126,000	262,000	320,000
NK Card (1915/ 1959)	NK department store	60,000	98,000	227,000	280,000

[a]Does not include T&E Cards, petrol and car rental companies' cards, but does include other companies' cards than the three largest specified here.
Sources DsFi 1983:9, Kontokortskommittén, *Identitets- och legitimationskontroll vid utfärdande och användande av kontokort: Delbetänkande* (Stockholm: Liber Förlag/Allmänna förlaget, 1983), 14; CfN, Kooperativa Förbundet (KF), Direktionens protokoll (Minutes of the Board of Directors), 1978 no. 16, 22 May 1978, Appendix 4: Anders Tenér and Åke Lindén, 'Förslag till Kooperativt kreditkort', 16 May 1978; *Kontokreditmarknaden på konsumentområdet* (Stockholm: Konsumentverket, 1980), 8–9; CfN, Erik Elinder's Papers, Elinder to Spencer Nilson, July 1979; 'Köpkort blir internationellt', *Köpmannen*, 12 July 1979, 3; 'Krögarnas kreditkort förlorar "monopolet"', *Veckans affärer*, 25 March 1971, 27

But the Swedish market favoured cards of Swedish origin such as Eurocard (1964), owned by the Swedish financing company Vendor and valid internationally, and its Swedish-only companion Rikskort (for hotels and restaurants). The international cards Diners Club and American Express did not enter the Swedish market until 1971, meaning that they were not offered to Swedish consumers until then, but some Swedish outlets accepted foreign Diners and American Express cards.[34]

Systematic statistics for credit cards are only available from the late 1970s on, and it is difficult to compare the notoriously scattered statistical information from the early years. It can be concluded, however, that the credit card companies' share of consumer credit grew steadily in the 1960s and 1970s. The credit card industry expanded in absolute terms as well, accelerating in the second half of the 1970s when both outstanding debt and the volume of credit card purchases rose by as much as 50 percent a year. Between 1968 and 1978, the Swedish card industry grew tenfold in terms of both credit volume (in relative value) and the number of cards in use (Fig. 4.1).[35]

Until the late 1970s the Swedish credit card companies flew under the legislative radar. The American financial economist Lewis Mandell, in his

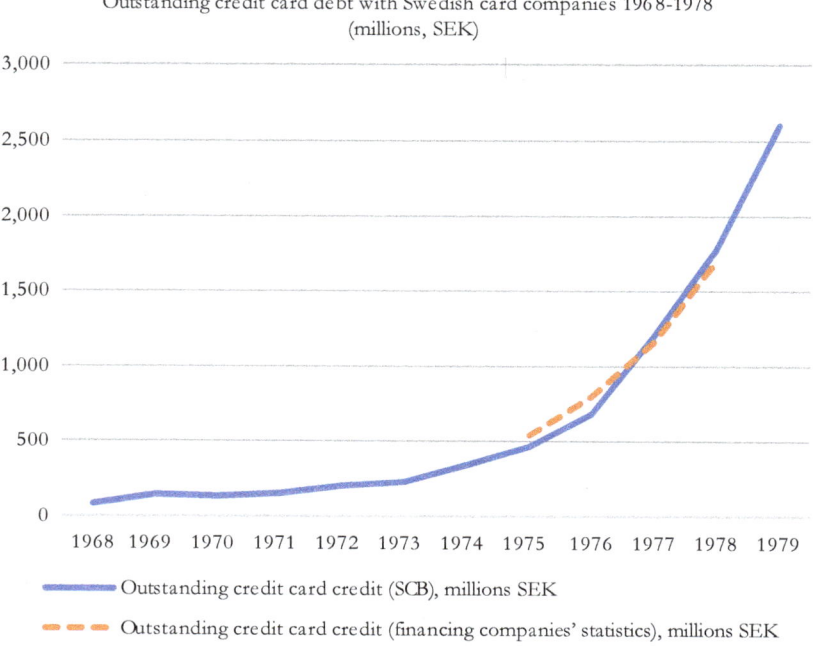

Fig. 4.1 Outstanding credit card debt with Swedish card companies 1968–1978 (SEK, millions). *Sources* SOU 1977:97, Finansieringsbolagskommittén, *Finansieringsbolag: Betänkande* (Stockholm: Liber Förlag/ Allmänna förlaget, 1977), 79 and DsFi 1984:10, Kontokortskommittén, *Kontokort. Slutbetänkande* (Stockholm: Liber, 1984), 66. The data is from Statistiska Centralbyrån (SCB, Statistics Sweden) and Finansieringsföretagens Förening (The Association of Financing Companies), and does not include all types of card companies

book on the early history of credit cards, writes that 'Swedish consumer credit legislation excluded cards as a payment mechanism', but this was in fact not the case.[36] Admittedly, regulatory legislation was constantly on the political agenda in the 1960s and 1970s. The critical reactions in the early 1960s even led to the appointment of a government inquiry into consumer credit. The commission worked from 1961 to 1966 and drew up a proposal for legislation, mainly to regulate instalment credit, but it was never acted on.[37] It was not until the late 1970s, following a second government inquiry and a new proposal, that new consumer credit legislation was introduced. However, the Consumer Credit Act, which came into force in 1979, concentrated on restricting traditional instalment credit and actually boosted the growth of the credit card industry.[38] Moreover, the strict credit restrictions imposed on the banks by the Riksbank in the 1960s and 1970s gave rise to a new type of financing company, to which the restrictions did not apply, and such companies became highly profitable in the 1970s. Some offered services such as leasing and factoring to businesses, while others gave credit card loans to individuals.[39] Thus, not only did credit card companies benefit indirectly from the general banking regulations of the 1960s; when more specific consumer credit regulations were introduced in the 1970s, they favoured credit cards over other forms of consumer credit. The first specific regulations on credit cards were introduced in 1984, only to be abolished less than a year later when the Swedish credit market was deregulated (Chapter 5). While legislation was important, it was not enough to create a market for credit cards; a cultural change was also needed.

Not Like American Cards: Culturalising Differences

The US example was important to those marketing the card, and there were plenty of temporal references to Sweden not having come 'as far as the United States' or 'being behind America'. But the domestication or 'Swedification' of the credit card was also seen as a matter of culture, morality and mentality.[40] 'It takes time to adjust the human soul to the most drastic novelties', Köpkort's managing director said in 1968 about credit cards.[41] The leading figures of the early Swedish credit card industry emphasised the political and social differences, and maintained that the distinctive cultural context required other market solutions and marketing strategies. As there were no European models to fall back on in the early 1960s, the Swedish case demonstrates how the first credit card companies met the challenge of not simply launching a financial product but also consciously attaching it to existing cultural values and practices. They both redesigned the credit card and tried to bring about a new way of thinking.

The managers of Köpkort AB were active in international collaborations such as the meetings organised by Eurofinas. The Swedish company claimed 'seniority' for having introduced credit cards on European soil (Table 4.2).[42] The young CEO of Köpkort, US-educated Sven Å. Cason,

Table 4.2 European bank credit cards, 1968

	Card system and year of introduction	International connection	Number of cards	Population (thousands)
UK	Barclay Card 1966	BankAmericard	1,200,000[a]	55,170
France	Carte Bleue 1967		310,000	49,650
	Carte d'Or 1968	Interbank	35,000	
Finland	OK-kort 1966		20,000	4,650
Sweden	Köpkort 1959/1962		125,000	7,940

[a]The UK numbers include non-active card users, as unrequested cards were sent out.
Source Sven Å. Cason, 'Kreditkorten i Europa', *Ekonomisk Revy*, 6 (1969), 334. These were the results of a survey conducted by the Swedish delegation of the European Bankers' Association in 1968. No other European countries reported having bank credit card systems. Historical population statistics from United Nations, World Population Prospects (2022)—processed by Our World in Data

was one of the keynote speakers at an international seminar on consumer credit organised by the Federation of Distributors in Brussels in 1967.[43] Cason devoted much of his talk to the differences between America and Europe in general as well as Sweden specifically. He pointed up the dissimilarities in values and attitudes. The task for the European card industry was not simply to embrace the American credit card as a model, he said, but to reshape and adapt the device to the specific cultural conditions in Europe.

His speech, along with abundant similar materials, reveals that the company's representatives consciously worked to domesticate the 'American' credit card in both a national and cultural sense. Cason warned against a straight import of the American practices. Based on the 'frustrations in many practical attempts to promote uncritically consumer credit in Sweden', he was convinced that consumer credit must be reconfigured to be accepted in Europe:

> Our expectation must … be realistically anchored to the specific conditions that, as a matter of fact, prevail in our part of the world. Consumer credit is certainly not an elastic balloon that can be readily inflated and then pushed free of any strings or restrictions as to attitudes and tradition. Consumer credit reflects basically a way of living, strung to the fundamental psychological traits and traditions of a nation and its people.

Cason's words about strings, psychology, attitudes, traditions and nation indicate an engagement in relational work; an ambition to carefully attach credit to the cultural context and to people's moral values, as well as to strategically inscribe it into the rhythm of daily life. He argued that, instead of employing aggressive marketing (which had failed in Sweden in 1960–1962), European companies should try to achieve a slower but longer-term change in attitudes, aiming at the next generation:

> We know ... by expensive experiences from Sweden that a broad acceptance of credit is basically not a matter of intensive marketing, it is a matter of the change of generation, where the ultimate success lies in an insistent promotion aimed at turning the up-growing generation positive to a continuous use of credit—to make them accept consumer credit—in its varying forms—as an up-to-date 'modus vivendi'—our day's way of living.[44]

This quote plainly spells out the aims of a bank-owned credit card company to change the minds of coming generations and accustom them to using credit on an everyday basis, as a way of life.

The ideas in Cason's speech probably came from an attitude survey conducted for Köpkort in 1965. It concluded that the earlier adverts had not resonated well with consumers, because 'ingrained prejudices had immunised them against the advertising message'. The survey, Köpkort's leadership reckoned, provided evidence of 'emotionally charged opinions about credit cards and their role in a market economy'. It also showed that negative opinions—described by the company as 'prejudices and misunderstandings'—were more prevalent among those on lower incomes, although such groups predominated among account holders. Despite the determined resistance, the survey concluded that there were signs that a generational shift was underway.[45]

So how did Köpkort move forward in its efforts to launch a Swedish card by changing general attitudes? How did the company start the long-term project of turning consumer credit into a 'new way of living'? A great deal of energy and money was invested in convincing retailers of the benefits of card payments, through personal visits, organised lectures, educational films and articles in various retail sectors' trade magazines. The company's CEO also appeared in the media, but the marketing aimed at the public hardly went beyond the traditional distribution of promotional leaflets, both by post and with the help of affiliated retailers and bank branches.[46] Because of the harsh tone of the debates in 1960–1962, advertising was cautious and sparse for a time.

In 1965, however, a full-page Christmas advert ran in all the major newspapers and attracted a great deal of attention (and criticism). It signalled not only a new advertising strategy, but also a new product design. The advert featured a young couple who seemed to have just used their Köpkort to buy a great number of Christmas presents. They were talking to an elderly lady, who asked them 'How can you really justify buying Christmas gifts on credit?' The younger woman replied:

> On credit! No, we bought with cash, even though we don't have to pay right away! ... And you know, Mum, we're actually really proud to have a card from Köpkort.[47]

Both the notion of cash payment and the pride in belonging to the group of those with a card were essential to the design of the new product, and point to the main de-vicing strategies: the credit card as a 'certificate of trust' and as 'modern money'. A third de-vicing strategy, the conceptualisation of the credit card as a device for financial planning, was alluded to in the small print of the same advert, which presented the card as a budgeting tool or 'service card' that gave its holder a new 'financial freedom'.

DE-VICING CREDIT: THE CARD AS A CERTIFICATE OF TRUST

Given the criticism in the early 1960s—or in Cason's words, the prevailing 'conservative spirit'—the key element of the cultural domestication of the credit card was to remove its stigma of shame. The card company hoped to achieve this with its product development in 1964–1965, which went under the name 'the new deal'. Instead of the blunt advertising of the early years or the cautious approach thereafter, Köpkort now sought to build into the card itself not only financial but also moral technologies.

The new deal was developed in collaboration with the retailers' organisation, and an advisory board with retail representatives was created. Shops would pay a fixed, semi-annual fee instead of a percentage of credit card sales, which simplified administration and reduced the retailers' costs, especially if the use of cards went up.[48] The most important news for consumers was that the new product design introduced the possibility to use the card in two ways. Besides revolving credit (allowing one to carry a balance from month to month), which was offered with interest and a small handling fee, Köpkort introduced another option: free-of-charge use of the card with full repayment of the balance on a monthly basis. Köpkort could thus be used as a traditional charge account, although offered by a third party, not a specific store. This function was also typical of the corporate cards, but for those there was a fee.[49] If one decided after a purchase to postpone the full payment for a longer period, the revolving credit function kicked in and interest was charged. Cason called the solution a 'nationwide optional account system', which according to him was unique in Europe at the time and was created from 'the American raw material' specifically to cater to the needs of the Swedish market.[50] Both the dual use and the centralisation into a single nationwide scheme were important. The choice of phrasing, such as 'raw material', illustrates that the Swedish marketers wanted to offer a fine-tuned national card solution.

The construction had two significant merits, which could be exploited when promoting the card. First, it blurred the line between credit as convenience—or even a social privilege—and credit as a necessity, and in so doing raised the credit card's prestige. Second, the boundary between cash payment and credit payment became unclear, which promoted the card as a simple payment instrument. The two parts were interlinked, and both were strategies for turning the card into a device that could destigmatise credit.

As to the first de-vicing strategy, in his Brussels talk Cason argued:

> It is … my firm belief that the promotion of consumer credit in the form of charge account and revolving credit service is an unrivalled way of fostering that faith and good-will without which consumer credit will not grow and render its inherent services to the public. Why you may ask. Because with charge account service, credit is combined with a feeling of prestige and a certain degree of status that the ownership of a credit card or charge account at a leading department store renders its entrusted bearer. And using the charge account on a revolving basis for part-payments [*sic*] over a longer period … you have entered the true field of consumer credit, *but with another mind and with no social inferiority complex or stigma.*[51]

He thus saw it as an important point to offer both a monthly account and revolving credit in the *same* product. The possibility of free monthly credit was deliberately created to evoke the first department stores' account system, which did not have the same stigma as instalment buying and other types of consumer credit. In the promotional brochures of the 1960s, the Köpkort card was therefore repeatedly described as a 'certificate of trust' *(förtroendebevis)*. This had multiple meanings: with its emphasis on trust it alluded to creditworthiness and to the card being a 'sign of good and well-managed personal finances', positively distinguished the cardholder from others with supposedly less well-managed finances, and signalled that its bearer could be trusted by others. At the same time, the promotional material stressed that the card would make its bearer trust in themselves, securing not only the confidence of others but self-confidence as well (Fig. 4.2).[52]

Fig. 4.2 'Köpkort inspires confidence, the Köpkort card boosts your confidence', advertising leaflet, early 1960s. CfN, Köpkort. Unknown photographer. Used with the permission of CfN

Here the de-vicing strategy built on the past to convey status, prestige and creditworthiness. Formalised credit systems were introduced early in department stores. American stores, for instance, ended their cash-only policy in the 1890s in favour of a charge account system.[53] In Sweden the department store NK introduced a charge account system in the 1910s, with a generous credit line, as it found that it could not refuse credit to its richest customers, who perceived it as a 'natural' privilege. Although not managed by a third party like the post-war systems, this credit scheme was highly professionalised. The elegant, numbered metal token (called an account plate, *kontobricka*) was presented at the cashier's desk and, unless the customer was known, a quick inquiry was sent via pneumatic tube to the credit office in the same building, the response arriving within minutes. Admittedly, in 1925 NK introduced a credit account with lower income requirements and a lower credit limit, explicitly offered to a group of carefully selected 'steady workers and lower officials'. But the standard accounts, which often belonged to the city's elite, already numbered over 25,000 in the mid-1930s and half of all purchases in the store were charged to a credit account. The NK card remained a significant player in the credit card market of the 1960s. Although made of plastic instead of metal after 1959, the NK card retained its prestigious image—an image the new credit card companies wanted to emulate.[54]

This was not an easy task, because Köpkort targeted a broader clientele and wanted to 'democratise' consumer credit, as it was often expressed. The double way of using the Köpkort card—both as a monthly overdraft account and as a card for longer-term loans with revolving credit payments—was intended to be a solution to the dilemma.[55] The fact that the cardholder did not have to decide at the time of purchase whether to use the extended credit was a key feature of the new product design, and aimed to erase the dividing line between credit as a convenience and credit as a necessity.

The notion of 'certificate of trust' and the association with the high-status department store accounts reveal a related aspect of the de-vicing strategy, whereby the card was configured as a membership card, signalling belonging to a select circle (similar to a Diners Club card). Again, this idea of a membership card needed to be broadened with the larger clientele in mind, so early marketing used the expression certificate of trust in the same sense as proof of identity occasionally promoting the card as an 'economic identity card'.[56] Credit cards have certainly played a role in the emergence of a financial identification system, as will be shown in Chapter 6; however, in the mid-1960s being asked to produce an ID document in everyday situations was still perceived as a slight and did not do much to enhance the credit card's image.

Neither did the classificatory aspect inherent in the metaphor 'certificate of trust' and in the practices of credit assessment resonate well with the Swedish public, except perhaps in the early years.[57] The deeply classificatory logic of credit reporting and credit rating has been highlighted in the American context by historians and social scientists. Marion Fourcade and Kieran Healy argue that contemporary credit scoring in the United States has replaced traditional class categorisations, while Josh Lauer and others have traced the long history of the system and through it the creation of the American 'financial identity' based on creditworthiness.[58]

Credit reporting developed in Sweden as well, keeping pace with the consumer credit industry. Individual credit limits were set after careful scrutiny before the card was issued, and in the earliest period the limits were indicated by numerical codes on the Köpkort card itself. By 1961, the new Kreditregister AB (founded in 1959) already had more than a million Swedes on its books, as mentioned in the debate that opened this chapter. It quickly became the largest Swedish credit bureau. The dominant American company Dun & Bradstreet entered the Swedish market in 1967 by buying several credit bureaus, including Kreditregister AB. By then the combined registers of the agencies already covered the entire Swedish population. However, in Sweden credit ratings did not assume the same historical importance as in the United States. The Swedish Credit Information Act (1973:1173) restricted the possibilities of credit ratings, for example, by limiting the type of information that could be collected and by prohibiting the sharing of records older than five years. It also banned foreign ownership of the credit reporting business. As the new regulations forced Dun & Bradstreet to cease its Swedish operations, credit rating practices like those in the United States did not develop in Sweden.[59] The banks would play an important role in this area as well, especially from the 1970s, as will be discussed in Chapter 6.

As for the discursive level, the promotion of the Köpkort card as an indicator of its holder's prestige and worth did not sit well with the otherwise egalitarian language of the social democratic welfare state, or with the ambition to 'democratise' the use of credit cards. In the mid-1960s, Swedish press commented on the 'ugly side' of American credit cards, describing them as the new indicators of personal worth, sorting people into categories. More credit cards meant greater prestige as they were evidence of a higher credit rating, it was reported, mostly in sharply critical terms.[60] So, ultimately, this strategy was not successful. Köpkort's attitude survey in the mid-1960s showed that the possession of credit cards was seen in an unfavourable light. Cards, even as proofs of creditworthiness, were still strongly associated with debt, and it was only when the credit part was downplayed that they became more widely accepted.

Köpkort AB dropped the 'certificate of trust' advertising slogan before 1970, in favour of the term 'modern money', which had also been introduced in the early 1960s. The contrast between Americans, who had several credit cards to prove their creditworthiness, and Swedes, who only needed to use one card—Köpkort's—as 'modern money' was exploited in its advertising, starting in the late 1960s.[61]

Credit Cards as Modern Money

The other key element built into the 1965 redesign of the Köpkort card pointed towards the future and aimed to erase the boundary between cash payments and credit purchases, framing the card as 'modern money'. Admittedly, interest-free monthly credit is also a loan in the strict sense, but by reference to this function the card was heavily marketed as a 'rational' and 'modern means of payment'. It helped that Köpkort was a national card, jointly owned by the commercial banks and with many affiliated retailers in a wide range of sectors, making it even easier to present it as 'modern money'.[62] The Swedish solution can be compared with the Carte Bleue bank card, which was introduced in France in 1967 as a simple monthly payment card to combat American-style revolving credit.[63] In contrast to the French card, Köpkort's dual design worked as a de-vicing strategy, whitewashing consumer credit both in practice and in the advertising message.

This solution had many advantages. In adverts it could be claimed that Köpkort, properly used, cost nothing. Especially for goods not obviously categorised as consumer durables, the card was presented as simply a new form of (cash) payment, as such smaller purchases were generally considered inappropriate to use credit for. By 1968 Köpkort was already envisaging the card's development into a 'universal' or 'all-purpose' card that could be used everywhere, even in food shops. The close cultural association with 'ready money' was key in these years before online payments became a reality.[64]

Another important goal for Köpkort was to make cash withdrawals possible for card users. This was mentioned in its policy documents in 1968 as a matter of 'fundamental importance', necessary to raise the status of the card—which, the company's management complained, was not yet accepted as a 'natural means of payment'. The expressions 'natural credit' and 'natural means of payment' were used recurrently and interchangeably, revealing an ambition to make the difference between credit and cash payment culturally invisible.[65] The 1965 attitude survey glimpsed signs of 'the beginning of a reassessment of credit cards from means of credit to service card'. One of the study's conclusions was otherwise that the new line for product development should be continued, because resistance to consumer credit was still so strong and almost a third of respondents said they had no 'need' for credit. It was these respondents, the company believed, who might be the new market for the card as a means of payment.[66]

In its advertising, the company continued to emphasise the card's use as a payment device rather than a credit instrument. An illustrated booklet, *Means of payment through the ages*, published in 1968, told the story of money from shells and precious metals via paper notes and cheques to the Köpkort card; and this publication, according to the company's marketing experts, was 'greatly appreciated' by the general public. In adverts the card was called, in addition to 'modern money', also 'Not money, but almost!', and was often marketed to both shops and individuals as a substitute for cheques.[67] As early as 1967 the Bankers' Association discussed the broad distribution of the Köpkort card to all holders of cheque accounts for wages or at least to the 'conscientious' ones (*skötsamma*), and even considered the possibility of replacing cheques entirely with the Köpkort credit card. This did not happen but invitations to sign up for Köpkort were sent out to selected groups of people with cheque-account wages. And later, during the cheque boycott by retailers in 1971–1972 (Chapter 2), advertisements and information material from banks encouraged all cheque account holders (most Swedish employees) to apply for the Köpkort's card as a solution.[68]

In these contexts, plastic cards were equated with cheques and cash, rather than other forms of credit, even though automatic debiting still lay in the future. 'It is credit cards instead of cash, and not credit cards instead of other credit varieties … that open a wide-angle perspective on the future', it was claimed in a manuscript for a lecture from 1969 used for internal training purposes, which also forcefully pointed out, that '[e]veryone doesn't have, God forbid, a constant need for credit—but definitely for money!' The goal, as it was formulated in this and many other documents, was to turn the credit card into a generally used means of payment. Still, at the same time Köpkort also exploited the allure of credit. After all, the card only really became profitable for the company when customers started using its credit function. Köpkort's representatives said that the credit card as a means of payment had been made especially attractive 'by being garnished with a credit facility'.[69]

Credit cards were eventually marketed as money plain and simple in the United States as well, but not until the early 1970s. The 1971 BankAmericard (later Visa) campaign, which used the slogan 'Think of it as money', has been described as the first in a range of US and international campaigns in the same spirit.[70] The powerful and seemingly self-evident metaphor of plastic money, since used in both popular and scholarly discourses, was consciously constructed and disseminated through the marketing efforts of the early credit card companies. Its de-vicing potential for consumer credit might explain its early appearance in the Swedish context. The credit card as simply a modern means of payment fed into the vision of a future cashless society, which became widespread in the international banking world in the 1960s and 1970s. It was especially popular in the Swedish banking sector, which in the 1960s was investing heavily in computer technology.[71] In this interpretation, the credit card appeared as something of a low-tech solution for cashlessness in anticipation of online payments becoming possible.

A Device for Financial Planning

Along with the two de-vicing strategies described above (the credit card as a certificate of trust and as modern money), there was a third one. It conceptualised the card—and consumer credit itself—as an instrument for financial planning. This strategy was also embedded in the construction of the cards and was emphasised in the marketing messages of several card companies in the 1960s and 1970s. Credit cards were advertised as tools for those who wanted to 'rationalise their accounting routines': the monthly statement of account offered an overview, helpful for the family's budget and bookkeeping, and all purchases could be paid for at the same time. In addition, the revolving credit function, the promotional leaflets said, turned the card into a 'financial instrument' with which 'the family's different expenses during the year could be balanced'. It was also called a 'liquidity reserve' for unforeseen events. And, as Köpkort's managing director put it in a technical-financial jargon, ordinary people could 'take advantage of the most favourable purchase opportunities in terms of price' without having to worry about their cash flow; in other words, they could buy when it was cheapest.

The promotional discourse presented budgets and credit cards in the same breath, suggesting that the two were similar devices for financial planning.[72] This resonated with ideas introduced by neoclassical economists around that time, such as 'consumption smoothing' (Chapters 2 and 5).[73] Köpkort was delivering the same seemingly objective message about 'financial planning', financial freedom and choice that the new cheque account holders were being taught by their banks. A similar argument, used by Köpkort and others from the early 1960s, was to present the credit card as an instrument for 'saving after the purchase' rather than before. This argument applies to all types of consumer credit, not just cards, and is known from other national histories of consumer credit.[74] Apparently, Köpkort was even reported to the Consumer Ombudsman for an advert with such a message as late as 1982, but this did not stop it (and other companies) from using this argument in different forms and settings.[75]

The framing of the card as a practical educational device belongs to this context as well. Credit cards taught people to manage their personal finances in a 'rational' way, it was claimed in the 1960s informational leaflets or, for example, in a promotional film: 'Through Köpkort, Svensson gains greater financial freedom of action and learns to plan his budget properly'. In these texts, the benefits of borrowing for consumption in times of inflation were also explained, as was the interest on the debt being tax-deductible.[76]

Financial knowledge and skills are hot topics today, and the concept of financial literacy is used by policymakers and social scientists alike.[77] The need for financial education has been emphasised by government agencies as an integral part of consumer protection in today's highly financialised society, but consumer information and financial education for empowering consumers were also discussed in the 1960s Sweden in the context of consumer and social policy. At the same time, banks and other financial companies also engaged in financial education, using it as a way to market their products (Chapters 2 and 3).[78] Financial education, as both marketing and consumer protection, was especially pronounced in the question of the effective interest rate. The new Consumer Credit Act, which came into force in 1979, required companies to give consumers clear information about the true cost of credit.[79] The Swedish Consumer Agency (Konsumentverket, founded in 1973) worked with the industry to develop a mathematical model to calculate the compound costs of credit, which included both interest and various fees. They produced easy-to-use tables and templates. This enabled consumers to compare different cards but also helped to normalise consumer credit, and triggered an advertising war between card companies trying to undercut one another.[80] The Consumer Agency was responsible for monitoring compliance with the law and informing the public about it. Now, for the first time, 'official' consumer information about credit was distributed through various channels, such as TV, radio, newspapers, posters and Consumer Agency leaflets along with the teaching materials it produced for schoolchildren.[81] The Consumer Agency was not the only communicator of information about credit cards, however. Financial and consumer journalists explained how cards worked and compared different card schemes, as did the card companies in their own adverts and brochures, often edited and designed in a style similar to that of the educational material produced by the Consumer Agency.

Overall, card companies welcomed the new legislation and claimed they were keen to provide consumers with understandable information. Such information included calculations of tax deductions and explanations of how inflation made buying on credit more attractive and financially justifiable.[82] Full-page adverts in 1979 by the card company Finax illustrated this strategy of advertising in the guise of financial education. The adverts, titled 'Challenge your economic prejudices' and 'Challenge your sense of economy', explained revolving credit in a straightforward way and compared the costs of the different forms of credit, admitting that a traditional bank loan was cheapest but noting that it was not readily available in times of credit restrictions. Referring to the Consumer Agency's model for calculating credit costs, the adverts detailed how they were tax-deductible. They then explained all the current wisdom about financial planning, talking of bringing structure, balance and liquidity to personal budgets.[83] Thus, this and the earlier marketing in the same vein sought to justify credit cards—and credit—as instruments of a new personal financial rationality.

InterConto and the Repersonalisation of the Credit Card

The old idea of the credit card as a certificate of trust in the sense of a membership card was reimagined in a modern, future-oriented way in the 1970s by a new company, ContoFöretagen (InterConto from 1978). Founded in 1971 on the basis of the former the retailer-owned card company Stockholms Konto-Ring, ContoFöretagen started its operations with only 3,000 cardholders but within a few years had become Köpkort's strongest competitor.[84] By 1979 it was managing 320,000 accounts, compared to Köpkort's 350,000. The owner and chairman of the board, Erik Elinder, was a marketing expert and entrepreneur with extensive experience from the advertising industry. Together with the managing director, computer expert Reine Olsson, Elinder built a modern company that offered a new type of credit card. The so-called selective card schemes that InterConto created and managed were specifically designed for different regions, consumer groups or retail sectors. They also offered private label card schemes for individual retail companies or chains. As late as the 1970s, ContoFöretagen/InterConto had to deal with the moral criticism of consumer credit. Former deputy managing director Gunilla Cronholm recalls that, when she joined the company in 1972, despite a brilliant career at a young age, she preferred not to say what she did for a living at social gatherings to avoid embarrassing reactions. It was only when the Ikea card, the Swedish furniture company's credit account managed by ContoFöretagen, was introduced nationwide in 1974 that she felt credit cards were becoming slightly less controversial.[85]

The selective cards were a way to turn a de-vicing strategy into a marketing tool for retailers. Elinder often referred to his company's credit cards as 'sales cards' ('*säljkort*'), in contrast to Köpkort's 'purchase cards' ('*köpkort*'). Advertising material was sent out with the account statements, so the selective account system could target the right group of customers. InterConto tried to instil a feeling in its account holders, if not of exclusivity, then of belonging, without being a loyalty card (these were introduced later) or an account card limited to one retailer.[86] For example, the Villa Conto card was offered to homeowners nationwide and could be used in a range of DIY shops and garden centres. As for the regional cards, a few select retailers from each sector were accepted while people were targeted based on where they lived. The case of Skåne

Conto is illustrative. This card was aimed mainly at residents of the city of Malmö, the main urban centre in southern Sweden (in the Skåne region), and was modelled on the Stockholm Conto and Gothenburg Conto in all but its name. The company's managers realised that, while Malmö residents would not mind being associated with Skåne, it would be difficult to market a card called Malmö Conto to residents of the surrounding smaller towns in this densely populated region. So instead of depersonalising credit, the Conto cards worked to repersonalise it.[87]

In this way, the card company reinterpreted trust and old-fashioned shop accounts, to offer a sense of belonging in the shape of a plastic credit card—and with the help of an advanced computer system. This strategy had similarities with the one used by the Diners Club card, which also conveyed a feeling of membership,[88] but instead of a 'club' and a message of exclusivity and high social status the InterConto cards played on differentiated identities. While building on traditional values such as local

Table 4.3 The card companies Köpkort and InterConto compared

Köpkort (est. 1962, bank-owned)	ContoFöretagen/InterConto (est. 1971, independent)
'Modern money' Compares to other *monies*, (such as cash and cheques)	'Membership card' Creates transactional identities; compares to other marketing channels and other credit possibilities
General credit card (as many retailers as possible) Nationwide use	Selective cards (a few selected stores for each branch) Local, regional, for specific groups or branches
Revolving credit and free-of-charge optional monthly accounts	Credit for periods fixed in advance (3–36 months), regular payments required
Targets the cash market (justification: a rational method of payment) Recruiting new customers for banks	Targets the credit market (justification: people's right to credit) Advertising on behalf of the retailers (for example in account statements)
'Purchase card', marketed to consumers	'Sales card', marketed to retailers as a marketing tool
Competes with 'price' (cheapest solution)	Competes with 'loyalty' (without being a proper loyalty card)
Vision of the future: 'cashless society'	Vision of the future: 'information card' with extensive knowledge about individual consumers

patriotism as part of strategies to destigmatise credit, at the same time the company was a pioneer in personalised marketing, exploiting differentiated card systems and the transactional identities they created—hence the internal nickname 'sales card'. For the serial entrepreneur Elinder, a selective card system was the first step towards an 'information card', as he put it, meaning a device for gathering and communicating knowledge about consumers that would eventually enable fully personalised sales. His ideas, though mostly limited to the pages of internal memos, were ahead of their time in the 1970s (see further in Chapter 6). Yet a cashless future was not an important part of InterConto's marketing narrative, and arguments presenting the card as the money of modern times were rarely used. Instead, Elinder repeatedly stated that his company was targeting the credit market, unlike Köpkort, which focused on the cash market. (See Table 4.3 for the differences between the two card schemes, including the different de-vicing strategies built into the cards).

THE MANY NAMES AND FACES OF THE CREDIT CARD

> He could talk for hours about credit cards without ever mentioning the word 'debt'. He firmly believed that the worst marketing mistake in history was calling it a 'credit card'; such a name, he felt, belittled its larger possibilities.[89]

This was said of Dee Hock, the first executive director of Visa Inc. (1970). Swedish bankers and card companies tried to avoid this 'mistake', even before Hock mentioned it. From the beginning they proposed other names, such as 'purchase card' (*köpkort*) and 'account card' (*kontokort*), which eventually became generic. The de-vicing strategies were not only evident in the functional design of the cards and the marketing arguments but were also reflected in the names used to denote the card itself. The word credit card (*kreditkort*) for this device was introduced in the late 1950s as a translation from English, but was used sparsely compared to other terms.[90] While credit card issuers eventually tended to avoid the exact wording in public contexts, critics used it to invoke its negative connotations.

Figure 4.3 illustrates the alternative terms used in major Swedish newspapers. The brand name Köpkort became *köpkort* (purchase card), a generic name for credit cards in the 1960s through to the late 1980s.

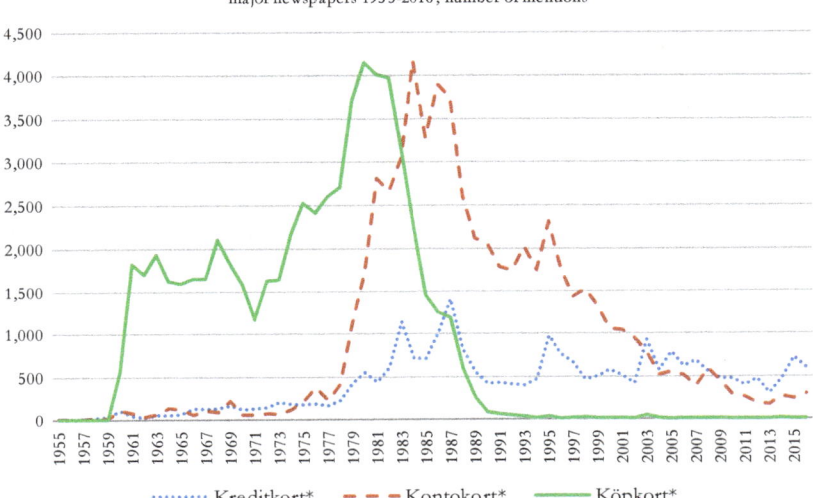

Fig. 4.3 Mentions of the words *kreditkort* (credit card); *kontokort* (account card); and *köpkort* (purchase card) in four major Swedish newspapers, 1955–2016. *Source Aftonbladet, Dagens Nyheter, Expressen, Svenska Dagbladet* in the digital database for Swedish daily newspapers, Kungliga biblioteket

It continued to be used, but only sporadically, as a synonym for the more common official term payment card (*betalkort*). The word *kontokort* (lit. account card, reminiscent of the name used by InterConto) existed as a generic, albeit less common, term in the early years of plastic cards; this became the main term for both credit and payment cards from the late 1970s. It was not until the new millennium that the word *kreditkort* (credit card) overtook it in everyday use.

There were also differences in the visual and material form of the cards. Admittedly, their shape and dimensions had been standardised since the 1970s. Both the smaller plastic model first offered by Köpkort and the larger ATM card were replaced by a uniform and later ISO-approved standard format (Chapter 6). But while Köpkort, like Visa and MasterCharge/MasterCard, aimed for a distinctive uniformity in the visual design of their own cards, InterConto's cards were given different patterns and logos, depending on the target group, alluding to regional and group identities. For example, the Stockholm Conto and Gothenburg Conto cards were decorated with emblematic images of the respective cities, while the Villa Conto cards featured an image of an archetypal Swedish red wooden house by the painter Carl Larsson.

In everyday use, the different names for plastic cards did not refer to specific functions, such as credit, debit or charge cards, but could rather describe all types of plastic cards in a more general sense. The distinction between the various cards was not entirely clear in the public mind, except for those used to withdraw cash from ATMs, which were considered completely different.[91] But it was not until 1980 that all the different functions (credit, debit and ATM withdrawals) actually merged when the Swedish savings banks introduced a combined card.

THE SAVINGS BANKS AND THE CONVERGENCE OF CREDIT AND PAYMENT

Although savings banks had been among the most vocal critics of credit cards in the early 1960s, Stockholm's Savings Bank started a collaboration with Erik Elinder in 1971 and secured the financing for ContoFöretagen/ InterConto. The savings banks also joined the commercial banks in the Köpkort consortium in 1973.[92] Then, in 1978, they played a significant role in the introduction of Visa to Sweden, again jointly with Elinder's company.[93]

Most importantly, the savings banks became the main drivers in a process whereby the infrastructures of cash and credit converged in the early 1980s. In 1979, they launched an experiment with direct card payments in the Blekinge region of southern Sweden. Card terminals were installed in department stores, food shops and other retail outlets, petrol stations and Systembolaget, the government-owned chain of off-licences. The media reacted with banner headlines to the prospect of buying alcohol with a credit card, which led to a flurry of critical comments.[94] The excitement was understandable; after all, until 1979 it was not even possible to use a credit card to pay for food, let alone alcohol. In reality, the cards used in this trial were not credit cards but the savings banks' own ATM cards equipped with an experimental debit card function, as representatives carefully explained in interviews.[95] The trial was not entirely successful, and online payments at shop terminals did not become the norm for quite a few years yet. However, when the new Sparbankskortet (Savings Banks' Card) was introduced in 1980, it meant that the savings banks' already widely used ATM cards—of which there were 750,000 in circulation in 1979—were upgraded with both a credit function and a (not yet online) debit function, and from then on could be used in shops (Fig. 4.5). This resulted in a sudden increase in the number of credit cards in Sweden.[96] Other card systems soon followed; for example, the Köpkort card added an automatic cash withdrawal function in the early 1980s. As the cards' functions became combined, the marketing narratives also converged.[97]

The savings banks' strategy of first issuing a large number of ATM cards and then adding new functions was the ultimate de-vicing strategy, or in a way the Swedish version of the famous and criticised credit card drops in the United States, where millions of unsolicited cards were sent out to the public. Here, the extensive de-vicing included the creation of a new infrastructure that merged the material practices of credit and regular payment.

The Breakthrough Years and the Internationalised Card Market

A few days before Christmas 1978, the newspaper *Sydsvenska Dagbladet* published an article with the title 'Breakthrough year for credit cards. The Swedes' Christmas—is it a Christmas on credit?', announcing a new era for cards in Sweden.[98] It was a message echoed across the media, and with good reason (Fig. 4.4). The Swedish credit card industry experienced an exceptional boom in the 1970s, as mentioned earlier. In 1977, three of the four most profitable companies in Sweden were credit card companies.[99]

The credit card as a device was also changing. By the end of the 1970s, cards began to be accepted in food shops, and holidays could be paid for by card—purposes that had previously been considered morally unacceptable for consumer credit. The terms and conditions of credit card accounts had originally made it clear that purchases of groceries, tobacco and alcohol were not permitted. In the early days, it was even printed on the cards themselves that they could not be used to buy food. Köpkort removed these restrictions in 1979.[100] Around the same time, even the consumer cooperative movement considered accepting credit cards, as the next chapter will show.

Visa was introduced in Sweden in 1978 by InterConto (in collaboration with the Stockholm Savings Bank), while MasterCharge (later

Fig. 4.4 'Christmas on credit', front page illustration in *Köpmannen*, 18 December 1978. Unknown photographer. Used with the permission of Svensk Handel

MasterCard) was introduced 1979 by Köpkort.[101] American credit card history portrays Sweden as a difficult market for the 'big two' to conquer, with reference to the country's restrictions on lending and strict financial and consumer regulations. However, the difficulties are better explained by the early existence of well-established national companies and their specific solutions for card use. In addition to the Köpkort (30 percent market share in 1978), InterConto (21 percent) and NK (21 percent) cards, Eurocard should also be mentioned among the Swedish cards, although this was an international system for corporate users. Eurocard was owned by the Swedish financing company Vendor (a subsidiary of Stockholms Enskilda Bank).[102] Some sources even suggest that it was 'out of consideration' for the powerful Wallenberg family, the majority owners of Vendor, that Köpkort did not respond to the many approaches it encountered from both MasterCharge and BankAmericard from the late 1960s.[103] It is noteworthy that shortly after Eurocard was sold to the Interbank Card Association in 1978, MasterCharge followed Visa by breaking into the Swedish market through a collaboration with Köpkort.[104]

But the remarkable increase in the Swedish credit card market in the 1970s preceded the arrival of the international card systems, and was not triggered by it, as one might assume in hindsight. The inflationary economy which made loans more profitable played a role, as did the legislative take on consumer credit. New computer technology was important, but the practical outcome with the possibility of online transactions at shop terminals (POS, point of sale system) came only later, in the 1980s, after the first trials in 1979. Clearly, a change in attitudes—carefully engineered sometimes by trial and error, and reinforced by an already bankified everyday life—was a substantial factor. *Sydsvenska Dagbladet*, in the article about a Christmas on credit quoted above, wrote that because of cards, 'for an ordinary person with an ordinary economy, buying on credit is becoming an everyday reality'. People changed and so did their wallets, which now had pockets for credit cards. Still, the newspaper added, most people were modest in their borrowing 'because of inherent moral principles'.[105]

By 1979 there were 1,800,000 credit cards in use (compared with 315,000 in 1971), even before the launch of the savings banks' card or the MasterCharge card (Table 4.1; Fig. 4.5). This increase and the intensive advertising of cards in 1978–1979 triggered a new moral panic. Another government inquiry was appointed and led to new, stricter regulations in 1984 aiming to limit card use. However, the regulations proved impossible to implement and were withdrawn within a year, when the entire Swedish banking and credit market was deregulated.[106] Plastic cards proliferated in the consumer-friendly 1980s and expanded even further in the 1990s, an era characterised by further deregulation and the internationalisation of the Swedish credit card industry. It was a different market, with many new players. Without looking back to the 1960s and

Fig. 4.5 'In the shadow of the Savings Banks' Card, all the other cards become small', full-page advertisement for the savings banks' combined credit and ATM card, *Köpmannen*, 21 April 1980. Artist unknown. Used with the permission of Swedbank

1970s, however, we cannot understand how the credit card as an everyday device was engineered—not only with financial and computer technologies but also with moral technologies—and how it was attached to the culture of everyday life and adapted to the Swedish context.

Reshaping the Moralities of Credit and Payment

In Sweden, early bankification and the early adoption of computer technologies were combined with strongly negative general attitudes towards consumer credit. Credit cards were introduced early by European standards, but had to be reconceptualised, reshaped and even renamed to gain general acceptance. The first attempt to popularise credit cards through intensive advertising, around 1960, failed. It was only by carefully exploiting and reinforcing the non-credit properties of the card that marketers could embed the credit card and the new uses of consumer credit into consumers' everyday practices.

Combining a Zelizerian approach to the moralities of markets with a focus on socio-technical devices, this chapter has shown how the plastic card itself became a tool for *de-vicing* consumer credit, making the use of credit a less immoral practice. I have highlighted the workings of three de-vicing strategies by looking at the material, technical and ultimately cultural-moral arrangements built into the card. First, as a 'certificate of trust', a kind of membership card, it evoked tradition and exclusivity, but also kept its association with the American practice of sorting people by their creditworthiness. Second, as a means of payment, essentially a modern form of money, it was presented as a promise of the future, being convenient, universally valid and easy to use. And third, it was also staged as a device that helped with household accounting and conveyed a new financial rationality. Financial planning and financial freedom that enabled consumer choice were part of what the new wisdom offered for a bankified life, and this was to be achieved with the help of the credit cards (as with cheque accounts).

The credit card blurred the boundaries between credit as a necessity and credit as a privilege, as well as between cash payments and credit purchases. For retailers, the card could be a marketing tool—and eventually a way to personalise their advertising. The configurations achieved through marketing arguments, denominations and actual material designs attached to the card notions such as rationality or social status, as well as a sense of belonging to a group, a region or a nation.

While this chapter's focus on a small national market has made the de-vicing strategies more visible, similar strategies were certainly used elsewhere as well. In Sweden, they were successful in the sense that they firmly established the use of plastic cards for payment, but the material device itself came to be more accepted than the consumer credit it originally represented. Early de-vicing strategies thus facilitated the later exploitation of the card's greater possibilities. Since the 1980s the debit card function has become the most common in Sweden, like most European countries and in contrast to the United States or Canada, where credit cards have dominated.[107] In the twenty-first century, with cash banned from many retail outlets, Swedes have been among the world's most frequent users of plastic cards for payment.[108] While in the late twentieth century cards were instrumental in changing payment practices and reorganising the moralities of debt—especially by blurring the boundaries between credit and cash—today cardless electronic transactions, with a new set of digital devices, are replacing both cash and card payments.

This chapter is also a contribution to the international history of credit cards, which has been dominated by the American story. Not only is Swedish credit card history missing from the literature; the few mentions that do figure there give the wrong picture, suggesting that credit cards were basically non-existent in Sweden until the late 1970s. My study has revealed something very different, with the early creation of a nationwide system and Swedish credit card industry representatives taking leading roles in European international organisations. A conventional view would also suggest that Sweden, with its highly regulated banking system and strong consumer protection policies, could not develop a credit card industry. Again, the opposite was the case. Although banking regulations made it difficult for the banks to grant loans, the new financial companies (including card companies) were not regulated by the same law. The consumer protection legislation of the 1970s restricted the older instalment credit, giving credit card companies the chance to develop. The main problem for the card companies was not the actual regulations but rather the moral attitude of the Swedish population. This means that the history of the spread of credit cards is also a history of moral change and the complex ways in which the moralities of credit have been rearranged. The next chapter explores how the ideological side of this change translated into practice in the late 1970s.

Open Access This chapter is licensed under the terms of the Creative Commons Attribution 4.0 International License (http://creativecommons.org/licenses/by/4.0/), which permits use, sharing, adaptation, distribution and reproduction in any medium or format, as long as you give appropriate credit to the original author(s) and the source, provide a link to the Creative Commons license and indicate if changes were made.

The images or other third party material in this chapter are included in the chapter's Creative Commons license, unless indicated otherwise in a credit line to the material. If material is not included in the chapter's Creative Commons license and your intended use is not permitted by statutory regulation or exceeds the permitted use, you will need to obtain permission directly from the copyright holder.

CHAPTER 5

Rewriting the History and Future of Consumer Credit: Ideological Change as a Marketing Strategy

In the autumn of 1978 and spring of 1979, credit cards were even more of a burning issue in the Swedish media than they had been in the early 1960s. Headlines such as 'Credit cards a social danger' or 'Burn them' were not uncommon, especially in the left-wing press.[1] At the same time, adverts for cards proliferated, introducing Visa in 1978, and then Master-Charge in 1979, and reminding the public about the existing Swedish card schemes. The number of cards in use continued to rocket. Gunnar Karneman, the managing director of Köpkort, complained about what he saw as ignorance and short-sightedness in the debate, or as he chose to call it, the credit card 'battle', which, he said in a talk, was raging on two levels. One was the ideological, political level where 'the pundits in the name of consumer protection and in a more or less patronising manner, tell others—consumers in general and the so-called underprivileged in particular—what is good for them'. These critics understood little about either the business or how credit cards worked, but wanted to regulate them anyway, Karneman sharply concluded. He added, 'The mainly ideologically oriented criticism is very wide of the mark'.[2]

The other level, according to Karneman, was the practical and economic level, 'where consumers find out on their own what suits them and then act accordingly'. The hysterical attacks on the marketing of cards and the demands to regulate them were exaggerated: today's consumers, he said, were well informed and had no difficulty making rational choices on their own.[3] Karneman chose to label only his opponents' line of thought as ideological, while claiming that he himself stood for what was practical and essentially self-evident. But clearly, there was an ideological divide in the credit card debate, with two opposing perspectives on consumers, on credit and on the role of the state versus the market.

In this chapter I examine how this ideological divide was handled—how the domestication process played out at a societal and political level. I analyse two illuminating cases from the late 1970s, both of which involved attempts to change once-dominant ideological preconceptions in society, and in both cases the circulation of knowledge was key. The first case deals with the credit card entrepreneur Erik Elinder's project to rewrite the history of consumer credit with the help of academic research. He mobilised the social sciences and humanities to reshape what he considered obsolete views and values in society and produce a new, scholarly legitimate narrative. The second case, which connects to and complements the first, tells the story of how the traditionally strongly credit-averse consumer cooperative movement decided not only to accept credit cards in their shops but to launch their own. This sensational U-turn was preceded by months of heated debate within the movement, described by observers as 'a clash between ideology and economy'. It involved the renegotiation of the cooperative ideology and a large-scale information campaign through the typical channels of a popular movement (*folkrörelse*), such as study circles and discussion groups, educational pamphlets and articles in the organisation's own magazine. Considering that almost 40 percent of Swedish households were co-op members and that every town had at least one cooperative shop—called Konsum shops—this change had a considerable impact.

CREDIT CARDS AND NEOLIBERALISM

Ideology crops up everywhere in the history of bankification. In the case of the cheque-account wages (Chapter 2), bankers actively sought to 'break down the ideological opposition' from the trade unions and also had to convince themselves to act against the ideologically ingrained reluctance to cater to workers by collecting union membership fees or inviting union representatives to join local bank boards.[4] At the women's banking conferences (Chapter 3), we saw how the banks and the representatives of the Taxpayers' Association—a non-partisan organisation, but with an openly ideological stance against the planned economy, high taxes and big government—worked together with the staff of government agencies.

Crossing and redrawing the ideological demarcation lines was even more important when it came to consumer credit and credit cards. In the literature, credit cards are associated with a neoliberal mindset: The concepts of consumer sovereignty and free consumer choice—key features of neoliberal capitalism—have often been used to justify credit cards and consumer credit. As part of the micro-infrastructure of everyday financialisation, the credit card represents neoliberalism in practice. Cards were marketed as devices for optimising consumer choice, by enabling consumption based on future income. Cards also helped with the move from public to private debt, and financialised everyday consumption by connecting it to larger financial markets. Third-party cards with revolving credit (Chapter 4) commodified credit and money itself. At least in the North American setting, credit cards ensured financial independence from both state and community, and were described as a substitute for welfare policies. Foucauldian interpretations highlight the self-disciplinary technology of credit cards and the challenge they pose to individuals in managing their own creditworthiness.[5] Moreover, in both the academic literature and popular narratives, the credit card emerges as a symbol of the consuming self.[6] Thus, it is clear from existing research that the credit card is and has historically been an ideologically charged artefact. This chapter charts not merely how credit cards (along with other financial instruments) were imbued with ideological preconceptions but also how contemporary actors tried to manage, negotiate and transform the ideological landscape and the role credit cards played within it.

THE CONSUMER IN THE WELFARE STATE

The late 1970s were a turbulent time in Swedish politics, with the Social Democrats losing power in 1976 for the first time in more than 40 years. A centre-right government took over, although the Social Democrats remained the largest party in Parliament. Like other Western economies, Sweden's was under stress with high inflation and the threat of rising unemployment, even if its inflation and unemployment levels were lower than in the United Kingdom, for example. Industry struggled with failing profit margins and low levels of investment. The once relatively calm relationship between organised capital and labour, built on a culture of corporatism and a spirit of consensus, had become strained.

The immediate cause of conflict was the wage-earner fund proposal, put forward by the Swedish Trade Union Confederation (LO) in 1975 and embraced, somewhat unwillingly, by the Social Democratic Party. Claiming to address both the industry's need for capital and the lack of economic democracy, the proposal suggested that part of the annual profits of all companies above a certain size be transferred to collective funds controlled by the trade unions to acquire shares. The hope—or the fear, depending on one's position—was that the workers would eventually gain collective control of the means of production, thus securing a true economic democracy. Wage-earner funds provoked massive opposition from the Swedish Employers' Association (SAF), which used them as an argument to mobilise popular support for the ideology of free enterprise and unregulated markets.[7]

One of the many arguments in these campaigns would pit the consumer against the wage earner.[8] In the later 1970s, the consumer policy of the welfare state was also under attack. As the opening quote from Karneman hints, consumer policy was often taken as an example to illustrate the patronising nature of the welfare state and the social engineering ambitions of Swedish reformism. The Swedish Consumer Agency (Konsumentverket), founded in 1973, had a broader mandate than its predecessors, the State Institute of Consumer Affairs (Statens Institut för Konsumentfrågor, 1957) and before that the Home Research Institute (Hemmens Forskningsinstitut, 1944). While the earlier consumer institutes had focused on research, information and education, the new Consumer Agency had a mandate to impose guidelines on producers. Instead of merely helping consumers to choose good products, it could now ensure that only good products were manufactured in the first place.[9] Marketing practices were also monitored, which, more than production guidelines, concerned credit card companies, as these were often criticised for misleading advertising and hidden credit costs.

This consumer policy was unique in the Western world, one Swedish observer claimed in the late 1970s.[10] It attracted considerable criticism from liberals. Instead of a weak consumer in need of protection, the critics envisaged a different ideal of a strong 'sovereign consumer'.[11] As the Danish historian Niklas Olsen has shown, the sovereign consumer is a key concept of neoliberalism. Figuring in economic theory and political rhetoric since the mid-twentieth century, it has become increasingly important since the late 1970s, often used to legitimise market-liberal reforms.[12] According to this notion, production in an unregulated market is governed by consumer demand. Consumers exercise their sovereignty through their choices and purchasing power and not, for example, by collectively taking over distribution. Liberal critics feared that freedom of choice and consumer interests would be subordinated to political and trade union demands in a 'politicised economy'.[13]

As explained in Chapter 4, in the mid-1970s consumer credit and credit cards were not directly regulated; only indirectly, through regulations on advertising, credit reporting and data protection.[14] But consumer credit legislation was on the way, and the consumer credit industry had reason to fear the outcome. It was well-known that the Social Democratic Party shared the co-op movement's hostility to consumer credit. For example, Prime Minister Tage Erlander attacked consumer credit at the Consumer Cooperative Union's national congress in 1961, in a statement reported in the press, but which triggered no responses; it was almost taken for granted at the time. Seventeen years later the social democratic criticism against consumer credit lingered, but the climate of the debate had changed. When former Social Democrat minister Thage G. Peterson wrote in an article in 1978 that 'such cards are the invention of capitalists only to increase sales and profits', it provoked sharp reactions in right-wing media.[15]

In 1975, a commission of inquiry appointed in 1971 by Olof Palme's government (he had succeeded Erlander as leader of the Social Democratic Party) presented a proposal for consumer credit legislation. It significantly limited the scope for consumer lending, for example requiring an initial down payment in cash when buying goods on credit. The proposal also included a duty to provide clear information to consumers on the effective interest rate and restrictions on companies offering instalment credit to hinder them from repossessing unpaid goods. However, this was only a proposal, and a change of government in 1976 gave the consumer credit industry some hope that the final legislation would not be as severe. This turned out to be the case, and the 1978 Consumer Credit Act was considerably watered down. Credit cards actually benefited from the changes, as they were exempt from the requirement for an initial cash deposit (Chapter 4).[16]

Preparations for consumer credit legislation, regulatory consumer policy and the criticism it provoked, together with the proliferation of credit cards and the stormy political climate of the 1970s, were the context for the two cases examined in this chapter. This was in addition to the hostile attitudes towards consumer credit, particularly on the political left. In both cases ideology—or rather the reshaping of ideological views on consumers and credit—was a central issue, and both cases involved negotiations and conflicts between economic and other values.

Part I

Rewriting History: *The Right to Credit*

The first part of this chapter explores a book project initiated in the mid-1970s by Erik Elinder (1912–1998), the charismatic entrepreneur and owner of the Swedish credit card company ContoFöretagen (later InterConto), mentioned in Chapter 4. The retailer-owned card company, Stockholms Konto-Ring (founded in 1959), was not part of the mergers of small credit card companies in the early 1960s. Instead, it continued to operate on a small scale until 1971, when it was bought by Elinder. Under a new name and starting with no more than 3,000 accounts in 1971, the company quickly grew to become Köpkort's main competitor (Fig. 5.1). Through clever marketing and the acquisition of older, smaller credit systems such as Göteborgs Ekonomicentral (Gothenburg Finance Centre), a former workers' credit union founded in 1929, Elinder turned his card business into a great success. In addition to its own cards, ContoFöretagen also managed private label cards for retailers including Ikea, as mentioned in Chapter 4. By 1978, when the company changed its name to InterConto and introduced Visa to Sweden, it already had 262,000 accounts, which would grow by more than 20 percent the following year to 320,000, securing second place close behind the bank-owned Köpkort with its 350,000 accounts.[17]

Elinder, struggling with what he described as the 'morally, psychologically, and politically charged' image of credit cards, commissioned two economic historians at the University of Gothenburg to write a book about 'small everyday loans' since 1800.[18] The working title, *The Right to Credit*, summed up the ideological message he wanted to convey about credit as an age-old moral right.[19] Elinder hoped this moral–ideological justification for consumer credit would find a wide readership:

> The book will be a classic, for the first time presenting a credit operation, which is of extraordinary importance for consumers, commerce, and social life. ... The better this book is, the more it will be read and the faster we will gain respect for the credit card operation and its social and economic role.[20]

5 REWRITING THE HISTORY AND FUTURE OF CONSUMER CREDIT   131

Fig. 5.1 'He bet on new cards—got 200 million in the pot', portrait of Erik Elinder in *Veckans affärer*, 27 January 1977. *Photo* Kjell Johansson. Used with the permission of photographer Kjell Johansson and the Bonnier Group

Aspirations were high, as reflected in the book's partly international scope and long historical perspective. Its target audience ranged from university researchers and students, politicians, journalists, bankers and teachers to people working in retail trade, trade union and co-op members, and participants in study circles.[21] However, the book project's scope, topic and realisation were all subject to negotiations and interpretations. The two historians abandoned the project in 1980 and the book, although almost finished, was never published. The manuscript, an extensive correspondence between Elinder and economic historian Jan Kuuse (one of the two authors), and a large number of letters and notes about the project, survive in Elinder's uncatalogued personal archive.[22] This rich documentation and the generosity of economic historians Jan Kuuse and Kent Olsson in sharing their memories present a rare opportunity to trace the aspirations, efforts, strategies and negotiations—the relational work—involved in the domestication of credit cards by influencing common ideologies. Elinder shared these ambitions with the entire industry, even if the methods used may have differed.

Narratives, Relational Work and the Domestication of Ideologies

'When trying to understand finance we should not only follow the money, we should also follow the story', advises the financial historian Per Hansen in an article on cultural approaches to financial history. Narratives, he argues, 'co-construct and legitimize [financial] regimes by framing the way we see the world. Narratives are not authorless discourses, but represent specific, powerful interests and make cultural capture by the financial sector of the political system possible'.[23] Other scholars from different disciplinary fields point out that narratives have been important in shaping, changing and legitimising the role of finance in society. Mary Poovey and Marieke de Goede, for example, have demonstrated the performative power that narratives—including literary accounts—have over the world of both high and low finance.[24] Hansen focuses on what he calls the grand narratives of finance in society, singling out two competing—and well-known—grand narratives in Western societies over the last century: the social state, or Keynesian narrative, gained momentum around 1930 and dominated until the late 1970s when it gave way to the market-liberal, or neoliberal, narrative. Hansen acknowledges the role of the social sciences, not least economics, in creating, shaping and legitimising these narratives. Still, he explains that other areas of cultural meaning production are also important and join in the creation of grand narratives, using Hollywood films as an example.[25]

While these scholars explore the (performative) impact of existing narratives, here I will unpack the explicit strategies and implicit ambitions in the process of *creating* a new popular and scholarly legitimate narrative as well as the negotiations, practical struggles and problems inherent in this narrative-making. The two grand narratives Hansen describes are both there. Although—as he argues—they are non-compatible, this did not stop the historical actors from trying to connect them, to domesticate the new by linking it to the old and familiar. In other words, relational work was also required at the narrative–ideological level.

Here the relational work was intertwined with what STS scholars have called 'boundary work'. Thomas Gieryn introduced this cartographical metaphor to analyse the efforts put into drawing symbolic demarcation lines between real and illegitimate science, between science and other epistemic authorities, and between science and external powers trying to exploit the authority and legitimacy of science, such as political or market forces.[26] Rather than exploring how academics establish and reinforce cultural boundaries, I train the spotlight on the other side of the symbolic border, namely the realm of business. In this sense, relational work is an inverted type of boundary work.

Gieryn focuses on natural scientists and technologists when scrutinising the relationship between the market and the industry on one side and university research on the other.[27] Within the discipline of history, it is more common to problematise 'the uses of history'. Commissioned company histories based on scholarly research, corporate storytelling and so-called history marketing are examples of history being 'used' by commercial actors.[28] Business history became a thriving field in economic history in Sweden in the 1970s, when large enterprises had their histories written by university-based historians. The economic historian Ulf Olsson describes a veritable upsurge in such projects from the mid-1970s, many of them commissioned by the Wallenberg group.[29] This prompted business historians to discuss the boundaries of academic research, which coincided with an ongoing debate on history and scientific methodology. Company histories were not sufficient per se; generalisations, theorising and a methodological awareness were deemed necessary for them to have scholarly credibility.[30]

In 1989 Karl-Gustav Hildebrand, a professor of economic history and the author of several corporate histories (including one on Handelsbanken), offered an unproblematic picture of the boundary work involved in writing corporate history. According to his argument, the transactions were rather straightforward: 'What the researcher offers the company is his working time and his scientific judgement, but the conclusions drawn are his own and no one else's'. In return, the historian gained access to valuable archival sources and interviews, as well as a financial reward. As for the corporation, Hildebrand writes, 'the PR effect lies in the fact that their company is considered deserving of a scientific presentation'. Sometimes the historical narrative also serves to strengthen a corporate identity; but, as he continues, both uses are based on a respect for 'the judgement of history'.[31] The present case offers a different scenario involving a business leader with no archival material, but a clear notion of the main argument of a commissioned book. Rather than respecting the judgement of history, Elinder wanted to rewrite it.

BREAKING DOWN IDEOLOGICAL BOUNDARIES: THRIFT REVISITED

> My toughest enemy in my present line of work is the Erik Elinder of the 1940s (i.e., the ingrained idea that you should save first and buy later). As you will remember, I was the head of *Lyckoslanten* [the savings banks' children's magazine] with [its stories about the characters] Thrift and Spendthrift and all that ideology. I built up the savings club movement, the household savings box movement, school savings activities and all this, which was a wonderfully nice and fun job in a world that seems quite distant from ours. This ideology/mythology from 1940 is what we must break down, and instead make people adapt to a new situation: a high-tax society with ever-increasing inflation ... Another ideology we must fight is the Herman Stolpe of the 1940s—we talked about this on the phone. The broad base of the cooperative movement is still against credit.[32]

This quote comes from a 1974 letter from Erik Elinder to Sven Rydenfelt, (neo)liberal economist, publicist, associate professor at Lund University and member of the Mont Pélerin Society, the international group founded by Friedrich von Hayek that gathered thought leaders around the ideology of free markets and neoliberalism.[33] This letter is a telling document in several ways. It was the first time Elinder explicitly mentioned publishing a book about consumer credit, asking Rydenfelt if he would write or edit this work. The choice of Rydenfelt indicates the book project's ideological affiliations, but the letter also highlights Elinder's background and contrasts it to his long-term ambitions.

Early in his career, Elinder, a Swedish pioneer in advertising and marketing, was head of the savings banks' Bureau of Information (Sparfrämjandet). He coordinated its savings campaigns and published the children's magazine *Lyckoslanten*, with its cartoon characters—the two young girls, Spara (Thrift), righteous and successful in all her undertakings, and her opposite Slösa (Spendthrift), irresponsible, lazy, causing endless trouble and not thinking twice before buying on credit. The two figures—with the moralities they embodied—became emblematic in the Swedish consciousness and everyday culture. In 1950, Elinder left the savings banks to head an advertising agency, which he later developed into Säljinstitutet, a large advertising chain. He sold the company around 1970 and was looking for new ventures when he joined the credit card business by buying the old Stockholms Konto-Ring.

As an advertising expert and not least due to his background in 'savings propaganda', as it was called in the mid-twentieth century, he was not only aware of the general negative attitudes towards consumer credit but also knew that it was possible to shape morals. After all, he had done that before, but from the opposite standpoint. Information, education and knowledge, as well as stories (such as those about Spara and Slösa), could be mobilised to change values and attitudes. The quote from his letter to Rydenfelt illustrates how he used a good story about himself working with savings campaigns in the past, clearly conscious of the fact that this added legitimacy to his new message.[34] This was true, even though—based on much of his writings, including notes not intended for publication—he seems to have been sincerely convinced of the merits of credit cards. The point here, however, is not Elinder's personal views but his strategy of shaping ideological beliefs in society.

Elinder repeatedly complained about the limited, 'obsolete' knowledge about consumer lending among Sweden's politicians and public, even bankers. He believed it to be both the cause and the consequence of persistent negative attitudes towards credit. The speedy development of the credit card business in the 1970s, and especially the prospects of its growth, motivated 'investments' in social science research, he argued; not just investments in computerisation and product development. The planned history book was important not only for raising the prestige of his company but also because, in Elinder's mind, it was a way to influence politicians, government agencies, banks and other businesses.[35] In writing to Rydenfelt and elsewhere, Elinder dwelt on the hostile attitude the Social Democratic Party had towards consumer credit (and advertising), as reflected in its party manifesto. As he wrote,

> Read SAP's [the Social Democratic Party's] latest platform, which is still stuck in the 1850s [*sic*] cooperative ideology, which sees consumer credit

as a danger to workers, debts as cruel and evil, while the right to buy on credit, which we argue is a benefit, is regarded as a shameless and dangerous seduction.[36]

Instead of the pitiful image of the commercially manipulated consumer forever trapped in a web of credit that emerged there, he wanted to bring forward a different figure: a rationally calculating, careful person who wanted to consume but not overconsume. He hoped to convince Social Democrats and the co-op movement that their fears were groundless, at least if credit provision was professionally organised. This aim became especially important in 1973–1975, when a government inquiry was working on a proposal for a new consumer credit legislation, and then again in 1980, when a new committee focused on the sole issue of credit cards. Elinder believed that to influence politicians he needed the credibility of (social) science: 'If we are to earn respect for our operations from the politicians of today and tomorrow, we have to move firmly forward with scientifically well-grounded publications highlighting the importance of our field of business'.[37] This conviction was probably based on the strong technocratic tradition and the role of scientific research in Swedish politics, where, the intellectual historian Per Wisselgren argues, official government inquiries served as boundary zones, opening the door for social science to influence political decisions.[38]

Elinder thus expected the dissemination of research-based knowledge to change both popular moralising and negative political attitudes. First, he wanted to show that the critics were wrong about the harmfulness of credit card use. In a society with high taxes, general welfare, relatively high incomes and high inflation, borrowing for consumption—for a higher standard of living—could be economically rational, even more so than saving. Or, as Elinder and his colleagues wanted to put it, consumer credit was a form of saving, but saving *after* the purchase rather than before. That credit cards were also useful to retailers was the least controversial part of the message.

Second, a historical account based on serious research, to Elinder's mind, would show that credit in everyday transactions was a 'natural right' or an age-old 'quality of life' that had been 'forgotten' and 'lost'.[39] Consumer lending and borrowing could, therefore, not be seen as problematic. These ideas regarding a natural moral right to credit, along with the ambition to influence government policy not to impede and even secure consumers' access to credit, resonated with the neoliberal notion of the sovereign consumer, who should be allowed to freely exercise their economic agency.[40]

At the same time, Elinder was well aware of the potential of advertising, the advances in applied marketing research, and how they could be used to map and influence consumer attitudes. In 1973 he wrote to Ernest Dichter, a well-known international pioneer in motivational marketing research and a key figure in twentieth-century advertising history.[41] Dichter—an old acquaintance of Elinder—replied, 'You asked whether I could help in finding out the attitudes of the Swedish people and how to change this attitude. The answer is yes'. After presenting the costs for a 'psychologically constructed interviewing guide', interviews and practical recommendations, he added, 'But having been in the advertising business yourself, you may not need too much of this help'.[42] Instead of hiring Dichter's firm, Elinder chose an original alternative: to change ideological attitudes and moral beliefs by rewriting the history of credit; or, more generally, by producing and distributing knowledge in collaboration with the *university-based* social, economic and not least historical sciences.

WHAT IS A HISTORY BOOK WORTH?

Although a historical study had been mentioned in Elinder's correspondence earlier, the first steps were taken in 1976.[43] His interest in the historical perspective awakened when he bought Göteborgs Ekonomicentral (Gothenburg Finance Centre). This was a small credit operation, a former credit union for workers, launched as a philanthropic project in 1929 by the financier and Olympic athlete Bruno Söderström. On the advice of one of his university contacts, Elinder got in touch with Professor Arthur Attman at the Department of Economic History at the University of Gothenburg. Attman recommended a younger colleague, Jan Kuuse, who he knew would be interested in a book project. Elinder was pleased with the idea. Not only did he find the young associate professor a nice and knowledgeable person; he also appreciated Kuuse having co-authored a book for the centenary of the telecom company LM Ericsson.[44]

Elinder gladly compared his project with Ericsson's anniversary book: 'I am aware that there are huge differences between LM Ericsson's resources and ours, but I do not think that our book has to be any less good for that'.⁴⁵ However, the book project on 'the right to credit' differed from the Ericsson book and other corporate history writing of the time. It might seem strange for a young company to commission a history book, but Elinder's aim was not to position his company in the mainstream historical narrative, or to produce a book as a monument to a glorious past. Rather, he wanted to write an alternative history in which consumer credit fitted better than in mainstream narratives.

Elinder duly met with Jan Kuuse, who suggested that he work with a colleague, Kent Olsson.⁴⁶ As Elinder had to get the book project accepted by ContoFöretagen's board, he presented it as an 'investment' in internal education and external information. The managing director Reine Olsson, a computer technology expert, wrote a sceptical comment about the cost of the project in the margin of Elinder's memo: 'I wholeheartedly support investing large amounts in personal development, but doubt the value of the concrete proposal. Can it be worth over SEK 100,000? What can we get for 25,000?'⁴⁷

The book project would go on to cost far over SEK 100,000 (SEK 450,000, €40,000 in today's money), including over 15 months of salary and a long research trip to the United States for the authors.⁴⁸ Looking at the bigger picture, Elinder later said that if the book influenced general attitudes and especially legislation, it would be valuable for an entire industry and definitely worth the money invested:

> Then our book, with all our fine arguments and all our valuable elucidation of the issue from 1800 to 1980, could become the introductory publication of the commission of inquiry on credit cards. It could affect developments in a way that nothing else could. Two researchers from a university department with great integrity would present the first objective, comprehensive, correct story of how consumer credit issues have been handled for 180 years, with an emphasis on the credit card developments in the 1970s, when most people had not yet seen the pattern. ... It's worth millions for our company alone and tens of millions for the whole industry if we can secure reasonable legislation and prevent much foolishness and much short-term patronising mentality.⁴⁹

The emphasis on the book as a scholarly product is plain ('objectivity' and 'integrity' being the keywords). This quote and Reine Olsson's comment also reveal that both men gauged the worth of the production and dissemination of ideologically favourable scholarly knowledge in terms of economic value. Elinder proposed a long-term and more visionary calculation, seeking to justify the considerable sums of money he had invested. But, as I will show, he also immediately used the knowledge, or rather the pieces of information, collected by the economic historians.

WHOSE BOOK? MESSAGE, STORY AND INFORMATION

'Our book', Elinder had said in the memo quoted earlier. Reading the exchanges between Elinder and Kuuse, in which the former replied to the latter's outline of the book with an 'alternative outline' and Elinder refused to budge in regard to the title 'The Right to Credit' (implying a ready-made message), one might wonder why the historians took on the task in the first place. Kuuse tells me that he and Kent Olsson were intrigued by the interesting research problem and the originality of the topic. Writing the history of consumer credit and credit cards in Sweden and working with both historical and contemporaneous material seemed like an opportunity not to be missed—not to mention that Elinder was persuasive, with a contagious enthusiasm.

Before looking more closely at the negotiations over the content and the intended circulation of the book, it should be noted that there were three aspects to the 'knowledge' produced in the process that Elinder, and to some extent the historians, spoke of: (1) *the argument* (ideological, or scientifically generalising), referred to as 'our argumentation', 'the message', 'the main line of argument', etc.; (2) *the story*, presented as a fascinating history, a narrative, 'thrilling like a novel', etc.; and (3) *the information* or *facts* referred to as such or sometimes just as 'knowledge' (*kunskaper*), a word that also denoted the entire package of argument, story and information. As Hayden White has pointed out, moralising is always present in any factual storytelling, in any narrative.[50] In this case, too, narrative, morality and fact were intertwined.

Elinder insisted on the ideological message from the outset, as I discussed above. As for the storyline, a big part of it was also plotted by Elinder early on. In a memo to the board of ContoFöretagen in 1977, he wrote that he had been looking for a historian to write a book for some time:

> Ever since we took over Göteborgs Ekonomicentral (Gothenburg Finance Centre), I have been absolutely fascinated by this company's origins and further development. I would, for my own information and because I believe that the story of this company has an exceptionally rare potential to

interest a broader audience, people who are otherwise uninterested in our world, want to present the company's background, start, development, etc. until this point. What makes Göteborgs Ekonomicentral interesting is: 1. The creator was a fascinating person; 2. Behind the initiative were workers' trade unions in an intimate collaboration with Gothenburg's merchants; 3. Idealism, economy, social responsibility, and economic innovation are mixed in a fascinating way.

Thus, to Elinder's mind the story was perfect because it included not only a celebrity, Bruno Söderström, but also poor, diligent, unionised workers. Both elements served to underscore the main argument. Addressing the trade unions was crucial:

> I feel that it is very important to have the unions and the Social Democratic Party with us in our efforts to develop an effective consumer credit system alongside the banking system. ... It's for this reason that I find it so exciting to have this history explained by an independent expert.[51]

The Swedish trade unions were a major force in society and formed an important target group for the card company, much like in the case of the cheque accounts for wages discussed in Chapter 2. So the historical narrative that was supposed to legitimise consumer credit had to include the workers.

Elinder might have been right about the possibilities of finding a wider audience with this story, if only the project had not outgrown its initial framework. It is evident that he insisted not only on a 'dramatic and exciting' story but also on a 'scientifically correct' one, at least in principle. Jan Kuuse has told me, 40 years on, that Elinder, although always generous and charming in his manners, had no understanding of scientific research or historical writing, that he went 'barging in', and involved himself too much in the writing process. According to Kuuse, they pushed back by referring to the established guidelines for research ethics: 'We wanted to ask the questions ourselves', he says.[52] This resonates with the boundary work of science which Gieryn describes.

Elinder's letters show him having plenty of ideas and opinions, which he relentlessly communicated. He was tenacious in making the main ideological argument more apparent, but was also engaged when telling a good story, which may not be surprising coming from a marketing man. On 30 May 1978, he wrote to Kuuse:

> Today, in the morning when I was cycling around Djurgården, I was thinking of your book. [It] contains a lot of valuable information, but which nevertheless doesn't involve me. It doesn't really stimulate me; it's not really as characteristically unique as I have dreamed of. [This is because] there are too few real people in your book. It is a stream of information flowing calmly and kindly. ... Let's put lively, exciting, vital people in every chapter.[53]

When criticising the manuscript, he called it 'your book' and wanted to add 'more drama', more events. In his next letter, the following day, Elinder linked the problem of a missing narrative to his feeling that the main line of argument about 'the right to credit' was disappearing as the manuscript progressed, and that the strategically important link to the trade unions had also faded. If only the economic historians would hold to the argumentation line, he wrote, both story and argument would be stronger:[54]

> The book can be as exciting as a detective novel if only the common thread of the story is sufficiently strong. It can be exciting without sacrificing objectivity. What we are writing is an economic history of ideas.[55]

In this clear example of trespassing onto the territory of independent academic research, he recognised that there were boundaries—hence his mentions of 'objectivity' and the 'economic history of ideas'—but also crossed them with the words '*we* are writing' and the comparison with a crime novel. Elinder and a small group of people at the company commented on the manuscript and suggested changes. One reader consistently deleted 'negative' words like 'debt collection' (*inkassering*, *indrivning*) and suggested 'softer', less unpleasant phrases. The word *köpkort*, which in the 1960s and 1970s became a generic term for a credit card, was also banned, probably because it was the company name of InterConto's main competitor. Admittedly, Elinder assured Kuuse that 'All I write and everything I comment on are my own spontaneous reactions, you are the one responsible for the content, you decide what should be in the book'.[56] However, considering Elinder's passionate engagement in the project, this sounds rather defensive as statements went—or it might have been a reaction to an earlier conversation. Still, it showed that despite constantly 'barging in', Elinder was keen to maintain the *idea* of scientific boundaries, because the credibility it could provide was valuable to him.

From the beginning there was an underlying conflict between the ideological ambitions and expected market(ing) value of the book and its academic worth. This conflict was not set down in writing, but Jan Kuuse and Kent Olsson recall that in a 1970s university setting it was controversial for them to take on a book project commissioned by a credit card company. The topic itself was dubious, especially to the intellectual left of the time, who would rather focus on issues such as indebtedness, overconsumption and the social dangers of buying on credit. Kuuse remembers the often critical media coverage of credit cards in 1978–1979 when they were working on the book.[57] For the same reasons, the political message became even more important to Elinder, and he wrote to Kuuse, presumably merely adding to the scholars' dilemmas:

> Neither the Social Democratic Party and the Consumer Ombudsman nor the banks and financial institutions have yet discovered this right [the right to credit]. This is why our story is dynamite, both politically and economically. That's why it must be written not as a war pamphlet, but as a depiction of a silent struggle, which isn't yet settled and where ContoFöretagen can be portrayed as the company that through its remarkable history is able to represent the interests of both the poor savers and the merchants in a very special way. Let's meet before you set out for America to talk more about this; if this line of argumentation is lost, we will miss the main point. The book will not have any message, the book gets no grip on the readers, and this we can't afford to risk.[58]

The economic historians had to strike a balance between academic criticism from their colleagues and the increasingly unambiguous ideological and business ambitions of their temporary employer.

FINDING THE RIGHT PUBLISHER: IDEOLOGY, SCIENCE OR GOOD WRITING?

In his earliest notes, Elinder stated that the book had to be published by a 'real publishing house', as this was the only way to attract enough readers and gain credibility.[59] In 1977 he therefore contacted a friend, P. A. Sjögren, who was the head of Rabén & Sjögren, the well-known publisher of Astrid Lindgren and other famous authors. Despite their friendship, the notion that Rabén & Sjögren might publish a book about 'the right to credit' was a bold one, as it was owned by the Consumer Cooperative Union (Kooperativa Förbundet, KF), the stronghold of anti-credit sentiment in society.

Still, Sjögren took Elinder's proposal seriously and responded that the topic—everyday economic issues—would in principle fit their profile. He also admitted that it represented a timely issue and that a historical study of consumer credit would contribute to the ongoing, intensifying debate on credit in society, and within the co-op movement. 'After the war, neither our country, nor the cooperative movement itself remained uninfluenced—uncontaminated!', Sjögren added with emphasis—'by the new views on consumer credit'. In a resolute tone, showing interest but clearly taking a stand against the commercial promotion of consumer credit in the shape of a book and (literally) underscoring the significance of a scholarly approach, he concluded:

> The premise, after all, is that the outline of the work is *scientific*—it describes and analyses economic historical processes and problems. The fact that the initiator is one of the most dynamic and successful promoters of consumer credit doesn't mean that the book will be a polemical pamphlet/ biased account of the unrestricted and unlimited growth of consumer credit.[60]

Elinder had taken this as a positive answer, and it probably confirmed his conviction that the book had to carry the hallmark of academic research. A few months later, he again wrote to Sjögren to confirm their mutual understanding that Rabén & Sjögren would publish the upcoming book. Only the publisher's answer is preserved, but it seems that Elinder argued for the increased timeliness of this book by referring to the Cooperative Union's plans to introduce their own credit card. Apparently, this was a relevant factor for the publisher as well, although he pointed out that the credit card issue was not yet resolved within the organisation. Not only was the question still under debate internally, but the negotiations were also far from public ('pretty secret'). The outcome, he agreed, was important for the book project—the required scientific objectivity becoming less crucial if the cooperative movement chose to accept and even issue credit cards:

> Should KF really go in for card credits, then a material that highlights the history of such credit is a good and important thing, and then it doesn't

matter all that much if the material is directly or indirectly characterised by a certain Elinderian enthusiasm for the credit card phenomenon. If, however, the negotiations within the cooperative movement were to lead to KF not wanting to embark on the credit card ship, this naturally forces us to take some extra care to ensure the objective character of this book.[61]

Again, we see an example of balancing the value of scholarly research against a moral–ideological deficit inherent in the topic. However, Sjögren stressed that the final decision would be based on the content and quality of the manuscript itself.

Five months later, the publisher hit a different note. The negotiations over the cooperative card were still ongoing, but Sjögren and his colleagues had now read the first four chapters and were not enthusiastic. Sjögren rejected the manuscript based on this partial reading. One reason for this, he said, was market-related. Despite Elinder paying for the publishing costs, they feared that the book would not be easy to sell or, as both Sjögren and Elinder had hoped, to use as a textbook for study circles. Sjögren quoted a reviewer who had said that some passages on economic theory, public debt and the quantitative reasoning on standards of living would be too heavy (did he mean too scientific?) and boring for a general readership. But, he added, the book became more fascinating when it discussed the everyday history of small-scale credit, and writing along this line more consistently would have made it more interesting for publication despite its obvious bias towards consumer credit.

What the reviewer and the publisher found most problematic, however, was not the quantitative reasoning or the 'propaganda' for consumer credit per se, but what they perceived as polemics against the Consumer Cooperative Union, or rather the historical accounts of the polemics back in the 1930s.[62] It would be strange, Sjögren argued, to publish a book that not only attacked the present beliefs of the publishing house's owners but also did so historically when the persons cited could no longer defend themselves.[63] This was a peculiar argument, as any historical investigation of the early twentieth-century debates on consumer credit would include both KF and those arguing against their cash-only policy—and the manuscript also voiced old cooperative ideologists and their attack on credit.[64] However, what Sjögren might have realised was that an overall positive historical narrative about consumer credit as a 'natural right' and an 'age-old quality of life' would redefine KF's historical struggle against it.

Clearly, the refusal was at least partly ideologically motivated. Also, the 'scientific' character of the book (political economy and social history) was becoming more of a burden than a free pass for publication, contrary to what had been said before. The rejection was a setback, but Elinder did not give up. He contacted the publishing house of SNS (Studieförbundet Näringsliv och Samhälle, the Centre for Business and Policy Studies), a think tank for collaborations between the business sector, decision-makers and academia, which provided a suitable, if less striking, context for the book.[65]

IMPORTING KNOWLEDGE FROM AMERICA

While the post-war criticism of consumer credit always included a strong hostility towards the American 'contamination' of Swedish society through credit cards, as reflected in the quote from P. A. Sjögren, the card companies looked at the American market with intense curiosity. Elinder was eager to learn more about American business practices. This eagerness, rather than their historical study, motivated a research trip in the summer of 1978 for the two economic historians. They had a busy schedule for their coast-to-coast journey, from New York to San Francisco, with a long list of people to visit at card companies, banks, consumer research centres and consumer organisations. Elinder acted as an intermediary for most of their contacts, but the fact that the travellers were academics rather than representatives of the card industry seems to have opened doors. In a presentation letter Elinder emphasised that Jan Kuuse, a 'prominent and well-known professor', had recently finished a monograph on the history of the telephone company Ericsson.[66]

Elinder had high expectations for the trip. He wanted the historians to gather information on 'the present situation' and asked for interviews 'about future perspectives' with key figures in the business. He also wanted to know whether the specific card product he had introduced in Sweden (selective card systems) could be exported to the United States. Elinder was well aware he was asking for more than academic historical research, but tried to defend his stance:

> I have often said that for you scholars, it must be immensely interesting to get as close to the real thing as possible while writing this particular book. I'm aware that it might be difficult for you to keep scientific research and economic journalism apart. For us, in our work, it's at the same time

immensely valuable that you at this very expansive stage are able to supply us with lots of important information.[67]

Knowledge—*information*—about contemporary American card businesses was thus 'immensely valuable' to Elinder's company in the expansive period of the late 1970s. Gathering this knowledge was not a typical task for historians, and nor was 'spreading the word' about InterConto, which they were also asked to do. Once again, the boundaries of academic historical research were blurred, which Elinder justified by referring to the (economic) value of this information for his business. Another letter reveals more details about Elinder's strategic use of the legitimacy of university research. He asked Kuuse to write and ask several key figures in the American card industry for information, in his capacity as an economic historian at the University of Gothenburg:

> If you write this on stationery with the University of Gothenburg letterhead, they will feel flattered and happy, and they will likely send you the manuscript ... This way, you acquire knowledge and so will I, and we both get contacts. ... Let's work together in this way so that you as a person and your department become a radar station for our knowledge acquisition.[68]

The correspondence reveals that Elinder had other motives with the book project than merely presenting a new interpretation of consumer credit based on a historical study. As hinted at earlier, contrary to traditional business history, while Elinder was keen to offer an interpretation (the argument) and suggest a good narrative (so that it would reach its audience), he also needed and asked for extensive information. He himself wanted to learn a great deal by using the historians as intermediaries. Kuuse had not only sent a detailed report of their encounters and experiences in America but also, at Elinder's request, ranked the usefulness of the information they had gathered. One of the top-ranked contacts, for example, was Ken Larkin, a long-time executive at Bank of America and a key figure in its BankAmericard/Visa operations.[69]

Dreaming Big: A Catalyst of Knowledge

Another task for Kuuse and Olsson on their trip was to buy a large number of books on consumer credit. This literature would not only be used as reference material in their historical study—Elinder had bigger dreams:

> I'm waiting with excitement for what you have to tell me when you come home, when you unpack all your tapes and notes and start reading all the books I hope you bought during your American trip, and which can serve as the basis for what I hope will become Sweden's most complete international library concerning small credits and particularly credit card systems and payment systems.[70]

The American books (a 30 kg parcel to start with) were to form the first cornerstone of a specialist library, open to researchers and students.[71] The library was part of one of Elinder's more quixotic plans for the creation of a smaller academic research centre in collaboration with one of the Swedish universities. As he recurrently put it, this would turn InterConto into a 'catalyst of knowledge' regarding consumer credit.[72] An upgraded version of this 'dream', as he called it, was the creation of an international research institution—including education and book publishing—financed by the Visa network, which his company was now part of. In his letter to Jan Kuuse about these ideas he again spelled out a desire to control the texts produced by the researchers, but now projected onto Visa: 'By Visa itself publishing this literature, one could always ensure that Visa is depicted in a correct way, as well as being able to monitor that Visa's competitors are depicted accurately with pace and taste and judgement'.[73]

On the one hand, Elinder's plans to create and coordinate a worldwide programme for research and education sound unrealistic, as they probably were. On the other hand, we know that he was a gifted entrepreneur with several successful ventures behind him. Also, he had taken some concrete steps in organising an international research network.[74] He corresponded with quite a few university scholars abroad, mainly Americans, including Lewis Mandell, one of the earliest historians of the credit card industry. He undertook a joint project with Elizabeth Hirschman, who would become a well-established professor in marketing. He also regularly exchanged letters and information on the consumer credit industry, and developed a friendly relationship, with Spencer Nilson, the editor and founder of a global newsletter for the credit and payment card industry, *The Nilson Report*, which still exists and has published statistics and information since 1970.

Among his many Swedish academic connections we find a long list of scholars who worked in business studies, economics, statistics, sociology, ethnology, numismatics and other fields. Regarding the book project and an idea for another, edited volume, he corresponded with scholars in prominent positions at Swedish universities and outside academia, in think tanks, government agencies as well as non-profit and other organisations. For example, with Hans Zetterberg, professor of sociology and director of the Swedish Institute for Opinion Research (SIFO), he discussed studies on the 'micro-thinking of consumers'.[75] Elinder's correspondence during the book project is evidence of his dense and varied network of academics, experts and opinion leaders. He even exchanged letters with Herman Stolpe, the arch-critic of credit cards, trying to convince him of people's natural right to credit and the benefits of plastic credit cards. Stolpe, an old acquaintance and former neighbour of Elinder's, replied in a long and polite letter arguing firmly for his unchanged stance.

Finally, yet another knowledge-related venture, also a by-product of the book project, deserves mention. InterConto—and Elinder personally—encouraged university students to write their theses on consumer credit, credit cards, payments in retail trade, or on InterConto itself. Elinder suggested topics and helped students working in fields of special interest to him.[76] Some university students received scholarships for trips abroad. This activity had already started in 1974, when a list of suggested research topics composed by Elinder was distributed among students writing their third-year theses in business studies at the University of Gothenburg.[77] He also discussed with Kuuse—as a 'spin-off' of the book project—the possibility of proposing topics for doctoral theses at the Department of Economic History. 'All this takes time, but once we have thrown the stone into the water, the ripples will continue for a long time to come', he wrote.[78]

Elinder's passionate interest in research on credit cards and consumer credit did not prevent him from explicitly characterising all research-related activities as PR. This kind of PR work, he wrote, was more important than straightforward advertising, especially in the early stages of creating a new market: it was vital to develop good products without attracting too much attention, and without risking—through blatant advertising—'irritating' the government, Parliament, the Consumer Agency or competitors.[79] All these academic contacts thus served a dual function: first, to provide the company and its owner with knowledge—knowledge regarding the consumer finance industry, social and moral attitudes, statistics and history; and second, through these contacts Elinder conveyed, put into circulation—with the added value of academic prestige—a new ideological view on consumer credit.

When Kuuse and Olsson, protecting their scholarly integrity, left the project in early 1980, Elinder tried to complete and publish the book without them (after all, the manuscript was only missing the final chapter) in collaboration with the SNS think tank. He even hoped to publish it as part of the inquiry into credit cards at the Ministry of Finance (Kontokortsutredningen 1980–1984).[80] In 1981, however, Erik Elinder sold InterConto, and his interest in the credit card industry began to wane.

Mr. Card and the Reshaping of Ideology as a Marketing Strategy

Efforts to create societal acceptance for consumer credit clearly went well beyond traditional marketing. The credit card company InterConto tried to reshape ideological views by circulating a new and scholarly legitimate narrative to convince policymakers and the public. As the marketing expert he was, Elinder believed this was more effective than 'noisy' advertising or direct promotional campaigns. He needed the credibility of university-based research, but wanted to control the main argument and the narrative of the book.[81]

Despite the manuscript not being published, some goals of the project were realised. The book project and its spin-off ventures, such as contacts with students, indirectly contributed to the domestication of consumer credit, although the effect might not have been immediate. The project was performative: the mere fact that work on a scholarly book was in progress could be used to circulate the message and dismantle some of the ideological obstacles to a widespread use of credit. Elinder became the public face of credit cards in Sweden, nicknamed Mr Card by the press. His own story—with an early career as one of the 'evangelists of thrift' at the savings banks' information service—was intriguing, and he did not hesitate to exploit it in his marketing, or rather his ideology-shaping efforts.[82]

As I mentioned, Lewis Mandell described Sweden as a peculiar card market, hard for the international companies to break into. He also wrote about Elinder as an innovative credit card pioneer, and InterConto as the only significant national card company in Sweden. Mandell's account omits Köpkort, despite the bank-owned company starting much earlier and dominating the Swedish market until the 1980s.[83] Now, Mandell was one of Elinder's international contacts, and his misinterpretation of the situation in 1970s Sweden might be explained by Elinder's determined enthusiasm.

More important, however, was the domestic context and the hope to produce a narrative that could relate to the lifeworlds of ordinary workers and at the same time provide a new ideology of consumer credit—aligned with what, in Per Hansen's words, could be called the grand narrative of neoliberalism. Elinder was keen to find points of connection with the trade unions and the co-op movement. Both organisations were not only important political forces but also had an exceptionally large membership base. And it is here that the two stories—that of Elinder's book project and KF's change of mind about credit cards—overlap. As the co-op movement was, alongside social democracy, the main guardian of anti-credit ideology, Elinder hoped to eventually influence cooperative views by publishing *The Right to Credit* with the KF-owned publishing house and that the book would be used by the co-op's study circles. This did not happen, but the study circles circulated new material familiarising their members with credit cards, to which I will now turn.

Part 2

Rewriting the Future? The Consumer Cooperative Credit Card

In November 1978, in time for the Christmas rush, the Stockholm department store PUB, owned by the Consumer Cooperative Union, KF—in everyday vernacular often called 'the Cooperation' (*Kooperationen*) or Konsum after the name of its food shops—decided to accept credit cards. The media also reported that the cooperative movement was considering introducing a credit card system of its own. This was quite a sensation, KF being the 'bastion of the cash economy in this country', as one newspaper put it, and it stirred up a veritable media storm.[84] The headlines included exclamations about failed ideals, a hopeless struggle against market competition, and the 'credit card psychosis that now also affected the Cooperation'.[85]

What the public did not know was that KF's national leadership had been discussing the issue for more than a year. An internal committee of inquiry found that 30 percent of KF members already had credit cards and that they used cards just as often as non-members. This implied that many members did at least some of their shopping at non-co-op shops. Credit card holders being on average younger gave a worrying indication of future trends. The investigation found a 'dramatic upsurge' in card use, and an exponential increase was expected in the coming years. Credit cards were still not used for groceries in Sweden (Chapter 4), but were widely accepted for other goods. In the largest department stores, for example, up to 50 percent of Christmas shopping was done by credit card. As KF was struggling with a sharp fall in profitability and trying to keep up with market competition, the committee recommended that credit card payments be accepted and preferably that the cooperative movement set up its own credit card system.[86]

A project to introduce a co-op credit card could not be done from one day to the next; it required a great deal of relational work. In addition, and in more practical terms, it also required a change in the organisation's founding statutes, which explicitly banned sales on credit. For this, a vote at two successive general meetings was needed.[87] I have already discussed the key arguments in KF's critique; it is clear that the 'war' against consumer credit was an essential part of the organisation's self-image and history.

The issue entailed a 'sharp clash between economy and ideology', as one newspaper put it.[88] During the last months of 1978 and until the summer of 1979, when the final decision was taken, the cooperative credit card was hotly debated at two national general meetings and at many local ones, as well as in KF's popular weekly *Vi* and in the daily press and other media outlets (Fig. 5.2). The question concerned both the many members and the general public, with the two groups largely overlapping.[89] The introduction of credit cards was strikingly at odds with the cooperative ideology, while it was justified by referring to market arguments. I will unpack what this 'clash' entailed, and how it was handled. How did KF deal with the ideological challenge posed by credit cards? How were consumer credit and the figure of the consumer reinterpreted? And what was the significance of the co-op credit card in the general societal debate and for the credit card market?[90]

The Rational Consumer and the Sovereign Consumer in the 1970s

Different views on credit purchases entail different views on the consumer. Two ideal-typical interpretations have emerged in the credit card debate: the rational consumer and the sovereign consumer. The former is associated with the co-op movement and, indeed, with Sweden's twentieth-century history as well as a Keynesian welfare state ideology, while the latter has been central to market-liberal and neoliberal thinking.

The historian Peder Aléx has characterised the ideological foundation of Swedish consumer cooperation using the key concept of the 'rational consumer'. Rationality was normatively defined and learned; it was not an inherent quality of the consumer as an economic actor. Instead, the individual consumer was perceived as fundamentally weak, vulnerable to the manipulative power of the market and advertising. The cooperative solution was that consumers should own the retail stores themselves, collectively. Eventually, KF also moved into industrial production. The organisation was a direct democracy, with each member having a vote. Consumers paid a small sum for their 'share' upon joining, and in return could expect dividends proportionate to their purchase, thus sharing in the profits.

In addition to distributing and eventually also producing 'the right goods', the co-op movement also aimed to educate consumers on everyday economic issues so that they could make rational and well-planned purchases based on their 'real needs'.[91] Therefore, KF conducted extensive informational and educational activities at its own training centre Vår gård, within its own correspondence institute Brevskolan, or through local study circles. As mentioned in the first part of the chapter, KF also owned a publishing house, Rabén & Sjögren, and, together with the Social Democrats and the Swedish Trade Union Confederation (LO), was a co-founder of the Workers' Educational Association (ABF, Arbetarnas Bildningsförbund) in 1912, it too an important institution in Swedish society.[92]

KF's ideal of rational consumption coincided with the direction taken by the consumer policy of the post-war welfare state. While the cooperative movement had its roots in British social liberalism in the mid-nineteenth century, and liberal beginnings in Sweden as well, it soon developed strong ties to social democracy and the labour movement. Leading cooperators were often active Social Democrats even in the

1970s, although some cracks between the interests of wage earners and consumers began to emerge.[93]

KF was still an important societal force in 1970s Sweden, with channels reaching broadly into society. The cooperative movement's popular weekly magazine, *Vi*, was one of the most widely distributed in the country, with a circulation of 320,000 (decreasing, but still a large number for a small country like Sweden).[94] With KF owning 20 percent of the retail market, a Konsum food shop could be found in every town and almost every neighbourhood, even if it often had to compete with a privately owned shop nearby. In addition, the department store chain Domus, established in the 1950s, and the Obs chain of supermarkets, established in the 1960s, also belonged to the cooperative movement. In the late 1970s, however, as KF saw declining sales, several stores were forced to close, and for the first time in its history many local societies could provide no dividends to their members.[95]

At the same time, a market-liberal criticism emerged that attacked the 'patronising' consumer policy of the welfare state and its implementation by the Swedish Consumer Agency. The same criticism also targeted KF, which, the critics claimed, was not a proper interest organisation. It could not give voice to independent consumers—who were supposed to steer production through their free consumption choices—as it not only had turned into a large business corporation but was also an uncritical supporter of the state's consumer policy.[96] Another ideal, that of a 'sovereign consumer', was emphasised in this criticism, which stressed that production should be governed by consumer demand rather than state regulation or normative morality. The consumer was portrayed as a strong figure whose actions were by definition rational—someone who exercised power through their choices and purchasing power, not through the collective takeover of distribution. Such a sovereign consumer does not need protection from above or normative ideas of the 'right' kind of consumption.[97]

Both the Consumer Ombudsman Sven Heurgren and KF's chairman Hans Alsén, also a Social Democrat politician, spoke out in the media to refute this liberal criticism. The Cooperative Union's policy programme for 1978 explicitly dismissed 'the common arguments in economic debates about the consumer's "sovereignty" in the market', citing that the individual consumer could not have all the information for their choice.[98] The two opposing views were splashed across the papers. Cooperative leaders made ironic remarks about consumers' 'sovereign' choices, asking for example 'Who ordered pop-rocks?', the popular American fizzy candy launched in the 1970s. In return, liberal debaters derided KF's practical but boring 'basic wardrobe', a line of clothing that was launched in the 1970s to refute superficial market trends but was not especially popular with consumers (in contrast to their more successful line of basic furniture).[99]

Thus, the Swedish co-op movement positioned itself, in principle and rhetorically, in opposition to the idea of the sovereign consumer. In official texts and contributions to the consumer policy debate it spoke of weak consumers, needs (not demand) and collective (not individual) solutions. However, in practice and in arguments about specifics, things could sound different. In the credit card issue, an ideological, cultural and even emotional relational work was carried out to find a balance between traditional cooperative ideals and a new financial market thinking, as well as between KF's notion of the (normatively) rational consumer and the (neo)liberal notion of the sovereign consumer.

INFORMATION—AS BEFITS A POPULAR MOVEMENT

The board was aware that a decision on credit cards would upset many members and likely be sensationalised in the press. So communication became a central concern. After initially publicly denying that the issue was under discussion KF's leadership wanted to 'control' the media debate, but this was easier said than done. In October 1978 a communications plan was drawn up, emphasising that the issue was 'very sensitive in terms of public opinion'.[100] It was equally sensitive among the membership, and fierce discussions were to be expected about this change to one of the co-op movement's core principles. Keen to introduce the card quickly to keep up with the competition, the chief financial officer, Stig Lundahl, suggested that it should be a simple board decision rather than involving the entire membership. After all, he argued, the Konsum shops already accepted cheque payments without knowing whether customers were in overdraft. If one sees credit cards as just another type of payment, then the whole issue is simply a practical matter, a technical innovation. He added that it would become increasingly difficult to distinguish between credit and cash payments in the future. In the meanwhile, 'It would be nice to avoid an exhausting discussion about our statutes', he told the board.[101]

However, chairman Alsén, although positive regarding the proposal and a cooperative credit card, insisted that it was not just a simple practical issue but a matter of principle that should be handled 'as befits a popular movement like ours', not as in a private company. The membership should be involved, and the matter decided at the general meeting. Alsén's proposal became the board's decision.[102]

Information for members was easier to manage than mass media coverage, and internal communications were carefully planned. 'Study materials' outlining the pros and cons of credit purchases were sent out ahead of local and regional meetings and before the general meetings in December and June. The discussions took place between December 1978, when the membership was first informed about the plans, and the summer of 1979, when the decision to change KF's statutes was voted through and the co-op credit card was launched. Informational activities appear as a massive communication campaign aimed at both cooperative members and the general public. The weekly magazine *Vi* extensively reported on opinions both for and against, while the mainstream media also covered the issue carefully. KF's leadership travelled around to local and regional meetings and also appeared in the press as well as on TV and radio. But, and this is my main point here, the information campaign directed at the membership relied largely on methods, such as study circles with discussion guides and organised debates, traditionally used by the cooperative movement—and other popular movements—for their educational campaigns. These educational channels were an organic part of the Swedish welfare society. Now, these means were used for an ideological reinterpretation of consumer credit, which in turn required a new view of the consumer.

Market Versus Ideology or Market Ideology?

The sources describe the debates on the co-op credit card in terms of economy versus ideology, but it is more accurate to say that two ideological standpoints stood against each other. On the one hand, the economic leadership of the cooperative movement around chief financial officer Lundahl argued for what I call a new financial rationality, which had clear similarities to neoliberal thinking about consumer sovereignty and the market as an objective order of information. To be sure, Lundahl claimed that his take on the matter had nothing to do with ideology but rather with the realities of high inflation, market competition and technological development. A credit card purchase, he argued, should not even be seen as a loan but as a form of payment or as post-purchase saving—views we recognise from the credit card companies' marketing messages. Here, in the context of the cooperative movement's own soul-searching about consumer credit, it is easier to pinpoint the inherent ideological conflict. While admitting that restrictions on credit card use might safeguard some consumers from poorly planned impulse purchases, at the general meeting in December 1978 Lundahl argued that KF should still allow credit cards, because this was what 'consumers themselves [had] chosen'. This statement reveals a shift from the traditional cooperative view of consumers as needing protection (against market forces) towards a new idea about free consumer choice as the main force that should govern not only the market but also the policies of the cooperative movement.

In the debates, the credit card advocates called their own arguments 'facts'. Lundahl and the business management of KF were keen to emphasise that their approach was the objective one, as opposed to other views, which they claimed were steeped in nostalgia, emotion and idealism. 'We must base our decisions on facts' was a key phrase in the information booklet distributed before the 1978 general meeting, and it was repeated countless times by credit card proponents.[103] For them, a financial logic based on individual profits—a variant of market logic—was synonymous with sound, objective thinking:

> In the current situation it's not profitable to save, but it's profitable to take tax deductions for interest on loans! You just have to face the facts. The young families look at the financial benefits of the cards in a straightforward way.[104]

On the other hand, a group of cooperative ideological 'traditionalists' argued against the arguments above by referring to cooperative ideology, collectivism and history. Instead of this 'new egoism' of the times, they said, the cooperative movement should stay true to its original goals and offer (collective) strength to the 'weakest consumers'. The consumer had to be protected from the lure of the credit card: it was 'terribly easy to fall into temptation once you have this card. Think how easy it is to buy the more expensive food item instead of the simpler one!'. Speaking against putting consumer choice first, the critics argued that before it was 'always one for all' but that now 'we have started to think individually'.[105] There was also an explicit attack on the new financial rationality emphasised by the business leadership of KF: 'Now we in the Co-op will also encourage each other not to let our consumption be limited by our income.'[106]

Equally important was the old criticism that credit created a 'serfdom' for consumers, a dependency—if not on the old type of mill owners, then on 'capitalists' in general. For some cooperators, the cash principle was an ideological cornerstone that could not be negotiated: it was what had made the organisation strong from the outset. The direction staked out by KF's business leadership would lead to 'the straight road to misery, both spiritual and economic'.[107] Some critics used class rhetoric, arguing that credit cards were only good for 'people from higher social classes' who could afford the interest rates and take advantage of the right to deduct part of it from their taxes. Rural areas were pitted against cities, with a representative from Northern Sweden saying that this 'vermin', this nuisance, the credit card, was only valid in the cities anyway. In a similar vein, the card was described—again—as a typical American invention that did not suit Swedes. And most importantly, several representatives stressed that KF was not a private company and should not think like one.[108]

Discussions also heated up in the general media. Polemical articles in newspapers on the left and centre of the political map explicitly politicised the debate, claiming that the co-op credit card was a sign of the labour movement's failure. A worker 'stuck in a credit quagmire' was unlikely to engage in collective action.[109] Others asked whether the consumer cooperative movement was on the verge of collapse, when it began to 'walk in the footsteps of private commerce' and when its own magazine 'depicted the credit card as a phenomenon subject to the laws of nature' and 'a natural right'.[110] These comments on what was also Erik Elinder's message bear witness to its inherent ideological power.

Most voices in the debate took a pragmatic stand between the two positions. While acknowledging that credit cards are ideologically problematic and may even be harmful to some consumers and to society, they argued that 'one can't live on ideology alone'; i.e. the co-op movement could not afford to say no to credit cards: 'Can we leave this to private commerce while we sit on our tails and talk about ideology?'[111] Against the idealism of the critics, they put forward a new line of market pragmatism, according to which KF should not let 'the capitalists' take all the profits from the card business. In a vulgarised vision of economic democracy, one KF representative argued:

Why should the cooperative movement not have the same opportunities that others have? The coin is round, but we must make sure it doesn't only roll in Wallenberg's direction. It should roll in our direction ... Our members shouldn't have to go to Wallenberg and Co. to sign up for credit cards.[112]

A related argument was that KF's entry would reshape the whole credit card market on a sounder basis.[113]

For the dominant market pragmatist line within KF the key was to adapt, however reluctantly, to market competition. They also reconsidered the importance of free consumer choice and held that mass consumer society had created a new type of consumer. People did not buy things they 'needed'; they bought things that were 'convenient to have at home' or 'pretty to wear'. So KF should not point fingers or assume an overprotective big brother attitude by 'holding up a hand as a stop sign in the mixed economy'.[114] After all, it was said, the choice to buy on credit is the responsibility of the individual.[115]

On a more practical note, the co-op credit card would also challenge the long-standing taboo of buying groceries on credit. In cooperative stores food was a dominant product category, and as several voices in the debate pointed out, it would be 'ridiculous' to sort out socks and sausages at the cashier's counter in a larger Konsum shop or an Obs (cooperative) supermarket. Chairman Alsén warned that selling food on credit would be a radical step, going beyond what KF's competitors were doing, but admitted that in practice it would be difficult to avoid. As one board member bluntly put it, 'ideology need not be associated with certain categories of goods'.[116]

As the quotes show, the tone of these discussions was emotionally charged. Some were angry and 'saw red', others were astonished and many expressed sadness. Comments, for instance that it 'stings the soul of many old faithful cooperators' or that the idea of the card 'leaves a bad taste in the mouth', were frequent, not only among credit card critics but also among market pragmatists.[117]

THE LAUNCH OF THE CO-OP CARD

Following the favourable vote at the general meeting in June 1979 (confirmed by an extraordinary meeting in August), KF's statutes were changed and the co-op credit card was launched in the major cities within a few months. The left-wing press took a negative and sometimes ironic tone in its commentary, saying that 'Konsum had betrayed its old ideals' and 'capitulated', recalling the war metaphors often used to describe the debate.[118] The right-wing newspaper *Svenska Dagbladet*, however, welcomed the decision, writing in line with the ideas of consumer sovereignty and a new financial rationality that the credit card was a good tool for 'creating order and regularity in the family economy' and that 'consumers should be allowed to decide for themselves how to finance their consumption' (Fig. 5.2).[119]

For the private credit card companies, KF's new card was anything but a disadvantage. They could use it as a moral justification for their own systems. Obviously, Erik Elinder also welcomed the decision.[120] Another company, Finax, used full-page adverts with headlines like 'Test your financial common sense' to claim that

> Credit cards have turned many old prejudices and inherited values upside down! ... Now, as we enter the 1980s, a million Swedes use credit cards every day. And KF-Konsum is launching its new credit card this autumn. *Nothing is as it used to be.*[121]

The monthly magazine of the Bankers' Association, *Ekonomisk Revy* (Economic Review), commented on the significance of the co-op credit card, stating that '[t]he previously deep-rooted aversion against credit card purchases is disappearing. With Konsum ... introducing its own card, the "credit card barrier" has now been crossed'.[122]

The co-op card was not hugely different from other credit cards; nor was it much cheaper. It never became a strong player in the Swedish credit card market. Still, the result of a pragmatic decision, it had a strong legitimising effect in a broader societal perspective, as the reactions show. Looking back, its cultural and symbolic significance seems to have been more important than its economic value to the cooperation or its actual spread in society. In addition to a moral endorsement of cards in general, it also sanctioned the use of credit to buy food, erasing what had been taboo for the older card systems.

New Regulations and Credit Cards in the Political Debate

The rapid growth of the credit card market, the industry's intensified marketing efforts and the controversy surrounding the cooperative's decision once again raised the question of regulation. Parliamentary motions by the Social Democrats and the Left Party (formerly the Communist Party) in late 1979 called for restrictive measures and an investigation into the matter. For Hans Pettersson in Hallstahammar, MP for the Left Party and member of the co-op, it was 'inconceivable how Konsum could introduce credit cards'. As well as blaming KF, Pettersson accused both the Social Democrats and the Conservatives of having too much faith in free market forces. The Social Democrat MP Roland Sundgren, also active in the cooperation, proposed with colleagues that the government appoint a commission of inquiry. He was also critical of credit cards but tried to justify the co-op card with the pragmatic arguments outlined above, stressing that it was at least a better kind of credit card, with a cooperative profile that tried to 'clean up the market'.[123]

Instead, it was the Minister for Economic Affairs and leader of the right-wing party Gösta Bohman—most probably not a co-op member—who defended KF's choice in Parliament: 'I have the highest appreciation for Konsum. They introduced the cards because they believed these were not only useful for KF in the competition with the private trade ... but also for the consumers'. Market competition and consumer choice were Bohman's key words. He argued, similar to KF's economic management, that buying on credit was simply 'saving afterwards' and that the campaign against credit cards in the press was exaggerated. He repeated the familiar objections to 'paternalism and finger-pointing'. He also linked consumer sovereignty to democracy, arguing that people who can choose parties and politicians in a parliamentary election should be trusted to make their own choices in other matters of life: 'Personally, I'm a supporter of free consumer choice', Bohman stressed in the debate, even though he agreed that the marketing of credit cards had become rather 'aggressive'.[124]

However, the centre-right government, which had been given a mandate by Parliament to intervene with restrictions if necessary, felt that certain measures were justified. On 1 July 1980, credit card companies were placed under the supervision of the Bank Inspection Board; and in the same year a committee within the Ministry of Finance, known as the Credit Card Committee, was appointed to investigate the impact of credit card use on society.

The increase in credit card borrowing had been halted when, in January 1981, a required initial down payment of 25 percent was introduced for credit card purchases (as for instalment purchases). However, the new rules were abolished in less than a year in return for a promise of restraint in advertising by the card industry.[125] The Credit Card Committee submitted its final report in 1984 (to the Social Democrat government since 1982).[126] Its proposal for new legislation included amendments to the Consumer Credit Act, which were to come into force on 1 May 1985. These regulations were abandoned after only a few months when the entire credit market was deregulated and the previous credit ceilings were lifted (the November Revolution, see Chapter 1).[127]

Card-Mindedness and Ideology

In his published talk, quoted at the beginning of this chapter, Gunnar Karneman, CEO of the company Köpkort, concluded in 1979 that the Swedish public was becoming 'card-minded'.[128] (Fig. 5.2) What he described as a general mental change had important ideological underpinnings. In this chapter I have argued that reshaping widely held and often taken-for-granted ideological views was a key aspect of the domestication of credit cards. Ideological relational work, already present in the case of cheque-account wages, became especially visible in the case of credit cards.

The chapter explored two settings in which 'ingrained' ideological beliefs were challenged in the late 1970s. The first sub-study has shown how a credit card company mobilised academic research to create a new historical narrative to justify the use of consumer credit. With this and other related projects, Erik Elinder, Sweden's Mr Card, aimed to influence politicians, leaders of popular movements such as the consumer cooperative movement and the labour movement, and ultimately their members, who largely overlapped with the Swedish population. He used compelling historical narratives about credit as an ancient right, a vehicle for social justice and a tool of financial common sense. He historicised the criticisms of the political left and presented these views as outdated and ideological, which he sought to counter with an 'objective' scientific approach, or with what was presented as simple common sense. However, it is clear

Fig. 5.2 Illustration for theme section 'Leva på lån' ('Living on credit') in the daily newspaper *Svenska Dagbladet*, 14 August 1979. Headlines on the same page include 'They just keep getting more and more'; 'New law favours credit cards'; and 'The Co-op is ready for credit cards'. Artist: Bengt Salomonsson. Used with the permission of Svenska Dagbladet

that Elinder's project was equally ideological, inspired by market-liberal views involving the sovereign consumer and free consumer choice. Influencing ideological beliefs was not Elinder's main goal but more a tool to create a market for his product. Establishing credit cards as a topic of academic research served the same purpose in the longer term, in addition to bringing legitimacy and respectability to the credit card business.

The second part of the chapter highlighted the ideological soul-searching of the consumer cooperative movement when it had to reconsider its historically entrenched critical stance on consumer credit. In an emotionally charged debate, proponents of credit cards—and of the new financial rationality the cards embodied—argued against those who defended traditional cooperative ideology. A market pragmatic line between the two, accepting the former message but emotionally sympathetic with the latter, emerged from the internal battles as the dominant one. Market pragmatics explained the need for change with reference to competition and consumer demand, abandoning not only the anti-credit stance but also the notion of the weak or vulnerable consumer in need of protection and collective action.

KF's acceptance of credit cards provided a symbolic consecration of the everyday use of credit. To understand this impact, it is important to bear in mind how culturally embedded the consumer co-operative movement was in Sweden, with its close links to the labour movement and not least because of the presence of Konsum food shops and Domus department stores throughout the country. The movement also mobilised its extensive communication channels—the weekly magazine, study material and study circles, and local, regional and national meetings for members—to spread information about credit cards.

The two cases are intricately intertwined. Elinder constructed his own narrative against the traditional cooperative credit ideology that he saw as still dominant in early 1970s' Sweden. It was the cooperative leadership and membership, along with the labour trade unions, that he wanted to reach out to, while it was the cards of InterConto and other companies that KF felt it had to compete with. There were also personal connections, Elinder's contact with the publishing house owned by KF or his correspondence with Herman Stolpe, the anti-credit opinion leader, being a few examples; many other points of contact, which fall outside the scope of this chapter, emerge from the source material.

This chapter thus shows that the domestication of credit cards and the new financial rationality they embodied involved relational work at an ideological level. I am not referring primarily to overt ideological confrontations such as political debates, although these also occurred around credit cards, but to a more mundane reshaping of ideological beliefs through academic research and new narratives (academic and popular), as well as through the channels of popular movements and new payment practices at the local Konsum shops.

Open Access This chapter is licensed under the terms of the Creative Commons Attribution 4.0 International License (http://creativecommons.org/licenses/by/4.0/), which permits use, sharing, adaptation, distribution and reproduction in any medium or format, as long as you give appropriate credit to the original author(s) and the source, provide a link to the Creative Commons license and indicate if changes were made.

The images or other third party material in this chapter are included in the chapter's Creative Commons license, unless indicated otherwise in a credit line to the material. If material is not included in the chapter's Creative Commons license and your intended use is not permitted by statutory regulation or exceeds the permitted use, you will need to obtain permission directly from the copyright holder.

CHAPTER 6

The Financialisation of Identity

The most tangible example of the banks' presence in Swedes' daily lives today is the digital BankID. It is used by virtually all adults (99.4 percent of those aged 18–67), not only for financial transactions but also for interactions with healthcare, schools and government agencies. The number of daily uses averages over 19 million (in a population of 10.5 million).[1] The hold that banks have on official identities has become so commonplace that it is hardly noticed anymore. Why is it the bank that identifies us when we act as patients, parents or citizens? A first thought is to look for the explanation in the rapid digitalisation process of recent decades. However, the story of the Swedish BankID did not begin in 2003 when a consortium of banks launched their digital solution but rather in the 1960s, when they started issuing plastic ID cards in connection with the new system of paying wages into cheque accounts that I discussed in Chapter 2 as the first step in the bankification of everyday life.

This chapter examines how Swedish banks came to manage the documentation of personal identities, a task historically associated with the state, and how the bank's new role was mediated to the public and eventually became naturalised. The topic places my study in the twofold context of the history of identity documents and of commercial surveillance. I argue that the bankification process created a new connection between personal finance and ID documents, and by extension between money and identity. This connection materialised in the shape of plastic cards—ID, credit, debit and loyalty cards—marking a *plastic regime* in the history of identification, partly overlapping a preceding paper-based regime and a succeeding digital regime. It was during this plastic regime that personal identities became financialised. I analyse the process and unpack both the nascent micro-infrastructure of financial surveillance and the cultural relational work that was required to forge the new link between money and identity and to embed it in everyday life.[2]

THE HISTORY OF IDENTIFICATION: STATE AND CHURCH

Commercial bodies and their role in identity management are largely absent from the historical literature on ID documents, as the British historian Edward Higgs has rightly observed.[3] Instead, research has focused on linking the history of documented and registered identities with the emergence of the bureaucratic state. Historians have traced the birth of identity documents to the organisation of society in times of war, to colonial administration and to the state's ambitions to control crime or simply the movements of its inhabitants. Identifying and recording criminals using fingerprints, bodily markers and later photography were part of this as science and new technology began to assist 'the memory of the state' in the authorities' desire to identify especially so-called dangerous elements in society already in the nineteenth century.[4]

Historians have also pointed out that ID documents—society's standardised definitions and formalised tracking of identities—have always had a cultural meaning. Such documents have been co-creators of the identities they sought to control. How the official question 'Who are you?' is posed and the expected answer shape how people think about questions like 'Who am I?', 'Who are we?' and 'Who are they?'[5] There are clear examples of this in Swedish history. Since it was the Church of Sweden that oversaw the population registers, the most common identity document was the *prästbetyg*, literally priest's certificate, which was issued by the parish priest and also served as a proof of good moral character. There were various types of priest's certificates, such as the *åldersbevis* (age certificate, similar to a birth certificate) or the *flyttningsbetyg* (change of address certificate), and until the mid-twentieth century the latter was still used for identification purposes. It was not necessarily a personal document—a man's papers often included his wife and children and was therefore also an expression of society's views on gender relations and the role of the family. The printed form, filled out by hand, was eventually updated with additions, corrections and crossings out.

The types of information varied over time, but along with name, place and date of birth there were typically also notes on occupation, religion, undergone confirmation, completed national military service and received vaccinations. Further back in time, literacy and respectable conduct was also included. The form's preprinted headings showed what was considered important for society to know, and provided a template into which individual identities were fitted.[6]

Of all identity documents, the passport's history has been the most studied, at least internationally; Swedish studies are still lacking. The main perspective in the narratives of this literature has been state surveillance and control, and the formation—or dismantling—of the nation state. This means that the passport has also been linked to the creation of national identities.[7] As with the priest's certificates, the passport reflects society's view on personal identities. Still in the early and mid-twentieth century, many Western countries' passports were issued for a family rather than an individual. They also included information on physical attributes such as height, eye and hair colour, face shape and sometimes skin colour. Such data thus became formalised identity markers.

The media historian Craig Robertson has highlighted how, in the nineteenth century, a paper-based documentary regime of verification replaced an older sensory regime that relied simply on person-to-person recognition in local communities. As this did not work in modern societies, where people typically moved around much more than before, paper documents were introduced to verify identities. Since the beginning of the twentieth century, such papers have usually included a photograph. These documents were the basis of a supposedly objective system—they gave identity 'a distinct, official shape'.[8] While Robertson writes about the United States, a similar change took place even earlier in Europe. The state wanted to create easily readable, registrable and stable official identities according to a bureaucratic logic. Identity documents were linked to local or central registers, which were also filed and stored on paper. It is only recently, with a paper-based regime having been replaced by a new digital one, that Robertson detects 'a move from the state' to commercial actors 'as the primary vendor of the verification of individual identity'.[9]

The History of Identification: The Market

While commercial actors had rarely been discussed in the literature on identity management in the past, the interest in the role of commercial forces in the contemporary digital era has exploded. In recent years, several scholars have highlighted how the digital world tracks, colonises and capitalises on our identities. Personal data, group memberships, taste preferences, health conditions, interests, values and political opinions are turned into commodities, sold and reused to create personalised and algorithmically tailored offers and messages.[10]

The American scholar and social critic Shoshana Zuboff takes this interest yet a step further. Her 2019 book on *Surveillance capitalism* argues for the emergence of a new kind of capitalism. While others claim that today's users of Google, Facebook and similar platforms have turned into products that these companies sell, Zuboff asserts that users' identities and lives are the raw material that these platforms extract. After algorithmic processing, the information can be refined into predictions and ultimately be used to shape behaviour in ways that generate economic profit.[11] She writes that we were 'wholly unprepared' for the threat of surveillance capitalism, as throughout history we have usually imagined that such threats come from the state rather than from 'new companies with imaginative names run by young geniuses that seemed to be able to provide us with exactly what we yearn for at little or no cost'.[12] Admittedly, there is a certain truth to that. Even in the Swedish debates on privacy in the early computer age, the discussions were more preoccupied with the authorities' new possibilities for surveillance than with what commercial actors could do.[13]

But there are objections, not least from a historical point of view. Is what Zuboff calls surveillance capitalism really something completely new that emerged suddenly with the rise of the internet in the twenty-first century? Or is it rather that capitalism has become technologically better at doing what it had already been doing earlier? Commercial companies had understood the (market) value of information about people's lives and behaviour long before computerisation. One example of this is the life insurance companies' extensive card registers of both customers and potential policyholders in early twentieth-century Europe and United States. In addition to basic personal data, such files also included family situation, income and wealth, hobbies and sometimes even dreams for the future. Another historical example can be found in the records of the first credit reporting agencies, although these delimited 'financial identities' were not yet competing with official identities.[14] So how did Swedish banks become issuers of quasi-official ID documents? Rather than today's digital surveillance capitalism, or the longer history of state surveillance of our identities, I am interested here in what lies in between, in the gap—or overlap—between the analogue documentary regime and the digital regime of identification. A closer look at the emergence of financial identification documents in Sweden from around 1960 on reveals exactly that.

This story is inevitably about the *market's way of seeing*. In an influential article, the sociologists Marion Fourcade and Kieran Healy analysed how market actors categorise and classify people in ways that ultimately have the potential to shape self-perceptions and behaviour. Their term 'seeing like a market' paraphrases the title of the political scientist James C. Scott's famous book *Seeing Like a State*, which explores the technocratic ambitions of the modern state. Passports, national identity documents and government records, both historically and today, are examples of how the state 'sees' its population and makes it 'legible'. While Fourcade and Healy illustrate the market's way of seeing with the contemporary American system of personal credit scoring as their empirical example, I write, from a historical perspective, about how such a market vision emerged through commercial identity documents and identification techniques.[15]

Zuboff's surveillance capitalism concerns the internet, but the 'datafication' of identity began earlier. Population registers, as well as other official registers and commercial personal registers of various kinds, were computerised in Sweden in the 1960s and 1970s. In media history research, this has been described as a transition from paper identities to computerised identities.[16] However, by focusing on registers rather than proofs of identity, researchers have overlooked a medium that was present in everyday life and played a key role in creating something of an 'identity economy' in the post-war Western world, namely the plastic card. If, from the 1960s on, plastic cards of various kinds—credit, debit and ID cards—have been, in a practical sense, carriers and transmitters of identifying personal information, in a more symbolic sense they also became carriers of feelings and opinions about the financialisation of identity.

The focus on cards, as both identity and payment devices, highlights how the banks entered yet another realm of life by issuing (quasi-)official means of identification and assuming responsibilities otherwise associated with the government authorities. In the early 1960s, bank staff were just as likely to be described as financial educators and advisors as they were to be called salesmen, selling financial products to a large new group of customers, as Chapters 2 and 3 has shown.[17] Sociologist Jeanne Lazarus argues that French banks, from the late 1960s, balanced between two poles: the old image of banks as official institutions for public service and the new one as commercial companies offering products and services for profit.[18] There was a similar tension in Sweden as well, but with an important difference: the image of the banks as public authorities was reinvented in a new form due to their role in the management of identification which, however, resulted exactly from their new consumer orientation.

In what follows, I first show how the cheque-account wages led to banks becoming involved in identity management, as well as how a new link between money and identity was created and naturalised. This is followed first by a discussion of the market for ID documents in Sweden and the banks' quasi-monopoly position there, and then by a section on the emergence of a financialised plastic regime of identification. The chapter concludes with the early visions of computerisation, online cashless transactions and customer registers, unpacking the uses of plastic cards as both identity and information devices.

From Diverse Identification Practices to Plastic Identity

As the new system of wage and salary payments through banks brought about a silent personal financial revolution (Chapter 2), the mass use of cheques created a need for identification documents. New cheque customers were expected to be 'bankminded', become financially knowledgeable and learn to use the new financial products offered to them, but it was not just about the bank customers' knowledge or lack thereof. The change also posed a twofold knowledge problem for the banks. On the one hand, with the new services banks now *knew* about almost every penny of their consumers' money. This was what a marketing expert at Handelsbanken in 1968 described as a truly 'intimate relationship between the customer and the bank'.[19] On the other hand, no matter how much the banks knew about their customers, it became impossible to recognise them all personally. Even less did retailers know whether the person paying with a cheque was the same person whose name was on it.

In the early years of the cheque-account wages many different proofs of identity were used—or, just as often, not used. The banks' in-house magazines mentioned several examples of documents and objects that had been presented to bank tellers for identification purposes in the late 1950s and early 1960s: social security certificates, membership cards for various professional associations and societies, firearm licences, change of address certificates, tax cards, business or visiting cards, or season tickets for the railway. Even uniforms and objects such as doctor's hats, inscribed wristwatches or wedding rings—symbols of identity of a different kind—were used and, until the early 1960s, often accepted as means of identification. Another—in retrospect dubious—method of identification used by bank clerks in the early years was to ask for a person's home address and look it up in the telephone directory.[20] Official documents were rare. People seldom carried passports but often had their driving licences with them. The latter was widely accepted—despite being easy to forge and not having an expiry date at the time—because it at least included a photograph.[21] On a smaller scale, post offices had issued paper identity cards since 1909 'for insured letters and parcels', in accordance with international postal regulations. These were considered a good solution until the late 1960s, albeit not as secure as the laminated bank ID cards, introduced a few years later.[22]

In 1961 *Remissan*, Handelsbanken's in-house magazine, told the story of a former employee. At the post office, lacking proper identification, he had shown the watch with his name engraved on it that he had received from Handelsbanken for his long and faithful service. The cashier accepted it with a smile. The magazine commented: 'It's not every day that Handelsbanken distributes identity documents'.[23] However, this is exactly what the bank would do shortly thereafter. Within 18 months, commercial banks such as Handelsbanken had started issuing and distributing their own 'secure' identity cards.

In 1962, a Bankers' Association working group developed the first version of a bank identity card (Fig. 6.1). It was to be issued to people 'whose identity is known to the bank or could with certainty be assured'. It included a photograph, a signature and a five-year expiry date, and was made of forgery-proof paper with a plastic cover.[24] It was the increase in cheque fraud cases that motivated the need for a special bank identity card; bank representatives stated that they would be 'less willing' to accept other proofs of identity in the future. These other types of identification were not banned, however, and it was up to the bank teller to decide case by case whether to accept them or not.²⁵

The banking world was generally ambivalent. In the magazine *Din Bank*, a bank lawyer wrote that the passport was not suitable as an everyday identity document because it was too valuable and too ungainly in shape to carry around all the time, and at the same time was also relatively easy to forge. There was therefore a great need for the new bank identity cards. 'Nonetheless', he argued, 'it would probably make more sense for a government agency to issue identity cards to citizens in general'.²⁶ Clearly, the bankers felt somewhat uneasy in their role as issuers of identity documents, which they saw more as a task for a public authority. A national card had been discussed in Parliament as early as the 1920s, and in 1944 a government committee of inquiry proposed a so-called citizen's card. However, the government seems to have been reluctant to embrace the idea of a national identity card, first delaying

Fig. 6.1 Posters announcing that the bank now issues identity cards, 1963, Uplands bank, Uppsala. *Photo* Uppsala-Bild and Upplandsmuseet. Used with the permission of Upplandsmuseet

and then later definitively rejecting all plans to introduce one.[27] When a private members' bill in Parliament in 1963 raised the issue again, it was voted down on the grounds that the banks had already begun to issue ID cards. This was despite the fact that the Bankers' Association, in its comments on the proposal, pointed out that the authorities should indeed play an active role in providing secure identity cards for the population.[28]

At this point the bankers still thought the distribution of bank ID cards would be gradual and slow, starting with new account holders, with bank clerks informing customers about identity cards over the counter rather than through a large-scale campaign.[29] But in 1965, when cheque fraud and the possible criminalisation of cheque misuse were brought to the fore in public debate (Chapter 2), the requirements for cheque use and identification practices became more rigorous. For example, the youngest employees and new hires were not immediately given chequebooks. An extensive information campaign was launched in the press to spread the stricter rules for cheque use, including rules for identity verification. People were strongly advised to keep their chequebooks safe, as there was a flourishing black market in stolen chequebooks. The cheque, promoted a few years earlier as an easy, convenient means of payment, was now hedged about with complicated rules, guidelines, restrictions and control mechanisms.[30] One of the new bank rules in 1965 involved compulsory identity checks, agreed on by the members of the Bankers' Association in consultation with the National Police Board (Rikspolisstyrelsen). Banks began to train their staff in how to confirm customers' identity. Most importantly, not all identity papers with a photo would henceforward be accepted but rather only a few types of 'secure' identity cards.[31] The retailers, through the Federation of Swedish Merchants (Köpmannaförbundet), also called for a uniform and easily verifiable means of identification. They maintained that it should be the banks' responsibility to supply all cheque account holders with such documents, considering that 'it was the banks that gave rise to this evil'.[32] All this meant that the banks started distributing their identity cards on a larger scale.[33] This was the beginning of a process that would end in standardised identity documents for all bank customers, or basically for all Swedish citizens.

The Shame of Identification

On many occasions, however, the real problem for bank staff and shop assistants was not unsatisfactory means of identification but that they had to ask for proof of identity in the first place. As the literature on the history of identity documents confirms, an inherent feature of identity verification is the suspicion of guilt.[34] This is an aspect that today, with advanced automated identification systems in many everyday contexts, is not necessarily obvious, being 'beneath the horizon of cultural visibility'.[35] But in the past, the cultural problems of identification were visible: it was shameful, and could be perceived as offensive, to be asked to identify oneself. In 1957 *Din Bank* quoted a customer, an accountant, who had felt insulted by the polite request that he identify himself when signing a cheque he wanted to cash: 'You ascribe to me a criminal act. You offend me by suspecting me of being a skilled criminal'.[36] The same topic was also debated in the daily papers, often in the letters to the editor. For example, in 1961 a letter to the daily newspaper *Göteborgstidningen* read:

> No one, however, asks the [the new cheque-salary] account holders what they think. They don't want the trouble and the discomfort of identification. It's unpleasant to have to show identity papers in order to dispose of their own money. ... 'Do I look so poor or suspect that I have to show papers for who I am?', think nine out of ten of those asked to identify themselves.[37]

Aware of the general attitudes, the working group for the development of identity documents stressed the importance of the public not perceiving their new secure 'bank ID card' as a 'police state measure'.[38] In this sense, its being issued by the banks was a clear advantage.

Although the banking press did not mention it, the initial negative feelings about identification might also have been influenced by the fact that another place where customers could be asked to identify themselves was Systembolaget, the government-owned off-licence. Between 1957 and 1964, suspect customers could be checked against the official blacklist of dealers and people convicted of drunkenness or drink driving. Then, in 1964, a notorious 'red lamp' to signal a random control was installed in Systembolaget's shops and anyone could be asked for identification. This, a former shop manager states, was greatly disliked on both sides of the counter. However, the requirements for secure identification documents were not high in these random checks, and many forms of ID were widely accepted.[39]

Skandinaviska Banken's in-house magazine launched an internal debate in 1962 concerning how to ask for identification. 'We can assure you that it's difficult, and many will feel offended when asked for some proof of identity', wrote the editor, introducing the subject. It was not only important to find the right tone and wording, but also to make the public understand that it was necessary, the standard phrase being 'This is to protect your money'.[40] Additionally, other banks as well as the Swedish Bankers' Association issued instructions and guidelines for shopkeepers, cashiers and shop assistants for how and when to ask for the ID card.[41] Shopkeepers and sales staff often pointed out that asking for identification was delicate. As late as 1968, in *Kontokuriren*, a newsletter distributed among Kreditbanken's cheque customers, a shop assistant brought up for debate the problematic issue of asking for an ID card. She complained about how often a request for identification was met with anger because it hurt the customer's feelings.[42] This recurrent topic in both banking and retail periodicals reveals an affective side to the formation of the new bankified subjects. While in the earlier period the possession of a chequebook could give the user a sense of pride and self-confidence, the demand for identification when paying by cheque was experienced as upsetting and shameful. Accounts of the feelings of shame triggered by the requests for identification also reinforce the insight that embedded identity and documented identity were interrelated in intricate ways.

In the 1960s, the way to handle the negative feelings in everyday commerce was often to give in and not confirm a cheque user's identity—but doing so could lead to financial consequences. The bank guarantee for forged, altered and bounced cheques (up to SEK 500, approx. €450 in today's value) was only valid if the sales assistant had verified the customer's identity and noted it on the back of the cheque. A study by the Swedish Bankers' Association in 1970 found that despite this rule, almost half the forged cheques passed in shops lacked a note on the signatory's identification.[43] The increasing rates of cheque fraud (Fig. 6.2) underlined the need for a secure, easily manageable form of identification and the destigmatisation of identity checks.

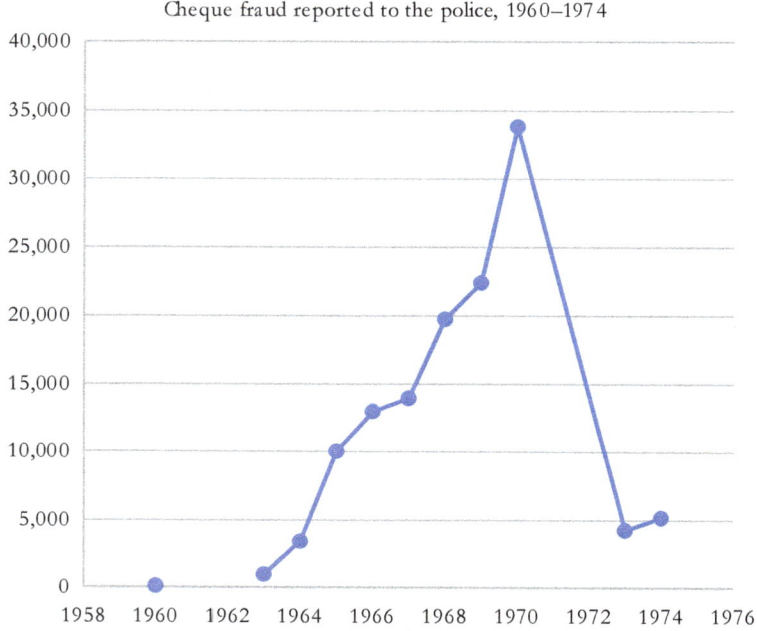

Fig. 6.2 Cheque fraud reported to the police, 1960–1974. *Source* DsFi 1971:12, 29, 32; DsFi 1975:7, 34; 'Infordrade statistiska uppgifter', in Riksarkivet, *Checklöneutredningen*. See also 'Skärpta bank-krav på legitimation', *Stockholms-Tidningen*, 25 February 1965

The Bank as Identifier

In the late 1950s, the banks envisioned tracking the new cheque account holders through the workplace, relying on employee numbers and the employers as indirect agents of surveillance (Chapter 2). A few years later, they found themselves not only issuing and distributing individual identity cards but also managing efforts for a national standard for identity documents. In 1965, representatives of the banks formed a new working group, now with representatives of the General Post Office and the National Police Board. The aim was to find a solution for secure identification practices.[44] Their work led to the creation in 1968 of the joint-stock company AB ID-kort (lit. ID card Ltd) to produce identity cards. Commercial banks and savings banks owned half of the company, and the state—through the General Post Office and two industrial companies (AB Ceaverken and AB Atomenergi)—owned the other half. AB Ceaverken was the only manufacturer of advanced photographic paper and X-ray film in Sweden, and the involvement of AB Atomenergi was probably motivated by the isotope technology that was used in the early period for easy mechanical checks of card expiry dates.[45] Thus, while the banks, along with post offices, were responsible for validating identity documents and at the same time also managed, issued and distributed the cards to the public, the state-owned companies had more influence on the technology and production process. The working group also discussed using one central register, but dismissed this in favour of the registers of the issuer (meaning the banks), even when it became clear that a partly state-owned company would be formed. Eventually, AB ID-kort ended up having a central register but an analogue one, which was not linked to the state population register and would not be computerised until the late 1970s.[46]

The new company produced three kinds of identity cards: the bank identity card, issued by banks or post offices; ID cards for private companies or public authorities (for officials who needed identification while on duty, such as policemen); and the new authorised driving licence, introduced in 1973. Only these cards, in addition to the passport, were henceforth to be accepted by banks, shops, post offices and public authorities. This essentially private solution for identity control based on a joint partnership of banks and the state seems to have been internationally unique.[47] It was somewhat peculiar in a longer perspective as well, and at odds with the typical twenty-first-century solutions highlighted by David Lyon, who describes the contemporary card cartels, whereby the state is responsible for issuing and validating ID cards but depends on the technology and software provided by tech companies.[48]

In the Swedish case, although it was partly involved in the production of cards the state played almost no role in authorisation or issuance. Instead, the banks served as gatekeepers and mediators of official identity. As AB ID-kort had no formal monopoly on manufacturing identity documents, the banks made sure that only 'bank-approved' ID documents were accepted. The Bankers' Association set up a Board for Identity Documents (Nämnden för legitimationshandlingar) as a consultative body in cases of inquiries for the approval of identity papers. In addition to representatives from commercial and savings banks, the board also included a representative from the Bank Inspection Board (a government authority) and a representative from trade and industry. The banks' impact was dominant, however.[49] This impact can be exemplified by the fact that the Board for Identity Documents denied the bank approval of cards from the American company Polaroid, despite its cards meeting the 1972 security requirements and being in use as company identification at Volvo.[50] Considering that an ID card that was not accepted in banks and shops would not be profitable to manufacture, Polaroid reported the Bankers' Association to the Antitrust Ombudsman for creating an 'ID monopoly'.[51] This ID monopoly was questioned by others as well, as will be seen.

In the early 1970s, a government inquiry into identity verification and cheque payments raised the question of a national supervisory authority for identity control. Despite strong support for the idea among the referral bodies, including the Bankers' Association itself, the inquiry did not propose the creation of this institution, and so identity documents remained unregulated by law. State supervision would be exercised only indirectly through the Bank Inspection Board's annual review of the banks' operations. This meant that the banks officially kept their dominant role in identifiaction.[52]

From Cheque Boycott to Mass Distribution of Identity Cards

Production of the new plastic bank ID cards began in 1970. Soon after, a general boycott of cheques within the retail trade and the resulting new rules for cheque use triggered a rapid, large-scale distribution—to virtually every adult in Sweden. How this distribution was handled and justified to the public was important in creating the link between money and identity.

As cheque fraud became a growing problem in the late 1960s (Fig. 6.2), at the recommendation of the National Police Board the banks abandoned their traditional guarantee for forged and altered cheques starting on 1 July 1971. In having them bear the costs of fraud, the idea was to force the recipients of cheque payments—shops, restaurants, hotels, etc.—to be more rigorous with their identity checks, even for small sums.[53] But the retailers, already unhappy at all the trouble the new system entailed, responded with a general boycott of cheques. Extensive negotiations were under way for more than a year between the banks and the retail trade organisations, including representatives of the Federation of Swedish Merchants, the Consumer Cooperative Union, department stores, hotels, restaurants and petrol stations. Trade unions were also involved in the discussions, representing employees with cheque account salaries.[54] An agreement, reached in late 1972, stated that the shops would revoke the boycott beginning in 1973 under certain conditions, such as fees on using cheques for smaller amounts.[55] The most important among these conditions was that by February 1973, the banks had to supply at least 90 percent of their cheque account customers with 'adequate' identity papers, meaning the new identity cards (or the soon to be introduced new driving licences) made by the new company AB ID-kort. All cheque purchases, regardless of amount, would henceforward require an inspection of identity documents. Production and distribution were therefore speeded up (Table 6.1).[56]

Even the government seemed only too happy to leave it to the banks to solve the problems of soaring cheque fraud and insufficiently rigorous ID practices. A government inquiry into possible measures to curb cheque fraud handed in its report in 1971, a few months into the cheque boycott. The lead investigator, an official at the Ministry of Finance, recommended that no measures be taken by the government because, as he argued, they had all been taken or decided on by the banks: the secure ID cards, informational campaigns on keeping chequebooks safe, name or personal identity number preprinted on cheques and so on.[57] Instead, in line with the initial directive from the Ministry of Finance, he suggested a decrease in the number of cheque accounts for wages and salaries:

> An efficient system of cheque accounts depends on the account holders possessing maturity, a sense of justice and a certain orderliness. Such properties cannot be guaranteed in all employees of a company. ... If we want to restore confidence in the cheque as a means of payment, it appears necessary to bring down the number of cheque accounts for wages.[58]

Phasing out the 'democratised' cheque system was not an option for the banks; quite the opposite, they worked to expand it (Chapter 2). Instead, the Bankers' Associations negotiated an end to the boycott by promising that the new ID cards would be quickly distributed to all bank customers.[59] Thus, not only did banks become issuers of identity documents but they also had to speed up the distribution to a very large public. Occasionally, employers helped their workforce (and the banks) through mass photography sessions and forms completed with the help

Table 6.1 Production of cards by AB ID-kort (ID Card Ltd), thousands

	1970	1971	1972	1973	1974[a]	Total 1 January 1970–31 August 1974
Swedish ID cards	195	413	637	1,514	465	3,225
Driving licences	–	–	–	445	1,350	1,795
Total	195	413	637	1,959	1,815	5,020

[a]The 1974 figures do not include the last four months of the year.
From 1970 the company also manufactured Danish ID cards, which are not included in the table.
In 1975 AB ID-kort started manufacturing bank cards and credit cards both for the Swedish market and for export.
Source 'När AB ID-kort startade tillverkningen', *ID-Nytt*, 3–4 (1974)

of computers for thousands of employees, as for example the telephone company LM Ericsson did in 1973.[60]

Over 5 million identity cards—in a country with a population of 8.1 million—were produced and distributed by the end of 1974 (Table 6.1). In the first round, all customers with bank salaries received an ID card for free. As there was some overlap between bank ID cards and driving licences, in 1974 AB ID-kort calculated that 1–2 million adults in Sweden were still without proper identification. These people—housewives, the retired and those still receiving cash wages—would soon receive ID cards, in most cases when they opened a current account at a bank.[61]

Finally, a nationwide advertising campaign in early 1974 reinforced the new link between identity and personal finances. Earlier information campaigns had included brochures and short films, training shop assistants and bank clerks to always ask for an ID card when accepting a cheque, not least to 'build up the habit' among the public, while large adverts urged customers to present their ID cards along with their cheques, saying this was necessary '[n]o matter how kind you look'. In contrast, the new campaign, targeting bank customers, was explicitly built around the slogan 'It's your money the ID card protects'. Adverts, flyers and posters spread the message across the country, and reminders were displayed in banks, post offices and shops.[62]

The ID card used as illustration in this campaign, and many others that followed in the years to come, featured the face of a young blonde woman in her twenties, named Maria Eriksson, who in both name and appearance conveyed the impression of the girl next door (Fig. 6.3). The plastic bank ID card was advertised with her photo on the demo cards,

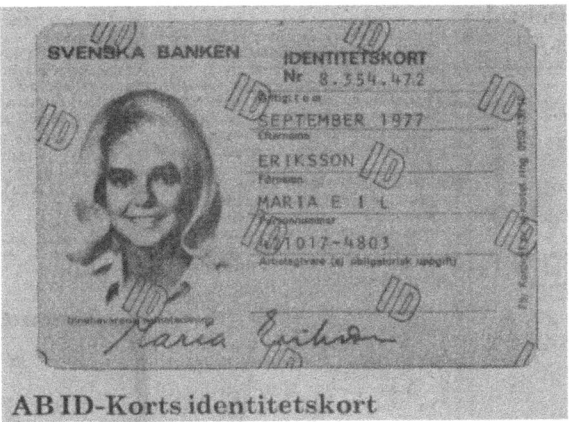

Fig. 6.3 The new plastic bank ID card as depicted in the commercial banks' information campaign, *Dagens Nyheter*, 13 November 1972. (Name and ID-number are fictional.) Used with the permission of Swedish Bankers

and with reassurances that the ID card was not only necessary in banks and shops but also useful in many other situations in life: 'No one says no to Maria'.[63] Identity checks eventually became commonplace, and by the mid-1970s the problem of shame and reluctance had mostly disappeared, to the point that it no longer warranted mention in the press or the bank archives. Bank identity was now domesticated. It was individual, it linked identity to money, and it was certified by banks (Fig. 6.4).

Plastic Identities and Plastic Money

'The ID card of the future will replace money', proclaimed an article in *Veckans affärer* in 1974.[64] It reported that the International Organisation for Standardisation (ISO) was preparing to adopt the same standard format for identity cards as the credit card already had (a format with the code CR80), and that cards with the new standard dimensions would have a three-track magnetic stripe as a data carrier. AB ID-kort already had the prototypes ready, but it would be a few years before the standard format was introduced in Sweden.[65] The article discussed the ID card and the credit card as basically the same phenomenon and announced

Fig. 6.4 'Wherever we are! Cheque + ID card = Money', poster by Kreditbanken, early 1970s. Unknown artist. Used with the permission of SEB

that, according to ISO, credit cards would soon have a photo and ID cards could be used for purchases.[66]

There was, indeed, a similarity between the two types of cards in function, context and material form. Introducing the plastic bank ID card had resolved the troubles in the payment system caused by the cheque boycott, but during the boycott commercial banks, including the state-owned Kreditbanken, had actively encouraged their cheque account customers to register for the banks' joint credit card system, Köpkort, as a practical solution.[67] Also, credit cards were sometimes conceptualised as economic identity cards (Chapter 4).

The mere material form of the bank-issued ID card, its resemblance to payment cards, underpinned the new link between identity and money. This was the era of plastics, the emblematic material of the post-war mass consumer society. The use of plastics in society began to expand in the 1950s, and the material came in handy for the production of credit cards and commercial ID cards. The sociologist Joe Deville has described how important the new cheap, lightweight material was for the mass introduction of credit cards in the United States from the late 1950s to the early 1970s. Unsolicited credit cards could be mailed out in envelopes to hundreds of thousands of Americans at little cost. Such mailings also occurred in Sweden in 1962, but on an exceedingly small scale.[68]

Plastic also had clear advantages when it came to identification. In the early 1960s, ID cards were already 'plastic-coated', but initially there were major security concerns as the plastic cover could be prised off and the photo removed. Lamination techniques improved over the years, though, and on newer cards the photo and data were a single photographic document. Plastic cards were technically more advanced and more difficult to forge than paper cards, and could more easily convey machine-readable information. This was important for both credit cards and the new ID documents. As early as 1963, *Dagens Nyheter* reported on the first generation of 'plastic-moulded' ID cards from the banks as a technological innovation: 'Identity cards of this type can be provided with coded characters that can be read by a central electro-brain's recognition system'.[69] A few years later, the more advanced bank identity cards from AB ID-kort were isotope-marked. A device read the authenticity of the card while confirming its validity in a way that was invisible to the human eye.[70]

The plastic card replaced not only paper documents but also the metal credit tokens used in early department store account systems, which sometimes, as in Sweden, looked more like a coin. In other cases, small square, card-like metal charge plates were used, embossed with text and numbers that could be transferred to paper using a machine. Embossing was possible, and even cheaper, with cards made of plastic. In Sweden this transition from metal to plastic happened in 1958–1959, about the same time as in the United States, where both American Express and BankAmericard (later Visa) launched their credit cards in 1958.[71] Plastic combined the advantages of paper and metal: it was both light and durable and could carry a great deal of visible information, including a photo, and at the same time be used for the mechanical transfer of data through embossing. And soon, machine-readable (optical and later digital) information on the plastic cards would secure the transfer.

In the 1960s and 1970s, Swedish banks considered using photos on credit cards to facilitate identity checks; by the late 1960s they had far-reaching plans for a new type of bank-issued identity card. Such a 'universal bank card', it was suggested, would function as both a proof of identity and a credit and debit card; it would have a photo, a barcode and, later, a magnetic stripe.[72] Another link between different types of plastic cards was that they were all produced by the same manufacturers. In late 1975, AB ID-kort acquired majority shares in IdentiData Sweden AB, which was the largest manufacturer of credit cards (and other transaction cards such as ATM cards and petrol company payment cards) not only in Sweden but in all of Europe. The similarities between credit cards and ID documents were emphasised in internal and external publications reporting on the merger.[73]

A closer look at the materialities thus reveals how proof of identity and money converged. Just as the credit card was a bridge between cash (both paper and metal) and today's increasingly cardless digital payments, the plastic ID card represented a transition between a paper-based documentary identification regime and a digital one. The plasticisation of identity starting in the late 1950s can with good reason be seen as a separate and financially dominated regime between the other two.

THE MARKET OF IDENTITIES

The 1974 *Veckans affärer* article on standardisation and ID cards as the money of the future also claimed that the key issue for the industry was to solve the problem of computerised *personal* identification. By this they did not mean numerical codes but rather biometric technologies such as voice recognition and machine reading of fingerprints or at least signatures. Machine reading of the cards themselves was already possible, although such equipment was not yet used in shops but only ATMs. 'There is big money in the ID card market', the newspaper concluded. And in this market, smaller national manufacturers competed with major international players such as IBM (with its magnetic stripe technology) and Polaroid (with its photo technology).[74]

It was, however, a Swedish company called Rollfilm that challenged the banks' quasi-monopoly. Rollfilm also appears in the 1974 article in *Veckans affärer* as one of the few companies with a possible solution for computers to recognise people. The company is interesting because it illustrates that identity documents and identification technologies became market goods as early as the 1960s, and that plastic cards mediated the transition between the older analogue documentary regime of identity verification and the new digital one. Rollfilm was founded by Eric Rothfjell, who in the 1940s had invented a new technology, the Antenna camera, which allowed for rapid mass photography while personal data was depicted on the same frame of film. The idea of combining portraits and data had come about when, during the Second World War, Rothfjell was tasked to photograph thousands of Finnish child refugees within a short time to provide them with identity papers. After the war, he patented and commercialised the technology. From the late 1950s, Rothfjell's company supplied plastic ID documents primarily to the corporate sector. Large industries were his first customers, but when Rollfilm started a collaboration with the security company Securitas, smaller companies and some government agencies also began to use his ID cards. Rollfilm's cards were also sold abroad: in 1970, for example, Rothfjell had exclusive rights to produce international student IDs. He introduced colour photos on ID cards, which was considered more secure and was advertised as the 'colour identity system of the computer age'.[75]

Other inventions followed, such as the automated facial recognition mentioned above, but were not implemented. The solution relied on the digital recognition of individually characteristic facial lines, which were included as a sophisticated line pattern on the back of the card. While the extent to which Rothfjell's method could have been useful in practice is difficult to gauge, he was one of the first to obtain a patent for this type of technology, in the United States, in 1974. Research on facial recognition and other biometric identity markers was still in its infancy, and its use was really only mooted in the late 1980s, by American card companies for example, and gained momentum in the 1990s when, as the media scholar Kelly Gates writes, 'biometric technologies promised to integrate bodies directly into transaction networks'.[76]

Until AB ID-kort began operations, Rollfilm's ID cards were used whenever reasonably secure identification was needed. Rollfilm was responsible for the production and technical design but it was the employers, or schools, who ensured people's identities and kept the registers on which the cards were based. Thus, until the 1960s, employers often acted as 'guarantors of identity'.[77] It was this role that banks took over in the early 1970s. Rothfjell's company therefore found itself in a difficult situation. Like Polaroid before him, he reported AB ID-kort and the Swedish Bankers' Association to the Antitrust Ombudsman (Näringfrihetsombudsman) for having created an 'ID monopoly', and even threatened to take his case to the Market Court (Marknadsdomstolen). The Ombudsman decided in favour of Rollfilm, but the opposition from the banks was strong. Although Rollfilm's ID card met the security requirements and was therefore approved by the Board for Identity Documents, the banks refused to distribute it, claiming it was important to minimise the number of card types in circulation. As a consequence, Rothfjell's ID card empire was threatened with bankruptcy.[78]

The 1970s saw several developments in Sweden's 'identity scandal'—as a newspaper called it—with many of those involved, including the banks, hoping that the government would set up a supervisory authority or legislate for a national government-issued card; but this did not happen.[79] Instead, the Bank Inspection Board remained indirectly responsible for supervising identification documents, which again reinforced the link between banks and identification. In the 1980s, certification (along with standardisation) became the solution, when both the banks and the state companies sold their share of AB ID-kort. However, the banks kept their role as guarantors of identities as the cards were still issued and distributed by the banks and the post offices' banking service.[80]

SEEING LIKE A BANK: A FINANCIAL INFORMATION SYSTEM

AB ID-kort's bank identity cards carried the cardholder's personal identity number (*personnummer*). This number was introduced in 1968, when a fourth digit was added to the three-digit serial number at the end of the old civil registration number (*folkbokföringsnummer*, introduced in 1947), making it more secure and useful for a broad range of purposes. The new *personnummer* revolutionised the banks' customer registers, which could now bring together all the information they had on an individual. Records had previously been kept by account, not by person, and customer records were only held at local branches. A former system development manager at Kreditbanken recalls:

For the first time you could see how customers behaved. When we introduced this system, we collected statistics, huge amounts of statistics; ... we now had an information system where we could see customer behaviour.

However, it was not until the 1980s that improved computer technology meant that banks were able to actually use the information they gathered in this way and took the step, as he said, 'from transaction system to information system'.[81]

The personal identity number also gave rise to a peculiar but common Swedish type of current account, the *personkonto*, which was yet another step towards a full-fledged financial information system and further strenghtened the connection between identity and money, as well as the banks' role as quasi-official authorities. When the state-owned commercial bank Kreditbanken merged with the Post Office Bank in 1974 the new bank, PK-Banken, offered a salary account called a *personkonto* (personal account). The account number was the same as the account holder's personal identity number, which simplified identity checks and the management of customer registers.[82] PK-Banken's *personkonto* could be used for cash withdrawals as well as cheque and giro payments, and also provided some limited credit. It became the most typical account for wages and salaries, especially as it was often used by default for public employees. In 1978, 1.2 million Swedes had a *personkonto*. Despite privacy issues being widely debated in the 1970s few critical voices were raised, probably because by the mid-1970s the link between personal finances and identification—between money and identity—had been naturalised.[83]

The personal identity number also prompted new ideas about online payments. In 1969 the Bankers' Association initiated a high-profile inquiry, the SIBOL project (Cooperation for an Integrated Online Payment System, Samarbete för integrerat betalningssystem online 1969–1971).[84] This strategic project actualised visions and practices for identity management, standardised ID checks and the registering of personal data—all parts of a future payments system. On an overarching level, the SIBOL plans concerned the role of banks in people's everyday financial life and in the entire "societal machinery" in the future. A 1969 policy document from the Bankers' Association stated:

> There are very strong reasons why the leadership of banks should be actively involved in the construction of the future payment system. This

will be an integral part of the future societal machinery. ... Should the banks not be able to gather around a common line of action, but instead allow a number of loosely knit systems to grow on their own, we could draw society's criticism upon ourselves, with the result that the government would take over control and management.[85]

In the media it was emphasised in a more neutral, pro-technology tone that the banks were working towards a cashless society (Fig. 6.5). Indeed, the objective was that at least some banks would start running the online SIBOL system as early as 1975, with all banks joining within ten years. The plans involved linking the banks' customer registers and credit reporting records with the databases of the bank-owned credit card companies. Identities would be verified with a combined ID, debit and credit card, the 'universal' bank card mentioned above. This was devised as a means of identification that could be checked both with the naked eye (photo, name, number) and automatically (machine-readable information and a personal code). The PIN was seen as an emergency solution—voice or fingerprint identification was envisioned. The SIBOL reports were emphatic that a standardised, universal bank card was 'a basic condition for the whole system'.[86] Identity, or at least proof of identity, thus became the 'money' of the imagined cashless society.

It was SIBOL's initial ambition to link the banks' registers also with official registers at the Riksbank and Statistics Sweden (Statistiska Centralbyrån, SCB) as well as with the stock exchange. But after three years of investigative work this was abandoned, as was eliminating cash in the near future. The latter remained a long-term goal, however, as work on a joint online payment system continued. The idea was to eventually patch in the retailers' terminals, and thereafter home terminals (a machine plugged into the telephone landline), to the payment system. The universal bank card was long a key feature of the discussions, but was ultimately rejected by the Swedish Bankers' Association in 1979 for practical reasons.[87]

When the Swedish Bankers' Association wrote its response to the report of the government inquiry on data and integrity in 1972, the bankers were keen to emphasise that 'the SIBOL project concerns only a pure transport system for payments, not an information system'.[88] Still, it is difficult to interpret the original SIBOL idea, with its interconnected registers and combined ID and payment and credit cards, as anything other than an attempt to create a comprehensive financial information system.

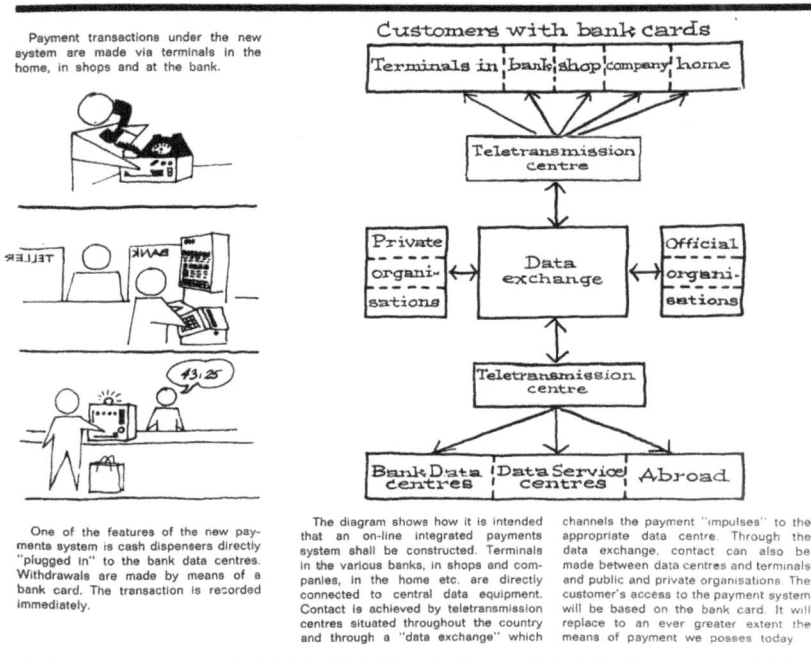

Fig. 6.5 The SIBOL system for online payments, 1971. Illustration in Svenska Bankföreningen, *Commercial Banking in Sweden* (Stockholm: Sv. Bankföreningen, 1971), 19. Unknown artist. Used with the permission of Swedish Bankers

Interestingly, the SIBOL plans from 1969 also included the integration of the commercial banks' credit reporting records into the envisioned online system, which in the early non-public sketches figured under the name of Upplysningscentralen (roughly: The Credit Reporting Central). As discussed in Chapter 4, credit reporting did not have the same significance in Sweden as in the United States, where credit scoring has been cited by scholars as the main example of the birth of financialised identities and of how 'seeing like a market' works in practice.[89] The Swedish Credit Reporting Act (1973:1173) restricted the possibilities to share credit records. It also excluded foreign companies. Dun & Bradstreet, a major international player which had set up shop in Sweden a few years before, was therefore forced to close down its Swedish operations. This left the most important Swedish credit reporting agency, ABAK, with something approaching a monopoly, but banks often operated on their own: savings banks traditionally relied on local credit records, while the commercial banks seem to have coordinated their work with credit information, at least from the 1960s.[90] Although their jointly run company, Upplysningscentralen (UC), was formally launched in 1977 with special permission from the new Data Inspection Board (established in 1973 under the Swedish Data Act), a unit with the same name had featured in Bankers' Association strategy documents a decade earlier and was part of the planned SIBOL system.[91] This suggests that the operation may have existed in some form before 1977, especially considering that already in its first (official) year of operation UC had nearly complete records on the Swedish population.[92] And while threats to personal privacy in the computer age were a hot topic at the time, the oft-expressed fears in the media and the many privacy scandals that went public almost exclusively involved the records kept by government agencies, not private companies. The banks' new customer registers continued to tick under the radar.[93]

While the historical material from the 1970s has little to say about banking professionals' visions for the further uses of these registers or the transactional data the banks were recording, early ideas about how such data could be commercially exploited were formulated in the credit card industry.

Information Cards

A closer look at the InterConto card company, discussed in the previous chapters, reveals that in the 1970s there was an interest in 'seeing like a market' when managing people's identities. Owner Erik Elinder jokingly called his credit card a 'sales card' (*säljkort*), to contrast it with the 'purchase card' (*köpkort*) of his major competitor (Chapter 4). His main ambition was not to provide 'modern money' as in Köpkort's advertising slogans. Instead, InterConto intended to use its 'selective account systems' to create a new marketing tool, a 'channel of communication' between retailers and consumers, based on the transactional identities that could be discerned from the data recorded by the cards. With the benefit of hindsight one is not surprised at the idea of using the information extracted from transactions such as the items bought, the choice of shops, or the frequency of similar purchases, but it was radical at the time. In 1973, the sociologist James Rule called BankAmericard's surveillance system one of the most advanced in the world, exactly because the company used transactional patterns recorded by its cards to determine whether to continue, extend or withdraw its customers' credit. But the thought of using these patterns in other ways was not discussed.[94]

Erik Elinder, with his background in advertising, realised early on that the future of his business was not in selling credit; the greatest potential lay instead in selling consumers, meaning the knowledge of buying behaviour recorded by the cards. In line with this, he also called the credit card an 'information card', and wanted to develop its functions even further. He returned to this idea in several internal memos in the 1970s, often referring to a 1972 conversation with his advisor and board member Gunnar Ehrlemark when the thought had first been raised:

> The credit card is a unique sales instrument—not because of the credit but because of the knowledge of the customer that a credit card, properly constructed, provides to the affiliated stores.
>
> [T]he cash customer cannot be identified—the cash customer is anonymous—the cash customer enters and leaves the shop without committing to anything. The cash customer is from this point of view uninteresting. In contrast, the credit card customer's name, address, telephone number, finances, buying habits, ability to pay, lifestyle, etc. are recorded in minute detail. This is not something terrible and dangerous, it is trivial from a security point of view, etc. However, it is a unique asset for a merchant who wants to provide extra service and who wants to take good care of his customers, who wants to satisfy the customer at a reasonable cost.
>
> What is it that we don't know about this person that can be of inestimable value to the merchant who wants to sell goods to him?[95]

This reveals an early vision of personalisation, or one-to-one marketing, which would not take hold in the marketing profession until the 1990s. Elinder's ambitions went beyond direct marketing based on the segmentation of consumers into target groups, the use of marketing surveys, or marketing that relied on register-based data (that is, marketing material sent out to a specific group of consumers selected through registers, for example new parents), which was becoming common in the 1970s and 1980s. Instead, he outlined future possibilities for personalised selling. He wanted to 'get to know' the individual customer, to get into their minds—even if only with the help of processing transactional data—and it was this customer knowledge he wanted to turn into his company's main product. In Elinder's view, commercial access to this knowledge was also beneficial to the consumer, who would receive better service. The new intimate relationship between financial companies and their customers, which Handelsbanken's marketers had pointed out back in 1968, was now to be packaged and resold.

While the media debate railed at the dangers of computerisation combined with large-scale public records creating 'register-people in a dehumanised society', for Elinder and his colleagues the goal was to know all their customers personally, albeit with the help of computers.[96] The anonymous, cash-based economy of the modern era would be transformed into a new personalised economy.[97] It was where the financial industries crossed into the market for identities, or at least recognised its promise long before the internet, social media and its surveillance capitalism. In this sense, the plastic card represented the market's (not the state's) desire to make people legible.

Elinder's ideas were further developed by others in the coming decades. I mentioned that InterConto managed the furniture manufacturer and retailer Ikea's credit account system in the 1970s. According to some sources, Elinder was the first to come up with the concept of the Ikea Family card, an early loyalty card system, introduced in 1984. It offered special products, previews and home insurance.[98] This was significant, because the typical customers of the low-price furniture store seldom bought on credit, but now the Ikea Family card gave the company access to similarly detailed personal data: customers' names, addresses, preferences, buying habits and financial and family situation. Designed to be more than 'a channel for direct contact' or a traditional loyalty reward system, in its first year the Ikea Family gained 200,000 new members, all without advertising and with only two Swedish stores affiliated. The system was launched both nationally and internationally in 1986.[99] Ikea's 1987 catalogue (published in 1986) presented it in a cheerful tone, welcoming everyone 'to the family'.[100] It was one of the world's first and largest modern loyalty cards systems, alongside American Airlines' Frequent Flyer programme launched in collaboration with Citibank in the early 1980s. By 2020, Ikea Family had 150 million members worldwide and over 3.2 million in Sweden.[101]

Other loyalty card programmes, launched later in the 1980s and 1990s in Sweden and elsewhere, were often called clubs rather than families. Ikea used a vocabulary of intimacy and belonging not one of exclusivity and prestige, which is what media scholars Josh Lauer and Lana Swartz have noted about other early loyalty schemes.[102] Initially, the 'fake' family rhetoric was seen as strange and met with criticism; there were jokes about spending time with 'new relatives' at the Ikea store, or that even a family could now be purchased in flat packaging. Within only few years, however, the Ikea Family card was a symbol of being an ordinary, down-to-earth person in the Swedish 'people's home', a member of the trade union and the Ikea Family.[103] True, Ikea was not (yet) a bank in the 1980s, but its collaboration with an insurance company connected its card to the financial services industry. Today, Ikano Bank, founded in 1994, manages the Ikea Family card. The new bank thus had an 'intimate relationship' from the start with many of its potential customers.

The Emergence of a Financial Identification Society

The bankification process created a link between identification and personal finances, or in more abstract terms, between identity and money. Highlighting the role of banks in the management of identification documents, and the significance of plastic cards (ID, credit and other cards), in this chapter I have argued that a financialisation of identity occurred during what I call the *plastic regime of identification*. In this intermediary regime, financial institutions and plastic cards helped the transition from a paper-based, documentary identification regime with the state as the primary monitor to a digital regime, typically described in the literature as dominated by various commercial forces. The cards were ascribed an important role in both in-person transactions and the emerging system of electronic payments. As the financialisation of identity found its material expression in the plastic card, the cards also triggered and channeled people's feelings about the new financial identification practices in society.

The link between money and identity required relational work, in addition to a new micro-infrastructure of everyday financial transactions. The introduction of the cheque-account wages in the 1960s—the first step in the bankification of everyday life—sparked a change in identification practices by creating a need for the banks to identify their new mass clientele. Being asked for an ID simply to access one's own money felt unfamiliar and even shameful, initially. The resentment evident in the source material confirms that the naturalisation of the everyday use of ID documents was a historically contingent process. However, bank-issued ID cards and the justifications for their use, associating them with everyday finances, successfully normalised ID checks in daily life. The bank campaigns appealed to the financial identity of the new account holders when they claimed 'It's your money the ID card protects'.[104]

While the role of banks in the management of identification is a specific Swedish story, the rise of the credit card is a more general one. Credit cards, as well, reinforced the new link between identification and personal finances. ID cards and credit cards became increasingly similar in form and function. From the 1970s on, both these types of plastic cards could be read by both humans and machines, and combined characteristics of paper documents and digital ID devices. They could function as proof of identity and as a form of money; their shape was adapted to the wallet, and the wallet to the cards. They were typically issued not by the authorities but by commercial actors, sometimes in partnership with government. The plastic card—in its form as a 'universal card', a combined ID, credit and debit card—was devised by Swedish banks to be the key to the financial informational system of the cashless society. Plastic cards were also at the centre of the dreams about commercial uses of transactional data, which illustrates how 'seeing like a market'—and seeing like a bank—worked in the 1970s setting. The cultural intimisation of people's relationship with financial institutions paved the way for intimate surveillance.

Today, cards are no longer needed as intermediary devices between computer systems and people; they are remnants of the plastic regime of identification. Identification can now be accomplished through digital BankID, fingerprints, facial recognition, Google ID or Facebook profile. The 'personal' part of these relationships endures in computer-generated personalisation, as imagined but not yet realised in the 1970s. However, a *historical* look at financial identification practices and their material-technical devices reveals the often invisible links between identity and money. From the perspective of the bankification of everyday life, and at a time when real-life interactions with banks and bank staff are increasingly rare, it is a crucial reminder that 'bankmindedness' and an intimate relationship with banks have historically been built into the everyday financial infrastructure and the official societal templates for identity verification.

The path from bank-issued plastic ID cards to today's digital BankIDs was not straight, though. In the 1980s Swedish banks continued to issue ID cards but gave up their control over their *production*, relying on standards and certifications.[105] In the early 2000s, both the Swedish and international landscape of identification documents changed. On the one hand, governments raced to engage with the issue of identification and national ID cards were introduced in many countries in the aftermath of 9/11. Like other European states, Sweden also had to adapt to European Union regulations, and in 2005 introduced a national plastic ID card valid in the Schengen area.[106] On the other hand, more important than ever before, digital identification in Sweden is once again driven and controlled by the banks. Digital BankID, launched in 2003, is used today on a daily basis as a quasi-official form of identification (although a few alternatives exist), and it was not until 2011 that a government agency was created to oversee electronic identification technologies. The dominance of the digital BankID in Sweden can be explained by the country's strong banking sector and the banks' ability to collaborate with each other and with the state; but also, as I have argued in this chapter, by the long-standing historical connections between everyday finances and identity management. This history also explains the difference contemporary ID experts have observed between a Nordic system of identification (which is managed mainly by financial institutions), the continental European tradition (which is state-dominated) and the Anglo-Saxon model (which uses a combination of commercial and public documents).[107]

Open Access This chapter is licensed under the terms of the Creative Commons Attribution 4.0 International License (http://creativecommons.org/licenses/by/4.0/), which permits use, sharing, adaptation, distribution and reproduction in any medium or format, as long as you give appropriate credit to the original author(s) and the source, provide a link to the Creative Commons license and indicate if changes were made.

The images or other third party material in this chapter are included in the chapter's Creative Commons license, unless indicated otherwise in a credit line to the material. If material is not included in the chapter's Creative Commons license and your intended use is not permitted by statutory regulation or exceeds the permitted use, you will need to obtain permission directly from the copyright holder.

CHAPTER 7

Conclusion

Many people living in Sweden today have not held a Swedish banknote or coin in their hands for years. In some neighbourhood shops and cafés, cash is no longer accepted. Almost all payments are digital—made using cards, mobile phones and computers—and therefore go through banks. Sweden has long been one of the world's most 'cashless societies', even if other countries are rapidly catching up. Banks also handle salaries and offer mortgages. As most banking transactions are conducted through mobile phones, people can access their bank accounts at any time of the day. They check their stock investments through easy-to-use apps from online banks such as Avanza, which was launched in 1999 and now has around two million customers. Small money transfers between friends and family members are done via the mobile phone app Swish (since 2012), a Swedish equivalent of the American Venmo, but unlike Venmo it is owned and developed by banks in cooperation with Sweden's Central Bank.[1] Swish is also used for payments online or in shops, and at most flea markets and jumble sales. It is also the banks, through the digital BankID (introduced in 2003), that secure personal identities in both economic and in non-economic situations online, for example when one makes a doctor's appointment or is in contact with municipal schools and government authorities. When it comes to the banks' dominance in the management of identity control, Sweden and the other Scandinavian countries are quite unique, even though the mundane omnipresence of banking institutions is a worldwide phenomenon. However, we rarely ask how this close—intimate—relationship developed in the first place; or if we do, we tend to look only at the digitalisation of the last two or three decades.

The historical process of the bankification of daily life that this book has explored is not a story specific to Sweden. But it was definitely embedded in a particular cultural, social, political and economic context that fundamentally shaped how the process unfolded. Moreover, the exceptionally early Swedish bankification clearly demonstrates that the phenomenon must be analytically distinguished from related processes that have received more attention in the literature: financialisation, deregulation, neoliberalisation, digitalisation, the depersonalisation of banking or the emergence of cashlessness, new forms of credit and commercial surveillance. More than just another word for the development of mass retail banking, the concept of the bankification of everyday life points to how all the above processes are intertwined with the changing role of banks, not only in society and in the financial sector as a whole but also in ordinary people's lifeworlds. It signals that this was a cultural change as well as an economic-financial one. The role of banks and other similar financial institutions in everyday life is often perceived as self-evident in contemporary societies. The Swedish case demonstrates how this sense of self-evidence has been historically created.

Bankification Between Financial and Cultural History

Between the late 1950s and the early 1980s, a silent personal financial revolution took place in Sweden. It turned virtually the entire population into consumers of various banking and financial services, thus reshaping the mundane financial routines of individuals and families as well as the role that banks and other financial companies played in them. It was an important transition that changed the everyday culture of money and paved the way for the financial transformations of subsequent decades. As contemporaneous bankers said, it moved 'people's wallets'—not just their savings—into bank accounts and created an intimate everyday relationship between the banks and their customers. This process, the bankification of everyday life, is an important part of both financial and cultural history, and also of the history of the Swedish welfare state. Yet it has been mostly overlooked by financial historians interested in larger institutional, economic and policy changes. Looking at what happened through the lens of cultural analysis a new pattern emerges, one that differs from the accounts of financial historians and also offers a different chronology of significant shifts. Cultural historians, for their part, have not typically been interested in topics like banking and financial matters. Even among historians of consumer culture, at least in Sweden, topics related to finance and credit have been rare. For historians of the welfare society the post-war period has been about social levelling, the emergence of gender equality, and state intervention in the lives of families through social and welfare legislation. In this context, questions about exactly how the new levelling wages or universal social benefits were paid out, and in what forms people spent or saved their money, seem secondary, whereas in my reading such questions and their answers lead to significant insights and open up an important field of study at the intersection of cultural and economic history.

Many historians see the late 1980s and early 1990s as a distinct turning point in Swedish history, marked by deregulations, the incipient retrenchment of the welfare state, neoliberalisation and globalisation, which also brought about significant changes to everyday financial practices. The 1980s have also been portrayed as the quintessential consumerist decade in this part of the world. These epochal narratives are not wrong and, admittedly, there is research that traces the beginnings of such processes back to the 1970s, both in Sweden and elsewhere. However, the argument in this book is that prior to the changes of the 1980s and 1990s a bankification process began in the 1950s and during the 1960s and 1970s established new practices, promoted a new mindset and created new devices and indeed a whole new micro-infrastructure for the handling of everyday finances. It was a profound but unremarkable transformation, best understood as a cultural shift rather than a political or economic one, even if it was entangled in both economy and politics. I have argued that the social democratic welfare state was an important contributing factor, even a 'condition of possibility' for the changes analysed in the book: because of the levelling of incomes and various new universal welfare provisions, the importance of the wage-earner subject, and the strict financial regulations that forced commercial banks to take an interest in the small deposits of ordinary households. But the bankification of everyday life, in particular with the financial educational efforts it entailed, was also intertwined with the long-term ambitions of important forces within the business community to foster an entrepreneurial and anti-socialist mindset among the population with a focus on individual financial agency.

The main interest of this book is not why, but how, the bankification of everyday life happened. I have identified and analysed a series of cultural challenges—in terms of class, gender, morality, ideology and identity—that had to be resolved along the way. I have argued that the new banking services and products, and the new practices they brought, needed to be linked to ordinary people's everyday concerns. They had to be domesticated, made familiar and eventually taken for granted. As sociologist Turo-Kimmo Lehtonen writes about the contemporary insurance products, '[t]hrough domestication, financial instruments can become part of our second nature'.[2] What I have described as the domestication of financial services was achieved through intricate cultural relational work, by which not only financial knowledge, practices and instruments were reshaped but also banks themselves and the financial identities of their customers.

Much of this relational work can be interpreted as market-engineering efforts by banks to create consumers for their new products. Sometimes counteracting—but often in practice intertwined with—the welfare state's social engineering ambitions, banks and other financial institutions were engaged in creating a new 'modus vivendi' for the population, as is especially evident in the case of credit cards.[3] However, beyond market engineering aimed at creating and introducing something new, the cultural relational work explored in this book involved combining the old and well-known with the new and as yet unfamiliar. The new financial subjects of the bankification project—the new cheque account holders, bank customers and credit card owners—were deeply rooted in and moulded onto the familiar subjects of the welfare state: the wage earner, the housewife and later the working woman, as well as the rational consumer of the cooperative movement.

Bankifying Everyday Life in Sweden

From the late 1950s Swedish commercial banks entered new areas of private and public life, among them the workplace. With the payment of wages came the task of collecting trade union fees and managing savings clubs and the welfare offices (*intressekontor*) of large industrial companies. As Chapter 2 shows, this was a major cultural clash in terms of not only class but also ideology, that both banks and trade unions, and probably the new account holders as well, had to deal with. With the new cheque accounts for wages and salaries, people's everyday money was handled by the banks, creating an intimate relationship between banks and households. New products and services, such as targeted savings-loan accounts or specific bank accounts for welfare payments, for instance the child benefit accounts, reinforced this intimacy. Family matters now became relevant to commercial banks, which had previously mainly served the business sector; and banks began giving advice on, for example, how husbands and wives should share their money between themselves. Newly appointed family economists *(familjeekonomer)* personified the banks' new expert role in family finances, offering counselling on household budgeting and pocket money as well as on stocks and shares, thus erasing the traditional boundaries between domestic money and market money. Chapter 3, through the study of the Golden Everyday women's conferences, highlights how the re-gendering of banking and finance helped to domesticate—familiarise—the new banking services by grounding them in family life and affectionate feelings, and by associating them with consumer skills.

Already with the mass distribution of cheque accounts, the banks became intermediaries in mundane consumer purchases; the introduction of credit cards was a further step in this direction. Both cheque accounts and credit cards presented a cultural challenge and involved a redefinition of these forms of money in terms of class. Credit cards in particular were at odds with prevailing moral values. The conventional anti-credit ethos fostered by the consumer cooperative movement, the savings bank movement and the labour movement had to be defied, or at least reinterpreted, for credit cards to succeed. Chapter 4 analyses how the new device, the card itself, was 'engineered' and defined as modern money, as a membership card certifying trust or as a budgeting device. The cultural technologies used to domesticate cards, together with the rapidly developing computer technologies, served to blur the conceptual boundaries between credit and cash payments. Notions such as 'post-purchase saving', 'consumption smoothing', 'allocating resources over time' and 'facilitating consumer choice' were introduced to the public from the 1960s to explain why buying on credit was not substantially different from cash purchases. These ideas were akin to the neoliberal reconceptualisation of finance and consumption, an economic-ideological thought complex, introduced in explicit form into the Swedish political discourse in the 1970s; but, as my study shows, the new financial practices of everyday bankification actualised such ideas earlier than this.

Chapter 5 moves a step away from the strictly defined banking sector and focuses on the ideological domestication of the credit card. The case of the card company InterConto showed how academic historical research was mobilised to reinterpret the prevalent cultural meanings of consumer credit as defined by social democracy and the consumer cooperative movement. A new history of consumer credit was therefore conceived in order to address politicians, cooperative members and unionised workers. At the same time, the Consumer Cooperative Union itself initiated a process that led to a reconsideration of the use of credit cards in everyday consumption. This required ideological relational work in the form of internal soul-searching within the cooperative movement and pragmatic reinterpretations as well as the unlearning of old financial rationalities and the learning of new ones. The circulation of knowledge about credit cards was carried out through the conventional channels of this large popular movement. Upon its launch, the cooperative credit card was interpreted by contemporaries as a general moral approval of consumer credit and an endorsement of a redefined financial rationality.

Chapter 6 places plastic cards in a broader context, showing how they came to embody a new concept of financial identity in their shape as bank-issued identity cards. This final empirical chapter picks up the thread from the first one. It shows how the cheque-account wages required a new approach to identity verification in everyday financial life, forcing the banks to issue ID documents and thus take on a role that typically belongs to government authorities. The conceptual and practical similarities between credit cards and ID cards, and the justifications used for the new routines of ID checks, created a new link between money and identity.

The analytical focus on bankification highlights an often-overlooked phase in the history of identification documents. The chapter argues that between a paper-based documentary identification regime dominated by the bureaucratic state and a digital regime that is typically assumed to be commercially driven, there was an intermediate plastic regime, during which identity became financialised. The development of computerisation, the banks' involvement in identity management and their work towards a new financial information and transaction system contributed to building the new intimate relationship between banks and their customers into the everyday financial infrastructure. As early as the 1970s, historical actors realised that this mass-managed intimacy held the promise of commercialising identities through the use of transactional data, for example for personalised sales offers.

Taken together, the chapters show how the bankification of everyday life created an intimate relationship between banks and the public, formed 'bankminded' customers and established a new personal financial rationality. Bankification introduced a range of devices that reshaped mundane financial practices, of which cheque accounts and credit cards were some of the most important. Banks made inroads into new spheres of public and private life, such as the workplace, the family, various consumer spaces and the world of social movements, and even took over the management of identity verification, a task that had traditionally belonged to the state (or the established Church). In the process, cultural boundaries of class, gender, morality and identity have been renegotiated, and the new role of banks has become virtually self-evident.

Needless to say, this book does not give a complete picture. It barely touches on three important phenomena that are often discussed in the financialisation of everyday life literature, and in which the banks have played a crucial role: home mortgages, pension insurance and popular stock investments. Housing loans in Sweden began increasing in both number and value after banks' lending ceilings were lifted in 1985. The issue of a new pension system partly based on individual investment choices became topical in the late 1990s. The popularisation of investment instruments for ordinary people started much earlier, with the banks playing a key role. The investment clubs, organised by commercial banks from 1957, and mutual investment funds launched the year after are mentioned but not explored in depth in the book. They are part of a separate story, in which different actors collaborated around initiatives to promote popular stock saving. In 1966, the Swedish Shareholders' Association (*Aktiespararna*) was founded with the aim of mobilising and representing small shareholders. In 1976 it initiated the creation of the Stock Promotion Foundation (*Aktiefrämjandet*), an organisation for the popularisation of equity investment, funded by Swedish businesses and also supported by the Bankers' Association.[4] The initiative, which aimed 'to turn all of us into small capitalists', was perceived by many contemporaries as one of the steps taken by organised business to counterbalance the much-contested trade union proposal for collectively owned wage-earner funds. Another step, two years later, was the tax-subsidised mutual fund savings scheme (*skattefonder*) introduced by the centre-right government.[5] As these mutual funds were mainly managed by banks, the reforms were easy enough to implement in a country where banks already had a rather 'intimate relationship' with the population. The distance between a highly politicised reform to a mundane practice was therefore short. The bankification of everyday life is a hitherto missing link, which explains how everyday financialisation could take hold of Swedish society relatively quickly.

The history of the mass investment culture became even more intertwined with the bankification of everyday life after the financial crisis of the early 1990s, and when the liberalisation of banking legislation made possible the opening of so-called niche banks or telephone banks, many of which specialised in stock market savings. Insurance companies and major retailers, such as Ikea and the food retail giants Konsum (Coop) and Ica, also started their own banking operations in the 1990s. Of course, these companies already had a close relationship with their large customer bases.

THE SWEDISH CASE IN AN INTERNATIONAL PERSPECTIVE

Bankminded describes the bankification of everyday life as a historical transition that in Sweden took place between the late 1950s and the mid-1980s. But the process has continued. The ties between banks and the everyday life of ordinary people multiplied when, in addition to salaries, diversified accounts, consumer payments and credit, the banks increasingly handled equity investments and mortgages and offered insurance products. The banks played an important role in everyday identification practices as early as the 1960s, but since the beginning of the 2000s, with the advent of digital BankID, this role has been forcefully renewed.

Looking back in history instead, some might argue for an earlier start of the bankification process, at least in Sweden. Taking into consideration traditional savings and occasional loans would lead back to the late nineteenth century, when large parts of the Swedish population were among the savings banks' clientele. As early as 1890, there were over a million accounts in the Swedish savings banks (and about a hundred thousand accounts in commercial banks). This was a large number in a country with a population of 4.8 million.[6] But a savings account in itself did not imply mundane interactions with a bank, and was not woven into everyday life in the same way as the later banking products were. So, in my interpretation, the bankification process must be dated to the post-war period.

Nevertheless, the mere possession of a bank account is a necessary condition for the bankification of everyday life, and statistics on the existence of bank connections in the population can give a clear indication of variations between countries. Historical comparisons are difficult to make, but the differences today are still enormous even if they are diminishing in a global perspective. According to the World Bank's financial inclusion statistics in 2021, over 76 percent of the world's adult population had an account at a bank or other regulated financial service provider, compared to only 51 percent in 2011. But while in countries such as Sweden and most European societies, as well as other high-income, developed countries like New Zealand, Canada or Japan, 95–100 percent of the population were banked in 2011—and even before that—financial inclusion rates are considerably lower in some other parts of the world, for example Afghanistan, 9 to 10 percent in the period 2011–2021, or the West Bank and Gaza, where the percentage increased from 20 to 34 percent in the same period. In some countries such as Ukraine, Chile, Venezuela or Kenya, the figures roughly doubled between 2011 and 2021 from about 40 to more than 80 percent, which the Global Financial Database explains with the emergence of digital financial instruments.[7] Countries with high levels of financial inclusion tend to be ones where the use of banking services is a daily routine.

However, similarly high levels of financial inclusion today say little about the different histories. The cultural, social and political underpinnings and ramifications of the bankification process varied in different national settings, even within Europe. Comparisons are not easy to make, as few studies have highlighted the bankification of everyday life as a specific process; the national histories of bankification can only be glimpsed through accounts of financialisation or stories of the banking industry and the development of retail banking. French scholars have noted that the 'bancarisation' in France of the late 1960s, rather than being part of a financialisation, was instead the result of a retail banking designed to preserve the 'definansialising' role of the welfare state. The new banking products were not connected to extended financial markets and did not bear financial risks.[8] In contrast, the literature on Britain does not speak of bankification as such, even when emphasising the role of banks and the spread of banking services among ordinary people. It is implied, however, that such a process was interwoven with the larger financialisation of daily life including, for example, the increase in consumer credit and an emerging mass investment culture.[9] This might partly be explained by the fact that in the United Kingdom the payment of wages by direct deposit or cheques was delayed. In 1979 over 50 percent of Britons still received their wages in cash, due to union resistance and older legislation protecting workers from unfair deductions. This deferred the bankification process, despite an advanced banking sector and well-developed computer technologies.[10] In the 1980s the affiliation of the remaining unbanked groups coincided with the development of a more globalised and financialised world, as well as a neoliberal shift in government. This would explain why bankification appears to be deeply intertwined with financialisation in the British case. Accounts of UK banking history have also emphasised the depersonalisation of banking, focusing on the disappearance of traditional gentlemanly bankers and the emergence of computerised interactions.[11] While the new intimate relationship between *banks* and their customers held the promise of algorithmic personalisation, as I have argued in this book, it did often entail an increasingly impersonal—or lacking—relationship between bank *staff* and customers.[12]

The Swedish case differs from both the French and British stories. Bankification in Sweden was early, even earlier than in France, and happened before financialisation fully took hold of the lives of ordinary people. It was deeply embedded in the welfare statist context, but was not 'definancialised' as scholars claim in regard to the French case. In addition to providing a micro-infrastructure for the later changes—for example new forms of credit and investment accounts—it was also instrumental in creating a new mindset, a new financial rationality, smoothly paving the way for a more financialised daily life. The change required considerable cultural relational work, as social, moral and ideological boundaries were blurred and cultural gaps smoothly and efficiently bridged within a few decades.

Some key elements of the Swedish bankification process, such as the initial role of wage and salary payments and the payment of welfare provisions, were similar to how banks became intimate agents of everyday life in Eastern Europe in the early 1990s. In the post-socialist countries, however, the change was more brutal and happened late but quickly, together with the transition to global capitalism. Salary accounts, credit cards, investment instruments and mortgages in Swiss francs were introduced to populations that were 'utterly unprepared'. As Alya Guseva and Akos Rona-Tas observe in their work on credit and payment cards, many of the financial instruments launched in 1990s Eastern Europe were perceived as going against the 'mentality' of the countries and 'banks had to change minds and habits and not just interest rates or annual fees'.[13]

The introduction of credit cards and cashless payments also emerges as an important part of the different national stories. While credit cards figure in all these contexts they are often associated with the United States, whereas in European countries plastic cards really took off when technology made it possible to use them for debit purchases. Sometimes—as in the case of China—salaries, social payments and payment cards are all controlled by the state, which makes the issue of financial surveillance, another important element of the bankification process, particularly salient.

Highlighting the bankification of everyday life as a distinct process, even if intertwined with some or all of the above mentioned changes, is the main contribution of this book. By exploring the exceptionally early Swedish case, I have shown that it was not only an economic and technological transition but also a political, social, moral and, not least, cultural one. It has not been recognised as an important historical process, even though the new financial practices and thinking it introduced have had a fundamental impact on everyday life. Whereas in the 1950s Swedes had to be urged and made to become bankminded, today the practices and thinking involved in this bankmindedness are so self-evident that not only is such a word unnecessary, sounding strange and obsolete, but we no longer reflect on the historical process that created it.

Open Access This chapter is licensed under the terms of the Creative Commons Attribution 4.0 International License (http://creativecommons.org/licenses/by/4.0/), which permits use, sharing, adaptation, distribution and reproduction in any medium or format, as long as you give appropriate credit to the original author(s) and the source, provide a link to the Creative Commons license and indicate if changes were made.

The images or other third party material in this chapter are included in the chapter's Creative Commons license, unless indicated otherwise in a credit line to the material. If material is not included in the chapter's Creative Commons license and your intended use is not permitted by statutory regulation or exceeds the permitted use, you will need to obtain permission directly from the copyright holder.

Notes

Notes to Chapter 1

1. Mary Poovey, 'Beneath the Horizon of Cultural Visibility', *Journal of Cultural Economy*, 1, 3 (2008), 337–347.
2. Centrum för Näringslivshistoria (Centre for Business History, hereafter CfN), Handelsbanken (hereafter HB), F4:11, internal memo 'Marketing Research', 29 March 1968. All translations are my own unless otherwise noted.
3. For example, 'Husmödrarna kan lätta på kreditrestriktionerna', *Norrlands-Posten*, 20 October 1956, press cutting in CfN, Skandinaviska Banken (hereafter SB), Ö1:2; 'Bankminded kvinna är samhällsgagnande', *Katrineholmskuriren*, 2 March 1959, press cutting in CfN, SB, Ö1:28. 'Limhamnarna skall göras bankminded', *Arbetet*, 19 April 1964.
4. For a similar interpretation of credit markets and the welfare state in France, see Helene Ducourant and Jeanne Lazarus, 'Credit in Society and in Sociology: On *The Bank and Its Customers* (Bourdieu, Boltanski, Chamboredon, 1963)', *European Journal of Sociology*, 64, 3 (2023), 385–416. On 'condition of possibility' see Michel Foucault, *The Birth of Biopolitics* (Basingstoke: Palgrave Macmillan, 2008), 160.
5. Randy Martin, *Financialization of Daily Life* (Philadelphia: Temple University Press, 2002); Paul Langley, *The Everyday Life of Global Finance: Saving and Borrowing in Anglo-America* (Oxford: Oxford University Press, 2008); the chapters in 'Part E—Techniques, Technologies and Cultures of Financialisation', in *The Routledge International Handbook of Financialization*, ed. by Philip Mader, Daniel Mertens, and Natascha van der Zwan (New York: Taylor & Francis, 2020), 345–410; Lena Pellandini-Simányi, 'The

Financialization of Everyday Life', in *The Routledge Handbook of Critical Finance Studies*, ed. by Christian Borch and Robert Wosnitzer (New York & London: Routledge, 2021), 278–299.

6. Greta R. Krippner, *Capitalizing on Crisis: The Political Origins of the Rise of Finance* (Cambridge, MA: Harvard University Press, 2011); Brett Christophers, 'The Limits to Financialization', *Dialogues in Human Geography*, 5, 2 (2015), 183–200; Mader, Mertens and van der Zwan, *The Routledge International Handbook of Financialization*. See also David Harvey, *A Brief History of Neoliberalism* (Oxford: Oxford University Press, 2007 [2005]), 33.

7. Martin, *Financialization of Daily Life*; Langley, *The Everyday Life of Global Finance*; Rob Aitken, *Performing Capital: Toward a Cultural Economy of Popular and Global Finance* (Basingstoke, UK: Palgrave Macmillan, 2007); Jeanne Lazarus, 'About the Universality of a Concept: Is There a Financialization of Daily Life in France?', *Civitas*, 17, 1 (2017), 26–42. See also Orsi Husz and David Larsson Heidenblad, 'The Making of Everyman's Capitalism in Sweden: Micro-Infrastructures, Unlearning, and Moral Boundary Work', *Enterprise & Society*, 24, 2 (2023), 425–454.

8. Martin, *Financialization of Daily Life*, 14; Langley, *The Everyday Life of Global Finance*; Donncha Marron, *Consumer Credit in the United States: A Sociological Perspective from the 19th Century to the Present* (Basingstoke, UK: Palgrave Macmillan, 2009), 110–114; Marion Fourcade and Kieran Healy, 'Classification Situations', *Accounting, Organizations and Society*, 38, 8 (2013), 559–572; Paul Langley and Andrew Leyshon, 'Financial Subjects: Culture and Materiality', *Journal of Cultural Economy*, 5, 4 (2012), 369–373.

9. Aitken, *Performing Capital*; Jeanne Lazarus 'Gouverner les conduites économiques par l'éducation financière: L'ascension de la financial literacy', in *Gouverner les conduits*, ed. by Sophie Dubuisson-Quellier (Paris: Presses de SciencesPo, 2016), 93–126.

10. Olivier Feiertag, 'La bancarisation de la société française dans les années 1968', in *Les Français et l'argent*, ed. by Alya Aglan, Olivier Feiertag, and Yannick Marec (Rennes: Presses Universitaires de Rennes, 2011), 163–175; Jeanne Lazarus, *L'épreuve de l'argent. Banques, banquiers, clients* (Paris: Calmann-Lévy, 2012), Ch. 1, esp. 28.

11. Lazarus, 'About the Universality of a Concept', 26–42.

12. Kristina Lilja, 'The Deposit Market Revolution in Sweden', in *The Swedish Financial Revolution*, ed. by Anders Ögren (Basingstoke, UK: Palgrave Macmillan, 2010), 41–59. See also Tom Petersson, *Mellan det lokala och det globala: Det svenska banksystemet ur ett historiskt perspektiv* (Norrtälje: Roslagens sparbank, 2009).

13. David Stafford and Susan King, 'Banking on the Unbanked', *International Journal of Bank Marketing*, 1, 2 (1983), 27–28 and Jacqueline Botterill, *Consumer Culture and Personal Finance* (Basingstoke, UK: Palgrave Macmillan, 2010), 103, 119. Aled Davies, Ben Jackson, and Florence Sutcliffe-Braitwaite (eds.), *The Neoliberal Age: Britain Since the 1970s* (London: UCL Press, 2021); Langley, *The Everyday Life of Global Finance*.
14. Zsuzsanna Vargha, 'Performing a Strategy's World: How Redesigning Customers Made Relationship Banking Possible', *Long Range Planning*, 51, 3 (2018), 480–494.
15. Mats Larsson, *Staten och kapitalet: det svenska finansiella systemet under 1900-talet* (Stockholm: SNS Förlag, 1998); Mats Larsson and Gabriel Söderberg, *Finance and the Welfare State: Banking Development and Regulatory Principles in Sweden, 1900–2015* (Cham: Palgrave Macmillan, 2017); Orsi Husz, 'Spara, Slösa och alla de andra', in *Signums svenska kulturhistoria, 1900-talet*, ed. by Jacob Christenson (Stockholm: Atlantis, 2009), 279–329.
16. While there are no official statistics on consumer credit from that time, newspapers and bankers reported from the meeting of Eurofinas, the organisation of European financial companies, that Sweden and Britain had the highest sums of consumer debt per capita in Europe in 1960–1961: 'Sverige, England störst i konsumtionskrediter', *Dagens Nyheter* (*DN*), 15 October 1961; 'Sverige tvåa som kreditland', *DN* 29 March 1960. On the lack of statistics, see *Index: Svenska Handelsbankens Ekonomiska Månadsöversikt*, 5 (1960).
17. CfN, Köpkort (hereafter KKA), vol. '1969', Sven Å. Cason, 'Samhälle utan check', manuscript for speech held 14 October 1968 at a conference organised by the Swedish Bankers' Association.
18. CfN, Erik Elinder's Papers (hereafter EEP), vol. 'Ehrlemark', Erik Elinder to Gunnar Ehrlemark, 24 October 1977.
19. On domestication in media and technology studies, see Thomas Berker et al. (eds.), *Domestication of Media and Technology* (Maidenhead: Open University Press, 2006); esp. Roger Silverstone, 'Domesticating domestication. Reflections on the life of a concept' in the same volume. On the adaptation of the concept to financial technologies: Turo-Kimmo Lehtonen, 'Domesticating Insurance, Financializing Family Lives: The Case of Private Health Insurance for Children in Finland', *Cultural Studies*, 31, 5 (2017), 685–711.
20. Léna Pellandini-Simányi, Ferenc Hammer, and Zsuzsanna Vargha, 'The Financialization of Everyday Life or the Domestication of Finance?', *Cultural Studies*, 29, 5–6 (2015), 733–759; Orsi Husz, 'Golden Everyday: Housewifely Consumerism and the Domestication of Banks in 1960s

Sweden', *Le Mouvement Social*, 250, 1 (2015), 41–63; for variegated financial subjects and hybrid subjectivities, see Léna Pellandini-Simányi and Adam Banai, 'Reluctant Financialization: Financialization without Financialised Subjectivities in Hungary and the United States', *Environment and Planning A: Economy and Space*, 53, 4 (2021), 785–808; Orsi Husz, David Larsson Heidenblad, and Elin Åström Rudberg, 'Wage Earners, Taxpayers or Everyman Capitalists? The Making of a Mutual Fund Culture in Sweden', in *Nordic Neoliberalisms*, ed. by Jenny Andersson and Chris Howell (forthcoming).

21. José Ossandón, Joe Deville, Jeanne Lazarus, and Mariana Luzzi, 'Financial Oikonomization: The Financial Government and Administration of the Household', *Socio-Economic Review*, 20, 3 (2022), 1473–1500.

22. Viviana Zelizer, 'How I Became a Relational Economic Sociologist and What Does That Mean?', *Politics & Society*, 40, 2 (2012), 149; Viviana Zelizer, *Economic Lives: How Culture Shapes the Economy* (Princeton: Princeton University Press, 2011), 407–408; Nina Bandelj, Paul James Morgan, and Elizabeth Sowers, 'Hostile Worlds or Connected Lives? Research on the Interplay Between Intimacy and Economy', *Sociology Compass*, 9, 2 (2015), 115–127.

23. Liz McFall, *Devising Consumption: Cultural Economies of Insurance, Credit and Spending* (Abingdon, Oxon: Routledge, 2015), 19, 28.

24. Karl-Gustaf Hildebrand, *Banking in a Growing Economy: Svenska Handelsbanken Since 1871* (Stockholm: Handelsbanken, 1971); Ulf Olsson, *Bank, familj, företagande: Stockholms Enskilda bank 1946–1971* (Stockholm: EHF-Handelshögskolan, 1986); Ulf Olsson, *I utvecklingens centrum: Skandinaviska Enskilda Banken och dess föregångare 1856–1996* (Stockholm: Skandinaviska Enskilda Banken, 1997); Petersson, *Mellan det lokala och det globala*; Ingvar Körberg, *Förnyelsen: Sparbankernas historia 1945–1980* (Stockholm: Ekerlid, 2006); Mats Larsson, *Staten och kapitalet*; Larsson and Söderberg, *Finance and the Welfare State*.

25. Tom Petersson, 'Samhälle och näringsliv med gemensamma mål', in *Det svenska näringslivets historia 1864–2014*, ed. by Lena Andersson-Skog and Mats Larsson (Stockholm: Dialogos, 2014), 475.

26. Anders Forsell, *Moderna tider i sparbanken: Om organisatorisk omvandling i ett institutionellt perspektiv* (Stockholm: Nerenius & Santérus, 1992), 87–100.

27. Olsson, *I utvecklingens centrum*, 188–189; Forsell, *Moderna tider i sparbanken*, 90; Körberg, *Förnyelsen*, 97–98.

28. The Post Office Savings Bank merged with Postgirot in 1960 to form Postbanken, which in turn merged with Kreditbanken to form PK-banken in 1974. Kurt Samuelsson, *Postbanken—postsparbank och postgiro* (Stockholm: Postverket, 1978).

29. Tom Petersson, 'Tillväxt, kriser och koncentration—det svenska banksystemet 1820–2005', in *Sverige—en social och ekonomisk historia*, ed. by Susanna Hedenborg and Mats Morell (Lund: Studentlitteratur, 2006), 383–387.
30. Forsell, *Moderna tider i sparbanken*, 90.
31. CfN, Bankföreningen (Swedish Bankers' Association, hereafter BF), Styrelsens protokoll (Minutes of the Board), 19 June 1968, §103 and Appendix 1.
32. Ibid. For ambitions to change British banks' image, see Botterill, *Consumer Culture and Personal Finance*; and Victoria Barnes and Lucy Newton, 'Women, Uniforms and Brand Identity in Barclays Bank', *Business History*, 64, 4 (2022), 801–830.
33. Petersson, 'Samhälle och näringsliv'.
34. Olsson, *I utvecklingens centrum*, 175–188.
35. Petersson, 'Tillväxt, kriser', 386; Olsson, *I utvecklingens centrum*, 175–177.
36. SPF 1955:416 (1955 års sparbankslag, Savings Banks Act of 1955); Forsell, *Moderna tider i sparbanken*, 126, 129; Körberg, *Förnyelsen*, 108–115, 277–289; Larsson and Söderberg, *Finance and the Welfare State*, 76–77.
37. Olsson, *I utvecklingens centrum*, 177.
38. The economic historian Lars Ahnland argues for a different view on financialisation in the Nordics, claiming that a first financialisation process occurred in the early twentieth century and a second one started in the 1980s. A similar argument is proposed by the Danish business historian Per Hansen. However, these longer perspectives do not change the interpretation of the financialisation process in the late twentieth century. See Lars Ahnland, 'Survey Article on Nordic Financialisation in the Long Run', *Scandinavian Economic History Review*, 71, 3 (2023), 247–257; and Per H. Hansen, 'From Finance Capitalism to Financialization: A Cultural and Narrative Perspective on 150 Years of Financial History', *Enterprise & Society*, 15, 4 (2015), 605–642.
39. Erik Andersson et al. (eds.), *Vardagslivets finansialisering* (Göteborg: Centrum för konsumtionsvetenskap, 2016), 9–10. For a review of Nordic studies on financialisation, see Ahnland, 'Survey Article on Nordic Financialisation'.
40. Alexis Stenfors, *The Swedish Financial System. Studies in Financial Systems No 13. FESSUD—Financialisation, Economy, Society and Sustainable Development* (2014), 152–155; see also Claes Ohlsson, *Folkets fonder? En textvetenskaplig studie av det svenska pensionssparandets domesticering* (Göteborg: Göteborgs universitet, 2007).
41. Stenfors, *The Swedish Financial System*, 15.
42. Claes Belfrage, 'Towards "Universal Financialisation" in Sweden?', *Contemporary Politics*, 14, 3 (2008), 277–296, esp. 281, 283, 290. For the notion

of 'risk shift', see Jacob S. Hacker, *The Great Risk Shift: The New Economic Insecurity and the Decline of the American Dream* (New York: Oxford University Press, 2008). On the British public pension scheme in the 1980s and the tensions between investor and consumer subjects, see Aled Davies, James Freeman, and Hugh Pemberton, '"Everyman Capitalist" or "Free to Choose"? Exploring the Tensions within Thatcherite Individualism', *The Historical Journal*, 61, 2 (2018), 477–501.

43. Some Swedish scholars—in the fields of ethnology, sociology and business studies—have written about the cultural changes in late twentieth-century Sweden in the aftermath of financialisation. Whether or not they use the concept of financialisation, their chronology is the same. See Mats Lindqvist, *Is i magen: Om ekonomins kolonisering av* vardagen (Stockholm: Natur och kultur, 2001); Fredrik Nilsson, *Aktiesparandets förlovade land: Människors möte med aktiemarknaden* (Eslöv: Symposion, 2003); Ohlsson, *Folkets fonder?*; Dick Forslund, *Hit med pengarna! Sparandets genealogi och den finansiella övertalningens vetandekonst* (Stockholm: Carlssons, 2008); Jane Pettersson, *Governing Citizens in the Age of Financialization: A Study of Swedish Financial Education* (Göteborg: Göteborgs universitet, 2022).

44. Torbjörn Hessling, *Att spara eller inte spara—vilken fråga!: Den sparfrämjande verksamheten 1820–1970*. (Stockholm: Sparfrämjandet, 1990). See also Körberg, *Förnyelsen* and Husz, 'Spara, Slösa och alla de andra'.

45. Orsi Husz, 'Privatekonomin och den borgerliga medelklassens identitetskris 1920–1970', *Fronesis*, 24 (2007), 116–130.

46. Rikard Westerberg, *Socialists at the Gate: Swedish Business and the Defense of Free Enterprise, 1940–1985* (Stockholm: Stockholm School of Economics, 2020); Jenny Andersson, 'Neoliberalism from within. The Business Fund and the Struggle for Market Ideology in Sweden', *Contemporary European History*, FirstView (2025), 1–17.

47. Quotes: Westerberg, *Socialists at the Gate*, 114; 116; see also 87–88.

48. Westerberg, *Socialists at the Gate*, 119.

49. Maria Grafström, *The Development of Swedish Business Journalism: Historical Roots of an Organisational Field* (Uppsala: Department of Business Studies, 2006); David Larsson Heidenblad, 'Marknadsleken', in *Marknadens tid. Mellan folkhemskapitalism och nyliberalism*, ed. by Jenny Andersson, Nikolas Glover, Orsi Husz, and David Larsson Heidenblad (Lund: Nordic Academic Press, 2023), 198–199.

50. William Sewell, 'A Strange Career: The Historical Study of Economic Life', *History and Theory*, 49, 4 (2010), 146–166. On the interest in everyday life within business history, see Kenneth Lipartito, 'Connecting the Cultural and the Material in Business History', *Enterprise & Society*, 14, 4 (2013), 686–704; and Andrew Popp, 'Histories of Business and the Everyday', *Enterprise & Society*, 21, 3 (2020), 622–637.

51. Tony Bennett, Liz McFall, and Mike Pryke, 'Editorial: Culture/Economy/Social', *Journal of Cultural Economy*, 1, 1 (2008), 1–7; McFall, *Devising Consumption*. For the concept of economic life, see especially Zelizer, *Economic Lives*.
52. For example, Lendol Calder, *Financing the American Dream: A Cultural History of Consumer Credit* (Princeton: Princeton University Press, 1999); Sean O'Connell, *Credit and Community: Working-Class Debt in the UK Since 1880* (Oxford: Oxford University Press, 2009); Jan Logemann (ed.), *The Development of Consumer Credit in Global Perspective* (New York: Palgrave Macmillan, 2012); Sabine Effosse, *Le crédit à la consommation en France, 1947–1965* (Paris: IGPDE, 2014); Gunnar Trumbull, *Consumer Lending in France and America* (New York: Cambridge University Press, 2014); Josh Lauer, *Creditworthy: A History of Consumer Surveillance and Financial Identity in America* (New York: Columbia University Press, 2017).
53. Julia Ott, *When Wall Street Met Main Street: The Quest for an Investors' Democracy* (Cambridge, MA: Harvard University Press, 2011); Janice M. Traflet, *A Nation of Small Shareholders: Marketing Wall Street after World War II* (Baltimore: Johns Hopkins University Press, 2013); see also Paul Crosthwaite et al., *Invested: How Three Centuries of Stock Market Advice Reshaped Our Money, Markets, and Minds* (Chicago: University of Chicago Press, 2022).
54. Amy Edwards, *Are We Rich Yet? The Rise of Mass Investment Culture in Contemporary Britain* (Oakland, CA: University of California Press, 2022). See also Davies et al., 'Everyman Capitalist'.
55. See for example, Viviana Zelizer, *The Social Meaning of* Money (Princeton, NJ: Princeton University Press, 1994); Bill Maurer, *How Would You Like to Pay? How Technology Is Changing the Future of Money* (Durham, NC: Duke University Press, 2015), 33–34; Bill Maurer and Lana Swartz (eds.), *Paid: Tales of Dongles, Checks, and Other Money Stuff* (Cambridge, MA: The MIT Press, 2017).
56. Bernardo Batiz-Lazo, Thomas Haigh, and David L. Stearns, 'How the Future Shaped the Past: The Case of the Cashless Society', *Enterprise & Society*, 15, 1 (2014), 103–131; Sean H. Vanatta, 'Citibank, Credit Cards, and the Local Politics of National Consumer Finance, 1968–1991', *Business History Review*, 90, 1 (2016), 57–80; Lauer, *Creditworthy*; Rachel O'Dwyer, 'Cache Society: Transactional Records, Electronic Money, and Cultural Resistance', *Journal of Cultural Economy*, 12, 2 (2019), 133–153.
57. Matt K. Matsuda, *The Memory of the Modern* (New York and Oxford: Oxford University Press, 1996), 121; Keith Hart, *The Memory Bank* (London: Profile Books, 1999); O'Dwyer, 'Cache Society'; Rachel

O'Dwyer, *Tokens: The Future of Money in the Age of the Platform* (London: Verso, 2023).
58. Melinda Cooper and Liz McFall, 'Ten Years After: It's the Economy and Culture, Stupid!', *Journal of Cultural Economy*, 10, 1 (2017), 1–7.
59. Marieke de Goede, *Virtue, Fortune, and Faith: A Genealogy of Finance* (Minneapolis: University of Minnesota Press, 2005), xxvi; de Goede builds on Jenny Edkins, *Poststructuralism & International Relations* (Boulder, CO: Lynne Rienner Publisher, 1999), 8.
60. Terry Cook, 'Remembering the Future: Appraisal of Records and the Role of Archives in Constructing Social Memory', in *Archives, Documentation, and Institutions of Social Memory: Essays from the Sawyer Seminar*, ed. by Francis X. Blouin and William G. Rosenberg (Ann Arbor: University of Michigan Press, 2006), 171. Quoted in Maria Cavallin-Aijmer and Samuel Edquist, 'Historikerna och arkiven i teori och praktik', in *Historikerna i samhället. Roller och förändringsmönster*, ed. by David Ludvigsson and Martin Åberg (Hedemora: Gidlunds, 2021), 144. See also Terry Cook, 'The Archive(s) Is a Foreign Country: Historians, Archivists, and the Changing Archival Landscape', *The American Archivist*, 74, 2 (2011), 613.

Notes to Chapter 2

1. 'Nu lever vi i bankåldern, välkommen!', *Kontokuriren*, 1b (1968). Parts of this chapter are based on my article 'From Wage Earners to Financial Consumers: Class and Financial Socialisation in Sweden in the 1950s and 1960s', *Critique Internationale*, 69, 4 (2015), 99–118. https://doi.org/10.3917/crii.069.0099.
2. Björn Thodenius (ed.), *Teknisk utveckling i bankerna* (Stockholm: Kungliga Tekniska Högskolan, 2008), 13.
3. Cf. Helene Ducourant and Jeanne Lazarus, 'Credit in Society and in Sociology: On *The Bank and Its Customers* (Bourdieu, Boltanski, Chamboredon, 1963)', *European Journal of Sociology*, 64, 3 (2023), 385–416.
4. Centrum för Näringslivshistoria (hereafter CfN), Handelsbanken (hereafter HB), F4b:22, Den stora kontojakten 1969, 6.
5. Svenska Handelsbanken, *Årsredovisning* (Annual Report) (1967), 26; Svenska Handelsbanken, *Årsredovisning* (1970), 16–17.
6. CfN, HB, F4b:22, Den stora kontojakten 1969, 9. However, this market research by Handelsbanken points out that reliable statistics from all banks on accountholders before 1968 are missing.

7. David Stafford and Susan King, 'Banking on the Unbanked', *International Journal of Bank Marketing*, 1, 2 (1983), 27–28; Jacqueline Botterill, *Consumer Culture and Personal Finance* (Basingstoke, UK: Palgrave Macmillan, 2010), 119. See also Victoria Barnes and Lucy Newton, 'Women, Uniforms and Brand Identity in Barclays Bank', *Business History*, 64, 4 (2022), 803.
8. In addition to published material from the period (reports of official government inquiries, parliamentary papers and a broad range of banking periodicals), this chapter builds on the archives of two of the largest commercial banks, Handelsbanken (HB) and Skandinaviska Banken (SB), along with those of the Bankers' Association (Bankföreningen, hereafter BF), all in CfN. The bank archives also contain rich collections of promotional material and newspaper cuttings. The periodicals studied are from the same banking institutions: *Remissan* (Handelsbanken), *Din Bank* (Skandinaviska Banken) and *Ekonomisk Revy* (the Bankers' Association).
9. Paul Langley, *The Everyday Life of Global Finance: Saving and Borrowing in Anglo-America* (Oxford: Oxford University Press, 2008); Paul Langley and Andrew Leyshon, 'Financial Subjects: Culture and Materiality', *Journal of Cultural Economy*, 5, 4 (2012), 369–373; Peter Miller and Nikolas Rose, *Governing the Present: Administering Economic, Social, and Personal Life* (Cambridge: Polity, 2008).
10. Rob Aitken, *Performing Capital: Toward a Cultural Economy of Popular and Global Finance* (Basingstoke, UK: Palgrave Macmillan, 2007); Randy Martin, *Financialization of Daily Life* (Philadelphia: Temple University Press, 2002); Gordon Clark, *Pension Fund Capitalism* (Oxford: Oxford University Press, 2000); Langley, *The Everyday Life of Global Finance*; Nikolas Rose, 'Government and Control', *British Journal of Criminology*, 40, 2 (2000), 321–339; Nikolas Rose, *Powers of Freedom* (Cambridge: Cambridge University Press, 1999), Chapter 7; Michel Foucault, '*Governmentality*', in *The Foucault Effect: Studies in Governmentality*, ed. by Graham Burchell, Colin Gordon, and Peter Miller (Chicago: University of Chicago Press, 1991), 87–104.
11. Viviana Zelizer, *The Social Meaning of* Money (Princeton, NJ: Princeton University Press, 1994); Viviana Zelizer, *Economic Lives: How Culture Shapes the Economy* (Princeton: Princeton University Press, 2011). See also Jeanne Lazarus, 'La méthode de Viviana Zelizer: La famille réconciliée avec l'économie', *Archives de Philosophie*, 85, 4 (2022), 11–27 and Bill Maurer, *Mutual Life, Limited: Islamic Banking, Alternative Currencies, Lateral Reason* (Princeton: Princeton University Press, 2005).
12. Cf. Marion Fourcade and Kieran Healy, 'Classification Situations', *Accounting, Organizations and Society*, 38, 8 (2013), 559–572, who argue

that contemporary credit scoring in the US replaced traditional class-based categorisations.
13. CfN, HB, F6:227, 'P.M. angående olika former av service och nya verksamhetsfält för banken'.
14. 'Åsikter om bankernas annonser och kundtjänst', Gallup poll February 1949, 8, 51 (http://snd.gu.se/gallup, retrieved 29 February 2019). For social groups and categorisations, see Orsi Husz, 'Att räkna värdighet. Privatekonomi och medelklasskultur i mitten av 1900-talet', *Scandia*, 79, 1 (2013), 87–121 and Carl-Filip Smedberg, 'Class Divisions in Use: The Swedish Social Group Taxonomy as Difference Technology, 1911–1970', *Contemporary European History*, 33, 4 (2024), 1352–1364.
15. Mats Larsson and Gabriel Söderberg, *Finance and the Welfare State: Banking Development and Regulatory Principles in Sweden, 1900–2015* (Cham: Palgrave Macmillan, 2017), 76–77; Anders Forsell, *Moderna tider i sparbanken: Om organisatorisk omvandling i ett institutionellt perspektiv* (Stockholm: Nerenius & Santérus, 1992), 93; Ulf Olsson, *I utvecklingens centrum: Skandinaviska Enskilda Banken och dess föregångare 1856–1996* (Stockholm: Skandinaviska Enskilda Banken, 1997), 175–177; Ingvar Körberg, *Förnyelsen: Sparbankernas historia 1945–1980* (Stockholm: Ekerlid, 2006), 185f.
16. Tom Petersson, 'Samhälle och näringsliv med gemensamma mål', in *Det svenska näringslivets historia 1864–2014*, ed. by Lena Andersson-Skog and Mats Larsson (Stockholm: Dialogos, 2014), 471–478; Torbjörn Hessling, *Att spara eller inte spara—vilken fråga!: Den sparfrämjande verksamheten 1820–1970* (Stockholm: Sparfrämjandet, 1990).
17. Björn Thodenius (ed.), *IT i bank- och finanssektorn 1960–1985* (Stockholm: Kungl. Tekniska högskolan, 2008), 45. CfN, HB, F4f:6, 'Inrättande av ett Fältråd 2/2 1962'. See also, Ulf Olsson, *Bank, familj, företagande: Stockholms Enskilda bank 1946–1971* (Stockholm: EHF-Handelshögskolan, 1986), 171–179; Körberg, *Förnyelsen*, 94–95.
18. Olsson, *Bank, familj, företagande*, 171; Körberg, *Förnyelsen*, 94–97; CfN, HB, F4f:7, 'Marknad 3.1 milj. löntagare', *Impuls*, 2 (1968); CfN, HB, F4:11, 'Marketing Research inom AMS', internal memo, 29 March 1968; CfN, HB, F4f:6, 'Intressekontorsverksamhet m.m.' Fältrådet, 28 August 1962.
19. Klas Åmark, *Hundra år av välfärdspolitik. Väfärdsstatens framväxt i Norge och Sverige* (Umeå: Boréa, 2005), 87–129; Gunnar Richardson, *Svensk utbildningshistoria* (Lund, Studentlitteratur (1999 [1977]). Hessling, *Att spara eller inte spara*, 241.
20. CfN, SB, B9661, ads for child benefit account.
21. Olsson, *Bank, familj, företagande*, 171; Petersson, 'Samhälle och näringsliv', 471–478; Körberg, *Förnyelsen*, 127.

22. CfN, HB, F4f:7, 'En ny organisation ger effektivitet och resultat', *Impuls*, 6–7 (1967) and '5 frågor till nya säljplaneringschefen', *Impuls*, 1 (1968). For a similar development in bank marketing in other countries, see Susana Martínez-Rodríguez and Bernardo Batiz-Lazo, 'Gender and bankarization in Spain, 1949–1970', *Business History*, FirstView (2023), 1–30; Barnes and Newton, 'Women, Uniforms', 823; Botterill, *Consumer Culture and Personal Finance*, 100–131.
23. 'Buss på kunderna', *Din Bank*, 1–2 (1956); 'Drive in bank', *Din Bank*, 3 (1957); CfN, HB, F4f:7, 'Se på dina bankfönster. Andra gör det', *Impuls*, 1 (1967). See also CfN, SB, 6529 ('Pressklipp, Kampanjer 1967–71'); and Ulf Olsson, *I utvecklingens centrum: Skandinaviska Enskilda Banken och dess föregångare 1856–1996* (Stockholm: Skandinaviska Enskilda Banken, 1997), 177–178, 189.
24. Tom Petersson, 'Tillväxt, kriser och koncentration—det svenska banksystemet 1820–2005', in *Sverige—en social och ekonomisk historia*, ed. by Susanna Hedenborg and Mats Morell (Lund: Studentlitteratur, 2006), 384; Olsson, *I utvecklingens centrum*, 178.
25. CfN, HB, F4f:7, *Impuls*, 3–4 (1967). The Swedish word 'lön' is used for both salaries and wages. It is therefore not always possible to distinguish between the two in the Swedish sources, which often mean both, especially as this was also a time when weekly wages were increasingly replaced with monthly salaries.
26. CfN, HB, F4f:6, Protokoll från Fältrådets sammanträde (Minutes of the Field Council meeting), 27 February 1962; See also CfN, HB, F4f:7, 'Marknad: 3.1 miljoner löntagare', *Impuls*, 2 (1968).
27. CfN, HB, F5:161, 'Utdrag ur betänkande avgivet av stadskamrer O. Forsberg', in 'Lönen på checkräkning', folder containing material for of Handelsbanken's 1958 promotional campaign.
28. Utredningen om sparstimulerande åtgärder, *Betänkande med förslag beträffande ändrade former för utbetalning av löner till i statens tjänst anställda* (Stockholm: Finansdepartementet, 1960), 5, 12–13, 17–18. See, however, the comments of the Bank Inspection Board on the committee's report, 'cheques should not be used by households for routine purchases of consumer goods', quoted in DsFi (Ministry of Finance Publication Series) 1971:12, Sture Lundell, *PM angående åtgärder för att motverka checkmissbruket* (Stockholm: Finansdepartementet 1971), 4, hereafter DsFi 1971:12.
29. CfN, BF, Styrelsens protokoll (Minutes of the Board of the Bankers' Association), 14 March 1962, §52.
30. Utredningen om sparstimulerande åtgärder, *Betänkande med förslag beträffande ändrade former för utbetalning av löner till i statens tjänst anställda*,

21–26, 27–28; Olsson, *Bank, familj, företagande*, 171–188; Körberg, *Förnyelsen*, 94–99.
31. Forsell, *Moderna tider i sparbanken*, 90; Hessling, *Att spara eller inte spara*, 239.
32. *Bankerna* 1974 (Stockholm: Kungl. Bankinspektionen, 1974), 14: Approx. 2,137,000 accounts in commercial banks including the new PK bank. Hessling (*Att spara eller inte spara*, 239) gives an estimate of 870,000 accounts for wages in savings banks in 1970. Handelsbanken estimated that in 1968 Sweden had 3.1 million people earning a salary or wage. See CfN, HB, F4f:7, 'Marknad 3.1 milj. löntagare', *Impuls*, 2 (1968). Population data from *Statistisk Årsbok för Sverige 1971* [*Statistical Abstract of Sweden*] (Stockholm, SCB [Statistics Sweden], 1971), 28, 67.
33. CfN, BF, F2b:7, 'Checklönekunden—attityder och vanor' 1966, (Attitude Survey conducted by the Bankers' Association and Statistics Sweden), first page unpag. The youngest employees, temporary, agricultural and domestic workers, small business owners and their employees were often excluded from the bank salaries.
34. Kristina Lilja, 'The Deposit Market Revolution in Sweden', in *The Swedish Financial Revolution*, ed. by Anders Ögren (Basingstoke, UK: Palgrave Macmillan, 2010), 41–59. See also Tom Petersson, *Mellan det lokala och det globala: Det svenska banksystemet ur ett historiskt perspektiv* (Norrtälje: Roslagens sparbank, 2009).
35. CfN, BF, F2b:7, 'Checklönekunden—attityder och vanor' 1966, Table 1.2 (34b).
36. Jeanne Lazarus, *L'épreuve de l'argent. Banques, banquiers, clients* (Paris: Calmann-Lévy, 2012), esp. 28; Olivier Feiertag, 'La bancarisation de la société française dans les années 1968', in *Les Français et l'argent*, ed. by Alya Aglan, Olivier Feiertag, and Yannick Marec (Rennes: Presses Universitaires de Rennes, 2011), 163–175.
37. Christopher Frank, 'Cashless Pay, Deductions from Wages, and the Repeal of the Truck Acts in Great Britain, 1945–1986', *Labor History*, 61, 2 (2020), 126; Botterill, *Consumer Culture and Personal Finance*, 103; cf. Bernardo Bátiz-Lazo, Tobias Karlsson, and Björn Thodenius, 'The Origins of the Cashless Society: Cash Dispensers, Direct to Account Payments and the Development of Online Real-Time Networks, c. 1965–1985', *Essays in Economic & Business History*, 32 (2014), 106.
38. For collective enrolment in the 1990s in Eastern Europe, see, Akos Rona-Tas and Alya Guseva, *Plastic Money. Constructing Markets for Credit Cards in Eight Postcommunist Countries* (Stanford, CA: Stanford University Press, 2014), 71. See also Gilles Laferté, 'Economic Identification: A Contribution to a Comparative Socio-History of Credit Markets', *Economic Sociology: The European Electronic Newsletter*, 15, 3 (2014), 5–11 about a different

NOTES TO CHAPTER 2   221

model in France, where workers received paycheques and therefore had to open bank accounts individually.
39. CfN, BF, F2b:7, 'Checklönekunden—attityder och vanor' 1966, first page unpag.
40. 'Kundkrets med checkar gör butiken till bank', *Fri Köpenskap*, 12 February 1958, press cutting in CfN, SB, F:71/43 (141).
41. Jan Wallander, *Forskaren som bankdirektör* (Stockholm: SNS, 1998), 31.
42. CfN, HB, F4f:7, 'Löneutbetalningar—grunden för fortsatt inlåning', *Impuls*, 2 (1968).
43. CfN, BF, F2b:7, 'Checklönekunden—attityder och vanor' 1966, Questions 11–14. See also CfN, BF, Styrelsens protokoll (Minutes of the Board of the Bankers' Association), 14 September 1966, §140.
44. CfN, SB, F:71/43 (141), 'P.M. angående löneckräkningar 19 Jan. 1959'. See also 'Hur har det lyckats', *Din bank*, 4 (1957) on the transition to bank salaries for the firm's white-collar employees; CfN, HB, F4f:7, 'Fackföreningar inom LO. Minneslista och argument', *Impuls*, 2 (1968).
45. Svenska Cellulosa AB and AB Hägglund & Söner.
46. CfN, HB, F5:161, 'Noteringar från direktionsberedning', 12 December 1963.
47. Ibid.
48. CfN, HB, F4f:6, 'Protokoll fört vid Handelsbankens Fältråds sammanträde', 2 May 1963.
49. Thodenius, *IT i bank- och finanssektorn*, 45.
50. CfN, HB, F4f:7, 'Löneutbetalningar—grunden för fortsatt inlåning', *Impuls*, 2 (1968).
51. 'Vi betalar med check', *Göteborgs Handels- och Sjöfartstidning (GHST)*, 27 January 1959, see also 'Checklön till 1,800 Volvoanställda', *Svenska Dagbladet (SvD)*, 31 January 1959, press cuttings in CfN, SB, Ö1:28.
52. 'Checklön populär', *Norrköpings tidningar*, 4 September 1964, press cutting in CfN, SB, vol. 'Tidningsurklipp 1964'. See also press cuttings in CfN, SB, Ö1:28 (1958–1959), for example: '400 på SAAB får lön på checkkonto', *Elfsborgs läns annonsblad*, 29 May 1958; 'Check istället för lönepåse', *Östergötlands Folkblad*, 5 February 1959.
53. 'Hur har det lyckats?', *Din Bank*, 4 (1957).
54. Tore Browaldh, 'Checken allmänheten och vi', *HB Remissan*, 7 (1958) and 'Hur har det lyckats?', *Din Bank*, 4 (1957).
55. This was discussed as early as 1953 by the bankers at Skandinaviska Banken. At that time, they rejected the idea of offering payment of wages by means of cheque accounts, exactly because of the control aspect. CfN, SB, F:71/43(141), 'Ang. lönebetalning hos företagen', 4 April 1953.
56. Hans Bergström, 'Check i snabbköpet—ingen utopi', *Din Bank*, 5–6 (1956).

57. CfN, SB, F:71/43(141), Letter from Bank Inspector Kurt Wulff to commercial banks, 8 April 1960; see also a commented press cutting 'Bank går till arbetsgivare om checkkonto överskrides', *GHST*, 26 March 1960 in the same volume.
58. '400 på SAAB får lön på checkkonto', *Elfsborgs läns annonsblad*, 29 May 1958, press cutting in CfN, SB, Ö1:28 (1958–1959); Bo Dahlgren, 'Checklön till tjänstemän', *Affärsekonomi*, 16 (1956), press cutting in CfN, SB, F:71/43 (141).
59. 'Allmänheten mera banksinnad genom checklön', *HB Remissan*, 4 (1959), 6–7.
60. 'Checken allmänheten och vi', *HB Remissan*, 7 (1958), 3; Advertisements in CfN, HB, F5:161 and CfN, SB, F:71/43 (141), see, for example, the promotional leaflet 'Check—bekväma pengar'.
61. CfN, HB, F5:161, for example folder 'Lön på checkräkning' (1958) and leaflet 'Låt oss betala Edra löner' (1958). See also Kungliga biblioteket (hereafter KB), Ephemera, Handelsbanken 1962–1965, 'Checklön—Högre lön'; 'Penningens sorti. Elektronisk plånbok kommer om femtio år', *Bankvärlden*, 2 (1959), 32. Cheques and cashlessness were also discussed in newspapers, for example 'Kontanter överflödiga om 20 år? Check och kreditkort istället', *Söderhamns Tidning*, 30 March 1960.
62. For shifts in financial ethos see Ducourant and Lazarus, 'Credit in Society and in Sociology'.
63. Ronny Ambjörnsson, *Den skötsamme arbetaren: idéer och ideal i ett norrländskt sågverkssamhälle 1880–1930* (Stockholm: Carlsson, 1988).
64. CfN, HB, F5:161, folder 'Lönen på checkräkning' and leaflet 'Låt oss betala edra löner'; CfN, SB, F:71/43 (141), a series of leaflets called 'Check-lön-ar sig'; KB, Ephemera, Handelsbanken 1962–1965, folder 'Checklön-Högre lön'.
65. CfN, SB, F:71/43 (141), 'Check—bekväma pengar', promotional leaflet 1962. 'Checklön populär', *Norrköpings tidningar*, 4 September 1964, press cutting in CfN, SB, 'Tidningsurklipp 1964'.
66. 'Lön på checkkonto', *Ny tid*, 15 January 1959, in CfN, SB, F:71/43 (141).
67. CfN, HB, F5:161, 'Utdrag ur betänkande avgivet av stadskamrer O. Forssberg, vilket sedan ledde till lönecheckräkningens införande i Kalmar' (Extract from the report presented by City Treasurer O. Forssberg, which led to the introduction of cheque salaries in the city of Kalmar), 5. See also advertisements in the same volume.
68. Tore Browaldh, 'Checken allmänheten och vi', *HB Remissan*, 7 (1958); CfN, HB, F5:161, Letter to branch office managers 1958 in the folder 'Lönen på checkräkning'; CfN, HB, F5:161, 'Utdrag ur betänkande avgivet av stadskamrer O. Forssberg', 5; 'Varför, Hur och Vad ska vi sälja' and 'Gör

varje kund till totalkund', both in *Din Bank*, 5 (1963). See also 'Vad är PR?', *Remissan*, 2 (1960); 'Här skall säljas!' *Remissan*, 9–10 (1964); and 'Bankernas nya aktietjänst ökar omsättningen på börsen', *Veckans affärer*, 25 July 1968.
69. 'Så arbetar Din Bank—Den är ett Varuhus i Ekonomi', in *Skånsk Marknad*, undated cutting 1966, in CfN, SB, Ö1:26. CfN, HB, F4f:7, 'Ett varuhus i tjänster', *Impuls*, 4 (1968). See also Orsi Husz, 'Golden Everyday: Housewifely Consumerism and the Domestication of Banks in 1960s Sweden', *Le Mouvement Social*, 250, 1 (2015), 41–63.
70. 'Sparpuritanen är död—leve målspararen. Bankerna fångar in spardrömmarna med konton i olika förpackning', *Veckans affärer*, 21 November 1968. See also 'Bankernas nya aktietjänst ökar omsättningen på börsen', *Veckans affärer*, 25 July 1968.
71. CfN, HB, F4f:7, 'Löneutbetlaningar—grunden för fortsatt inlåning', *Impuls*, 2 (1968). See also Hessling, *Att spara eller inte spara*, 131; Wallander, *Forskaren som bankdirektör*, 31.
72. 'Sparpuritanen är död—leve målspararen', *Veckans affärer*, 21 November 1968.
73. 'Bankernas nya aktietjänst ökar omsättningen på börsen', *Veckans affärer*, 25 July 1968.
74. Orsi Husz, David Larsson Heidenblad, and Elin Åström Rudberg, 'Wage Earners, Taxpayers or Everyman Capitalists? The Making of a Mutual Fund Culture in Sweden', in *Nordic Neoliberalisms*, ed. by Jenny Andersson and Chris Howell (forthcoming).
75. Turo-Kimmo Lehtonen and Mika Pantzar, 'The Ethos of Thrift: The Promotion of Bank Saving in Finland During the 1950s', *Journal of Material Culture*, 7, 2 (2002), 211–231.
76. In 1965, KF had approximately 1.36 million members (compare to 2.8 million households in Sweden). Kooperativ krönika, online history resource; *Statistisk Årsbok 1968* (Stockholm: SCB, 1968), 143.
77. Utredningen om sparstimulerande åtgärder, *Betänkande med förslag beträffande ändrade former för utbetalning av löner till i statens tjänst anställda*, 11, 13; SOU 1961:2, Utredningen om sparstimulerande åtgärder, *Sparstimulerande åtgärder: Betänkande* (Stockholm: Esselte, 1961), 52–53.
78. On similar discussions in Great Britain: Botterill, *Consumer Culture and Personal Finance*, 126; Edward Higgs, *Identifying the English: A History of Personal Identification 1500 to the Present* (London: Bloomsbury, 2011), 175.
79. CfN, SB, Ö1:27, 'PM betr. pressen och lördagsstängningen', commentary by the Bankers' Association 21 September 1964. For critical articles, see press cuttings in the same volume: 'Dålig bankservice', *Köpmannen*, 4 June

1964; 'Aldrig på en lördag', *Sydsvenska Dagbladet*, 28 July 1964; 'Checklön besvärligt vi är inte vana ännu att vara utan pengar', *Örebrokuriren*, 29 June 1964; 'Skandalöst med stängda banker', *Sydsvenska Dagbladet*, 4 June 1964.

80. 'Allmänheten och affärsbankerna', *Ekonomisk Revy*, 4 (1965); CfN, SB, Ö1:27, 'Pressen och bankernas lördagsstängning' (commentary by the Bankers' Association 23 August 1966); see also press cuttings in the same volume: P.G. Bergström, 'Är checklönen obekväm?', *Dagens Nyheter (DN)*, 6 April 1965; 'Klart för kvällsöppet', *Aftonbbladet (AB)*, 1 June 1965.

81. For example, press cuttings in CfN, SB, Ö1:27, 'Bankfri lördag ej enda serviceförsämringen', *DN*, 8 July 1966; 'Banktrötta butiksägare hotar med checkbojkott', *DN*, 13 August 1966; 'Bankerna sviker sina nya kunder', *Expressen*, 28 June 1966; 'Bankbojkott', *Sydsvenska Dagbladet*, 28 June 1966; 'Obekväm checklön', *DN*, 4 April 1965; 'Obekväm checklön' by Olof Rundin, *DN*, 27 April 1965; 'Inget slut på checklöneeländet', *ST Ekonomi*, 11 February 1965; 'Checksystemet' (letter to the editor), *Sydsvenska Dagbladet*, 28 April 1964.

82. 'Ströms startar 'bankservice' för kontokunderna', untitled cutting, 18 December 1966, in CfN, SB, F:71/43 (141).

83. For example, 'Dragkamp om checken', *Göteborgstidningen*, 9 April 1961, press cutting in CfN, SB, F:71/43 (141).

84. 'Checklön besvärligt vi är inte vana ännu att vara utan pengar', *Örebrokuriren*, 29 June 1964.

85. CfN, BF, F2b:7, 'Checklönekunden—attityder och vanor' 1966, p. 1 and Teknisk del (Technical part), p. 16, Questionnaire VI.46, Table 1.1.

86. See, for example, CfN, SB, F:71/43 (141), 'Check—bekväma pengar', promotional leaflet 1962.

87. 'Vad göra åt bankerna?', *Köpmannen*, 4 August 1966, press cutting in CfN, SB, Ö1:27. See also DsFi 1971:12, 42.

88. Olof Ernsell, 'Checklöneräkningen—ett räntabilitetsproblem', *Ekonomisk Revy*, 2 (1965).

89. 'Checklöneavgift inte aktuell', *Enköpings-Posten*, 11 March 1965, press cutting in CfN, SB, Ö1:27.

90. 'allmän ilska', 'en vilja att missförstå', in 'Checklöneavgift inte aktuell', *Enköpings-Posten*, 11 March 1965, press cutting in CfN, SB, Ö1:27. See also 'Löntagarna vill inte vara med om bankerna tar checklöneavgift', *GHST*, 4 February 1965, and similar articles in the same volume.

91. 'Dödsdom över checklönen', *Kvällsposten*, 20 March 1965, press cutting in CfN, SB, Ö1:27.

92. 'Allmänheten och bankerna', *DN*, 4 May 1965, press cutting in CfN, SB, Ö1:2.

93. For example 'Avgift på checklön', *Stockholms-Tidningen (ST)*, 4 February 1965; 'De privatägda', *AB*, 3 February 1965; 'Hysch-hysch kring checklönerna', *Köpmannen*, 11 February 1965; 'Bankbojkott', *Sydsvenka Dagbladet*, 28 June 1966, press cuttings in CfN, SB, Ö1:27. See also CfN, BF, F2b:6, 'Postverket och checksystemet med särskilt hänsyn till checklönen' (October 1966), 14.
94. Tekniska Museet, Från datamaskin till IT (From computing machines to IT), Interview 127 (Ingvar Anderberg), 17 October 2007, 11.
95. 'Bankerna vill ta checkavgift—en bromsar', *ST,* 3 February 1965; 'Checklöneavgift inte aktuell', *Enköpings-Posten*, 11 March 1965, press cuttings in CfN, SB, Ö1:27; 'Allmänheten och affärsbankerna', Editorial in *Ekonomisk Revy*, 4 (1965). See also 'Allmänheten och bankerna', *DN*, 4 May 1965, press cutting in CfN, SB, Ö1:2.
96. The parliamentary committee (*Första lagutskottet*) assigned to prepare the matter did not recommend criminalisation. Motion i Andra kammaren (Private Member's Bill in the Second Chamber) 1965 no. 380, by Börjesson; Första lagutskottets utlåtande (Statement of the first Parliamentary Committee on Law) 1965 no. 23.
97. See press cuttings from 1965 in CfN, SB, Ö1:27.
98. Motion i Andra Kammaren (Private Member's Bill in the Second Chamber) 1965 no. 380, by Börjesson. For the criticism, see press cuttings from 1965 in CfN, SB, Ö1:27; and Första lagutskottets utlåtande (Statement of the first Parliamentary Committee on Law) 1965 no. 23, statements from referral bodies, p. 10. Another measure the banks were urged to undertake was to provide cheque account holders with secure identity documents. See further in Chapter 6.
99. Första lagutskottets utlåtande 1965 no. 23, 12 and 'Dödsdom över checklönen', *Kvällsposten*, 20 March 1965, press cutting in CfN, SB, Ö1:27.
100. 'The Government's directives' (1968) for the Inquiry into cheque wages, see DsFi 1971:12, 2.
101. CfN, BF, F2b:6, 'PM ang. checkrörelsen och regeringsrådet Lundells utredning', 17 September 1971, 2.
102. For example, 'Debatt: Barnens fickpengar' and 'Rätt frys, god affär för familj', *Kontokuriren*, 3 (1967); 'Svårt att beräkna den exakta räntan' and 'Räkna själv ut kreditkostnaden!', *Kontokuriren*, extra issue (1967); 'Vill ni ha hjälp med deklarationen', *Kontokuriren*, 1 (1971).
103. 'Kung Konsument har fritt val. Utnyttja chansen i egen favör'; 'Vad ser banken på när den bedömer?'; 'Topp i utgifter kan delas. Den ger handlingsfrihet' and 'Lånerätt ger balans i budgeten', all in *Kontokuriren*, 1b (1968); 'Ni tjänar mer på pengarna ju mer ni vet om dem', *Kontokuriren*, 3b (1968); 'Aktieaktuellt'; 'Vill ni ha Köpkort', *Kontokuriren*, 4 (1968); 'Är det fult att låna pengar' and 'Sprid kostnad

med Köpkort', *Kontokuriren*, 1c (1969). For neoliberalism, consumer credit and consumer sovereignty see Donncha Marron, *Consumer Credit in the United States: A Sociological Perspective from the 19th Century to the Present* (Basingstoke, UK: Palgrave Macmillan, 2009); Christopher Payne, *The Consumer, Credit and Neoliberalism: Governing the Modern Economy* (London: Routledge, 2012); Niklas Olsen, *The Sovereign Consumer: A New Intellectual History of Neoliberalism* (Cham, Switzerland: Palgrave Macmillan, 2019).

104. Fourcade and Healy, 'Classification situations'.
105. 'Checken blir åter giltig i handeln', *SvD*, 11 November 1972; 'Småcheckar—missbruk', *SvD*, 23 December 1978; 'Vanlig löntagare dyr kund', *DN*, 28 December 1978.
106. Björn Thodenius, Bernardo Batiz-Lazo, and Tobias Karlsson, 'The History of the Swedish ATM: Sparfrämjandet and Metior', in *History of Nordic Computing 3: Third IFIP WG 9.7 Conference*, ed. by Giuseppe Impagliazzo et al. (Heidelberg: Springer, 2011), 92–100. For ATMs, see Bernardo Batiz-Lazo, *Cash and Dash: How ATMs and Computers Changed Banking* (Oxford: Oxford University Press, 2018).
107. DsFi 1971:12, 66; see also informational leaflets for Köpkort and letters to and from *Konsumentombudsmannen* (the Consumer Ombudsman) about the banks' advertisements for Köpkort as a substitute for cheques, in Riksarkivet (Swedish National Archives), Checklöneutredningen (Government Inquiry into Cheque Account Salaries and Wages). See also ads by *Kreditbanken* for Köpkort, *Kontokuriren*, 1 (1968) and 4 (1968). CfN, BF, Styrelsens protokoll (Minutes of the Board of the Bankers' Association), 20 September 1967, §164.

NOTES TO CHAPTER 3

1. This chapter builds in part on the following articles: Orsi Husz, 'Golden Everyday: Housewifely Consumerism and the Domestication of Banks in 1960s Sweden', *Le Mouvement Social*, 250, 1 (2015), 41–63; Orsi Husz, 'The Birth of the Finance Consumer: Feminists, Bankers and the Re-Gendering of Finance in Mid-Twentieth-Century Sweden', *Contemporary European History*, 33, 4 (2024), 1332–1351.
2. Rob Aitken, *Performing Capital: Toward a Cultural Economy of Popular and Global Finance* (Basingstoke, UK: Palgrave Macmillan, 2007), 201.
3. In addition to Aitken, *Performing Capital* see, for example, Randy Martin, *Financialization of Daily Life* (Philadelphia: Temple University Press, 2002), esp. 14; Gordon Clark, *Pension Fund Capitalism* (Oxford: Oxford University Press, 2000); Paul Langley, *The Everyday Life of Global Finance: Saving and Borrowing in Anglo-America* (Oxford: Oxford University Press,

2008); Ismail Erturk et al., 'The Democratisation of Finance? Promise, Outcomes and Conditions', *Review of International Political Economy*, 14, 4 (2007), 553–575; Paul Langley and Andrew Leyshon. 'Financial Subjects: Culture and Materiality', *Journal of Cultural Economy*, 5, 4 (2012), 369–373.

4. Viviana Zelizer, 'How I Became a Relational Economic Sociologist and What Does That Mean?', *Politics & Society*, 40, 2 (2012), 145–174; Viviana Zelizer, *Economic Lives: How Culture Shapes the Economy* (Princeton: Princeton University Press, 2011), 407–408; Nina Bandelj, Paul James Morgan, and Elizabeth Sowers, 'Hostile Worlds or Connected Lives? Research on the Interplay Between Intimacy and Economy', *Sociology Compass*, 9, 2 (2015), 115–127.

5. In Handelsbanken's archives (hereafter HB) at the Centrum för Näringslivhistoria (Centre for Business History, Stockholm, CfN) the materials from the women's conferences are collected in three unsorted volumes, all marked 'Marknadsavdelningen F4:43'. They include, for example, internal memos, photographs, synopses, manuscripts of talks and diary entries by one of the speakers. Audience reception was indirectly documented in the media coverage, in surveys and by the conference speakers. Additional materials from the archives of HB and of Skandinaviska Banken (hereafter SB) were used, and I also searched the banking press for topics related to women and banking.

6 For example, Jacqueline Botterill, *Consumer Culture and Personal Finance* (Basingstoke, UK: Palgrave Macmillan, 2010), 100–101; Sabine Effosse, 'Financial Empowerment for Married Women in France', *Quaderni Storici*, 56, 1 (2021), 117–141; Victoria Barnes and Lucy Newton, 'Women, Uniforms and Brand Identity in Barclays Bank', *Business History*, 64, 4 (2022), 801–830; Susana Martínez-Rodríguez and Bernardo Batiz-Lazo, 'Gender and Bankarization in Spain, 1949–1970', *Business History*, FirstView (2023), 1–30.

7. Kajsa Holmberg and Maria Stanfors, *Setting a Trend: Feminisation of the Commercial Bank Sector in Sweden, 1864–1975* (Stockholm: EHF, 2011); Tom Petersson, 'Women, Money and the Financial Revolution', in *Women and Their Money 1700–1950*, ed. by Anne Laurence, Josephine Maltby, and Janette Rutterford (London: Routledge, 2009).

8. See Swedish banking adverts from the 1940s in CfN, SB, B7a:3 and CfN, HB, F6v:3. For women being afraid of banks, see also 'Kan ni hålla allt i huvudet', illustrated advert by Skandinaviska Banken and 'Har ni bankskräck?', ad by Handelsbanken, both in *Hertha*, 43, 4 (1956).

9. Husz, 'The Birth of the Finance Consumer'.

10. Effosse, 'Financial empowerment for married women'.

11. Martínez-Rodriguez and Batiz-Lazo, 'Gender and bankarization in Spain'.

12. Nancy M. Robertson, 'The Principle of Sound Banking and Financial Noblesse Oblige: Women's Departments in US Banks at the Turn of the Twentieth Century', in *Women and Their Money: Essays on Women and Finance*, ed. by Anne Laurence, Josephine Maltby, and Jeanette Rutherford (London and New York: Routledge, 2009), 243–249. The Swedish banking literature reported with interest about women's departments in banks, seen as an American PR feature, 'Allmänheten och bankerna i USA', *Ekonomisk revy*, 5 (1950), 449–52. Debra Michals, 'The Buck Stops Where? 1970s Feminist Credit Unions, Women's Banks, and the Gendering of Money', *Business and Economy On-line*, 16 (2018); and 'Women's Bank Sets Trust Company Plan', *New York Times*, 27 November 1973.
13. The law applied to marriages effectuated after 1920. Kari Melby, Anna-Birte Ravn, and Christina Carlsson Wetterberg (eds.), *Gender Equality and Welfare Politics in Scandinavia* (Bristol: The Policy Press, 2009), 231 or more in detail: Chapters 1–3, 7. See also Zara Bersbo, '*Rätt för kvinnan att blifva människa–fullt och helt': Svenska kvinnors ekonomiska medborgarskap 1921–1971* (Växjö: Linnéuniversitetet, 2012); Christina Florin and Lars Kvarnström (eds.), *Kvinnor på gränsen till medborgarskap: Genus, politik och offentlighet 1800–1950* (Stockholm: Atlas, 2001); Åsa Lundqvist, *Familjen i den svenska* modellen (Umeå: Boréa, 2007).
14. Bersbo, '*Rätt för kvinnan*', Part 4.
15. See statistics in Melby et al., *Gender Equality and Welfare Politics*, 232. Women's labour force participation in percent of the female population, Sweden (compared to OECD Europe): 1960: 50.1 percent (cf. 44 percent in OECD Europe); 1968: 56.6 percent (cf. 43 percent in OECD Europe); 1974: 64.9 percent (cf. 46 percent in OECD Europe).
16. Martínez-Rodriguez and Batiz-Lazo, 'Gender and bankarization in Spain'.
17. For a similar argument, see Barnes and Newton, 'Women, uniforms': in the late 1970s Barclays bank used female personal bankers to signal and offer friendliness and a welcoming, warm atmosphere.
18. Quote from CfN, HB, F6v:9, 'Handelsbankens reklamsituation 1954/55'. See also discussion on 'dynamic advertising' ('dynamisk reklam') in CfN, HB, F6v:8, 'Ojusterade anteckningar från sammanträde med reklamkommittén i Svenska Handelsbanken', 12 January 1955, 2.
19. CfN, HB, F6v:3, 'Noteringar från Bidragskommitténs sammanträde, 17 november 1947, å Bankföreningen'; 'PM angående bankens reklam'; 'Rapport över en marknadsundersökning beträffande AB Svenska Handelsbankens annonsering' 1949. See also Tom Björklund, *Reklamen i svensk marknad 1920–1965* (Stockholm: Norstedt & Söner, 1967), 89 on the general tendency in the late 1940s among advertising companies to reduce the number of goodwill adverts. This was especially valid for banks.
20. CfN, HB, F6v:3, 'PM angående bankens reklam'.

21. Ibid.
22. CfN, HB, F6v:3, Letter by Enfrid Browaldh, 19 March 1948. For the opinion-shaping activities by organised business interests in the name of free enterprise, see Rikard Westerberg, *Socialists at the Gate: Swedish Business and the Defense of Free Enterprise, 1940–1985* (Stockholm: Stockholm School of Economics, 2020); and on the idea of the market economy in this mobilisation, see Jenny Andersson, 'Neoliberalism from Within. The Business Fund and the Struggle for Market Ideology in Sweden', *Contemporary European History*, FirstView (2025), 1–17. The concept of public relations had just about been introduced in Sweden, see *Företagets Public Relations. Föredrag hållna 17–18 November 1948* (Svenska Reklamförbundet: Stockholm, 1949).
23. For example, adverts for bank accounts for the child benefit in CfN, SB, unsorted advertising material. Jan Wallander, *Forskaren som bankdirektör* (Stockholm: SNS, 1998), 31; 'Sparpuritanen är död—leve målspararen, Bankerna fångar in spardrömmarna med konton i olika förpackning', *Veckans affärer*, 21 November 1968. See also CfN, HB, F4f:7, 'Sälj & välj', *Impuls*, 5 (1967).
24. Gøsta Esping-Andersen, *The Three Worlds of Welfare Capitalism* (Cambridge: Polity, 1990); Klas Åmark, *Hundra år av välfärdspolitik. Väfärdsstatens framväxt i Norge och Sverige* (Umeå: Boréa, 2005), 87–127.
25. There are other points of connection between consumer banking and the Swedish system of social welfare, such as the pension system and the new holiday legislation in 1963, which gave rise to a range of holiday accounts combining savings and loans. Admittedly, the savings banks' 'savings propaganda' had included images of children and families earlier, but the only product they offered at the time was the savings account.
26. CfN, HB, F6v:9, 'Handelsbankens reklamsituation vid årskiftet 1954/55'.
27. 'Åsikter om bankernas annonser och kundtjänst', Gallup-poll February 1949, 8, 51 (http://snd.gu.se/gallup, retrieved 29 February 2019).
28. Klas Åmark, 'Familj, försörjning och livslopp under 1900-talet', in *Familjeangelägenheter: Modern historisk forskning om välfärdsstat, genus och politik*, ed. by Helena Bergman and Peter Johansson (Eslöv: Symposion, 2002), 243–258, esp. 252–253.
29. 'Kvinnor och pengar', see newspaper cuttings from 1958 in CfN, SB, Ö1:28, for example 'Kvinnor lär sig ekonomi', *Göteborgs Tidningen*, 4 February 1958. See also 'PR på sitt sätt', *Din Bank*, 5–6 (1961).
30. Husz, 'The Birth of the Finance Consumer'. For FBA, see Ulla Manns, *Den sanna frigörelsen* (Eslöv, Symposion, 1997). See also Pernilla Jonsson and Silke Neusinger, *Gendered Money. Financial Organization in Women's Movement* (New York: Berghahn Books, 2012).

31. For example, 'Hushållspengar i banken bättre än i handväskan', *Lunds Dagblad*, 20 March 1958, press cutting in CfN, SB; Ö1:28; 'bankminded' women in 'Husmödrarna kan lätta på kreditrestriktionerna', *Norrlands-Posten*, 20 October 1956, press cutting in CfN, SB, Ö1:2. 'Bankminded kvinna är samhällsgagnande', *Katrineholmskuriren*, 2 March 1959, press cutting in CfN, SB; Ö1:28.
32. Husz, 'The Birth of the Finance Consumer'.
33. Husz, 'The Birth of the Finance Consumer'; CfN, SB, Ö1:2, Programme, planning, memos, press cuttings.
34. 'Charm och pengar', *Norrländska Socialdemokraten*, 10 October 1956, press cutting in CfN, SB, Ö1:2; 'Charm och pengar lockade fullsatta hus', *Din Bank*, 5–6 (1956).
35. The production of such films continued until the early 1970s. Boel Berner, *Sakernas tillstånd: Kön, klass, teknisk expertis* (Stockholm: Carlsson, 1996), Ch. 4; Anne Marit Myrstad, 'Thrift and Traces of Work: On Housewife Films and Sales Talk', in *Twentieth-Century Housewives: Meanings and Implications of Unpaid Work*, ed. by Gro Hageman and Hege Roll-Hansen (Oslo: Oslo Academic Press, 2005), 110.
36. CfN, HB, F4:43, 'Kontakt med kvinnoorganisationer', memo 30 June 1960 from Lennart Oscarsson to Dir. Erik Lindström; CfN, HB, F4:43, 'Förslag till Gyllene Vardagar' 1963; CfN, HB, F4:10, 'Anteckningar från sammanträde om GV. Försäljning till kvinnliga målgrupper', 8 April 1969.
37. CfN, HB, F4:43, Proposal from the PR department of the evening newspaper *Expressen*, undated.
38. CfN, HB, F4:43, 'Inledningsanförande till Svenska Handelsbankens "Gyllene Vardag"'.
39. CfN, HB, F4:43, 'Dagboksanteckningar från Färgrika och Gyllene vardagar' (diary entries) by Maud Retuerswärd.
40. Ibid.
41. CfN, HB, F4:43, for example: 'Internt meddelande ang: Gyllene Vardag, Uddevalla'; 'Minneslista'; 'P.M. Gyllene vardag Örnsköldsvik'.
42. 'Varför konsulenter—hur arbetar de?', *Remissan*, 8 (1965).
43. Ibid.; '19 män på fältet', *Din Bank*, 6 (1962); Wallander, *Forskaren som bankdirektör*, 124.
44. CfN, HB, F4:43, 'Kontakt med kvinnoorganisationer', memo 30 June 1960 from L. Oscarsson to Dir. E. Lindström.
45. CfN, HB, F4:43, 'Dagboksanteckningar från Färgrika och Gyllene vardagar' by Maud Reuterswärd.
46. CfN, HB, F4:43, 'Gyllene vardagsdeltagare—en profilundersökning'.
47. See, for example, CfN, HB, F4:43, Programme for Conference 'Gyllene vardagskväll' in Huddinge 24 November 1965; 'Gyllene vardagskväll', *Jönköpingsposten*, 22 April 1966, press cutting in the same volume.

48. CfN, HB, F4:43, 'Dagboksanteckningar från Färgrika och Gyllene vardagar' by M. Reuterswärd.
49. For Maud Reuterswärd, see https://sverigesradio.se/artikel/3838168; 'Maud Reuterswärd 1920–1980', in *Svenskt kvinnobiografiskt lexikon* (Online resource, article by Birger Hedén), www.skbl.se/en/article/MaudReutersward (retrieved 2 May 2024).
50. Viviana Zelizer, *The Purchase of Intimacy* (Princeton & Oxford: Princeton University Press, 2005), for example, 20–29.
51. On these two persons and the consumer discourses of the period, see Orsi Husz, 'Passionate About Things: The Swedish Debate on Throwawayism', *Nordic Historical Review/Revue d'histoire Nordique*, 12, 1 (2011), 135–160.
52. CfN, HB, F4:43, Versions of printed programmes and preparatory notes.
53. Brita Lövgren, *Hemarbete som politik: Diskussioner om hemarbete, Sverige 1930–40-talen och tillkomsten av Hemmens Forskningsinstitut* (Stockholm: Almqvist & Wiksell, 1993); Brita Åkerman et al. (eds.), *Kunskap för vår vardag: Forskning och utbildning för hemmen* (Stockholm: Akademilitteratur, 1984); Orsi Husz, 'Spara, Slösa och alla de andra', in *Signums svenska kulturhistoria, 1900-talet*, ed. by Jacob Christenson (Stockholm: Atlantis, 2009), 279–329; Iselin Theien, 'Shopping for the "People's Home": Consumer Planning in Norway and Sweden After the Second World War', in *The Expert Consumer*, ed. by Alain Chatriot, Marie-Emmanuelle Chessel, and Matthew Hilton (Adelshot: Ashgate, 2006).
54. Helena Mattsson, 'Designing the Reasonable Consumer: Standardization and Personalization in Swedish Functionalism', in *Swedish Modernism: Architecture, Consumption and the Welfare State*, ed. by Helena Mattsson and Sven-Olov Wallenstein (London: Black Dog Publishing, 2010), 74.
55. Peder Aléx, *Den rationella konsumenten: KF som folkuppfostrare 1899–1939* (Stockholm/Stehag: Symposion, 1994); Peder Aléx, *Konsumera rätt—ett svenskt ideal: Behov, hushållning och* konsumtion (Lund: Studentlitteratur, 2003); Orsi Husz, 'The Morality of Quality: Assimilating Material Mass Culture in Twentieth Century Sweden', *Journal of Modern European History*, 10, 2 (2012), 152–181. See also Yvonne Hirdman, *Att lägga livet till rätta: Studier i svensk folkhemspolitik* (Stockholm: Carlssons, 1990), 95–99, 197–203.
56. Richard Swedberg, 'The Centrality of Materiality', in *Living in a Material World: Economic Sociology Meets Science and Technology Studies*, ed. by Trevor J. Pinch and Richard Swedberg (Cambridge, MA: MIT Press, 2008), 80; see also Nancy Berlage, 'The Establishment of an Applied Social Science. Home Economics, Science and Reform at Cornell University, 1870–1930', in *Gender and American Social Science: The Formative Years*, ed. by Helene Silverberg (Princeton: Princeton University Press, 1998);

Nancy Folbre, *Greed, Lust & Gender: A History of Economic Ideas* (Oxford: Oxford University Press, 2009), 258–260.
57. Berner, *Sakernas tillstånd*, 246. It was not until 1977 that the institution originally called the School of Domestic Economics (1895, Fackskolan för huslig ekonomi), and later the School of Domestic Education (1961, Seminariet för huslig utbildning), became a university department in Domestic Science, in Uppsala. The profile of all these institutions, however, was nutrition, textiles and childcare rather than finances, and today the academic discipline is split into Food and Nutrition studies and Textile studies. (https://www.uu.se/institution/kostvetenskap/om-oss/historik, retrieved 3 May 2024).
58. Lövgren, *Hemarbete som politik*; Berner, *Sakernas tillstånd*; Åkerman et al., *Kunskap för vår vardag*; Hirdman, *Att lägga livet till rätta*; Cf. Joy Parr and Gunilla Ekberg, 'Mrs Consumer and Mr Keynes in Postwar Canada and Sweden', *Gender & History*, 8, 2 (1996), 212–230.
59. Husz, 'Passionate About Things'.
60. CfN, HB, F4:11, 'Memo from the Marketing Department of Handelsbanken', 29 March 1968.
61. 'Varför, Hur och Vad ska vi sälja' and 'Gör varje kund till totalkund', both in *Din Bank*, 5 (1963). See also: Tore Browaldh, 'Checken allmänheten och vi', *HB Remissan*, 7 (1958) and CfN, HB, F5:161, Letter to branch office managers in Handelsbanken (1958) in the folder, 'Lönen på checkräkning'.
62. '19 män på fältet', *Din Bank*, 6 (1962); 'Information som alla begriper. Från försäljningskonferensen i Strömstad', *Din Bank*, 4 (1963); 'Varför, Hur och Vad skall vi sälja?', *Din Bank*, 5 (1963); 'Sälj, sälj, sälj', *Remissan*, 1 (1965); 'Kundtjänst—bara för våra damer?', *Remissan*, 3 (1965); 'Välmatad konsulentträff i Norrtälje', *Remissan*, 7 (1965); 'Varför konsulenter—hur arbetar de?', *Remissan*, 8 (1965).
63. 'Varför, Hur och Vad skall vi sälja?', *Din Bank*, 5 (1963).
64. Bengt Senneby, 'Banktjänster till salu', *Din Bank*, 3 (1958).
65. Gerard Enckell, 'Går vi för långt?', *Din Bank*, 2 (1962); See further 'Gick vi för långt?', *Din Bank*, 4–5 (1962); Editorial by managing director Lars Erik Thunholm: 'Konkurrens och service inom bankerna', *Din Bank*, 6 (1962). For the same topic CfN, HB, F4f:7, 'Är försäljning så svårt', *Impuls*, 3–4 (1967).
66. For example, CfN, HB, F4f:7, 'Är vi en jippobank?', *Impuls*, 2 (1969) and 'Banker manipulerar inte. Vi för saklig diskussion' (interview with Jan Wallander), *DN*, 28 February 1970; Wallander, *Forskaren som bankdirektör*, 32.
67. CfN, HB, F4:43, 'Gyllene vardagsdeltagare—en profilundersökning'; 'Gyllene vardag i Hässleholm', *Norra Skåne*, 5 May 1966; 'Vad vet mamma

om pengar. Gyllene vardag i Hässleholm', *Arbetet*, 5 May 1966. For Elsa Nygren, see also 'Kvinna utsedd till bankdirektör', *DN*, 12 March 1966.
68. CfN, HB, F4:43, Talks and synopsis; 'Annorlunda "vardag" i Göteborg', *Remissan*, 9 (1965).
69. 'Annorlunda "vardag" i Göteborg', *Remissan*, 9 (1965).
70. CfN, SB, B7A:5, adverts; Wallander, *Forskaren som bankdirektör*, 29, 31.
71. CfN, SB, Ö1:26, Folder 'Bankens egna publikationer' and 'Så arbetar Din Bank—Den är ett Varuhus i Ekonomi', *Skånsk Marknad* (undated cutting) 1966. See also 'Ett varuhus i tjänster', advert for HB in *Sunt Förnuft*, 5 (1963).
72. 'Ge barnen andelar i framtiden—ge dem aktier!', advert by Handelsbanken featuring Elsa Nygren, *Hertha*, 6 (1957).
73. Savings loans, mentioned above, were a new form of consumer credit that offered individuals loans for twice the amount they saved and were introduced in the 1950s.
74. See Sabine Effosse, *Le crédit à la consommation en France, 1947–1965* (Paris: IGPDE, 2014), 209–222.
75. Aitken, *Performing Capital*, 44 and 206 on budgets as calculative devices.
76. 'Medlemsantalet i SBF', *Sunt Förnuft*, 6 (1968).
77. Orsi Husz, 'Privatekonomin och den borgerliga medelklassens identitetskris 1920–1970', *Fronesis* 24 (2007), 116–130.
78. Personal communication by Gunnel Petre's daughter, 6 February 2014.
79. See also Gunnel Petre, *På grön kvist med budget?* (Stockholm: Handelsbanken, 1964), 5.
80. Barnes and Newton, 'Women, uniforms'.
81. 'Diskutera familjeekonomin först efter en god måltid!', *Arbetet*, 14 October 1965; 'Svenska Handelsbanken uppmanade kvinnor att sätta färg på vardagen', *Helsingborgs Dagblad*, 14 October 1965, press cuttings in CfN, HB, F4:43.
82. Viviana Zelizer, *The Social Meaning of* Money (Princeton, NJ: Princeton University Press, 1994); Zelizer, *The Purchase of Intimacy*. See also Melinda Cooper, *Family Values: Between Neoliberalism and the New Social Conservatism* (New York: Zone Books, 2017) for an analysis of a neoliberal take on such a reconciliation.
83. CfN, HB, F4:43, manuscripts of talks.
84. For gender equality and allocations of money, see Zelizer, *The Social Meaning of* Money; Nancy Folbre, *Who Pays for the Kids?: Gender and the Structure of Constraint* (London: Routledge, 1994); Carole B. Burgoyne, 'Introduction: Special Issue on the Household Economy', *The Journal of Socio-Economics*, 37, 2 (2008), 455–457; Jan Pahl, 'His Money, Her Money: Recent Research on Financial Organisation in Marriage', *Journal of Economic Psychology*, 16, 3 (1995), 361–376. For the history and politics of

economic gender equity, Alice Kessler-Harris, *In Pursuit of Equity: Women, Men, and the Quest for Economic Citizenship in 20th-Century America* (Oxford: Oxford University Press, 2001).
85. 'Familjeekonomisk preparandkurs', *Ekonomisk Revy*, 3 (1961), 249. For 'future savings', see also Rebecca Pulju, *Women and Mass Consumer Society in Postwar France* (Cambridge: Cambridge University Press, 2011), 77 and Effosse, *Le crédit à la consommation*, 220–222.
86. CfN, HB, F4:43, Internal message with the GE programme attached, 21 February 1962.
87. CfN, HB, F4:43, 'Vad är lagom hushållspengar?'; 'Vad ska ungdomarna betala hemma?'; 'Vad kostar barnen?'; 'På grön kvist med budget', several editions exist, 1964–1969, and KB, Ephemera, Handelsbanken.
88. *Hon och Handelsbanken* (1966), 8–9, 10.
89. 'Pr på sitt sätt', *Din Bank*, 5–6 (1961).
90. Cf. Pulju, *Women and Mass Consumer Society*, 198.
91. Berner, *Sakernas tillstånd*, 228.
92. Around 1960, basic knowledge about budgeting and financial services at credit institutes made its way into the school curriculum. See Ulla Johansson, *Sparsamhetsfostran i 1900-talets svenska obligatoriska skolor* (Umeå: Pedagogiska rapporter, 1988), 26 about the curricula of 1955 and 1962.
93. CfN, HB, F4:10, 'Anteckningar från sammanträde om GV. Försäljning till kvinnliga målgrupper', 8 April 1969; 'Internt meddelande', by Gunnel Petre, Subject: 'Saldon på Gyllene vardags konton', 20 January 1970 and 'Saldogruppering av vissa försäljningskodade konton', 1 October 1969, by AMS/Marknadsanalys.
94. Wallander, *Forskaren som bankdirektör*, 124, 150. All central advertising stopped, and consultants as a category also disappeared. The former consultants (60 persons) were transferred to regular positions. These radical changes in marketing occurred only at Handelsbanken and not at the other banks.
95. Åmark, 'Familj, försörjning', 166, 267; Christina Florin and Bengt Nilsson, '"Something in the Nature of a Bloodless Revolution": How New Gender Relations Became Gender Equality Policy in Sweden', in *State Policy and Gender System in the Two German States and Sweden 1945–1989*, ed. by Rolf Torstendahl (Uppsala: Historiska institutionen, 1999), 11–77.
96. Eva Moberg, 'Kvinnans villkorliga frigivning', in *Unga liberaler* (Stockholm: Bonniers, 1961); Nancy Eriksson, *Bara en hemmafru* (Stockholm: Forum, 1964).
97. Petre, *På grön kvist med budget?*, 10.
98. Gunnel Petre, *Lagen och pengarna i hemmet* (Stockholm: Handelsbanken, 1969), 9 and 11.

99. CfN, HB, F4:10, 'Anteckningar från sammanträde om GV. Försäljning till kvinnliga målgrupper', 8 April 1969.
100. Martin, *Financialization of Daily Life*, 2 and 55.
101. Zelizer, *The Social Meaning of* Money; Zelizer, *The Purchase of Intimacy*; and see also for example, Paul Crosthwaite et al., *Invested: How Three Centuries of Stock Market Advice Reshaped Our Money, Markets, and Minds* (Chicago: University of Chicago Press, 2022).
102. Cf. Robertson, 'The Principle of Sound Banking', 248–249.
103. Amy Edwards, *Are We Rich Yet? The Rise of Mass Investment Culture in Contemporary Britain* (Oakland, CA: University of California Press, 2022).

Notes to Chapter 4

1. 'Kontokrediterna—välsignelse eller landsfara?', *Affärsekonomi*, 16 (1961); 'Tummen ner för kreditkorten', *Dagens Nyheter* (*DN*), 23 February 1961; 'Kooperationen vill ej införa förbud mot konsumtionskredit', *Svenska Dagbladet* (*SvD*), 23 February 1961. See also 'TV: Är det farligt att köpa på kredit' (debate between Lettström and Stolpe), *DN*, 5 May 1961; 'Svensk ordförande i Eurofinas', *DN*, 30 May 1963. Note, however, that the interpretations of the debate were strikingly different in the various newspapers. Parts of this chapter are based on my article, Orsi Husz, 'Money Cards and Identity Cards: De-vicing Consumer Credit in Post-war Sweden', *Journal of Cultural Economy*, 14, 2 (2021), 139–158.
2. 'Kontokrediterna—välsignelse eller landsfara?', *Affärsekonomi*, 16, (1961); 'Kooperationen vill ej införa förbud mot konsumtionskredit', *SvD*, 23 February 1961.
3. *Veckojournalen/Idun*, 8 (1964) portrayed Willy Maria Lundberg as 'a wailing wall for consumers, a fury against negligent manufacturers, impossible to silence'. See also 'TV: Kreditkortsystemet', *DN*, 21 October 1960.
4. David Rune, 'Att leva på plast: Hot eller möjlighet? En studie av svensk kreditkortsdebatt 1979–87', BA thesis (Stockholm: Department of History, Stockholm University, 2007); see also Chapter 5 in this book.
5. For the savings banks' informational activities, see Torbjörn Hessling, *Att spara eller inte spara—vilken fråga!: Den sparfrämjande verksamheten 1820–1970* (Stockholm: Sparfrämjandet, 1990). For 'Spara' and 'Slösa', Orsi Husz, 'Spara, Slösa och alla de andra', in *Signums svenska kulturhistoria, 1900-talet*, ed. by Jacob Christenson (Stockholm: Atlantis, 2009), 279–329; Dick Forslund, *Hit med pengarna! Sparandets genealogi och den finansiella övertalningens vetandekonst* (Stockholm: Carlssons, 2008).
6. Peder Aléx, *Den rationella konsumenten: KF som folkuppfostrare 1899–1939* (Stockholm/Stehag: Symposion, 1994); Husz, 'Spara, Slösa och alla de

andra'; Mats Larsson and Gabriel Söderberg, *Finance and the Welfare State: Banking Development and Regulatory Principles in Sweden, 1900–2015* (Cham: Palgrave Macmillan, 2017), Ch. 6.

7. The analysis is based mainly on Köpkort's company archives and the personal archives of the entrepreneur Erik Elinder, who owned the card company ContoFöretagen (founded in 1971, renamed InterConto in 1978). Both archival collections are unregistered, and mostly lack distinctive volume names. For citations I use the abbreviations KKA (Köpkort archives) and EEP (Erik Elinder's Papers). This is supplemented by other archival material (banking archives and collections of ephemera at Kungliga biblioteket (KB, the Swedish National Library), reports from several government commissions of inquiry and general press as well as specialist business press.

8. For example, CfN, Skandinaviska Banken (hereafter SB), F:71 101 (494), 'Utredning om kreditkortsystem' January 1960, 1; 'Skyldig' and 'Lev gott på plastepngarna', *Kvällspressen*, 2 August 1978. For guilt and debt, see also Nigel Dodd, *The Social Life of Money* (Princeton: Princeton University Press, 2014), 144.

9. Viviana Zelizer, *Morals and Markets: The Development of Life Insurance in the United States* (New York: Columbia University Press, 1979); Viviana Zelizer, *The Social Meaning of Money* (Princeton, NJ: Princeton University Press, 1994).

10. Zelizer, *Morals and Markets*, 153.

11. Francis Lee and Claes-Fredrik Helgesson, 'Vices and De-vicing in Making Valuable Data: Algorithms and Anxieties in High Throughput Biomarker Screening', article manuscript (Uppsala University/Linköping University, 2016).

12. Michel Callon (ed.), *The Laws of the Markets* (Oxford: Blackwell, 1998); Michel Callon and Fabian Muniesa, 'Peripheral Vision: Economic Markets as Calculative Collective Devices', *Organization Studies*, 26, 8 (2005), 1229–1250; Michel Callon, Yuval Millo, and Fabian Muniesa (eds.), *Market Devices* (Oxford: Blackwell, 2007). Eve Chiapello, 'Financialization as a Socio-Technical Process', in *The Routledge International Handbook of Financialization*, ed. by Philip Mader, Daniel Mertens, and Natascha van der Zwan (London: Routledge, 2020), 81–91.

13. Zsuzsanna Vargha, 'Assembling Lines: Queue Management and the Production of Market Economy in Post-socialist Services', *Journal of Cultural Economy*, 11, 5 (2018), 420–439.

14. Liz McFall, *Devising Consumption: Cultural Economies of Insurance, Credit and Spending* (Abingdon, Oxon: Routledge, 2015), 19, 28, esp. 4–5; Franck Cochoy, Joe Deville, and Liz McFall (eds.), *Markets and the Arts of Attachment* (London: Routledge, 2017), 6–11; Bruno Latour,

Reassembling the Social (Oxford & New York: Oxford University Press, 2005).
15. For good or viable matches, see Zelizer, 'How I Became a Relational Economic Sociologist'; see also McFall, *Devising Consumption*, 86.
16. Husz, 'Spara, Slösa och alla de andra'.
17. Tekniska Museet, Från datamaskin till IT (From computing machines to IT), Interview 127 (Ingvar Anderberg), 17 October 2007. See also 'Våra konkurrenter. Dagligvaror på kredit', *Kooperatören*, 6 (1978).
18. Lewis Mandell, *The Credit Card Industry: A History* (Boston: Twayne, 1990); Joe Nocera, *A Piece of the Action: How the Middle Class Joined the Money Class* (New York: Simon & Shister, 2013 [1994]); George Ritzer, *Expressing America: A Critique of the Global Credit Card Society* (Thousand Oaks: Pine Forge Press, 1995); Robert Manning, *Credit Card Nation* (New York: Basic, 2000); Donccha Marron, *Consumer Credit in the United States: A Sociological Perspective from the 19th Century to the Present* (Basingstoke, UK: Palgrave Macmillan, 2009); David L. Stearns, *Electronic Value Exchange. Origins of the Visa Electronic Payment System* (London: Springer 2011); Joe Deville, 'Paying with Plastic: The Enduring Presence of the Credit Card', in *Accumulation: The Material Politics of Plastic*, ed. by Jennifer Gabrys, Gay Hawkins, and Mike Michael (London: Routledge, 2014).
19. Only recently have social scientists begun to explore the different national histories. Cf. Akos Rona-Tas and Alya Guseva, *Plastic Money. Constructing Markets for Credit Cards in Eight Postcommunist Countries* (Stanford, CA: Stanford University Press, 2014); José Ossandón, 'My Story Has No Strings Attached: Credit Cards, Market Devices and a Stone Guest', in *Markets and the Arts of Attachment*, ed. by Franck Cochoy, Joe Deville, and Liz McFall (London: Routledge, 2017); Henning Jensen, *Historien om Dankort* [Published by the author] 2016; Bernardo Batiz-Lazo and Gustavo A. Del Angel, 'The Ascent of Plastic Money: International Adoption of the Bank Credit Card, 1950–1975', *Business History Review*, 92, 3 (2018), 509–533.
20. Jan Logemann, 'Credit Access and the American Welfare State', in *The Development of Consumer Credit in Global Perspective*, ed. by Jan Logemann (New York: Palgrave Macmillan, 2012); Andreas Wiedemann, *Indebted Societies: Credit and Welfare in Rich Democracies* (Cambridge: Cambridge University Press, 2021).
21. Kungliga biblioteket (KB), Ephemera Collection, vol. Möbel-Ikéa 1950–1970, 'Bosättningslån', pamphlet from 1963.
22. Carl-Johan Bouveng, Sven Sannesson, and Arne Ögren, *Konsumtionskrediter i Sverige* (Stockholm: SNS, 1963), 30–32; CfN, SB, F:71 101 (494) 'Utredning om kreditkortsystem', January 1960.

23. Bouveng, *Konsumtionskrediter*, 30–32; CfN, KKA, vol. '1969', Sven Å. Cason, 'Konsumtionskrediter, Köpkort, Kontokort', *Handelsutbildning*, 4 December 1966.
24. CfN, SB, F:71 101 (494), 'Utredning om kreditkortsystem', January 1960.
25. Mandell, *The Credit Card Industry*, 31.
26. CfN, Handelsbanken (hereafter HB), F12:58, 'City- och Shoppingkonto'; CfN, SB, F:71 101 (494), 'Utredning om kreditkortssystem'.
27. CfN, HB, F12:58, 'Protokoll fört vid sammanträde med styrelsen för City-Shoppingkonto AB', 28 October 1960; see also job advert in *Dagens Nyheter*, 24 September 1960. For the problem of two-sided markets, see Rona-Tas and Guseva, *Plastic Money*, 57–59.
28. Herman Stolpe, *Kredit och reklam på avvägar* (Stockholm: Rabén & Sjögren, 1961), esp. 29; K.P., 'Konsumtionskrediter i förvirrad tappning', *Ekonomisk revy*, 5 (1961), 374–376 and Herman Stolpe, 'Om konsumtionskrediter' incl. reply by KP, *Ekonomisk revy*, 7 (1961), 507–509. See also CfN, KKA, vol. '1969', manuscripts of polemical speeches as response to the criticism.
29. Orsi Husz, 'The Morality of Quality: Assimilating Material Mass Culture in twentieth Century Sweden', *Journal of Modern European History*, 10, 2 (2012), 152–181. The lead critic of throwawayism was the consumer journalist Willy Maria Lundberg, mentioned in the introduction of the chapter. The Swedish debate was influenced by the American one, see Vance Packard, *The Hidden Persuaders* (New York: David McKay, 1957), and idem., *The Waste Makers* (New York: David McKay, 1960).
30. See, for example, Ritzer, *Expressing America*; 'Våra kreditkort missbrukas inte', *DN*, 20 February 1962.
31. Bouveng, *Konsumtionskrediter*, 95f; CfN, KKA, vol. '1969', Sven Å. Cason, 'Konsumtionskrediter, Köpkort, Kontokort', *Handelsutbildning*, 4 (1966); SOU 1966:42, Konsumtionskreditutredningen, *Konsumtionskrediter i Sverige: Betänkande* (Stockholm: Esselte, 1966), 19, 224, herafter SOU 1966:42.
32. SOU 1966:42, 16–18; *Kreditkorten och konsumenten*, Delrapport III, KoV 1981:6–04 (Vällingby: Konsumentverket, 1981), 3, 37; 'Moderna pengar', *Rateko*, 10 (1978), press cutting in CfN, KKA, 'Tidningsklipp 1978'; CfN, KKA, vol. '1969–1971', various marketing and informational material; KB, Ephemera, vol. Köpkort AB, informational leaflets.
33. Sweden's population in 1979 was 8.2 million. For statistical data on cards, see SOU 1966:42, 59–60; SOU 1977:97, Finansieringsbolagskommittén, *Finansieringsbolag: Betänkande* (Stockholm: Liber Förlag/Allmänna förlaget, 1977), 34, 80, hereafter SOU 1977:97; 'Satsade på nya kort', *Veckans affärer*, 10 January 1977; Sven Å. Cason, 'Kontokort—marknad med perspektiv!', *MMM tidningen*, 10 (1967), press cutting in

CfN, KKA, vol. '1969'; CfN, EEP, Erik Elinder to Spencer Nilsson, June 1979.
34. 'Eurocard—ett kreditkort som gäller i hela Europa', *DN*, 18 November 1964; 'Gunnar Åkerlund död. Byggde upp och utvecklade Finans-Vendor', Obituary, *DN*, 19 November 1982; 'Krögarnas kreditkort förlorar "monopolet"', *Veckans affärer*, 25 March 1971.
35. *Kreditkorten och konsumenten*, 2; *Kontokreditmarknaden på konsumentområdet* (Stockholm: Konsumentverket, 1980), 6–9; SOU 1975:63, Kreditköpkommittén, *Konsumentkreditlag m.m.: Betänkande* (Stockholm: Liber Förlag/ Allmänna förlaget, 1975), 47, hereafter SOU 1975:63; SOU 1977:97, 79.
36. Mandell, *The Credit Card Industry*, 45–46.
37. SOU 1966:42.
38. SOU 1975:63; *Kontokreditmarknaden på konsumentområdet*; 'Kontoföretagen går mot en ny vår när den nya kreditlagen träder i kraft', *Köpmannen*, 1 May 1978.
39. For financing companies, see Lars Ramklint, 'Tjänar pengar på bristen på pengar. Riksbankens priskontroll gäller inte de lönsamma finansbolagen', *DN*, 12 February 1978.
40. For example, 'Sverige tvåa som kreditland', *DN*, 29 March 1960; 'Sverige, England störst i konsumtionskrediter', *DN*, 15 October 1961. For Swedification, see Billy Ehn, Jonas Frykman, and Orvar Löfgren, *Försvenskningen av Sverige: Det nationellas förvandlingar* (Stockholm: Natur och kultur, 1993).
41. CfN, KKA, vol. '1969', 'Samhälle utan check', manuscript of speech at the conference of the Swedish Bankers' Association, 14 October 1968.
42. Fredrik Lettström, *Konsumentkrediter: Föreläsning vid Stockholms Universitet* (Stockholm, 1976), 52f; 'Svensk ordförande i Eurofinas', *DN*, 30 May 1963; Sven Å. Cason, 'Kreditkorten i Europa', *Ekonomisk revy*, 6 (1969).
43. CfN, KKA, vol. 'Reklam 1967', Sven Å. Cason, 'Swedish Experience in the Field of Charge Accounts and Revolving Credit', Speech at the Seminar on Consumer Credit, organised by Fédération Internationale des Grandes Entreprises de Distribution (FIGED), Brussels, 7–8 March 1967.
44. Ibid.
45. CfN, KKA, vol. 'Säljutbildn. 2/6', 'Sammanfattning av resultatet från statistik- och attitydundersökningar', Köpkort AB, 12 August 1965.
46. CfN, KKA, vol. 'Reklam 1967', transcript of television debate, see also article manuscripts and adverts in the same volume.
47. Advert, for example in *DN*, 5 December 1965 and in *AB*, 12 December 1965.
48. CfN, KKA, vol. '1969–1970', 'PM för beslut i policyfrågor', 27 March 1968.

49. Cf. Gunnar Trumbull, *Consumer lending in France and America* (New York: Cambridge University Press, 2014); Rona-Tas and Guseva, *Plastic Money*.
50. CfN, KKA, vol. 'Reklam 1967', Cason, 'Swedish experience'; Sven Å. Cason, 'Köpkortssystemets marknadsanpassning', *Ekonomisk revy*, 5 (1966).
51. CfN, KKA, vol. 'Reklam 1967', Cason, 'Swedish experience', my emphasis.
52. See, for example, CfN, KKA, vol. 'Reklam 1967', 'Köpkort ger förtroende—Köpkortet inger förtroende', advert.
53. William Leach, *Land of Desire: Merchants, Power, and the Rise of a New American Culture* (New York: Pantheon, 1993); Lendol Calder, *Financing the American Dream: A Cultural History of Consumer Credit* (Princeton: Princeton University Press, 1999); Marron, *Consumer Credit*, 46–48; Department store credit schemes are still important in some parts of the world, see José Ossandón, 'Sowing Consumers in the Garden of Mass Retailing in Chile', *Consumption Markets & Culture*, 17, 5 (2014).
54. Orsi Husz, *Drömmars värde: Varuhus och lotteri i svensk konsumtionskultur, 1897–1939* (Hedemora: Gidlunds, 2004), 94–95, 153–154. CfN, EEP, transcript of telephone call between Erik Elinder and Göran Oldenburg (credit manager at NK), 1970s; Göran Oldenburg, 'Kontobrickorna ersätts av plastkort', *Kompanirullan*, 3 (1959), 13.
55. CfN, KKA, vol. 'Säljutbildn. 2/6', 'Sammanfattning av resultatet från statistik-och attitydundersökningar', 12 August1965. See also 'Kreditkort klarar kris åt statussvensk utan pengar i fickan', *DN*, 15 July 1967.
56. In the 1960s, classification and identification were intertwined in the card's functions. Classification requires identification, as the French sociologist Gilles Laferté argues highlighting the role of contemporary consumer credit in what he calls an 'economic identification economy', in which economic transactions are no longer based on face-to-face interactions, but depend on advanced identification systems. Gilles Laferté, 'Economic Identification: A Contribution to a Comparative Socio-History of Credit Markets', *Economic Sociology: The European Electronic Newsletter*, 15, 3 (2014); Orsi Husz, 'Bank Identity: Banks, ID Cards, and the Emergence of a Financial Identification Society in Sweden', *Enterprise & Society*, 19, 2 (2018), 391–429.
57. CfN, KKA, vol. '1969', manuscript, speech by Sven Å. Cason to the congress of Sveriges Köpmannaförbund (Federation of Swedish Merchants) 4–8 June 1967; CfN, KKA, vol. 'Trycksaker från utställningen', Promotional pamphlet, 1970s. Cf. Trumbull, *Consumer Lending*, 48.
58. Marion Fourcade and Kieran Healy. 'Classification Situations', *Accounting, Organizations and Society*, 38, 8 (2013), 559–572; Josh Lauer, *Creditworthy: A History of Consumer Surveillance and Financial Identity in America* (New York: Columbia University Press, 2017); Martha Poon,

'Scorecards as Devices for Consumer Credit: The Case of Fair, Isaac & Company Incorporated', in *Market Devices*, ed. by Michel Callon, Yuval Millo, and Fabian Muniesa (Oxford: Blackwell, 2007); Akos Rona-Tas and Stefanie Hiss, 'The Role of Ratings in the Subprime Mortgage Crisis: The Art of Corporate and the Science of Consumer Credit Rating', in *Markets on Trial*, ed. by Michael Lounsbury and Paul M. Hirsch (Badford: Emerald, 2010), 115–155. See also José Ossandón, 'Quand le crédit à la consommation classe les gens et les choses: Une revue de littérature et un programme de recherche', *Revue française de socio-economie*, 9, 1 (2012), 83–100.

59. DsFi1984:10, 42; SOU 1966:42, 69; Bouveng, *Konsumtionskrediter*, 37; SOU 1972:79, Kreditupplysningsutredningen, *Kreditupplysning och integritet. Betänkande* (Stockholm: Berling, 1972), 35–36, 38. The implementation of the Credit Reporting Act was supervised by a new authority, the Data Inspection Board (1973, *Datainspektionen*), the first of its kind in the world.
60. See, for example, 'Kunder utan kreditkort "misstänkta"', *SvD*, 11 December 1965; 'Kreditkort klarar kris åt kontantlös', *DN*, 15 July 1967; 'Pengar nej tack, vi tar bara kontokort!', *Veckorevyn*, 44 (1978).
61. CfN, KKA, vol. 'Trycksaker från utställningen', Promotional pamphlet, 1970s.
62. CfN, KKA, vol. '1969', 'Köpkort—modern konto- och betalningsservice', newspaper cutting, 1968–1969; CfN, KKA, vol. 'Reklam 1967', Adverts; CfN, KKA, vol. 'Trycksaker från utställningen', 'Varsågod. Inte Pengar. Men Nästan!', direct advert pamphlet, April 1975.
63. Trumbull, *Consumer Lending*, 67–68.
64. CfN, KKA, vol. '1969–1971', 'PM för beslut i policyfrågor', 27 March 1968.
65. Ibid. and CfN, KKA, vol. 'Trycksaker från utställningen', promotional pamphlets and invitations to sign up for Köpkort, 1964–1965.
66. CfN, KKA, vol. 'Säljutbildn. 2/6', 'Sammanfattning av resultatet från statistik-och attitydundersökningar', 12 August 1965, 3 and 5.
67. CfN, KKA, vol. '1969', 'Redovisning av Köpkorts marknadsföringsåtgärder'; CfN, KKA, vol. 'Trycksaker från utställningen', 'Varsågod. Inte Pengar. Men Nästan!', direct advert pamphlet, April 1975; CfN, KKA, vol. '1969', 'Köpkort—modern konto- och betalningsservice', newspaper cutting, 1968–1969; CfN, KKA, vol. 'Reklam 1967', Adverts; CfN, KKA, vol. '1969', Sven Å. Cason, 'Konsumtionskrediter, Köpkort, Kontokort', *Handelsutbildning*, 4 (1966).
68. CfN, Bankföreningen (Swedish Banker's Association, hereafter BF), A2a:62, Minutes of the Board, 20 sept 1967, §164 and Appendixes 6 and 7. *Kontokuriren* 1971–1972.

69. CfN, KKA, vol. 'Säljutbildning 6/6', 'Kreditkortets roll i framtidens betalförmedling', manuscript, 10 September 1969; CfN, KKA, vol. '1969', 'Den amerikanska konsumtionskreditens nya dimensioner', manuscript by Sven Å. Cason, 23 April 1968.
70. Stearns, *Electronic Value Exchange*, 68; Paul Chutkov, *VISA. The Power of an Idea* (Chicago: Harcourt, 2001); Mandell, *The Credit Card Industry*, 39.
71. Bernardo Batiz-Lazo, Thomas Haigh, and David L. Stearns, 'How the Future Shaped the Past: The Case of the Cashless Society', *Enterprise & Society*, 15, 1 (2014), 103–131; Björn Thodenius, Bernardo Batiz-Lazo, and Tobias Karlsson, 'The History of the Swedish ATM: Sparfrämjandet and Metior', in *History of Nordic Computing 3: Third IFIP WG 9.7 Conference*, ed. by Giuseppe Impagliazzo et al. (Heidelberg: Springer, 2011), 92–100; CfN, KKA, vol. '1969', 'Den amerikanska konsumtionskreditens nya dimensioner', manuscript by Sven Å. Cason, 23 April 1968.
72. See other similar material, for example CfN, KKA, vol. 'Reklam 1967', 'Budget, budgetering' advert leaflet 1967; or KB, Ephemera, vol. Köpkort AB, adverts. See also CfN, KKA, vol. 'Svenskt Köpkort, Shoppingkonto 1960–61', script for promotional film; Gunnar Karneman, *Kontokort: en väg för finansplanering även för hushållen* (Stockholm: Finansieringsföretagens förening, 1976); Gunnar Karneman 'Moderna pengar', *Rateko*, 19 (1976).
73. Milton Friedman, *A Theory of Consumption Function* (Princeton, NJ: Princeton University Press, 1957).
74. Calder, *Financing the American Dream*.
75. CfN, KKA, vol. 'Trycksaker från utställningen', Advert with note.
76. CfN, KKA, vol. 'Svenskt Köpkort, Shoppingkonto 1960–61', Script for promotional film and 'Försäljningargument för köpkort gentemot konsumenten'.
77. Jeanne Lazarus, 'Gouverner les conduites économiques par l'éducation financière: L'ascension de la financial literacy', in *Gouverner les conduits*, ed. by Sophie Dubuisson-Quellier (Paris: Presses de SciencesPo, 2016), 93–126; Jeanne Lazarus, 'Financial Literacy Education', in *The Routledge International Handbook of Financialization*, ed. by Philip Mader, Daniel Mertens, and Natascha van der Zwan (London: Routledge, 2020), 390–399; Charlotta Bay, Bino Catasús, and Gustav Johed, 'Situating Financial Literacy', *Critical Perspectives on Accounting*, 25, 1 (2014); *OECD/INFE International Survey of Adult Financial Literacy* (OECD, 2020).
78. SOU 1966:42, 175.
79. Konsumentkreditlagen (Consumer Credit Act) 1977:981; see also Rasmus Fleischer, 'Kreditkonsumtion i Sverige, 1945–1985', *Historisk Tidskrift*, 136, 4 (2016), 626–657.

80. 'Räntekrig om kontokort,' *DN*, 5 November 1979; 'Nytt 'bankkrig' om kreditkorten', *DN*, 20 October 1979.
81. 'Nya lagen för köp på kredit—den ska ingen missa', *Ica Nyheter*, 19 October 1978, press cutting in CfN, KKA, vol. 'Tidningsklipp 1978'; 'Ta på krita—vad kostar det? Så här svarar konsumentverket', *DN*, 3 April 1979.
82. 'Så väljer du rätt bland Sveriges alla kontokort!', *Privata Affärer*, 2 (1978), 21–29 press cutting in CfN, KKA, vol. 'Tidningsklipp 1978'.
83. CfN, EEP, vol. 'Conto-kriget-79', 'Testa dina ekonomiska fördomar'; and CfN, EEP, vol. Helsidesannonser, 'Testa ditt ekonomiska sinne'. See also E. O. Holm, *Kontokort och kreditsystem i detaljhandeln* (Göteborg: Länssparbanken, 1980).
84. *Kontokreditmarknaden på konsumentområdet*, 10–11. When not stated otherwise, this section builds on material concerning InterConto and its precursors in Erik Elinder's Papers (EEP). No list of records exists, and the volumes are not distinctly marked.
85. Personal communication, 26 April 2018.
86. The company InterConto offered these as well. They in fact pioneered the development of the loyalty card system, and offered ready-made solutions for private-label card systems.
87. Cf. Viviana Zelizer, *The Social Meaning of Money* (Princeton, NJ: Princeton University Press, 1994); Keith Hart, *The Memory Bank* (London: Profile Books, 1999), Ch. 6; Dodd, *The Social Life of Money*, 305–310.
88. Lana Swartz, 'Cards', in *Paid: Tales of Dongles, Checks, and Other Money Stuff*, ed. by Bill Maurer and Lana Swartz (Boston: MIT Press, 2017).
89. Nocera, *A Piece of the Action*, 63.
90. 'Avarterna hotar kredithandeln', *DN*, 4 September 1959 (interview with F. Lettström).
91. *Kreditkorten och konsumenten*, 2, 4.
92. CfN, KKA, vol. 'Trycksaker från utställningen', untitled. For examples of the savings banks' earlier criticism of credit cards see 'Kreditkort klarar kris åt statussvensk utan pengar på fickan', *DN*, 15 June 1967; 'Modehus lockar kunder med kreditkort i brev', *Aftonbladet*, 6 December 1962.
93. Through the financing company Tornet, which belonged to the savings banks' sphere of interest and owned 50 percent of the shares in Visa Sweden. See volumes on Visa in CfN, EEP and 'Visa', *Sparbankerna*, 15 (1978).
94. CfN, KKA, vol. Tidningsklipp 1978, see for example 'Systemet börjar snart sälja sprit på kontokort', placard for the evening paper *Aftonbladet* (*AB*) (date missing); 'Spritköp på kontokort,' *AB*, 28, November 1978; 'Systemet inför nu kontokort!', *Skövde nyheter*, 29 November 1978; 'Hoppsan! Kontokort på Systemet!', *Östra Småland*, 29 November 1978.

95. 'Sparbanken kommer med eget köpkort', *SvD*, 20 October 1978; CfN, EEP, vol. 'Tidningsurklipp 1976–1979', 'Sparbankutspel: Inför eget köpkort' (newspaper cutting, title and date missing); CfN, EEP, vol. 'Conto-kriget –79', 'Sparbankerna sätter allting på ett kort,' *Västerviks tidning*, November (date missing).
96. Ingvar Körberg, *Förnyelsen: Sparbankernas historia 1945–1980* (Stockholm: Ekerlid, 2006), 348–367; 'Sparbankerna tar ledningen', *Affärsvärlden*, 8 (1979), press cutting in CfN, EEP, vol. 'Tidningsurklipp 1976–1979'.
97. *Kontokreditmarknaden på konsumentområdet*, 29.
98. 'Genombrottsår för kontokorten. Svenskarnas jul, är det en jul på kredit?', *Sydsvenska Dagbladet*, 21 December 1978.
99. Köpkort had first turned a profit in 1965, see CfN, KKA, vol. '1969–1971', 'Köpkort AB och framtiden—underlag för policydiskussion', April 1969. The company had in 1977 40 percent of the card market, and was Sweden's second-most profitable company after Systembolaget (the government owned chain of liquor stores). In third and fourth place came two other finance companies (Finax and Kundkredit). 'Så väljer du rätt bland Sveriges alla kreditkort!', *Privata Affärer*, 2 (1978); 'Många förlorare, men det finns också vinnare. Storföretagens resultat 1977', *Affärsvärlden*, 21 (1978). See also 'Moderna pengar', *Rateko*, 10 (1978); 'Skyldig?' *Kvällsposten*, 2 September 1978, press cuttings in CfN, KKA, vol. 'Tidningsklipp 1978'.
100. *Kontokreditmarknaden på konsumentområdet*, 12 and 'Köpform som kommer: Livsmedel på kreditkort', *Arbetet*, 23 May 1978. 'Livsmedel på kredit på väg tillbaka?', *Hallandsposten*, 24 May 1978; 'Succé för resor på krita—men är det etiskt?', *Skånska Dagbladet*, 27 July 1978. CfN, KKA, vol. 'Trycksaker från utställningen', 'Ansökan om Köpkort' and other similar material.
101. *Kontokreditmarknaden på konsumentområdet* 1980, 10–11.
102. Ibid., 8–9, measured as a share of outstanding loans.
103. CfN, BF, Styrelsens protokoll (Minutes of the Board of the Bankers' Association), 20 September 1967, Appendix 6: 'Rapport från kommittén för utredning av frågan om kreditkort och därmed jämförliga instrument'; CfN, EEP, vol. 'Kontoboken', Letter from Erik Elinder to Professor Nils Melander, 18 August 1978.
104. For example, 'Eurocard säljs till bankgrupp', *DN*, 21 April 1978.
105. 'Genombrottsår för kontokorten. Svenskarans jul, är det en jul på kredit?', *Sydsvenska Dagbladet*, 21 December 1978.
106. Rune, 'Att leva på plast'; Fleischer, 'Kreditkonsumtion'; Orsi Husz, 'Kreditkortskriget: Kooperativa Förbundet och den finansiellt rationella konsumenten', in *Marknadens tid. Mellan folkhemskapitalism och nyliberalism*, ed. by Jenny Andersson, Nikolas Glover, Orsi Husz, and David Larsson Heidenblad (Lund: Nordic Academic Press, 2023), 215–242.

107. *Kortbetalningarnas betydelse i samhället* (Stockholm: Svenska Bankföreningen, 2013); Bruce Carruthers and Laura Ariovich, *Money and Credit: A Sociological Approach* (Cambridge: Polity, 2010), 112; Mathias Drehman, Charles Goodhart and Malte Krueger, 'The Challenges Facing Currency Usage', *Economic Policy*, 17 April (2002), 195–227, 202.
108. *Svenska folkets betalningsvanor 2018* (Stockholm: Sveriges Riksbank, 2018); Svenska folkets betalningsvanor 2023 (Stockholm: Sveriges Riksbank), online resource (www.riksbank.se/sv/statistik/statistik-over-betaln ingar-sedlar-och-mynt/betalningsvanor/); VISA Europe Sweden. Press Release, 'Annual Results', 28 January, 2013.

NOTES TO CHAPTER 5

1. 'Kontokort en samhällsfara? Hört i radio', *Vestmanlands läns tidning*', 23 March 1978; 'Bränn dom!', *Norrländska socialdemokraten*, 13 December 1978. This chapter builds in part on two previous publications: Orsi Husz, 'The Entrepreneur's Dream: Credit Card History Between PR and Academic Research', in *Histories of Knowledge in Postwar Scandinavia: Actors, Arenas and Ambitions*, ed. by Johan Östling, David Larsson Heidenblad, and Niklas Olsen (London: Routledge, 2020), 127–151; and Orsi Husz, 'Kreditkortskriget: Kooperativa Förbundet och den finansiellt rationella konsumenten', in *Marknadens tid. Mellan folkhemskapitalism och nyliberalism*, ed. by Jenny Andersson, Nikolas Glover, Orsi Husz, and David Larsson Heidenblad (Lund: Nordic Academic Press, 2023), 215–242.
2. Gunnar Karneman, *Kontokort—en väg för finansplanering även för hushållen* (Stockholm: Finansieringsföretagens förening, 1979).
3. Ibid.
4. Centrum för Näringslivshistoria (hereafter CfN), Handelsbanken (HB), F4f:6, Protokoll från Fältrådets sammanträde (Minutes of the Field Council meeting), 11 May 1963.
5. Donccha Marron, *Consumer Credit in the United States: A Sociological Perspective from the 19th Century to the Present* (Basingstoke, UK: Palgrave Macmillan, 2009), 110–112, 185; Christopher Payne, *The Consumer, Credit and Neoliberalism: Governing the Modern Economy* (London: Routledge, 2012), 10, 60–67; Niklas Olsen, *The Sovereign Consumer: A New Intellectual History of Neoliberalism* (Cham, Switzerland: Palgrave Macmillan, 2019), 249; see also Paul Langley, *The Everyday Life of Global Finance: Saving and Borrowing in Anglo-America* (Oxford: Oxford University Press, 2008), 185–193; Paul Langley and Andrew Leyshon, 'Financial Subjects: Culture and Materiality', *Journal of Cultural Economy*, 5, 4 (2012), 369–373.

6. See, for example, George Ritzer, *Expressing America: A Critique of the Global Credit Card Society* (Thousand Oaks: Pine Forge Press, 1995).
7. Rikard Westerberg, *Socialists at the Gate: Swedish Business and the Defense of Free Enterprise, 1940–1985* (Stockholm: Stockholm School of Economics, 2020), 241–294; Stig-Björn Ljunggren, *Folkhemskapitalismen: Högerns programutveckling under efterkrigstiden* (Stockholm: Tiden, 1992); Hans de Geer, *I vänstervind och högervåg: SAF under 1970-talet* (Stockholm: Allmänna förlaget, 1989); Bo Stråth, *Mellan två fonder: LO och den svenska modellen* (Stockholm: Atlas, 1998); Jenny Andersson, 'Neoliberalism from Within. The Business Fund and the Struggle for Market Ideology in Sweden', *Contemporary European History*, FirstView (2025), 1–17.
8. Kurt Samuelsson, 'Politiker och facket hotar konsumentens frihet. Syn på konsumentkreditlagen', *Konsumenträtt & Ekonomi*, 4 (1978), press cutting in CfN, Köpkort (KKA), vol. 'Tidningsklipp 1978'.
9. Orsi Husz and Karin Carlsson, 'Marketing a New Society or Engineering Kitchens', in *Consumer Engineering: Marketing Between Planning Euphoria and the Limits of Growth, 1930s–1970s*, ed. by Jan Logemann et al. (Washington, DC: Palgrave Macmillan, 2019), 215–243; Sophie Elsässer, *Att skapa en konsument: Råd & Rön och den statliga konsumentupplysningen* (Göteborg: Makadam 2012).
10. Kersti Gylling, 'Riktlinjer som producentpåverkan—ett samhällsintresse', in *Måste konsumenten gå till Verket?*, ed. by Fride Antoni and Ann-Charlotte Plogner (Stockholm: Industriförbundet, 1978), 69.
11. Olle Wästberg, 'Ämbetsverk konsumenthot', *Svenska Dagbladet*, 16 March 1978; Fride Antoni and Ann-Charlotte Plogner (eds.), *Måste konsumenten gå till Verket?* (Stockholm: Industriförbundet, 1978).
12. Olsen, *The Sovereign Consumer*.
13. Kurt Samuelsson, 'Politiker och facket hotar konsumentens frihet. Syn på konsumentkreditlagen', *Konsumenträtt & Ekonomi*, 4 (1978), press cutting in CfN, KKA, vol. 'Tidningsklipp 1978'. See also above and Olle Wästberg, 'Självständiga beslut från konsumenterna: Nej till förmyndarsamhället', *Köpmannen*, 20 November 1978.
14. See especially the Swedish Credit Information Act (Kreditupplysningslagen) 1973:1173 and the Marketing Act (Marknadsföringslagen) 1975: 1418.
15. 'Peterson kastar masken', *Svenska Dagbladet (SvD)*, 12 May 1978.
16. SOU 1975:63, Kreditköpkommittén, *Konsumentkreditlag m.m.: Betänkande* (Stockholm: Liber Förlag/Allmänna förlaget, 1975); DsFi 1984:10, Kontokortskommittén, *Kontokort: Slutbetänkande* (Stockholm: Liber Förlag/Allmänna förlaget, 1984), 25f.
17. Orsi Husz, 'Att sälja kredit som pengar: Kreditkortets domesticering i 1960-talets Sverige', in *Vardagslivets finansialisering*, ed. by Erik Andersson, Oskar Broberg, Marcus Gianneschi, and Bengt Larsson (Göteborg:

Centrum för konsumtionsvetenskap, 2016), 45–57; CfN, HB, F12:58, 'Protokoll fört vid sammanträde med styrelsen för City-Shoppingkonto AB', 28 October 1960. See also CfN, Skandinaviska Banken (SB), F:71 101(494), 'Utredning av kreditkortsystem', January 1960.
18. CfN, EEP, Erik Elinder to Professor Nils Meinander, Finland, 18 August 1978, 4.
19. CfN, EEP, vol. 'Kontoboken', Erik Elinder (EE) to Jan Kuuse (JK), Stockholm, 9 January 1979; and CfN, EEP, vol. 'Rätten till kredit' (RTK), 'PM beträffande den nya boken "Rätten till kredit—en glömd livskvalitet"', undated.
20. CfN, EEP, vol. 'Kuuse', EE to Erik Landberg, 12 November 1980. Swedish quotes translated by the author.
21. CfN, EEP, vol. 'RTK', EE Memo, 18 May 1978.
22. My main source material consists of ten volumes of Erik Elinder's archives as well as interviews with economic historians Jan Kuuse and Kent Olsson: March and November 2018 by telephone with JK, and 12 April 2019 in a meeting with both of them.
23. Per H. Hansen, 'From Finance Capitalism to Financialization: A Cultural and Narrative Perspective on 150 Years of Financial History', *Enterprise & Society*, 15, 4 (2015), 636.
24. Mary Poovey, *Genres of the Credit Economy: Mediating Value in Eighteenth- and Nineteenth-Century Britain* (Chicago: University of Chicago Press, 2008); Marieke de Goede, *Virtue, Fortune, and Faith: A Genealogy of Finance* (Minneapolis: University of Minnesota Press, 2005). See also the seminal work of Donald MacKenzie on the performativity of financial models: Donald A. MacKenzie, *An Engine, Not a Camera: How Financial Models Shape Markets* (Cambridge, MA: MIT Press, 2006).
25. Hansen, 'From Finance Capitalism', 605–642.
26. Thomas Gieryn, *Cultural Boundaries of Science: Credibility on the Line* (Chicago: Chicago University Press, 1999), esp. 12–35.
27. See also Kalle Grandin, Nina Wormbs, and Sven Widmalm, *The Science-Industry Nexus: History, Policy, Implication* (Sagamore Beach, MA: Science History Publications/USA, 2004); Ingemar Pettersson, 'The Nomos of University', *Minerva*, 56, 3 (2018), 381–403.
28. See Håkan Lindgren (ed.), 'Företagshistoria' (Business history, Special Issue), *Historisk tidskrift*, 99, 3 (1979); and Karl-Gustaf Hildebrand, *Om företagshistoria* (Uppsala: Uppsala University, 1989). For the uses of history in general, see Peter Aronsson, *Historiebruk: Att använda det förflutna* (Lund: Studentlitteratur, 2004). For corporate storytelling and the role of historical narratives in businesses, see Mads Mordhorst and Stefan Schwarzkopf, 'Theorising Narrative in Business History', *Business History*, 59, 8 (2017), 1155–1175; William M. Foster et al., 'The Strategic Use

of Historical Narratives: A Theoretical Framework', *Business History*, 59, 8 (2017), 1176–1200. See also Sara Kristoffersson, *Design by IKEA: A Cultural History* (London: Bloomsbury, 2014).
29. For example, historical monographs on companies such as Alfa Laval, Stockholms Enskilda Bank and ASEA, as well as a series of biographies on members of the Wallenberg family.
30. Lindgren, 'Företagshistoria'; Hildebrand, *Om företagshistoria*; Ulf Olsson, *En värdefull berättelse*. Göteborg Papers in Economic History, no. 16 (Gothenburg: Department of Economic History, Göteborg University, 2013), 4. See also Göran B. Nilsson, 'Historia som vetskap', *Historisk tidskrift*, 125, 2 (2005), 203.
31. Hildebrand, *Om företagshistoria*, 5–6.
32. CfN, EEP, vol. 'Conto Forskning', EE to Sven Rydenfelt, 30 September 1974.
33. Nils Erik Sandberg, 'Svensk ärkeliberal', *DN*, 21 January 2011. Philip Mirowski and Dieter Plehwe (eds.), *The Road from Mont Pèlerin: The Making of the Neoliberal Thought Collective* (Cambridge: Harvard University Press, 2009).
34. For further examples, see CfN, EEP, vol. 'Kontoboken', EE to Professor Niels Meinander, Finland, 18 August 1978 and *Newsletter from ContoFöretagen* 1 (1972).
35. CfN, EEP, vol. 'Kontoboken', EE, 'PM beträffande nödvändigheten av forskning och ökad information', April 1977; About the lack of knowledge see also CfN, EEP, vol. 'ContoForskning', EE to Sven Rydenfelt, 30 September 1974.
36. CfN, EEP, vol. 'Kontoboken', EE, 'PM beträffande nödvändigheten av forskning och ökad information', April 1977. For similar phrases see also CfN, EEP, vol. 'Kontoboken', EE to Professor Niels Meinander, Finland, 18 August 1978; and CfN, EEP, vol. 'ContoForskning', EE to Sven Rydenfelt, 30 September 1974.
37. CfN, EEP, vol. 'Kontoboken', EE, 'PM beträffande nödvändigheten av forskning och ökad information', April 1977.
38. Per Wisselgren, 'Vetenskap och/eller politik? Om gränsteorier och utredningsväsendets vetenskapshistoria', in *Mångsysslare och gränsöverskridare*, ed. by Bosse Sundin and Maria Göransdotter (Umeå: Umeå universitet, 2008), 114.
39. Preliminary titles and key expressions in the presentations of the book project.
40. Christopher Payne, *The Consumer, Credit and Neoliberalism*, 10, 60–67; Niklas Olsen, *The Sovereign Consumer*, 249.

41. Jan Logemann, *Engineered to Sell. European Emigrés & the Making of Consumer Capitalism* (Chicago: University of Chicago Press, 2019), 254–260. Stefan Schwarzkopf and Rainer Gries, *Ernest Dichter and Motivation Research* (New York: Palgrave Macmillan, 2010); Daniel Horowitz, *The Anxieties of Affluence: Critiques of American Consumer Culture, 1939–1979* (Amherst: University of Massachusetts Press, 2004), 51–56. Dichter also figures in Vance Packard's emblematic book from 1957 on the advertising industry, *The Hidden Persuaders* (New York: David McKay).
42. CfN, EEP, vol. 'ContoForskning', Ernest Dichter to EE, 14 November 1973.
43. CfN, EEP, vol. 'ContoForskning', Bo Wickström to EE, 8 October 1974.
44. Artur Attman, Jan Kuuse, and Ulf Olsson, *LM Ericsson 100 Years* (Stockholm: Telefon AB LM Ericsson, 1977 [in Swedish 1976]).
45. CfN, EEP, vol. 'Kontoboken', EE, 'PM beträffande nödvändigheten av forskning och ökad information', April 1977.
46. CfN, EEP, vol. 'Kontoboken', EE, 'PM beträffande nödvändigheten av forskning och ökad information', April 1977; Interview with Kuuse 2018.
47. CfN, EEP, vol. 'Kuuse', EE to Gunnar Ehrlemark, Roland Norle, Reine Olsson, Stockholm, 25 April 1977.
48. CfN, EEP, vol. 'Kuuse', Contract. See also JK to EE, 20 September 1978.
49. CfN, EEP, vol. 'Kuuse', EE to Reine Olsson, 21 August 1980.
50. Hayden White, *The Content of the Form* (Baltimore: The Johns Hopkins University Press, 1987), 14, 25; Niklas Stenlås, 'Vem syr kejsarens kläder?', *Arbetarhistoria*, 3–4 (2002), 51–56.
51. CfN, EEP, vol. 'Kuuse', EE to Gunnar Ehrlemark, Roland Norle, Reine Olsson, 25 April 1977.
52. Interview with Jan Kuuse and Kent Olsson, 12 April 2019.
53. CfN, EEP, vol. 'Kuuse', EE to JK, 30 May 1978.
54. CfN, EEP, vol. 'Kuuse', EE to JK, 31 May 1978.
55. Ibid.
56. CfN, EEP, vol. 'Kuuse', EE to JK, 9 August 1978.
57. CfN, KKA, vol. 'Tidningsklipp 1978'.
58. CfN, EEP, vol. 'Kuuse', EE to JK, 31 May 1978.
59. CfN, EEP, vol. 'Kontoboken', EE, 'PM beträffande nödvändigheten av forskning och ökad information', April 1977.
60. CfN, EEP, vol. 'Kuuse', PA Sjögren to EE, 18 November 1977, original emphasis.
61. CfN, EEP, vol. 'Kontoboken', PA Sjögren to EE, 17 February 1978. About a meeting between Elinder and KF see also CfN, EEP, vol. 'Ehrlemark', Letter from EE to Gunnar Ehrlemark 22 December 1977.
62. CfN, EEP, vol. 'Kuuse', PA Sjögren to EE, 5 July 1978.
63. CfN, EEP, vol. 'Kuuse', PA Sjögren to EE, 5 July 1978.

64. CfN, EEP, vol. 'RTK', RTK manuscript, Chapter 2, 11.
65. CfN, EEP, vol. 'Kuuse', EE, memo to Reine Olsson, 21 August 1980.
66. CfN, EEP, vol. 'RTK', PM by JK; CfN, EEP, vol. 'Kontoboken', EE to a long list of American contacts, 7 July 1978.
67. CfN, EEP, vol. 'Kuuse', EE to JK, 9 August 1978.
68. CfN, EEP, vol. 'RTK', EE to JK, Stockholm, 25 August 1978.
69. For Larkin, see Joe Nocera, *A Piece of the Action: How the Middle Class Joined the Money Class* (New York: Simon & Shister, 2013 [1994]), 22, 32, 55–56; Paul Chutkov, *VISA. The Power of an Idea* (Chicago: Harcourt, 2001), 103; David Stearns, *Electronic Value Exchange: Origins of the Visa Electronic Payment System* (London: Springer, 2011), 20, 47 on Larkin as 'synonymous with the BankAmericard program' at Bank of America.
70. CfN, EEP, vol. 'Kuuse', EE to JK, 9 August 1978; see also EE to JK, 29 September 1978.
71. CfN, EEP, vol. 'Kuuse', EE to JK, 29 September 1978; and vol. 'Kontoboken', EE to a long list of international contacts, February 1979.
72. CfN, EEP, vol. 'Kontoboken', 'Betr. 'Conto 79'', 19 December 1978. Memo from EE to Gunilla Cronholm and others. EE to Professor Niels Meinander, Finland, 18 August 1978.
73. CfN, EEP, vol. 'Kuuse', EE to JK, 29 September 1978.
74. CfN, EEP, vol. 'Memoarer', Dr. G.J. Weisensee, Zurich, to EE, 13 July 1979, about an international book project.
75. CfN, EEP, vol. 'Kontoboken', EE to Hans Zetterberg, 27 August 1979.
76. CfN, EEP, vol. 'Kontoboken', 'Förslag till uppsats'. See also CfN, EEP, vol. 'ContoForskning', Professor Bo Wickström to EE, 8 October 1974 on topics for bachelor/master theses.
77. CfN, EEP, vol. 'ContoForskning', Wickström to EE, 8 October 1974.
78. CfN, EEP, vol. 'Kontoboken', EE, 'PM beträffande nödvändigheten av forskning och ökad information', April 1977.
79. CfN, EEP, vol. 'Kontoboken', EE to RO, 8 June 1979.
80. CfN, EEP, vol. 'Kuuse', EE to Erik Landberg, 12 November 1980.
81. CfN, EEP, vol. 'Kontoboken', EE to RO, 8 June 1979.
82. 'Från tornsvala till Mr Card', *SvD*, 5 June 1990. In a history of the savings banks' informational activities Elinder is described as one of the 'evangelists of thrift', see Torbjörn Hessling, *Att spara eller inte spara—vilken fråga!: Den sparfrämjande verksamheten 1820–1970* (Stockholm: Sparfrämjandet, 1990), 177, 187.
83. Lewis Mandell, *The Credit Card Industry: A History* (Boston: Twayne, 1990), 44.
84. CfN, KKA, vol. 'Tidningsklipp 1978', 'Kredikort—nytt vapen hos Konsum', *Blekinge läns tidning*, 18 October 1978.

85. 'credit card psychosis' (kontokortsspykos), CfN, KKA, vol. 'Tidningsklipp 1978', *Arbetarbladet* (Gävle) 1978 (undated); see also 'Hopplöst kämpa mot kreditkorten', *Göteborgs-Tidningen* (*GT*), 20 November 1978; 'Det blir kontokort hos Konsum', *Aftonbladet* (*AB*), 16 May 1979.
86. Anders Tenér and Åke Lindén, 'Förslag till Kooperativt kreditkort', 16 May 1978, in CfN, Kooperativa Förbundet (herafter KFA), Direktionens protokoll (Minutes of the Board of Directors), 1978 no. 16, 22 May 1978, Appendix 4; CfN, KFA, Förbundsstämmans protokoll (Minutes of the General Meeting), 4 December 1978, Appendixes 8 and 9. 'Kontokorten…' and 'Ska vi ha kontokort i Konsum?', *Kooperatören*, 1 (1979), 12–15 and 17–21, respectively.
87. 'Ändringar i stadgar och handlingsprogram', *Kooperatören*, 2 (1979), 41. Admittedly, in 1946 KF had introduced a limited form of consumer loan, Låneköp, which, however, was combined with savings and applied only to select durables. See Tenér and Lindén (1978), 'Förslag till Kooperativt kreditkort' and Fredrik Sandgren, 'Introducing Co-operative Consumer Credit: The Case of Loan-purchases and the Swedish Consumer Co-operative Movement in 1945' (Nordiska historikermötet: Aalborg, 2017).
88. 'Så fungerar kontokortet', *Hudiksvalls-Tidningen*, 7 December 1978, press cutting in CfN, KKA, vol. 'Tidningsklipp 1978'.
89. SOU 1979:62, Kooperationsutredningen. *Kooperationen i Sverige: betänkande* (Stockholm: Liber Förlag/Allmänna förlaget, 1979), 38–39.
90. My sources include archival material from KF, as well as press and political material from 1978 to 1980.
91. Peder Aléx, *Den rationella konsumenten: KF som folkuppfostrare 1899–1939* (Stockholm/Stehag: Symposion, 1994); Orsi Husz, 'Spara, Slösa och alla de andra', in *Signums svenska kulturhistoria, 1900-talet*, ed. by Jacob Christenson (Stockholm: Atlantis, 2009), 279–299; Helena Mattsson, 'Designing the Reasonable Consumer: Standardization and Personalization in Swedish Functionalism', in *Swedish Modernism: Architecture, Consumption and the Welfare State*, ed. by Helena Mattsson and Sven-Olov Wallenstein (London: Black Dog Publishing, 2010), 74–99. For weak consumers see CfN, KFA, Förbundsstämmans protokoll (Minutes of KF's General Meeting), June 1979, inaugural speech by chairman Hans Alsén, 11 June 1979, 5.
92. 'Handelns historia: Kooperativa Förbundet: Konsumenskooperationen år för år' (The history of commerce: The Cooperative Union), http://www.handelnshistoria.se/handelsforetag/kf/konsumentkooperationen-ar-for-ar/ (retrieved 28 June 2023).
93. For example, KF criticised the wage-earner fund proposal arguing that it did not take the consumer perspective into consideration. CfN, KFA, Bilaga till Direktionens protokoll (Appendix to the minutes of the Board

of Directors), 12 March 1979, 'Kooperationens konsumentpolitiska roll' (1978).
94. SOU 1979:62, 186.
95. SOU 1979:62, 38–39. See also the online historical encyclopedia of Kooperativa Förbundet, https://kf.se/uppslagsverk/antalet-medlemmar-minskade-i-konsumentforeningarna/; Sara Kristoffersson, 'A Brand for Everyone', in *Design Culture: Objects and Approaches*, ed. by Guy Julier et al. (London: Bloomsbury, 2019); 'Första fem basmöblerna färdiga', *Köpmannen*, 28 August 1978; and CfN, KKA, vol. Förbundsstämmans protokoll (Minutes of KF's General Meeting), June 1979, inaugural speech by chairman Hans Alsén, 11 June 1979, 5.
96. Antoni and Plogner, *Måste konsumenten*; Olle Wästberg, 'Ämbetsverk som konsumenthot', *SvD*, 16 March 1978; Olle Wästberg, 'Självständiga beslut från konsumenterna: Nej till förmyndarsamhället', *Köpmannen*, 20 November 1978; Sven Heurgren, 'Privata konsumentgrupper behövs ej', *SvD*, 14 February 1978. Husz and Carlsson, 'Marketing a New Society'; Elsässer, *Att skapa en konsument*, 266, 277–278, 321; Sun-Joon Hwang, *Folkrörelse eller affärsföretag* (Stockholm: Stockholms universitet, 1995), 103–130.
97. See above and Olsen, *The Sovereign Consumer*.
98. Sven Heurgren, 'Privata konsumentgrupper behövs ej', *SvD*, 14 February 1978. CfN, KFA, Bilaga till Direktionens protokoll (Appendix to the Minutes of the Board of Directors), 12 March 1979, 'Kooperationens konsumentpolitiska roll' (1978), 18, 27.
99. Olle Wästberg, 'Självständiga beslut från konsumenterna', *Köpmannen*, 20 November 1978; Husz, 'Kreditkortskriget', 218–219.
100. CfN, KFA, Förbundsstyrelsens protokoll (Minutes of the KF Board), 1978 no. 83. (27 October).
101. CfN, KFA, Förbundsstyrelsens protokoll (Minutes of the KF Board), 1978 no. 81 (1 September), 21, 24.
102. CfN, KFA, Förbundsstyrelsens protokoll (Minutes of the KF Board), 1978 no. 83. (27 October).
103. CFN, KFA, Förbundsstämmans protokoll (Minutes of the General Meeting), December 1978, Appendix 9, *Kontokort på Konsum?*, 1. Informational booklet for the membership.
104. CfN, KFA, Förbundsstämmans protokoll (Minutes of the General Meeting), December 1978, 69.
105. Ibid., 49.
106. Ibid., 71; and CfN, KFA, Förbundsstämmans protokoll (Minutes of the General Meeting), June 1979, 91.
107. CfN, KFA, Förbundsstämmans protokoll (Minutes of the General Meeting), December 1978, 44.

108. Ibid., 35–37; 'Vem tjänar på kontokort', *Vi*, 13 (1979) 29 March; 'Kontokortet kommer', *Vi*, 25 (1979) 21 June, 10–11. See also quotes such as: 'Kreditkorten är ekonomins narkotika' ('The credit card is the narcotics of the economy') and 'Kontantprincipen är KFs främsta princip' ('The cash-only policy is KF's main principle'), both in 'Säj nej till kontokort!', *Vi*, 12 (1979) 22 March, 28.
109. 'Skulden som bojor', *Aftonbladet*, 1 December 1979; 'Kreditkorten—ett strupgrepp på löntagarna', *DN*, 26 November 1979.
110. 'KF hänger med', *Nerikes Allehanda*, 8 November 1978.
111. CfN, KFA, Förbundsstämmans protokoll (Minutes of the General Meeting), December 1978, 52 and June 1979, 92.
112. The Wallenberg family were the most influential financiers in Sweden. They also owned—through the Swedish company Vendor—Eurocard (established 1965), an international payment card for professionals and businesses. 'Kontokortet kommer. Röster för och emot på stämman', *Vi*, 25 (1979) 21 June, 10–11; 'Kontokorten kan bredda kooperationen', *Kooperatören*, 5 (1979).
113. 'Ja till kontoköp', *Vi*, 32–33 (1979) 9 August, 38; 'Kontokortet kommer', *Vi*, 25 (1979) 21 June.
114. CfN, KFA, Förbundsstämmans protokoll (Minutes of the General Meeting), December 1978, 59–60, 67 and 78.
115. 'Det är inte Konsums sak att vara förmyndare', *Vi*, 24 (1979) 14 June, 28; 'Vi ska inte låsa oss fast vid föråldrade principer' and 'Konsums kontokort skiljer sig från övriga kreditkort', *Vi*, 12 (1979) 23 March; 'Vi kan inte ställa oss som våra medlemmars förmyndare', *Göteborgs-Posten*, 15 May 1979; 'Kontokort–under ansvar', *SvD*, 4 November 1979; 'Kontokorten kan bredda kooperationen', *Kooperatören*, 5 (1979), 44.
116. CfN, KFA, Förbundsstyrelsens protokoll (Minutes of the KF Board), 1978 no. 83, 20, 26 and 19.
117. For example, *Vi*, 48 (1978) 30 November, 38; CfN, KFA, Förbundsstämmans protokoll (Minutes of the General Meeting), December 1978, 40.
118. 'Konsum sviker de gamla idealen', *Göteborgs-Tidningen*, 20 September 1979; 'Kreditkorten—ett strupgrepp på löntagarna', *DN*, 26 November 1979; see also 'Mat på kredit', *Aftonbladet*, 11 August 1979.
119. 'Kontokort—under ansvar', *SvD*, 4 November 1979; 'Kontoklart för KF', *SvD*, 14 August 1979.
120. Husz, 'The Entrepreneur's Dream'; Erik Elinder, 'Kontokort—en förmån eller fara?', *Köpmannen*, 17 December 1979.
121. CfN, EEP, vol. 'Contokriget', Finax whole-page adverts, original emphasis. See also large adverts in the private retail trade's own magazine *Köpmannen* 1979–1980.

122. Bo Gunnarsson, 'Betalkort—teknik eller behov?', *Ekonomisk Revy*, 6 (1979), 256.
123. Riksdagens protokoll (Minutes of the Parliament), 1979/1980 no. 48, 10 December 1979: 'Om kreditkortens roll i samhällsekonomin', 11, 13–16, 18–22.
124. Ibid., 16, 21.
125. DsFi 1984:10, 139–140; Rasmus Fleischer, 'Kreditkonsumtion i Sverige, 1945–1985', *Historisk Tidskrift*, 136, 4 (2016), 653; David Rune, 'Att leva på plast: Hot eller möjlighet? En studie av svensk kreditkortsdebatt 1979–87', BA thesis (Stockholm: Department of History, Stockholm University, 2007).
126. DsFi 1984:10.
127. Fleischer, 'Kreditkonsumtion', 653–654.
128. Karneman, *Kontokort*.

Notes to Chapter 6

1. BankID statistics, https://www.bankid.com/om-oss/statistik (retrieved 26 February 2024). This chapter draws on two of my previous studies: Orsi Husz, 'Bank Identity: Banks, ID Cards, and the Emergence of a Financial Identification Society in Sweden', *Enterprise & Society*, 19, 2 (2018), 391–429, and Orsi Husz, *The Identity Economy* (Stockholm: Riksbankens Jubileumsfond with Makadam förlag, 2022).
2. In addition to bank archives, the Bankers' Association's records, Erik Elinder's Papers, trade journals and the mainstream media, I also use material from the company *AB ID-kort* and from government committees.
3. Edward Higgs, 'Consuming Identity and Consuming the State in Britain, c. 1750', in *Identification and Registration Practices in Transnational Perspective*, ed. by Ilsen About, James Brown, and Gayle Lonergan (Basingstoke, UK: Palgrave Macmillan, 2013), 164. The bias is tellingly illustrated in two edited volumes (Caplan and Torpey, *Documenting Individual Identity*; About et al. *Identification and Registration*), published as surveys of the historical research on documented identity. Of the 35 essays between the two volumes, only Higgs's in the latter one mentions the role of commercial actors.
4. Matt K. Matsuda, *The Memory of the Modern* (New York and Oxford: Oxford University Press, 1996), 121; See esp. Jon Agar, 'Modern Horrors: British Identity and Identity Cards', in *Documenting Individual Identity*, ed. by Jane Caplan and John Torpey (Princeton, NJ: Princeton University Press, 2001), 101–120; Anne M. Joseph, 'Anthropometry, the Police Expert and the Deptford Murders', in Caplan and Torpey, *Documenting Individual Identity*, 164–183; John Torpey, 'The Great War and the Birth of the Modern Passport System', in Caplan and Torpey, *Documenting*

Individual Identity, 256–270. See also Simon A. Cole, *Suspect Identities: A History of Fingerprinting and Criminal Identification* (Cambridge, MA: Harvard University Press, 2001); David Lyon, *Identifying Citizens: ID Cards as Surveillance* (Cambridge: Polity Press, 2009), 27–35; Ilsen About, James Brown, and Gayle Lonergan (eds.), *Identification and Registration Practices in Transnational Perspective: People, Papers and Practices* (Basingstoke, UK: Palgrave Macmillan, 2013).

5. For example, Caplan and Torpey, *Documenting Individual Identity*; Craig Robertson, 'A Documentary Regime of Verification', *Cultural Studies*, 23, 3 (2009), 329–354; Craig Robertson, *The Passport in America: The History of a Document* (New York: Oxford University Press, 2010); Edward Higgs, *Identifying the English: A History of Personal Identification 1500 to the Present* (London: Bloomsbury, 2011); Colin Koopman, *How We Became Our Data: A Genealogy of the Informational Person* (Chicago: University of Chicago Press, 2019).

6. Gösta Lext, *Studier i svensk kyrkobokföring 1600–1946* (Göteborg: Landsarkivet, 1985). See Koopman, *How We Became Our Data*, 13 for the 'formatting' of identity.

7. John Torpey, *The Invention of the Passport: Surveillance, Citizenship and the State* (Cambridge: Cambridge University Press, 1999). See also Higgs, *Identifying the English*. For older Swedish travel documents, see Anna-Brita Lövgren, *Staten och folk på väg: Pass i Sverige från Gustav Vasas tid till 1860* (Lund: Nordic Academic Press 2018).

8. Robertson, 'Documentary Regime'; Robertson, *The Passport in America*. Quote from Craig Robertson, "You Lie!' Identity, Paper, and the Materiality of Information', *The Communication Review*, 17, 2 (2014), 71.

9. Robertson, 'Documentary Regime', 347. See also Kelly Gates, *Our Biometric Future: Facial Recognition Technology and the Culture of Surveillance* (New York: New York University Press, 2011), 34–37, who connects the financial interests in *documented* identities (the 'securitization of identity') to the computerisation and neoliberalisation process of the 1980s and 1990s.

10. See, for example, David Lyon (ed.), *Surveillance as Social Sorting: Privacy, Risk, and Digital Discrimination* (London: Routledge, 2003); Daniel Solove, *The Digital Person: Technology and Privacy in the Information Age* (New York: New York University Press, 2004). Nick Couldry and Ulysses A. Meijas, *The Costs of Connection: How Data Is Colonizing Human Life and Appropriating It for Capitalism* (Stanford: Stanford University Press, 2019); Celia Lury and Sophie Day, 'Algorithmic Personalization as a Mode of Individuation', *Theory, Culture & Society*, 36, 2 (2019), 17–37.

11. Shoshana Zuboff, *The Age of Surveillance Capitalism: The Fight for the Future and the New Frontier of Power* (London: Profile Books, 2019). See

also Sue Curry Jansen and Jefferson Pooley, 'Blurring Genres and Violating Guild Norms: A Review of Reviews of the Age of Surveillance Capitalism', *New Media & Society*, 23, 9 (2021), 2839–2851.
12. Zuboff, *Surveillance Capitalism*, 53.
13. For selective direct advertising based on state registers, see SOU 1972:47, Offentlighets- och sekretesslagstiftningskommittén, *Data och integritet: betänkande* (Stockholm: Allmänna Förlaget, 1972), 187. See also Lars Ilshammar, *Offentlighetens nya rum: Teknik och politik i Sverige 1969–1999* (Örebro: Örebro universitet, 2002); Johan Fredrikzon, *Kretslopp av data: Miljö, befolkning, förvaltning och den tidiga digitaliseringens kulturtekniker* (Lund: Mediehistoriskt arkiv, 2011), Ch. 6.
14. For examples of early commercial interest in data collection and surveillance by insurance and credit reporting businesses, see Alf Sjöblom, *Trygghet som handelsvara: privat folkförsäkring i det framväxande välfärdssamhället 1900–1950* (Stockholm: Historiska institutionen, Stockholms universitet, 2016); Josh Lauer, *Creditworthy: A History of Consumer Surveillance and Financial Identity in America* (New York: Columbia University Press, 2017); Koopman, *How We Became Our Data*. For an empirical example from Swedish sources, see Einar Hellners, *Kurs för livförsäkringsacquisitörer* (Malmö: Hermods, 1932), Letter 9. p. 16.
15. Marion Fourcade and Kieran Healy, 'Seeing Like a Market', *Socio-Economic Review*, 15, 1 (2017), 9–29. See also Sarah E. Igo, *The Known Citizen: A History of Privacy in Modern America* (Cambridge, MA: Harvard University Press, 2018), 56.
16. Robertson, *The Passport in America*; Fredrikzon, *Kretslopp av data*, 235–236.
17. For advisors and educators see, for example, Tore Browaldh, 'Checken allmänheten och vi', *HB Remissan*, 7 (1958); Centrum för näringslivshistoria (Centre for Business History, CfN), Handelsbanken (HB), F5:161, circular letter to branch office managers at Handelsbanken; folder *Lönen på checkräkning* and 'Utdrag ur betänkande avgivet av stadskamrer O. Forssberg', 5. For salesmen, see 'Varför, Hur och Vad ska vi sälja' and 'Gör varje kund till totalkund', *Din Bank*, 5 (1963).
18. Jeanne Lazarus, *L'épreuve de l'argent. Banques, banquiers, clients* (Paris: Calmann-Lévy, 2012), Ch. 1.
19. See Chapter 1 and CfN, HB, F4:11, internal memo 'Marketing Research', 29 March 1968.
20. All examples from *HB Remissan/Remissan* and in *Din Bank*, 1958–1963.
21. 'Hur har det lyckats?', *Din Bank*, 4 (1957); 'Kan ni legitimera er?', *Din Bank*, 2 (1962); 'Kan ni legitimera er' (Part 2), *Din Bank*, 3 (1962); 'Dödsdom över checklönen', *Kvällsposten*, 20 March 1965, press cutting in CfN, Skandinaviska Banken (SB), Ö1:27.

22. Motion i Andra Kammaren (Private Members' Bill in the Second Chamber) 1963 no. 683; Allmänna beredningsutskottets utlåtande (Drafting Committee's Report) 1963 no. 15.
23. 'Han hade legitimationshandlingarna runt handleden', *Remissan*, 9–10 (1961), 39.
24. 'Ny banklegitimation mot checkbedragare', *Stockholms-Tidningen (ST)*, 17 November 1962, press cutting in CfN, SB, Ö1:27; 'Får jag be om legitimation', *Din Bank*, 4 (1963); Allmänna beredningsutskottets utlåtande (Drafting Committee's Report) 1963 no. 15.
25. 'Får jag be om legitimation', by Lennart Börnforss (in charge of the Bankers' Association's work with ID cards), *Din Bank*, 4 (1963).
26. Gunnar Herlitz, 'Rätt och skyldighet att kräva legitimation', *Din Bank*, 4 (1963).
27. SOU 1944:52; DsFi 1975:7, *Förslag till Lag om identitetskontroll vid inlösen av check* (Stockholm: Liber Förlag/Allmänna förlaget, 1975); 'Medborgarkort', *Dagens Nyheter (DN)*, 5 January 1950; 'Medborgarkort dröjer ytterligare', *Svenska Dagbladet (SvD)*, 17 November 1951.
28. Motion i Andra Kammaren (Private Members' Bill in the Second Chamber), 1963 no. 683; Allmänna beredningsutskottets utlåtande (Drafting Committee's Report), 1963 no. 15; Andra Kammarens protokoll (Records of the Proceedings in the Second Chamber), 1963 no. 16, 53.
29. 'Får jag be om legitimation', *Din Bank*, 4 (1963), see the section 'Hjälp till att snabbt sprida ID-korten.'
30. In addition to the limited possibility to cash cheques in shops, it was no longer possible to write a cheque to a 'third party', i.e. another private person. 'Ny bankregel i tysthet om "spärr" för privatcheck', *SvD*, 24 September 1966. See also DsFi 1971:12, Sture Lundell, *PM angående åtgärder för att motverka checkmissbruket* (Stockholm: Finansdepartementet, 1971).
31. 'Ert checkhäfte värt 4000 kronor "svart"', *Kvällsposten*, 7 October 1966, press cutting in CfN, SB, Ö1:27; 'Nu minskar checkbrotten', *Folket*, 18 February 1965; 'Checkbedrägerier minskar', *Aftonbladet*, 23 March 1965, press cutting in CfN, SB, Ö1:2. See also DsFi 1971:12, 41–42.
32. 'Broms på skojet', *Köpmannen*, 8 December 1966; see also 'Enhetlig legitimation krav från rikspolisen', *DN*, 26 February 1965; 'Skärpta bank-krav på legitimation', *ST*, 25 February 1965; 'Skärpt kamp mot checkskoj. Förslag om medborgarkort', *DN*, 4 March 1965, press cuttings in CfN, SB, Ö1:2.
33. 'Bistrare tider för checkskojare. Bankerna skärper kontrollen', *Folket*, 18 February 1965; 'Enhetlig legitimation', *DN*, 26 February, 1965; 'Skärpta bank-krav på legitimation', *ST*, 25 February 1965, press cuttings in CfN,

SB, Ö1:2; 'Svårare att få ut checklön', *ST Ekonomi*, 12 June 1965, press cutting in CfN, SB, Ö1:27.
34. Torpey, *Invention of the Passport*, 166; Lyon *Identifying Citizens*, 14, 70; Robertson, 'Documentary Regime', 348. For fingerprinting and the association with criminality, see Cole, 'Suspect Identities.'
35. Mary Poovey, *Genres of the Credit Economy: Mediating Value in Eighteenth- and Nineteenth-Century Britain* (Chicago: University of Chicago Press, 2008), 4.
36. 'Hur har det lyckats?', *Din Bank*, 4 (1957).
37. 'Dragkamp om checken', *Göteborgstidningen*, 9 April 1961, press cutting in CfN, SB, F:71/43 (141).
38. CfN, Bankföreningen (Swedish Banker's Association, hereafter BF), Styrelsens protokoll (Minutes of the Board of the Bankers' Association), 19 July 1968, §104.
39. Jenny Björkman, 'Systemskiftet.' *Populär Historia*, 12 (2004). Starting in 1964, customers in the state monopoly's liquor shops were legally required to show an ID document that included a photo. See, for example, campaign adverts 'Klart vi har FOTO-legitimation', *Expressen*, 22 January 1964; and 'Systemlegitimation gäller ej på bank', *SvD*, 25 January 1964.
40. 'Kan ni legitimera er', *Din Bank*, 2 (1962); 'Kan ni legitimera er?' (Part 2), *Din Bank*, 3 (1962). Also mentioned in these articles are different means of identification used in everyday practice. The same slogan was used later in a large national campaign for the use of ID cards, see *ID-Nytt*, 1 (1975). See also the humorous articles by Åke Cato, 'Jahapp sa löntagaren', *Aftonbladet*, 28 December 1978, and 'Plastkort luktar inte', *Aftonbladet*, 10 November 1977.
41. Information folders, instruction booklets, and instructional films in Riksarkivet (RA), Checklöneutredningen 1968–1971 (Government Inquiry into Cheque Account Salaries and Wages), for example leaflets and adverts such as 'Varsågod–check och legitimation'; 'Vid betalning med check. Information till kassa- och butikspersonal'; 'Klara besked om check och legitimation'; and 'Gör det till en vana.'
42. 'Varför ilska när jag ber om ID-kort?', *Kontokuriren*, 2 (1968), 1.
43. DsFi 1971:12, 33.
44. DsFi 1975:7, 6; 'Post scriptum: Sju frågor om identitetshantering', *ID-Nytt*, 1 (1977), 2.
45. DsFi 1975:7, 6; CfN, BF, Styrelsens protokoll (Minutes of the Board of the Bankers' Association), 19 June 1968, §104 and Appendixes 2 and 3, 'Protokoll fört vid sammanträde den 4/6 1968 med arbetsgruppen för ID kort'. CfN, BF, F2b:3, 'Promemoria 14/11 1966', and 'Slutrapport 13/11 1968' by Arbetsgruppen för utredning av legitimationshandlingar.

46. CfN, BF, F2b:3, 'Promemoria 14/11 1966', and 'Slutrapport 13/11 1968' by Arbetsgruppen för utredning av legitimationshandlingar; 'AB ID-korts arkiv', *ID-Nytt*, 2 (1974).
47. See 'Post scriptum: Sju frågor om identitetshantering', *ID-Nytt*, 1 (1977); 'När AB ID-kort startade tillverkningen', *ID-Nytt*, 3–4 (1974). See also CfN, BF, Styrelsens protokoll (Minutes of the Board of the Bankers' Association), 19 June 1968, §104 and Appendixes 2 and 3, 'Protokoll fört vid sammanträde den 4/6 1968 med arbetsgruppen för ID kort'.
48. Lyon, *Identifying Citizens*, 63–81.
49. The industry was represented on the board by two organisations: Sveriges Industriförbund (Federation of Swedish Industry) and Näringslivets säkerhetsdelegation (Business Sector's Security Delegation). DsFi 1975:7, 9–10.
50. Ibid., 25.
51. 'Bankföreningen anmäld till NO', *DN*, 24 February 1973.
52. DsFi 1975:7; SOU 2007:100, Id-kortsutredningen, *Id-kort för folkbokförda i Sverige. Betänkande* (Stockholm: Fritze, 2007), 36. Regulations were developed in the form of standards in 1981 by the Swedish Standards Institute (SiS), a nonprofit association. See also *ID-Nytt*, 3 (1975) and Justitieutskottet, *Förbättrad kontroll av legitimationshandlingar. Betänkande* (Committee of Justice's Report), 1988/1989:JuU3 (Riksdagen/Parliamentary Papers, 1989).
53. Overdrafts were still the bank's risk while the fraudulent use of stolen cheques, if unreported, was the account holder's responsibility.
54. DsFi 1975:7, 5; CfN, SB, F:71/43, internal memos and correspondence with the Bankers' Association. For cheque fraud, see also Johannes Knutson and Eckart Külhorn, *När checkbedrägerierna försvann*, BRÅ Rapport (Stockholm: Liber Förlag/Allmänna förlaget, 1980), 19–25.
55. No interest was paid on the account if the client used more than seven cheques a month. In addition, banks had to contribute to a fund for fighting cheque fraud and compensate retailers' losses in certain cases. A SEK 1 handling fee was charged for cheques under SEK 50. See 'Checken blir åter giltig i handeln', *SvD*, 11 November 1972; 'Småcheckar–missbruk', *SvD*, 23 December 1978; 'Vanlig löntagare dyr kund. Nu ska vi ut ur bankerna', *DN*, 28 December 1978.
56. DsFi 1975:7, 4–5; 'Säkrare ID-kort skyddar era pengar', *Kontokuriren*, 1 (1970), 1.
57. DsFi 1971:12, 44–45.
58. Ibid., 1–2.
59. CfN, BF, F2b:6, 'PM ang checkrörelsen och regeringsrådet Lundells utredning' (17 September 1971), memo from P. Modigh.
60. 'Checkens återkomst kräver nya ID-kort', *Kontakten*, 2 (1973), the in-house magazine at LM Ericsson.

61. 'Bästa läsare', *ID-Nytt*, 1 (1975).
62. 'Editorial' and 'Det är dina pengar ID-kortet vill skydda!', *ID-Nytt*, 1 (1975); 'Säkrare ID-kort skyddar era pengar', *Kontokuriren*, 1 (1970); and KB, Ephemera, AB ID-kort, Posters and other informational material. See also recurring adverts in *Ekonomisk Revy* under the year 1971.
63. 'Till Maria säger ingen nej', *Ekonomisk Revy*, recurring (1974); and KB, Ephemera, AB ID-kort, similar adverts as well as adverts for the savings banks' ID card in campaigns to schoolchildren. See also 'ID-kort och koder, nycklar till livet', *DN*, 16 February 1984.
64. 'Framtidens ID-kort ersätter pengar', *Veckans affärer*, 5 December 1974, 33.
65. 'Sju frågor om framtiden', *ID-Nytt*, 4 (1976); 'Svensk standard för transaktionskort', *ID-Nytt*, 3–4 (1977); 'Förslag till ny Svensk standard för identitetskort i strolek ID1', *ID-Nytt*, 4 (1980); CfN, BF, F3a:30, 'Förslag till nytt ID-kortsystem', 1 November 1979.
66. 'Framtidens ID-kort ersätter pengar', *Veckans affärer*, 5 December 1974, 33.
67. DsFi 1971:12, 66. For the Köpkort credit card as a substitute for cheques, see advertising and informational leaflets and letters to and from Konsumentombudsmannen (the Consumer Ombudsman) in RA, Checklöneutredningen 1968–1971 (Government Inquiry into Cheque Account Salaries and Wages). For promotion of Köpkort by state-owned Kreditbanken, see adverts in *Kontokuriren*, 1 (1968) and 4 (1968).
68. Joe Deville, 'Paying with Plastic: The Enduring Presence of the Credit Card', in *Accumulation: The Material Politics of Plastic*, ed. by Jennifer Gabrys, Gay Hawkins, and Mike Michael (London: Routledge, 2014), 87–104; Joe Nocera, *A Piece of the Action: How the Middle Class Joined the Money Class* (New York: Simon & Shister, 2013 [1994]). For a Swedish 'card drop', 'Modehus lockar kunder med kreditkort i brev', *Aftonbladet*, 6 December 1962; and CfN, EEP, vol. 'Kontoboken', transcript of telephone call 26 April 1978 between Erik Elinder and Göran Oldenburg about the NK card.
69. 'Plastgjutna identitetskort i stor säkerhetskampanj', *DN*, 15 January 1963.
70. For example, KB, Ephemera, AB ID-kort, 'Apparat för isotopkontroll', Informational leaflet.
71. Deville, 'Paying with Plastic'; Bernardo Batiz-Lazo and Gustavo A. Del Angel, 'The Ascent of Plastic Money: International Adoption of the Bank Credit Card, 1950–1975', *Business History Review*, 92, 3 (2018), 509–533; Orsi Husz, 'Money Cards and Identity Cards: De-vicing Consumer Credit in Post-war Sweden', *Journal of Cultural Economy*, 14, 2 (2021), 139–158. Diners Club, often referred to as the world's first credit card system, was established in 1950, but the cards were initially made of cardboard.

For the introduction of plastic for cards in Sweden: Göran Oldenburg, 'Kontobrickorna ersätts av plastkort', *Kompanirullan*, 3 (1959).

72. For the bank card, see 'Bankerna vill inte avskaffa kontanter', *DN*, 5 September 1972; CfN, BF, Styrelsens protokoll (Minutes of the Board of the Bankers' Association), 16 April 1969, §74 and Appendixes 6–13, for example: 'Bankkortets standardisering är ett grundläggande villkor för hela det skissade systemet' and 'Elektroniskt betalningssystem', Memo, 20 March 1969, 5. 'Checkhanteringen kan göras mycket enklare', *Köpmannen*, 3 March 1980. CfN, BF, Styrelsens protokoll (Minutes of the Board of the Bankers' Association), 21 November 1979, §197.
73. KB, Ephemera, AB ID-kort, Brochures from AB ID-kort 1974–1976; 'Köp utan kontanter. Handeln storsatsar', *DN*, 11 July 1980.
74. 'Framtidens ID-kort ersätter pengar', *Veckans affärer*, 5 December 1974.
75. 'Han plåtar oss nästan alla', *DN, 30 December 1970*; Advertisement for example in *DN*, 30 March 1971; Birger Kock (ed.), *Från idé till produkt. En samling kända svenska uppfinnare berättar om sitt arbete* (Stockholm: Styrelsen för teknisk utveckling i samarbete med Sv. Uppfinnareföreningen, 1981), 57–63. 'Nytt ID-kort för Rothfjell', *DN*, 2 July 1975; 'Skarp NO-kritik för ID-monopol', *DN*, 18 September 1975; 'Striden om ID-korten. Konkurrenten Rollfilm hotas av kronofogden', *DN*, 23 September 1975.
76. Rolf Eric Rothfjell, *Method for Indentifying Individuals Using Selected Characteristic Body Curves*. US Patent 3,805,238, 16 April 1974. Kelly Gates, 'The Securitization of Financial Identity and the Expansion of the Consumer Credit Industry', *Journal of Communication Inquiry*, 34, 4 (2010), 423.
77. 'Plastgjutna identitetskort i stor säkerhetskampanj', *DN*, 15 January 1963.
78. 'Framtidens ID-kort ersätter pengar',*Veckans affärer*, 5 December 1974; 'ID-kortstriden', *DN*, 25 September 1975; 'Bankerna måste ta Rollfilmkort', *DN*, 1 February 1979.
79. For the identity scandal ('identitetshärvan'), see 'Framtidens ID-kort ersätter pengar', *Veckans affärer*, 5 December 1974.
80. Husz, 'Bank Identity'. The state sold its shares in ID-kort to LM Ericsson in 1984. KB, Ephemera, AB ID-kort, Leaflet 'ID-kort' (1986); 'AB ID-kort–ett helprivat företag', *DN*, 16 February 1984. See also 'Id-kort och koder nycklar till livet', *DN*, 16 February 1984.
81. Gunnar Enroth, in Björn Thodenius (ed.), *Teknisk utveckling i bankerna* (Stockholm, Kungliga Tekniska Högskolan, 2008), 15. Cf. Gates, 'Securitization of Financial Identity', 422 about the proliferation of financial transactional data in the American credit card industry of the 1980s; and Thomas Haigh, '"Veritable Bucket of Facts": Origins of the Database Management System', *SIGMOD Record*, 35, 2 (2006), 33–49 about database technology.

82. Postbanken had been practising the system for a few years by then. 'Idag startar PK banken', *DN*, 1 July 1974; 'Personnumret – nyckel till kontroll', *DN*, 13 July 1973; 'Datalag ska skydda privatliv, men än säljs vi som nummer', *DN*, 13 July 1973.
83. KB, Ephemera, PK-banken 1974–1979, Broschures about Personkonto. See also 'Det blev julpengar fast datorn slog till', *DN*, 14 December 1978.
84. SIBOL, *[Samarbete för integrerat betalningssystem on-line]-systemet* (Stockholm: SIBOL, 1972), volumes 1–4; Thodenius, *Teknisk utveckling*, 14.
85. CfN, BF, Styrelsens protokoll (Minutes of the Board of the Bankers' Association), 16 April 1969, §74, Appendix 12 (5) 'Policyfrågor'.
86. 'Bankerna vill inte avskaffa kontanter', *DN*, 5 September 1972; CfN, BF, Styrelsens protokoll (Minutes of the Board of the Bankers' Association), 16 April 1969, §74 and Appendixes 6–13, for example 'Bankkortets standardisering är ett grundläggande villkor för hela det skissade systemet' and 'Elektroniskt betalningssystem', Memo, 20 March 1969, 5.
87. CfN, BF, Styrelsens protokoll (Minutes of the Board of the Bankers' Association), 16 April 1969, §74, Appendix 9, 'Elektroniskt betalningssystem'; CfN, BF, Styrelsens protokoll (Minutes of the Board of the Bankers' Association), 21 November 1979, §197, Appendix, 'Förslag till nytt ID-kortssystem', 6 November 1979; CfN, BF, F3 a:30, 'PM med komplettering av beslutsunderlag i bankkortsfrågan (del 2)', 6 November 1979. It was said that it would be easier to retract or deny the transaction card of a negligent bank customer if the card did not also serve as an ID card.
88. CfN, BF, Styrelsens protokoll (Minutes of the Board of the Bankers' Association), 18 October 1972, §228, Appendix, Referral response (*remissvar*) to the Ministry of Justice, 18 October 1972; For the report see SOU 1972:47.
89. Lauer, *Creditworthy*; Fourcade and Healy, 'Seeing like a market'.
90. SOU 1972:79, 38–53. ABAK is short for AB Automatisk Kontokontroll.
91. For UC see CfN, BF, Styrelsens protokoll (Minutes of the Board of the Bankers' Association), 14 May 1968, §92 and Appendix 5; 20 November 1974, §203; and 20 March 1979, §60. For SIBOL/electronic payment systems, see CfN, BF, Styrelsens protokoll (Minutes of the Board of the Bankers' Association), 16 April 1969, §74 and Appendixes 6–8.
92. SOU 1978:54, Datalagstiftningskommittén, *Personregister—datorer—integritet: översyn av datalagen: delbetänkande* (Stockholm: Liber Förlag/Allmänna förlaget, 1978), 114; CfN, BF, Styrelsens protokoll (Minutes of the Board of the Bankers' Association), 25 April 1979, §60 and Appendix 1: 'Upplysningscentralen (UC)'.
93. Ilshammar, *Offentlighetens nya rum*, 137; Kajsa Klein (ed.), *Integritetsdebatten åren kring 1984: Transkript av ett vittnesseminarium vid Tekniska museet i Stockholm den 30 november 2007* (Stockholm: KTH, Avdelningen

för teknik- och vetenskapshistoria, 2008), 37–39, transcript of a witness seminar on the privacy debate around 1984; For privacy debates see also Fredrikzon, *Kretslopp av data*.
94. James B. Rule, *Private Lives and Public Surveillance* (London: Allen Lane, 1973), 265.
95. CfN, EEP, vol. 'Memoarer', Quotes from notes by Elinder, 9 August 1978 and 29 August 1978. The same issue was discussed both earlier (1972) and later (1980).
96. 'Effektivitet måste vägas mot integritetsskyddet', *DN*, 29 April 1971.
97. See Gates, 'Securitization of Financial Identity', 423, for how transaction data collected by American credit card companies in the 1980s and 1990s 'became a valuable commodity in itself'. Josh Lauer, 'Plastic Surveillance: Payment Cards and the History of Transactional Data, 1888 to Present', *Big Data & Society*, 7, 1 (2020) points to the long history behind transactional data as a commodity, using the example of credit reporting agencies and—from the 1980s—loyalty cards.
98. 'Från tornsvala till Mr Card', *SvD*, 5 June 1990; 'Erik Elinder', obituary, *SvD*, 16 July 1998.
99. 'Välkommen in i familjen!' (Welcome to the Family!), Editorial for the 1987 Ikea catalogue (published 1986), 2.
100. In 1986, the Ikea catalogue had a global circulation of 45 million and was published in ten languages.
101. Lauer, 'Plastic surveillance'; https://www.ingka.com/newsroom/ikea-family-reaches-150-million-members/ (retrieved 14 March 2024).
102. Lauer, 'Plastic Surveillance'; Lana Swartz, *New Money: How Payment Became Social Media* (New Haven, CT: Yale University Press, 2020), 58–59.
103. 'Bli en maktfaktor, bli medlem', *Aftonbladet*, 21 September 1985; 'Möbeldröm. Släkten är värst', *Aftonbladet*, 28 June 1985; Åke Cato, 'Ikeologen och risken med IF', *Aftonbladet*, 31 August 1988; 'Försoffade kändisar på möblernas Café Opera!, *Aftonbladet*, 12 October 1991.
104. Editorial, *ID-Nytt*, 1 (1975). For the banks' new ID card 'protecting' people's money and thus being necessary for everyone, see 'Säkrare ID-kort skyddar era pengar', *Kontokuriren*, 1 (1970).
105. A proposal for state regulation by an expert committee within the Department of Finances was not realised. See DsFi 1975:7; and SOU 2007:100, 36. KB, Ephemera, AB ID-kort, Leaflet 'ID-kort' (1986); and 'AB ID-kort–ett helprivat företag', *DN*, 16 February 1984.
106. SOU 2007:100, 32, 65–70. For the growing interest in national identification schemes post-9/11, see Lyon, *Identifying Citizens*, 71, 72.
107. SOU 210:104; David Birch, *Identity Is the New Money* (London: Publishing Partnership, 2014), 44.

Notes to Chapter 7

1. On Venmo, see Lana Swartz, *New Money: How Payment Became Social Media* (New Haven, CT: Yale University Press, 2020), 21–23.
2. Turo-Kimmo Lehtonen, 'Domesticating Insurance, Financializing Family Lives: The Case of Private Health Insurance for Children in Finland', *Cultural Studies*, 31, 5 (2017), 707.
3. For 'modus vivendi', see CfN, KKA, vol. 'Reklam 1967', Sven Å. Cason, 'Swedish Experience in the Field of Charge Accounts and Revolving Credit', Speech at the Seminar on Consumer Credit, organised by Fédération Internationale des Grandes Entreprises de Distribution (FIGED). Brussels, 7–8 March 1967.
4. David Larsson Heidenblad, "Marknadsleken: Aktie-SM och populariseringen av aktiesparande", in *Marknadens tid. Mellan folkhemskapitalism och nyliberalism*, ed. by Jenny Andersson, Nikolas Glover, Orsi Husz, and David Larsson Heidenblad (Lund: Nordic Academic Press, 2023), 193–213.
5. The subsidised mutual fund saving scheme was continued in renewed form as *allemansfonder*, in English Everyman's funds, by the Social Democrats in the 1980s. See Orsi Husz, David Larsson Heidenblad, and Elin Åström Rudberg, 'Wage Earners, Taxpayers or Everyman Capitalists? The Making of a Mutual Fund Culture in Sweden', in *Nordic Neoliberalisms*, ed. by Jenny Andersson and Chris Howell (forthcoming); 'Den nybildade Aktiefrämjandet vill göra oss till småkapitalister', *Dagens Nyheter*, 20 June 1976.
6. Kristina Lilja, 'The Deposit Market Revolution in Sweden', in *The Swedish Financial Revolution*, ed. by Anders Ögren (Basingstoke, UK: Palgrave Macmillan, 2010), 50.
7. World Bank, The Global Findex Database 2021: Financial Inclusion, Digital Payments, and Resilience in the Age of COVID-19 Online resource. https://www.worldbank.org/en/publication/globalfindex.
8. Jeanne Lazarus, 'About the Universality of a Concept: Is There a Financialization of Daily Life in France?', *Civitas*, 17, 1 (2017), 26.
9. Amy Edwards, *Are We Rich Yet? The Rise of Mass Investment Culture in Contemporary Britain* (Oakland, CA: University of California Press, 2022); Paul Langley, *The Everyday Life of Global Finance: Saving and Borrowing in Anglo-America* (Oxford: Oxford University Press, 2008); Pål Vik, '"The Computer Says No": The Demise of the Traditional Bank Manager and the Depersonalisation of British Banking, 1960–2010', *Business History*, 59, 2 (2016), 231–249.
10. Christopher Frank, 'Cashless Pay, Deductions from Wages, and the Repeal of the Truck Acts in Great Britain, 1945–1986', *Labor History*, 61, 2 (2020), 127.

11. Vik, 'The Computer Says No'; Bernardo Batiz-Lazo, *Cash and Dash: How ATMs and Computers Changed Banking* (Oxford: Oxford University Press, 2018).
12. Zsuzsanna Vargha, 'Markets from Interactions: The Technology of Mass Personalization in Consumer Banking' (March 2009). Available at SSRN: http://dx.doi.org/10.2139/ssrn.1351624.
13. Akos Rona-Tas and Alya Guseva, *Plastic Money. Constructing Markets for Credit Cards in Eight Postcommunist Countries* (Stanford, CA: Stanford University Press, 2014), 33, 120.

Bibliography

Archives

Centrum för Näringslivshistoria, CfN (Centre for Business History)
Erik Elinder's Papers, EEP (Uncatalogued archival collection)
Handelsbanken, HB
Köpkort AB, KKA (Uncatalogued archival collection)
Kooperativa Förbundet, KFA (Consumer Cooperative Union)
Skandinaviska Banken, SB
Svenska Bankföreningen, BF (Swedish Bankers' Association)

Kungliga biblioteket, KB (Swedish National Library Stockholm)
Vardagstryck (Ephemera collections): *AB ID-kort, Köpkort, Svensk Köpkort, PK-banken, Handelsbanken, Möbel Ikéa*

Riksarkivet, RA (Swedish National Archives)
Checklöneutredningen 1968–1971 (Government Inquiry into Cheque Wages)

Tekniska Museet
Från datamaskin till IT (From computing machines to IT, Documentation project)

Newspapers and Periodicals

(Press cuttings retrieved from the archival collections are cited with reference to the archival volumes)

Aftonbladet (AB)
Bankvärlden 1956–1982
Dagens Nyheter (DN)
Din Bank (in-house magazine of Skandinaviska Banken) 1956–1975
Ekonomisk Revy (review published by the Bankers' Association) 1956–1982
Expressen
ID-Nytt (in-house magazine of the company AB ID-kort) 1974–1983
Kontokuriren (periodic publication for the cheque account clients of Kreditbanken) 1967–1971
Kooperatören (journal of the Consumer Cooperative Union) 1978–1980
Köpmannen (weekly journal of the Federation of Swedish Merchants) 1978–1983
Remissan (*HB Remissan* until 1960, in-house magazine of Handelsbanken) 1956–1980
Sunt Förnuft 1950–1970
Svenska Dagbladet (SvD)
Svenska Handelsbankens Årsredovisningar (Annual Reports of Handelsbanken) 1963–1979
Veckans affärer (Business Weekly) 1965–1980
Vi (popular weekly magazine, published by the Consumer Cooperative Union) 1978–1980

Interviews

Jan Kuuse and Kent Olsson (Gothenburg, 12 April 2019)
Gunilla Cronholm (Stockholm, 26 April 2018)

Websites

Galluparkivet, Svenska Gallupundersökningar från 1942 till 1956. Svensk Nationell Datatjänst (Swedish National Data Service) https://snd.se/sv/gallup
Kooperativ Krönika, www.kf.se/historiskt-uppslagsverk/
Svenskt kvinnobiografiskt lexikon, www.skbl.se/en
Svenska folkets betalningsvanor, Sveriges Riksbank, https://www.riksbank.se/sv/statistik/statistik-over-betalningar-sedlar-och-mynt/betalningsvanor/
World Bank, The Global Findex Database 2021: Financial Inclusion, Digital Payments, and Resilience in the Age of COVID-19, www.worldbank.org/en/publication/globalfindex

Books, Chapters, Articles and Other Published Works

About, Ilsen, James Brown, and Gayle Lonergan (eds.). *Identification and Registration Practices in Transnational Perspective: People, Papers and Practices* (Basingstoke, UK: Palgrave Macmillan 2013).

Agar, Jon. 'Modern Horrors: British Identity and Identity Cards', in *Documenting Individual Identity*, ed. by Jane Caplan and John Torpey (Princeton, NJ: Princeton University Press, 2001), 101–120.

Ahnland, Lars. 'Survey Article on Nordic Financialisation in the Long Run', *Scandinavian Economic History Review*, 71, 3 (2023), 247–257.

Aitken, Rob. *Performing Capital: Toward a Cultural Economy of Popular and Global Finance* (Basingstoke, UK: Palgrave Macmillan, 2007).

Åkerman, Brita et al. (eds.). *Kunskap för vår vardag: Forskning och utbildning för hemmen* (Stockholm: Akademilitteratur, 1984).

Aléx, Peder. *Den rationella konsumenten: KF som folkuppfostrare 1899–1939* (Stockholm: Symposion, 1994).

Aléx, Peder. *Konsumera rätt—ett svenskt ideal: behov, hushållning och konsumtion* (Lund: Studentlitteratur, 2003).

Allmänna beredningsutskottets utlåtande (Drafting Committee's Report) no. 15, in *Bihang till Riksdagens Protokoll år 1963* (Parliamentary Papers) (Stockholm: Riksdagen, 1963).

Åmark, Klas. 'Familj, försörjning och livslopp under 1900-talet', in *Familjeangelägenheter: Modern historisk forskning om välfärdsstat, genus och politik*, ed. by Helena Bergman and Peter Johansson (Eslöv: Symposion, 2002).

Åmark, Klas. *Hundra år av välfärdspolitik. Väfärdsstatens framväxt i Norge och Sverige* (Umeå: Boréa, 2005).

Ambjörnsson, Ronny. *Den skötsamme arbetaren: idéer och ideal i ett norrländskt sågverkssamhälle 1880–1930* (Stockholm: Carlsson, 1988).

Andersson-Skog, Lena, and Mats Larsson (eds.). *Det svenska näringslivets historia 1864–2014* (Stockholm: Dialogos, 2014).

Andersson, Erik, Oskar Broberg, Marcus Gianneschi, and Bengt Larsson (eds.). *Vardagslivets finansialisering* (Göteborg: Centrum för konsumtionsvetenskap, 2016).

Andersson, Jenny, Nikolas Glover, Orsi Husz, and David Larsson Heidenblad (eds.). *Marknadens tid. Mellan folkhemskapitalism och nyliberalism* (Lund: Nordic Academic Press, 2023).

Andersson, Jenny. 'Neoliberalism from Within: The Business Fund and the Struggle for Market Ideology in Sweden', *Contemporary European History*, FirstView (2025), 1-17.

Andra Kammarens protokoll (Records of the Proceedings in the Second Chamber) no. 16, in *Riksdagens protokoll år 1963, Andra kammaren* (Parliamentary Papers) (Stockholm: Riksdagen, 1963).

Antoni, Fride, and Ann-Charlotte Plogner (eds.). *Måste konsumenten gå till Verket?* (Stockholm: Industriförbundet, 1978).

Aronsson, Peter. *Historiebruk: Att använda det förflutna* (Lund: Studentlitteratur, 2004).

Attman, Artur, Jan Kuuse, and Ulf Olsson. *LM Ericsson 100 Years* (Stockholm: Telefon AB LM Ericsson, 1977 [in Swedish 1976]).

Bandelj, Nina, Paul James Morgan, and Elizabeth Sowers. 'Hostile Worlds or Connected Lives? Research on the Interplay Between Intimacy and Economy', *Sociology Compass*, 9, 2 (2015), 115–127.

Bankerna (Stockholm: Kungl. Bankinspektionen, 1968–1983).

Barnes, Victoria, and Lucy Newton. 'Women, Uniforms and Brand Identity in Barclays Bank', *Business History*, 64, 4 (2022), 801–830.

Batiz-Lazo, Bernardo, and Gustavo A. Del Angel. 'The Ascent of Plastic Money: International Adoption of the Bank Credit Card, 1950–1975', *Business History Review*, 92, 3 (2018), 509–533.

Batiz-Lazo, Bernardo, and Gustavo Del Angel. *The Dawn of Plastic Jungle: The Introduction of the Credit card in Europe and North America, 1950–1975*, Economics Working Paper 16107 (Stanford: Hoover Institution, 2016).

Batiz-Lazo, Bernardo, Thomas Haigh, and David L. Stearns. 'How the Future Shaped the Past: The Case of the Cashless Society', *Enterprise & Society*, 15, 1 (2014), 103–131.

Batiz-Lazo, Bernardo, Tobias Karlsson, and Björn Thodenius. 'The Origins of the Cashless Society: Cash Dispensers, Direct to Account Payments and the Development of Online Real-Time Networks, c. 1965–1985', *Essays in Economic & Business History*, 32 (2014), 100–137.

Batiz-Lazo, Bernardo. 'ATMs', in *Paid: Tales of Dongles, Checks and Other Money Stuffs*, ed. by Bill Maurer and Lana Swartz (Cambridge, MA: The MIT Press, 2017).

Batiz-Lazo, Bernardo. *Cash and Dash: How ATMs and Computers Changed Banking* (Oxford: Oxford University Press, 2018).

Bay, Charlotta, Bino Catasús, and Gustav Johed. 'Situating Financial Literacy', *Critical Perspectives on Accounting*, 25, 1 (2014), 36–45.

Belfrage, Claes. 'Towards "Universal Financialisation" in Sweden?', *Contemporary Politics*, 14, 3 (2008), 277–296.

Bennett, Tony, Liz McFall, and Mike Pryke. 'Editorial: Culture/Economy/Social', *Journal of Cultural Economy*, 1, 1 (2008), 1–7.

Berggren, Henrik, and Lars Trägårdh. *Är svensken människa?: gemenskap och oberoende i det moderna Sverige* (Stockholm: Norstedt, 2006).

Berker, Thomas, Maren Hartman, Yves Punie, and Katie J. Ward (eds.). *Domestication of Media and Technology* (Maidenhead: Open University Press, 2006)

Berlage, Nancy. 'The Establishment of an Applied Social Science. Home Economics, Science and Reform at Cornell University, 1870–1930', in *Gender and American Social Science: The Formative Years*, ed. by Helene Silverberg (Princeton: Princeton University Press, 1998).

Berner, Boel. *Sakernas tillstånd: kön, klass, teknisk expertis* (Stockholm: Carlsson, 1996).

Bersbo, Zara. *'Rätt för kvinnan att blifva människa—fullt och helt': Svenska kvinnors ekonomiska medborgarskap 1921–1971* (Växjö: Linnéuniversitetet, 2012).

Birch, David. *Identity Is the New Money* (London: Publishing Partnership, 2014).

Björklund, Tom. *Reklamen i svensk marknad 1920–1965* (Stockholm: Norstedt & Söner, 1967).

Björkman, Jenny. 'Systemskiftet', *Populär Historia*, 2 (2004).

Blyth, Mark. *Great Transformations: Economic Ideas and Institutional Change in the Twentieth Century* (New York: Cambridge University Press, 2002).

Botterill, Jacqueline. *Consumer Culture and Personal Finance* (Basingstoke, UK: Palgrave Macmillan, 2010).

Bouveng, Carl-Johan, Sven Sannesson, and Arne Ögren. *Konsumtionskrediter i Sverige* (Stockholm: SNS, 1963).

Burgoyne, Carole B. 'Introduction: Special Issue on the Household Economy', *The Journal of Socio-Economics*, 37, 2 (2008), 455–457.

Calder, Lendol. *Financing the American Dream: A Cultural History of Consumer Credit* (Princeton: Princeton University Press, 1999).

Callon, Michel (ed.). *The Laws of the Markets* (Oxford: Blackwell, 1998).

Callon, Michel, and Fabian Muniesa. 'Peripheral Vision: Economic Markets as Calculative Collective Devices', *Organization Studies*, 26, 8 (2005), 1229–1250.

Callon, Michel, Yuval Millo, and Fabian Muniesa (eds.). *Market Devices* (Oxford: Blackwell, 2007).

Caplan, Jane, and John C. Torpey (eds.). *Documenting Individual Identity: The Development of State Practices in the Modern World* (Princeton, NJ: Princeton University Press, 2001).

Carruthers, Bruce, and Laura Ariovich. *Money and Credit: A Sociological Approach* (Cambridge: Polity, 2010).

Cason, Sven Å. 'Konsumtionskrediter, Köpkort, Kontokort', *Handelsutbildning*, 4 (December 1966a).

Cason, Sven Å. 'Köpkortssystemets marknadsanpassning', *Ekonomisk Revy*, 5 (1966b).

Cason, Sven Å. 'Kreditkorten i Europa', *Ekonomisk Revy*, 6 (1969).

Cato, Åke. 'Jahapp sa löntagaren', *Aftonbladet*, 28 December, 1978.

Cato, Åke. 'Plastkort luktar inte', *Aftonbladet*, 10 November, 1977.

Cavallin-Aijmer, Maria, and Samuel Edquist. 'Historikerna och arkiven i teori och praktik', in *Historikerna i samhället. Roller och förändringsmönster*, ed. by David Ludvigsson and Martin Åberg (Hedemora: Gidlunds, 2021).

'Checkens återkomst kräver nya ID-kort', *Kontakten*, 2 (1973).

Chiapello, Eve. 'Financialization as a Socio-Technical Process', in *The Routledge International Handbook of Financialization*, ed. by Philip Mader, Daniel Mertens, and Natascha van der Zwan (London: Routledge, 2020), 81–91.

Christophers, Brett. 'The Limits to Financialization', *Dialogues in Human Geography*, 5, 2 (2015), 183–200.

Chutkov, Paul. *VISA. The Power of an Idea* (Chicago: Harcourt, 2001).

Clark, Gordon. *Pension Fund Capitalism* (Oxford: Oxford University Press, 2000).

Cochoy, Franck, Joe Deville, and Liz McFall (eds.). *Markets and the Arts of Attachment* (London: Routledge, 2017).

Cole, Simon A. *Suspect Identities: A History of Fingerprinting and Criminal Identification* (Cambridge, MA: Harvard University Press, 2001).

Cook, Terry. 'Remembering the Future: Appraisal of Records and the Role of Archives in Constructing Social Memory', in *Archives, Documentation, and Institutions of Social Memory: Essays from the Sawyer Seminar*, ed. by Francis X. Blouin and William G. Rosenberg (Ann Arbor: University of Michigan Press, 2006).

Cook, Terry. 'The Archive(s) Is a Foreign Country: Historians, Archivists, and the Changing Archival Landscape', *The American Archivist*, 74, 2 (2011), 600–632.

Cooper, Melinda, and Liz McFall. 'Ten Years After: It's the Economy and Culture, Stupid!', *Journal of Cultural Economy*, 10, 1 (2017), 1–7.

Cooper, Melinda. *Family Values: Between Neoliberalism and the New Social Conservatism* (New York: Zone Books, 2017).

Couldry, Nick, and Ulysses A. Meijas. *The Costs of Connection: How Data Is Colonizing Human Life and Appropriating It for Capitalism* (Stanford: Stanford University Press, 2019).

Crosthwaite, Paul, Peter Knight, Nicky Marsh, Helen J. Paul, and James Taylor. *Invested: How Three Centuries of Stock Market Advice Reshaped Our Money, Markets, and Minds* (Chicago: University of Chicago Press, 2022).

Curry Jansen, Sue, and Jefferson Pooley. 'Blurring Genres and Violating Guild Norms: A Review of Reviews of the Age of Surveillance Capitalism', *New Media & Society*, 23, 9 (2021), 2839–2851.

Davies, Aled, Ben Jackson, and Florence Sutcliffe-Braitwaite (eds.). *The Neoliberal Age: Britain since the 1970s* (London: UCL Press, 2021).

Davies, Aled, James Freeman, and Hugh Pemberton. '"Everyman Capitalist" or "Free to Choose"? Exploring the Tensions within Thatcherite Individualism', *The Historical Journal*, 61, 2 (2018), 477–501.

De Geer, Hans. *I vänstervind och högervåg: SAF under 1970-talet* (Stockholm: Allmänna förlaget, 1989).
De Goede, Marieke. *Virtue, Fortune, and Faith: A Genealogy of Finance* (Minneapolis: University of Minnesota Press, 2005).
Deleuze, Gilles. 'Postscript on the Societies of Control', *October*, 59, 4 (1992), 3–7.
Deville, Joe. 'Paying with Plastic: The Enduring Presence of the Credit Card', in *Accumulation: The Material Politics of Plastic*, ed. by Jennifer Gabrys, Gay Hawkins, and Mike Michael (London: Routledge, 2014).
Dodd, Nigel. *The Social Life of Money* (Princeton: Princeton University Press, 2014).
Drehman, Mathias, Charles Goodhart, and Malte Krueger. 'The Challenges Facing Currency Usage', *Economic Policy*, 17, April (2002), 195–227.
DsFi (Ministry of Finance Publication Series) 1971:12. Sture Lundell. *PM angående åtgärder för att motverka checkmissbruket* (Stockholm: Finansdepartementet, 1971).
DsFi 1975:7. *Förslag till Lag om identitetskontroll vid inlösen av check* (Stockholm: Liber Förlag/Allmänna förlaget, 1975).
DsFi 1983:9. Kontokortskommittén. *Identitets- och legitimationskontroll vid utfärdande och användande av kontokort: Delbetänkande* (Stockholm: Liber Förlag/Allmänna förlaget, 1983).
DsFi 1984:10. Kontokortskommittén. *Kontokort: Slutbetänkande* (Stockholm: Liber Förlag/Allmänna förlaget, 1984).
Ducourant, Helene, and Jeanne Lazarus. 'Credit in Society and in Sociology: On the Bank and Its Customers (Bourdieu, Boltanski, Chamboredon, 1963)', *European Journal of Sociology*, 64, 3 (2023), 385–416.
Edkins, Jenny. *Poststructuralism & International Relations* (Boulder, CO: Lynne Rienner Publisher, 1999).
Edwards, Amy. *Are We Rich Yet? The Rise of Mass Investment Culture in Contemporary Britain* (Oakland, CA: University of California Press, 2022).
Effosse, Sabine. 'Financial Empowerment for Married Women in France', *Quaderni Storici*, 56, 1 (2021), 117–141.
Effosse, Sabine. *Le crédit à la consommation en France, 1947-1965* (Paris: IGPDE, 2014).
Ehn, Billy, Jonas Frykman, and Orvar Löfgren. *Försvenskningen av Sverige: Det nationellas förvandlingar* (Stockholm: Natur och kultur, 1993).
Elsässer, Sophie. *Att skapa en konsument: Råd & Rön och den statliga konsumentupplysningen* (Göteborg: Makadam, 2012).
Eriksson, Nancy. *Bara en hemmafru* (Stockholm: Forum, 1964).
Erturk, Ismail et al. 'The Democratisation of Finance? Promise, Outcomes and Conditions', *Review of International Political Economy*, 14, 4 (2007), 553–575.

Esping-Andersen, Gøsta. *The Three Worlds of Welfare Capitalism* (Cambridge: Polity, 1990).
Feiertag, Olivier. 'La bancarisation de la société française dans les années 1968', in *Les Français et l'argent*, ed. by Alya Aglan, Olivier Feiertag, and Yannick Marec (Rennes: Presses Universitaires de Rennes, 2011), 163–175.
Fleischer, Rasmus. 'Kreditkonsumtion i Sverige, 1945–1985', *Historisk Tidskrift*, 136, 4 (2016), 626–657.
Florin, Christina, and Bengt Nilsson. '"Something in the Nature of a Bloodless Revolution": How New Gender Relations Became Gender Equality Policy in Sweden', in *State Policy and Gender System in the Two German States and Sweden 1945–1989*, ed. by Rolf Torstendahl (Uppsala: Historiska institutionen, 1999).
Florin, Christina, and Lars Kvarnström (eds.). *Kvinnor på gränsen till medborgarskap: Genus, politik och offentlighet 1800–1950* (Stockholm: Atlas, 2001).
Folbre, Nancy. *Greed, Lust & Gender: A History of Economic Ideas* (Oxford: Oxford University Press, 2009), 258–260.
Folbre, Nancy. *Who Pays for the Kids? Gender and the Structure of Constraint* (London: Routledge, 1994).
Företagets Public Relations. Föredrag hållna 17–18 november 1948 (Svenska Reklamförbundet: Stockholm, 1949).
Forsell, Anders. *Moderna tider i sparbanken: Om organisatorisk omvandling i ett institutionellt perspektiv* (Stockholm: Nerenius & Santérus, 1992).
Forslund, Dick. *Hit med pengarna! Sparandets genealogi och den finansiella övertalningens vetandekonst* (Stockholm: Carlssons, 2008).
Första lagutskottets utlåtande (Statement of the first Parliamentary Committee on Law) no. 23, in *Bihang till Riksdagens Protokoll år 1965 (Parliamentary Papers)*, (Stockholm: Riksdagen, 1965).
Foster, William M. et al. 'The Strategic Use of Historical Narratives: A Theoretical Framework', *Business History*, 59, 8 (2017), 1176–1200.
Foucault, Michel. 'Governmentality', in *The Foucault Effect: Studies in Governmentality*, ed. by Graham Burchell, Colin Gordon, and Peter Miller (Chicago: University of Chicago Press, 1991), 87–104.
Foucault, Michel. *The Birth of Biopolitics: Lectures at the Collège de France 1978–79*, ed. by Michel Senelhart (Basingstoke: Palgrave Macmillan, 2008).
Fourcade, Marion, and Kieran Healy. 'Classification Situations', *Accounting, Organizations and Society*, 38, 8 (2013), 559–572.
Fourcade, Marion, and Kieran Healy. 'Seeing Like a Market', *Socio-Economic Review*, 15, 1 (2017), 9–29.
Frank, Christopher. 'Cashless Pay, Deductions from Wages, and the Repeal of the Truck Acts in Great Britain, 1945–1986', *Labor History*, 61, 2 (2020), 122–137.

Fredrikzon, Johan. *Kretslopp av data: Miljö, befolkning, förvaltning och den tidiga digitaliseringens kulturtekniker* (Lund: Mediehistoriskt arkiv, 2021).
Friedman, Milton. *A Theory of Consumption Function* (Princeton, NJ: Princeton University Press, 1957).
Frohman, Larry. 'Virtually Creditworthy: Privacy, the Right to Information, and Consumer Credit Reporting in West Germany', in *The Development of Consumer Credit in Global Perspective*, ed. by Jan Logemann (New York: Palgrave Macmillan, 2012), 129–154.
Gates, Kelly. *Our Biometric Future: Facial Recognition Technology and the Culture of Surveillance* (New York: New York University Press, 2011).
Gates, Kelly. 'The Securitization of Financial Identity and the Expansion of the Consumer Credit Industry', *Journal of Communication Inquiry*, 34, 4 (2010), 417–431.
Gieryn, Thomas F. *Cultural Boundaries of Science: Credibility on the Line* (Chicago: University of Chicago Press, 1999).
Grafström, Maria. *The Development of Swedish Business Journalism: Historical Roots of an Organisational Field* (Uppsala: Department of Business Studies, 2006).
Grandin, Kalle, Nina Wormbs, and Sven Widmalm. *The Science-Industry Nexus: History, Policy, Implication* (Sagamore Beach, MA: Science History Publications/USA, 2004).
Gylling, Kersti. 'Riktlinjer som producentpåverkan—ett samhällsintresse', in *Måste konsumenten gå till Verket?*, ed. by Fride Antoni and Ann-Charlotte Plogner (Stockholm: Industriförbundet, 1978).
Hacker, Jacob S. *The Great Risk Shift: The New Economic Insecurity and the Decline of the American Dream* (New York: Oxford University Press, 2008).
Haigh, Thomas. '"Veritable Bucket of Facts": Origins of the Database Management System', *SIGMOD Record*, 35, 2 (2006), 33–49.
Hansen, Per H. 'From Finance Capitalism to Financialization: A Cultural and Narrative Perspective on 150 Years of Financial History', *Enterprise & Society*, 15, 4 (2015), 605–642.
Hart, Keith. *The Memory Bank* (London: Profile Books, 1999).
Harvey, David. *A Brief History of Neoliberalism* (Oxford: Oxford University Press, 2005).
Hellners, Einar. *Kurs för livförsäkringsacquisitörer* (Malmö: Hermods, 1932).
Hessling, Torbjörn. *Att spara eller inte spara—vilken fråga!: Den sparfrämjande verksamheten 1820–1970* (Stockholm: Sparfrämjandet, 1990).
Higgs, Edward. 'Consuming Identity and Consuming the State in Britain, c. 1750', in *Identification and Registration Practices in Transnational Perspective*, ed. by Ilsen About, James Brown, and Gayle Lonergan (Basingstoke, UK: Palgrave Macmillan, 2013), 164–182.

Higgs, Edward. *Identifying the English: A History of Personal Identification 1500 to the Present* (London: Bloomsbury, 2011).
Hildebrand, Karl-Gustaf. *Banking in a Growing Economy: Svenska Handelsbanken Since 1871* (Stockholm: Handelsbanken, 1971).
Hildebrand, Karl-Gustaf. *Om företagshistoria* (Uppsala: Uppsala University, 1989).
Hirdman, Yvonne. *Att lägga livet till rätta. Studier i svensk folkhemspolitik* (Stockholm: Carlssons, 1990).
Holm, E. O. *Kontokort och kreditsystem i detaljhandeln* (Göteborg: Länssparbanken Göteborg, 1980).
Holmberg, Kajsa, and Maria Stanfors. *Setting a Trend: Feminisation of the Commercial Bank Sector in Sweden, 1864–1975* (Stockholm: EHF, 2011).
Horowitz, Daniel. *The Anxieties of Affluence: Critiques of American Consumer Culture, 1939–1979* (Amherst: University of Massachusetts Press, 2004).
Husz, Orsi, and David Larsson Heidenblad. 'The Making of Everyman's Capitalism in Sweden: Micro-Infrastructures, Unlearning, and Moral Boundary Work', *Enterprise & Society*, 24, 2 (2023), 425–454.
Husz, Orsi, and Karin Carlsson. 'Marketing a New Society or Engineering Kitchens', in *Consumer Engineering: Marketing Between Planning Euphoria and the Limits of Growth, 1930s–1970s*, ed. by Jan Logemann, Gary Cross, and Ingo Köhler (Washington, DC: Palgrave Macmillan, 2019), 215–243.
Husz, Orsi, David Larsson Heidenblad, and Elin Åström Rudberg. 'Wage Earners, Taxpayers or Everyman Capitalists? The Making of a Mutual Fund Culture in Sweden', in *Nordic Neoliberalisms*, ed. by Jenny Andersson and Chris Howell (forthcoming).
Husz, Orsi. 'Att räkna värdighet. Privatekonomi och medelklasskultur i mitten av 1900-talet', *Scandia*, 79, 1 (2013), 87–121.
Husz, Orsi. 'Att sälja kredit som pengar: Kreditkortets domesticering i 1960-talets Sverige', in *Vardagslivets finansialisering*, ed. by Erik Andersson, Oskar Broberg, Marcus Gianneschi, and Bengt Larsson (Göteborg: Centrum för konsumtionsvetenskap, 2016), 45–57.
Husz, Orsi. 'Bank Identity: Banks, ID Cards, and the Emergence of a Financial Identification Society in Sweden', *Enterprise & Society*, 19, 2 (2018), 391–429.
Husz, Orsi. 'From Wage Earners to Financial Consumers: Class and Financial Socialisation in Sweden in the 1950s and 1960s', *Critique Internationale*, 69, 4 (2015), 99–118.
Husz, Orsi. 'Golden Everyday: Housewifely Consumerism and the Domestication of Banks in 1960s Sweden', *Le Mouvement Social*, 250, 1 (2015), 41–63.
Husz, Orsi. 'Kreditkortskriget: Kooperativa Förbundet och den finansiellt rationella konsumenten', in *Marknadens tid. Mellan folkhemskapitalism och*

nyliberalism, ed. by Jenny Andersson, Nikolas Glover, Orsi Husz, and David Larsson Heidenblad (Lund: Nordic Academic Press, 2023), 215–242.

Husz, Orsi. 'Money Cards and Identity Cards: De-vicing Consumer Credit in Post-war Sweden', *Journal of Cultural Economy*, 14, 2 (2021), 139–158.

Husz, Orsi. 'Passionate About Things: The Swedish Debate on Throwawayism', *Nordic Historical Review/Revue d'histoire Nordique*, 12, 1 (2011), 135–160.

Husz, Orsi. 'Privatekonomin och den borgerliga medelklassens identitetskris 1920–1970', *Fronesis*, 24 (2007), 116–130.

Husz, Orsi. 'Spara, Slösa och alla de andra', in *Signums svenska kulturhistoria, 1900-talet*, ed. by Jacob Christenson (Stockholm: Atlantis, 2009), 279–329.

Husz, Orsi. 'The Birth of the Finance Consumer: Feminists, Bankers and the Re-Gendering of Finance in Mid-Twentieth-Century Sweden', *Contemporary European History*, 33, 4 (2024), 1332–1351.

Husz, Orsi. 'The Entrepreneur's Dream: Credit Card History Between PR and Academic Research', in *Histories of Knowledge in Postwar Scandinavia: Actors, Arenas and Ambitions*, ed. by Johan Östling, David Larsson Heidenblad, and Niklas Olsen (London: Routledge, 2020), 127–151.

Husz, Orsi. 'The Morality of Quality: Assimilating Material Mass Culture in Twentieth Century Sweden', *Journal of Modern European History*, 10, 2 (2012), 152–181.

Husz, Orsi. *Drömmars värde. Varuhus och lotteri i svensk konsumtionskultur, 1897–1939* (Hedemora: Gidlunds, 2004).

Husz, Orsi. *The Identity Economy* (Stockholm: Riksbankens Jubileumsfond with Makadam förlag, 2022).

Hwang, Sun-Joon. *Folkrörelse eller affärsföretag* (Stockholm: Stockholms universitet, 1995).

Igo, Sarah E. *The Known Citizen: A History of Privacy in Modern America* (Cambridge, MA: Harvard University Press, 2018).

Ilshammar, Lars. *Offentlighetens nya rum: Teknik och politik i Sverige 1969–1999* (Örebro: Örebro Universitet, 2002).

Index: Svenska Handelsbankens Ekonomiska Månadsöversikt, 5 (1960).

Jensen, Henning. *Historien om Dankort* (Published by the author, 2016).

Johansson, Ulla. *Sparsamhetsfostran i 1900-talets obligatoriska svenska skolor* (Umeå: Pedagogiska inst., Umeå universitet, 1988).

Jonsson, Pernilla, and Silke Neusinger. *Gendered Money: Financial Organization in Women's Movement* (New York: Berghahn Books, 2012).

Joseph, Anne M. 'Anthropometry, the Police Expert and the Deptford Murders', in *Documenting Individual Identity*, ed. by Jane Caplan and John Torpey (Princeton, NJ: Princeton University Press, 2001), 164–183.

Justitieutskottet, *Förbättrad kontroll av legitimationshandlingar. Betänkande* (Committee of Justice's Report), 1988/89:JuU3 (Riksdagen/Parliamentary papers, 1989).

K.P. 'Konsumtionskrediter i förvirrad tappning', *Ekonomisk revy*, 5 (1961), 374–376.

Karneman, Gunnar. 'Moderna pengar', *Rateko*, 19 (1976).

Karneman, Gunnar. *Kontokort: en väg för finansplanering även för hushållen* (Stockholm: Finansieringsföretagens förening, 1979).

Kessler-Harris, Alice. *In Pursuit of Equity: Women, Men, and the Quest for Economic Citizenship in 20th-Century America* (Oxford: Oxford University Press, 2001).

Klein, Kajsa (ed.). *Integritetsdebatten åren kring 1984: Transkript av ett vittnes-seminarium vid Tekniska museet i Stockholm den 30 november 2007* (Stockholm: KTH, Avdelningen för teknik- och vetenskapshistoria, 2008).

Knutson, Johannes, and Eckart Külhorn. *När checkbedrägerierna försvann (BRÅ Rapport)* (Stockholm: Liber Förlag/Allmänna förlaget, 1980).

Kock, Birger (ed.). *Från idé till produkt. En samling kända svenska uppfinnare berättar om sitt arbete* (Stockholm: Styrelsen för teknisk utveckling i samarbete med Sv. uppfinnareföreningen, 1981).

Kontokreditmarknaden på konsumentområdet, KoV 1980:7 (Stockholm: Konsumentverket, 1980).

Koopman, Colin. *How We Became Our Data: A Genealogy of the Informational Person* (Chicago: The University of Chicago Press, 2019).

Körberg, Ingvar. *Förnyelsen: Sparbankernas historia 1945–1980* (Stockholm: Ekerlid, 2006).

Kortbetalningarnas betydelse i samhället (Stockholm: Svenska Bankföreningen, 2013).

Kreditkorten och konsumenten Delrapport III, KoV 1981:6–04 (Vällingby: Konsumentverket, 1981).

Krippner, Greta R. *Capitalizing on Crisis: The Political Origins of the Rise of Finance* (Cambridge, MA: Harvard University Press, 2011).

Kristoffersson, Sara. 'A Brand for Everyone', in *Design Culture: Objects and Approaches*, ed. by Guy Julier et al. (London: Bloomsbury, 2019).

Kristoffersson, Sara. *Design by IKEA: A Cultural History* (London: Bloomsbury, 2014).

Laferté, Gilles. 'Economic Identification: A Contribution to a Comparative Socio-History of Credit Markets', *Economic Sociology: The European Electronic Newsletter*, 15, 3 (2014).

Langley, Paul, and Andrew Leyshon. 'Financial Subjects: Culture and Materiality', *Journal of Cultural Economy*, 5, 4 (2012), 369–373.

Langley, Paul. *The Everyday Life of Global Finance: Saving and Borrowing in Anglo-America* (Oxford: Oxford University Press, 2008).

Larsson Heidenblad, David. 'Marknadsleken: Aktie-SM och populariseringen av aktiesparande', in *Marknadens tid. Mellan folkhemskapitalism och nyliberalism*, ed. by Jenny Andersson, Nikolas Glover, Orsi Husz, and David Larsson Heidenblad (Lund: Nordic Academic Press, 2023), 193–214.

Larsson, Mats, and Gabriel Söderberg. *Finance and the Welfare State: Banking Development and Regulatory Principles in Sweden, 1900–2015* (Cham: Palgrave Macmillan, 2017).

Larsson, Mats. *Staten och kapitalet: det svenska finansiella systemet under 1900-talet* (Stockholm: SNS Förlag, 1998).

Latour, Bruno. *Reassembling the Social* (Oxford & New York: Oxford University Press, 2005).

Lauer, Josh. 'Plastic Surveillance: Payment Cards and the History of Transactional Data, 1888 to Present', *Big Data & Society*, 7, 1 (2020).

Lauer, Josh. 'The Good Consumer: Credit Reporting and the Invention of Financial Identity in the United States, 1840–1940', *Enterprise & Society*, 11, 4 (2010), 686–694.

Lauer, Josh. *Creditworthy: A History of Consumer Surveillance and Financial Identity in America* (New York: Columbia University Press, 2017).

Lazarus, Jeanne. 'About the Universality of a Concept: Is There a Financialization of Daily Life in France?', *Civitas*, 17, 1 (2017), 26–42.

Lazarus, Jeanne. 'Financial Literacy Education', in *The Routledge International Handbook of Financialization*, ed. by Philip Mader, Daniel Mertens, and Natascha van der Zwan (London: Routledge, 2020), 390–399.

Lazarus, Jeanne. 'Gouverner les conduites économiques par l'éducation financière: L'ascension de la financial literacy', in *Gouverner les conduits*, ed. by Sophie Dubuisson-Quellier (Paris: Presses de SciencesPo, 2016), 93–126.

Lazarus, Jeanne. 'La méthode de Viviana Zelizer: La famille réconciliée avec l'économie', *Archives de Philosophie*, 85, 4 (2022), 11–27.

Lazarus, Jeanne. *L'épreuve de l'argent. Banques, banquiers, clients* (Paris: Calmann-Lévy, 2012).

Leach, William. *Land of Desire: Merchants, Power, and the Rise of a New American Culture* (New York: Pantheon, 1993).

Lee, Francis, and Claes-Fredrik Helgesson. 'Vices and De-vicing in Making Valuable Data: Algorithms and Anxieties in High Throughput Biomarker Screening', article manuscript (Uppsala University/Linköping University, 2016).

Lehtonen, Turo-Kimmo, and Mika Pantzar. 'The Ethos of Thrift: The Promotion of Bank Saving in Finland During the 1950s', *Journal of Material Culture*, 7, 2 (2002), 211–231.

Lehtonen, Turo-Kimmo. 'Domesticating Insurance, Financializing Family Lives: The Case of Private Health Insurance for Children in Finland', *Cultural Studies*, 31, 5 (2017), 685–711.

Lettström, Fredrik. *Konsumentkrediter: Föreläsning vid Stockholms Universitet* (Stockholm, 1976).

Lext, Gösta. *Studier i svensk kyrkobokföring 1600–1946* (Göteborg: Landsarkivet, 1985).
Lilja, Kristina. 'The Deposit Market Revolution in Sweden', in *The Swedish Financial Revolution*, ed. by Anders Ögren (Basingstoke, UK: Palgrave Macmillan, 2010), 41–63.
Lindgren, Håkan (ed.). 'Företagshistoria' (Business history, Special Issue), *Historisk tidskrift*, 99, 3 (1979).
Lindqvist, Mats. *Is i magen: Om ekonomins kolonisering av vardagen* (Stockholm: Natur och kultur, 2001).
Lipartito, Kenneth. 'Connecting the Cultural and the Material in Business History', *Enterprise & Society*, 14, 4 (2013), 686–704.
Ljunggren, Stig-Björn. *Folkhemskapitalismen: Högerns programutveckling under efterkrigstiden* (Stockholm: Tiden, 1992).
Logemann, Jan (ed.). *The Development of Consumer Credit in Global Perspective* (New York: Palgrave Macmillan, 2012).
Logemann, Jan. 'Credit Access and the American Welfare State', in *The Development of Consumer Credit in Global Perspective*, ed. by Jan Logemann (New York: Palgrave Macmillan, 2012).
Logemann, Jan. *Engineered to Sell: European Emigrés & the Making of Consumer Capitalism* (Chicago: University of Chicago Press, 2019).
Lövgren, Anna-Brita. *Staten och folk på väg: Pass i Sverige från Gustav Vasas tid till 1860* (Lund: Nordic Academic Press 2018).
Lövgren, Brita. *Hemarbete som politik: Diskussioner om hemarbete, Sverige 1930–40-talen och tillkomsten av Hemmens Forskningsinstitut* (Stockholm: Almqvist & Wiksell, 1993).
Lundqvist, Åsa. *Familjen i den svenska modellen* (Umeå: Boréa, 2007).
Lury, Celia, and Sophie Day. 'Algorithmic Personalization as a Mode of Individuation', *Theory, Culture & Society*, 36, 2 (2019), 17–37.
Lyon, David (ed.). *Surveillance as Social Sorting: Privacy, Risk, and Digital Discrimination* (London: Routledge, 2003).
Lyon, David. *Identifying Citizens: ID Cards as Surveillance* (Cambridge: Polity Press, 2009).
MacKenzie, Donald A. *An Engine, Not a Camera: How Financial Models Shape Markets* (Cambridge, MA: MIT Press, 2006).
Mader, Philip, Daniel Mertens, and Natasha van der Zwan (eds.). *The Routledge International Handbook of Financialization* (New York: Taylor & Francis, 2020).
Maixé-Altés, J. Carles. 'ICT the Nordic Way and European Retail Banking', in *History of Nordic Computing 4, Fourth IFIP WG 9.7 Conference, Revised Selected Papers*, ed. by Christian Gram, Per Rasmussen, and Søren Duus Østergaard (Heidelberg: Springer, 2015), 249–262.
Mandell, Lewis. *The Credit Card Industry: A History* (Boston: Twayne, 1990).

Manning, Robert. *Credit Card Nation* (New York: Basic, 2000).
Manns, Ulla. *Den sanna frigörelsen* (Eslöv: Symposion, 1997).
Marron, Donncha. *Consumer Credit in the United States: A Sociological Perspective from the 19th Century to the Present* (Basingstoke, UK: Palgrave Macmillan, 2009).
Martin, Randy. *Financialization of Daily Life* (Philadelphia: Temple University Press, 2002).
Martínez-Rodríguez, Susana, and Bernardo Batiz-Lazo. 'Gender and Bankarization in Spain, 1949–1970', *Business History*, FirstView (2023), 1–30.
Matsuda, Matt K. *The Memory of the Modern* (New York and Oxford: Oxford University Press, 1996).
Mattsson, Helena. 'Designing the Reasonable Consumer: Standardization and Personalization in Swedish Functionalism', in *Swedish Modernism: Architecture, Consumption and the Welfare State*, ed. by Helena Mattsson and Sven-Olov Wallenstein (London: Black Dog Publishing, 2010), 74–99.
Maurer, Bill, and Lana Swartz (eds.). *Paid: Tales of Dongles, Checks, and Other Money Stuff* (Cambridge, MA: The MIT Press, 2017).
Maurer, Bill. *How Would You Like to Pay? How Technology Is Changing the Future of Money* (Durham: Duke University Press, 2015).
Maurer, Bill. *Mutual Life, Limited: Islamic Banking, Alternative Currencies, Lateral Reason* (Princeton: Princeton University Press, 2005).
McFall, Liz. *Devising Consumption: Cultural Economies of Insurance, Credit and Spending* (Abingdon, Oxon: Routledge, 2015).
Melby, Kari, Anna-Birte Ravn, and Christina Carlsson Wetterberg (eds.). *Gender Equality and Welfare Politics in Scandinavia* (Bristol: The Policy Press, 2009).
Michals, Debra. 'The Buck Stops Where? 1970s Feminist Credit Unions, Women's Banks, and the Gendering of Money', *Business and Economy On-line*, 16 (2018).
Miller, Peter, and Nikolas Rose. *Governing the Present: Administering Economic, Social, and Personal Life* (Cambridge: Polity, 2008).
Mirowski, Philip, and Dieter Plehwe (eds.). *The Road from Mont Pèlerin: The Making of the Neoliberal Thought Collective* (Cambridge: Harvard University Press, 2009).
Moberg, Eva. 'Kvinnans villkorliga frigivning', in *Unga liberaler* (Stockholm: Bonniers, 1961).
Mordhorst, Mads, and Stefan Schwarzkopf. 'Theorising Narrative in Business History', *Business History*, 59, 8 (2017), 1155–1175.
Motion i Andra Kammaren (Private Member's Bill in the Second Chamber) no. 380, in *Bihang till Riksdagens Protokoll år 1965, Andra kammaren (Parliamentary Papers)* (Stockholm: Riksdagen, 1965).

Motion i Andra kammaren (Private Members' Bill in the Second Chamber) no. 683, in *Bihang till Riksdagens Protokoll år 1963, Andra kammaren (Parliamentary Papers)* (Stockholm: Riksdagen, 1963).

Myrstad, Anne Marit. 'Thrift and Traces of Work: On Housewife Films and Sales Talk', in *Twentieth-Century Housewives: Meanings and Implications of Unpaid Work*, ed. by Gro Hageman and Hege Roll-Hansen (Oslo: Oslo Academic Press, 2005).

Nilsson, Fredrik. *Aktiesparandets förlovade land: Människors möte med aktiemarknaden* (Eslöv: Symposion, 2003).

Nilsson, Göran B. 'Historia som vetskap', *Historisk tidskrift*, 125, 2 (2005).

Nocera, Joe. *A Piece of the Action: How the Middle Class Joined the Money Class* (New York: Simon & Schuster, 2013 [1994]).

O'Connell, Sean. *Credit and Community: Working-Class Debt in the UK Since 1880* (Oxford: Oxford University Press, 2009).

O'Dwyer, Rachel. *Tokens: The Future of Money in the Age of the Platform* (London, 2023).

O'Dwyer, Rachel. 'Cache Society: Transactional Records, Electronic Money, and Cultural Resistance', *Journal of Cultural Economy*, 12, 2 (2019), 133–153.

OECD/INFE *International Survey of Adult Financial Literacy* (OECD, 2020).

Ohlsson, Claes. *Folkets fonder?: En textvetenskaplig studie av det svenska pensionssparandets domesticering* (Göteborg: Göteborgs universitet, 2007).

Oldenburg, Göran. 'Kontobrickorna ersätts av plastkort', *Kompanirullan*, 3 (1959).

Olsen, Niklas. *The Sovereign Consumer: A New Intellectual History of Neoliberalism* (Cham, Switzerland: Palgrave Macmillan, 2019).

Olsson, Ulf. *Bank, familj, företagande: Stockholms Enskilda bank 1946–1971* (Stockholm: EHF-Handelshögskolan, 1986).

Olsson, Ulf. *I utvecklingens centrum: Skandinaviska Enskilda Banken och dess föregångare 1856–1996* (Stockholm: Skandinaviska Enskilda Banken, 1997).

Ossandón, José, Joe Deville, Jeanne Lazarus, and Mariana Luzzi. 'Financial Oikonomization: The Financial Government and Administration of the Household', *Socio-Economic Review*, 20, 3 (2022), 1473–1500.

Ossandón, José. 'My Story Has No Strings Attached: Credit Cards, Market Devices and a Stone Guest', in *Markets and the Arts of Attachment*, ed. by Franck Cochoy, Joe Deville, and Liz McFall (London: Routledge, 2017).

Ossandón, José. 'Quand le crédit à la consommation classe les gens et les choses: Une revue de littérature et un programme de recherche', *Revue française de socio-economie*, 9, 1 (2012), 83–100.

Ossandón, José. 'Sowing Consumers in the Garden of Mass Retailing in Chile', *Consumption Markets & Culture*, 17, 5 (2014).

Ott, Julia. *When Wall Street Met Main Street: The Quest for an Investors' Democracy* (Cambridge, MA: Harvard University Press, 2011).

Packard, Vance. *The Hidden Persuaders* (New York: David McKay, 1957).
Packard, Vance. *The Waste Makers* (New York: David McKay, 1960).
Pahl, Jan. 'His Money, Her Money: Recent Research on Financial Organisation in Marriage', *Journal of Economic Psychology*, 16, 3 (1995), 361–376.
Parr, Joy, and Gunilla Ekberg. 'Mrs Consumer and Mr Keynes in Postwar Canada and Sweden', *Gender & History*, 8, 2 (1996), 212–230.
Payne, Christopher. *The Consumer, Credit and Neoliberalism: Governing the Modern Economy* (London: Routledge, 2012).
Pellandini-Simányi, Léna, and Adam Banai. 'Reluctant Financialization: Financialization without Financialized Subjectivities in Hungary and the United States', *Environment and Planning A: Economy and Space*, 53, 4 (2021), 785–808.
Pellandini-Simányi, Léna, Ferenc Hammer, and Zsuzsanna Vargha. 'The Financialization of Everyday Life or the Domestication of Finance?', *Cultural Studies*, 29, 5–6 (2015), 733–759.
Pellandini-Simányi, Léna. 'The Financialization of Everyday Life', in *The Routledge Handbook of Critical Finance Studies*, ed. by Christian Borch and Robert Wosnitzer (New York & London: Routledge, 2021), 278–299.
'Pengar nej tack, vi tar bara kontokort!', *Veckorevyn*, 44 (1978).
Petersson, Tom. *Mellan det lokala och det globala: Det svenska banksystemet ur ett historiskt perspektiv* (Norrtälje: Roslagens sparbank, 2009).
Petersson, Tom. 'Samhälle och näringsliv med gemensamma mål', in *Det svenska näringslivets historia 1864–2014*, ed. by Lena Andersson-Skog and Mats Larsson (Stockholm: Dialogos, 2014), 471–478.
Petersson, Tom. 'Tillväxt, kriser och koncentration—det svenska banksystemet 1820–2005', in *Sverige—en social och ekonomisk historia*, ed. by Susanna Hedenborg and Mats Morell (Lund: Studentlitteratur, 2006).
Petersson, Tom. 'Women, Money and the Financial Revolution', in *Women and Their Money 1700–1950*, ed. by Anne Laurence, Josephine Maltby, and Janette Rutterford (London: Routledge, 2009).
Petre, Gunnel. *Lagen och pengarna i hemmet* (Stockholm: Handelsbanken, 1969).
Petre, Gunnel. *På grön kvist med budget?* (Stockholm: Handelsbanken, 1964).
Pettersson, Ingemar. 'The Nomos of University', *Minerva*, 56, 3 (2018), 381–403.
Pettersson, Jane. *Governing Citizens in the Age of Financialization: A Study of Swedish Financial Education* (Göteborg: Göteborgs universitet, 2022).
Poon, Martha. 'Scorecards as Devices for Consumer Credit: The Case of Fair, Isaac & Company Incorporated', in *Market Devices*, ed. by Michel Callon, Yuval Millo, and Fabian Muniesa (Oxford: Blackwell, 2007).
Poovey, Mary. 'Beneath the Horizon of Cultural Visibility', *Journal of Cultural Economy*, 1, 3 (2008), 337–347.

Poovey, Mary. *Genres of the Credit Economy: Mediating Value in Eighteenth- and Nineteenth-Century Britain* (Chicago: University of Chicago Press, 2008).
Popp, Andrew. 'Histories of Business and the Everyday', *Enterprise & Society*, 21, 3 (2020), 622–637.
Pulju, Rebecca. *Women and Mass Consumer Society in Postwar France* (Cambridge: Cambridge University Press, 2011).
Richardson, Gunnar. *Svensk utbildningshistoria* (Lund: Studentlitteratur, 1999 [1977]).
Ritzer, George. *Expressing America: A Critique of the Global Credit Card Society* (Thousand Oaks: Pine Forge Press, 1995).
Robertson, Craig. 'A Documentary Regime of Verification', *Cultural Studies*, 23, 3 (2009), 329–354.
Robertson, Craig. *The Passport in America: The History of a Document* (New York: Oxford University Press, 2010).
Robertson, Craig. '"You Lie!" Identity, Paper, and the Materiality of Information', *The Communication Review*, 17, 2 (2014).
Robertson, Nancy M. 'The Principle of Sound Banking and Financial Noblesse Oblige: Women's Departments in US Banks at the Turn of the Twentieth Century', in *Women and Their Money: Essays on Women and Finance*, ed. by Anne Laurence, Josephine Maltby, and Jeanette Rutherford (London and New York: Routledge, 2009).
Rona-Tas, Akos, and Alya Guseva. *Plastic Money: Constructing Markets for Credit Cards in Eight Postcommunist Countries* (Stanford, CA: Stanford University Press, 2014).
Rona-Tas, Akos, and Stefanie Hiss. 'The Role of Ratings in the Subprime Mortgage Crisis: The Art of Corporate and the Science of Consumer Credit Rating', in *Markets on Trial*, ed. by Michael Lounsbury and Paul M. Hirsch (Badford: Emerald, 2010), 115–155.
Rose, Nikolas. 'Government and Control', *British Journal of Criminology*, 40, 2 (2000), 321–339.
Rose, Nikolas. *Powers of Freedom* (Cambridge: Cambridge University Press, 1999).
Rothfjell, Rolf Eric. *Method for Indentifying Individuals Using Selected Characteristic Body Curves*. US Patent 3,805,238, 16 April 1974.
Rule, James B. *Private Lives and Public Surveillance* (London: Allen Lane, 1973).
Rune, David. 'Att leva på plast: Hot eller möjlighet? En studie av svensk kreditkortsdebatt 1979–87', BA thesis, Dept. of History, Stockholm University, 2007.
Samuelsson, Kurt. *Postbanken – postsparbank och postgiro* (Stockholm: Postverket, 1978).

Sandgren, Fredrik. 'Introducing Co-operative Consumer Credit: The Case of Loan-Purchases and the Swedish Consumer Co-operative Movement in 1945' (Nordiska historikermötet: Aalborg, 2017).
Schwarzkopf, Stefan, and Rainer Gries. *Ernest Dichter and Motivation Research* (New York: Palgrave Macmillan, 2010).
Sewell, William. 'A Strange Career: The Historical Study of Economic Life', *History and Theory*, 49, 4 (2010), 146–166.
SIBOL [Samarbete för integrerat betalningssystem on-line]-systemet (Stockholm: SIBOL, 1972).
Silverstone, Roger. 'Domesticating Domestication. Reflections on the Life of a Concept', in *Domestication of Media and Technology*, ed. by Thomas Berker et al. (Maidenhead: Open University Press, 2006).
Sjöblom, Alf. *Trygghet som handelsvara: privat folkförsäkring i det framväxande välfärdssamhället 1900–1950* (Stockholm: Historiska institutionen, Stockholms universitet, 2016).
Smedberg, Carl-Filip. 'Class Divisions in Use: The Swedish Social Group Taxonomy as Difference Technology, 1911–1970', *Contemporary European History*, 33, 4 (2024), 1352–1364.
Söderlind, Åsa. *Personlig integritet som informationspolitik: Debatt och diskussion i samband med tillkomsten av Datalag (1973:289)* (Borås/Gothenburg: Institutionen Biblioteks- och informationsvetenskap, 2009).
Solove, Daniel. *The Digital Person: Technology and Privacy in the Information Age* (New York: New York University Press, 2004).
SOU (Swedish Government Official Reports) 1944:52. Folkbokföringskommittén. *Folkbokföringskommitténs betänkande med förslag till omorganisation av folkbokföringen* (Stockholm, 1944).
SOU 1961:2. Utredningen om sparstimulerande åtgärder. *Sparstimulerande åtgärder: Betänkande* (Stockholm: Esselte, 1961).
SOU 1966:42. Konsumtionskreditutredningen. *Konsumtionskrediter i Sverige: Betänkande* (Stockholm: Esselte, 1966).
SOU 1972:47. Offentlighets- och sekretesslagstiftningskommittén. *Data och integritet: Betänkande* (Stockholm: Allmänna Förlaget, 1972).
SOU 1972:79. Kreditupplysningsutredningen. *Kreditupplysning och integritet: Betänkande* (Stockholm: Berling, 1972).
SOU 1975:63. Kreditköpkommittén. *Konsumentkreditlag m.m.: Betänkande* (Stockholm: Liber Förlag/Allmänna förlaget, 1975).
SOU 1977:97. Finansieringsbolagskommittén. *Finansieringsbolag: Betänkande* (Stockholm: Liber Förlag/Allmänna förlaget, 1977).
SOU 1978:54. Datalagstiftningskommittén. *Personregister—datorer—integritet: Översyn av datalagen: Delbetänkande* (Stockholm: Liber Förlag/Allmänna förlaget, 1978).

SOU 1979:62. Kooperationsutredningen. *Kooperationen i Sverige: Betänkande* (Stockholm: Liber Förlag/Allmänna förlaget, 1979).
SOU 2007:100. Id-kortsutredningen. *Id-kort för folkbokförda i Sverige: Betänkande* (Stockholm: Fritze, 2007).
SOU 2010:104. Utredningen om bildande av en e-legitimationsnämnd. *E-legitimationsnämnden och svensk e-legitimation: Betänkande* (Stockholm: Fritze, 2010).
Stafford, David, and Susan King. 'Banking on the Unbanked', *International Journal of Bank Marketing*, 1, 2 (1983), 27–40.
Statistisk Årsbok för Sverige/Statistical Abstract of Sweden (Stockholm: SCB, 1965–1979).
Stearns, David L. *Electronic Value Exchange: Origins of the Visa Electronic Payment System* (London: Springer, 2011).
Stenfors, Alexis. *The Swedish Financial System. Studies in Financial Systems No 13. FESSUD – Financialisation, Economy, Society and Sustainable Development* (2014).
Stenlås, Niklas. 'Vem syr kejsarens kläder?' *Arbetarhistoria*, 3–4 (2002), 51–56.
Stolpe, Herman. 'Om konsumtionskrediter', incl. reply by KP, *Ekonomisk revy*, 7 (1961), 507–510.
Stolpe, Herman. *Kredit och reklam på avvägar* (Stockholm: Rabén & Sjögren, 1961).
Stolpe, Herman. *Kredit och reklam på avvägar: En diskussionshandledning för gruppstudier* (Stockholm: Rabén & Sjögren, 1961).
Stråth, Bo. *Mellan två fonder: LO och den svenska modellen* (Stockholm: Atlas, 1998).
Sveriges Riksbank. *Svenska folkets betalningsvanor 2018* (Stockholm: Sveriges Riksbank, 2018).
Swartz, Lana. 'Cards', in *Paid: Tales of Dongles, Checks, and Other Money Stuff*, ed. by Bill Maurer and Lana Swartz (Boston: MIT Press, 2017).
Swartz, Lana. *New Money: How Payment Became Social Media* (New Haven, CT: Yale University Press, 2020).
Swedberg, Richard. 'The Centrality of Materiality', in *Living in a Material World: Economic Sociology Meets Science and Technology Studies*, ed. by Trevor J. Pinch and Richard Swedberg (Cambridge, MA: MIT Press, 2008), 80.
Theien, Iselin. 'Shopping for the "People's Home": Consumer Planning in Norway and Sweden after the Second World War', in *The Expert Consumer*, ed. by Alain Chatriot, Marie-Emmanuelle Chessel, and Matthew Hilton (Adelshot: Ashgate, 2006).
Thodenius, Björn (ed.). *IT i bank- och finanssektorn 1960–1985* (Transcript of witness seminar at Tekniska museet) (Stockholm: Kungl. Tekniska högskolan, 2008).

Thodenius, Björn (ed.). *Teknisk utveckling i bankerna fram till 1985* (Transcript of witness seminar at Tekniska museet) (Stockholm: Kungl. Tekniska högskolan, 2008).
Thodenius, Björn, Bernardo Batiz-Lazo, and Tobias Karlsson. 'The History of the Swedish ATM: Sparfrämjandet and Metior', in *History of Nordic Computing 3: Third IFIP WG 9.7 Conference*, ed. by Giuseppe Impagliazzo et al. (Heidelberg: Springer, 2011), 92–100.
Torpey, John. 'The Great War and the Birth of the Modern Passport System', in *Documenting Individual Identity*, ed. by Jane Caplan and John Torpey (Princeton, NJ: Princeton University Press, 2001).
Torpey, John. *The Invention of the Passport: Surveillance, Citizenship and the State* (Cambridge: Cambridge University Press, 1999).
Traflet, Janice M. *A Nation of Small Shareholders: Marketing Wall Street after World War II* (Baltimore: Johns Hopkins University Press, 2013).
Trumbull, Gunnar. *Consumer Lending in France and America* (New York: Cambridge University Press, 2014).
Uppgifter om bankerna (Stockholm: Kungl. Bank- och fondinspektionen, 1954–1967).
Utredningen om sparstimulerande åtgärder. *Betänkande med förslag beträffande ändrade former för utbetalning av löner till i statens tjänst anställda* (Official Report of the Inquiry into Measures for Stimulating Thrift) (Stockholm: Finansdepartementet, 1960).
Vanatta, Sean H. 'Citibank, Credit Cards, and the Local Politics of National Consumer Finance, 1968–1991', *Business History Review*, 90, 1 (2016), 57–80.
Vargha, Zsuzsanna. 'Assembling Lines: Queue Management and the Production of Market Economy in Post-socialist Services', *Journal of Cultural Economy*, 11, 5 (2018), 420–439.
Vargha, Zsuzsanna. 'Markets from Interactions: The Technology of Mass Personalization in Consumer Banking' (March 2009). Available at SSRN: https://doi.org/10.2139/ssrn.1351624.
Vargha, Zsuzsanna. 'Performing a Strategy's World: How Redesigning Customers Made Relationship Banking Possible', *Long Range Planning*, 51, 3 (2018), 480–494.
Vik, Pål. '"The Computer Says No": The Demise of the Traditional Bank Manager and the Depersonalisation of British Banking, 1960–2010', *Business History*, 59, 2 (2016), 231–249.
VISA Europe Sweden. Press Release, 'Annual Results', 28 January 2013.
'Visa', *Sparbankerna*, 15 (1978).
Wallander, Jan. *Forskaren som bankdirektör* (Stockholm: SNS Förlag, 1998).
Westerberg, Rikard. *Socialists at the Gate: Swedish Business and the Defense of Free Enterprise, 1940–1985* (Stockholm: Stockholm School of Economics, 2020).

White, Hayden. *The Content of the Form* (Baltimore: The Johns Hopkins University Press, 1987).

Wiedemann, Andreas. *Indebted Societies: Credit and Welfare in Rich Democracies* (Cambridge: Cambridge University Press, 2021).

Wisselgren, Per. 'Vetenskap och/eller politik? Om gränsteorier och utredningsväsendets vetenskapshistoria', in *Mångsysslare och gränsöverskridare* ed. by Bosse Sundin and Maria Göransdotter (Umeå: Umeå universitet, 2008).

'Women's Bank Sets Trust Company Plan', *New York Times*, 27 November 1973.

Zelizer, Viviana. 'How I Became a Relational Economic Sociologist and What Does That Mean?', *Politics & Society*, 40, 2 (2012), 145–174.

Zelizer, Viviana. *Economic Lives: How Culture Shapes the Economy* (Princeton: Princeton University Press, 2011).

Zelizer, Viviana. *Morals and Markets: The Development of Life Insurance in the United States* (New York: Columbia University Press, 1979).

Zelizer, Viviana. *The Purchase of Intimacy* (Princeton, NJ: Princeton University Press, 2005).

Zelizer, Viviana. *The Social Meaning of* Money (Princeton, NJ: Princeton University Press, 1994).

Zuboff, Shoshana. *The Age of Surveillance Capitalism: The Fight for the Future and the New Frontier of Power* (London: Profile Books, 2019).

Index

A
advertising, 8, 10, 12, 32, 34, 42, 46, 55, 65–67, 85, 95, 102, 107, 111, 112, 119, 121, 128, 134, 135, 137, 148, 149, 152, 161, 180, 190–192
Aléx, Peder, 152
algorithm (algorithmic etc.), 92, 168, 206
Alsén, Hans, 153, 155, 158, 251, 252
American Airlines, 192
American Express, 97, 183
Anderberg, Ingvar, 93, 225, 237
anti-credit, 50, 163
　anti-credit discourse, 90
　anti-credit ethos, 91, 201
　anti-credit ideology, 150
　anti-credit norms, 50
　anti-credit sentiments, 143
anti-socialist (agenda, ideology, mindset), 17, 84, 88, 200
Antitrust Ombudsman, 178, 186
Arbetarnas Bildningsförbund, Workers' Educational Association (ABF), 152
ATM, ATM cards, 11, 58, 93, 115–117, 184
Atomenergi AB, 177
Attman, Arthur, 137
Avanza bank, 197

B
bancarisation, 6, 205
BankAmericard, 95, 109, 119, 146, 183, 191
bank bus, 34
bank consultant, 72, 73, 78, 82
bank customers, 23, 29, 49, 53, 55, 57, 79, 84, 86, 87, 170, 173, 179, 180, 200
Bankers' Association, Swedish (Svenska Bankföreningen), 12, 21, 37, 39, 40, 52, 53, 55, 108, 159, 171, 173, 175, 177–179, 186–188, 190, 203
BankID, 1, 25, 165, 194, 195, 197, 204
bank identity cards, 171, 172, 177, 183, 186

bankification, 6, 7, 13, 14, 16, 19, 22, 26, 30, 57, 93, 165, 199, 202, 203, 205, 206
bankification of everyday life, 4, 6, 15, 19, 22, 23, 26, 30, 31, 56, 57, 62, 165, 193, 194, 198–200, 203–205, 207
Bank Inspection Board (Bankinspektionen), 12, 45, 54, 55, 160, 178, 186, 219
bankminded, 3, 9, 26, 46, 55, 69, 170, 203, 207
bank staff, 48, 170, 174
  bank clerk(s), 171, 173, 180
  bank employee(s), 51
  bank official(s), 3, 77, 78, 85
  bank teller(s), 171, 172
Barclays Bank, 58
Belfrage, Claes, 15
Berggren, Henrik, 15
biometric identification, 185
Board for Identity Documents, 177, 178, 186
Bohman, Gösta, 160
boundary work, 25, 133, 140
boycott of cheques. *See* cheque boycott
breadwinner–homemaker, 47, 74
  breadwinner–homemaker family, 64
  breadwinner–homemaker household, 85
Brevskolan (the correspondence institute of the consumer cooperative movement), 152
Britain, 7, 14, 19, 30, 39, 58, 87, 205, 211, 215, 220, 223, 234, 246, 253, 256, 262, 263. *See also* United Kingdom
budget, 19, 47, 55, 80–86, 92, 102, 109–111, 201
  budget consultant, 24, 83
  budget expert, 81, 83, 84

budget templates, 81, 83, 85, 92
household budgets, 12, 81, 82, 201
Budget Bureau, Taxpayers', 17, 81
budgeting, 55, 81, 102, 201
Bureau for Economic Information, 17
business history, 10, 19, 133, 146

C
Canada, 121, 205
Carte Bleue, 100, 107
cash, 31, 33, 35–39, 45, 46, 50–52, 58, 67, 96, 102, 108, 114, 116, 117, 121, 122, 129, 150, 157, 180, 184, 187, 188, 191, 192, 197, 201, 206
  cash-only policy, 50, 105, 144
  cash payment(s), 24, 51, 58, 102, 103, 107, 108, 121, 154, 201
  substitute for cash, 46
cashless, 114, 170, 207
  cashlessness, 109, 198
  cashless society, 19, 46, 109, 188, 194, 197
Cason, Sven Å., 8, 10, 99–103
Ceaverken, AB, 177
Central Bank, 188, 197. *See also* Riksbank
central register, 167, 177
charge account, 103, 105
charge plates, 183
cheque(s), 8, 16, 23, 31, 32, 37, 39–58, 65, 79, 108, 154, 170, 175, 178–180, 187, 200, 206
  cheque account(s), 2, 20, 23, 26, 29, 31, 35–45, 47–49, 51, 53–57, 79, 83, 86, 108, 110, 121, 140, 165, 173, 201, 203
  cheque accounts for wages (incl. cheque-account wages), 2, 7, 23, 25, 30, 34, 48, 50, 51, 58, 65, 73, 126, 140, 161, 170, 171, 179, 193, 201, 202

INDEX 291

chequebook, 19, 23, 29, 35, 37, 39–42, 44, 45, 47, 55, 57, 92, 173, 175, 179
cheque boycott, 58, 108, 178, 179, 182
cheque fraud, 52, 54, 171, 173, 175, 178, 179
child benefit, 33, 64, 66, 67
child benefit account (*barnbidragskonto*), 16, 49, 66, 201
Chile, 205
China, 207
Citibank, 192
citizen's card, 172
civil registration number (*folkbokföringsnummer*), 186
class, 3, 10, 11, 19, 23, 30–33, 42, 44, 45, 52, 57, 106, 157, 200, 203
class-based categorisations, 57
collective bargaining agreements (*kollektivavtal*), 40
collectivism, 156
commercial banks, 2, 11–13, 16, 18, 21, 23, 24, 29, 30, 32, 33, 40–43, 48, 51, 53, 54, 56, 58, 63–65, 67–69, 79, 84, 87, 95, 107, 116, 171, 177, 182, 190, 200, 201, 203, 204
commercial surveillance, 19, 165, 198
computer, 112, 169, 177, 180, 185, 192, 197
computer age, 168, 185, 190
computerisation, 26, 42, 135, 168, 170, 192, 202
computerised personal identification, 184
computer system, 113, 194
computer technology(ies), 7, 24, 109, 119, 120, 138, 187, 201, 206

connected lives, 9, 62
conscientious worker (*skötsamma arbetaren*), 47
consultant. *See* bank consultant
Consumer Agency (The Swedish Consumer Agency, Konsumentverket), 111, 128, 148, 153
consumer choice, 121, 127, 156, 158, 160, 162
consumer cooperative movement, 12, 16, 56, 58, 76, 90, 117, 126, 157, 161, 162, 201, 202
Consumer Cooperative Union (Kooperativa Förbundet, KF), 21, 25, 50, 89, 143, 150
consumer credit, 2, 5, 7, 8, 13, 16, 18, 19, 24, 25, 60, 55–58, 80, 89–112, 119–121, 126–130, 134–151, 155, 156, 161, 162, 202, 205
consumer credit legislation, 98, 99, 136, 161
criticism of consumer credit, 90, 91, 112, 145
opposition against consumer credit, 154
Consumer Credit Act, 99, 110, 129, 161
consumer debt, 19, 92
consumer demand, 129, 153, 163
consumer education, 16, 69, 75–77, 87
consumer experts, 75, 79, 87
Consumer Institute. *See* State Institute of Consumer Affairs
consumerism, 7, 19, 48, 57, 96
consumerist decade, 199
Consumer Ombudsman, 110, 142, 153
consumer policy, 7, 13, 87, 90, 128, 129, 152–154

consumer protection, 110, 122, 125
consumption smoothing, 56, 58, 110, 201
ContoFöretagen, 95, 96, 112, 116, 130, 138, 139, 142. *See also* InterConto
Cook, Terry, 21
cooperative credit card, co-op card, 151, 155, 202
cooperative ideology, 126, 151, 156, 162
cooperative movement. *See* consumer cooperative movement
cooperative shops, 50, 90
Cooper, Melinda, 20
co-op movement. *See* consumer cooperative movement
CR80 format, 181
credit. *See also* consumer credit
  credit as convenience, 103, 105
  credit as natural right, natural credit, 108, 136, 144, 148, 157
  credit as necessity, 103, 105, 121
  credit-critical voices, 91
  credit criticism, 90
credit bureau, 89, 90
credit card(s)
  credit card as a certificate of trust, 24, 102, 104–107, 109, 112, 121
  credit card as modern money, 24, 102, 107–109
  credit card drops, 117
  credit card industry, 89, 91, 97, 99, 117, 119, 122, 147, 149, 190
  credit cards statistics, 97
  criticism of credit cards (incl. opposition against, aversion against), 90, 159
Credit Information Act, 106
credit regulation(s), 30, 33, 99

credit reporting, 106, 169, 188, 189
Credit Reporting Act, 189
credit restrictions, 49, 91, 95, 99, 111
credit scoring, 57, 106, 169, 189
creditworthiness, 5, 104, 105, 107, 121, 127
Cronholm, Gunilla, 112
Cronsioe, Frideborg, 68, 69, 82, 84
cultural economy, 18, 20
cultural history, 4, 10, 198
cultural technologies, 20, 201
current accounts, 7, 19, 23, 29, 32, 42, 45, 49, 68
customer registers, 170, 186–188, 190

D
Data Act, the Swedish, 190
Data Inspection Board, 190
debit cards, 116, 121, 184, 194
definancialised, 6, 206
de Goede, Marieke, 20, 132
department store credit, 240
department stores, 84, 93, 96, 103, 105, 116, 151, 163, 179
depersonalisation of banking, 198
deregulation, 3, 4, 14, 16, 22, 29, 119, 198, 199
destigmatisation (incl. destigmatise, destigmatising), 2, 19, 24, 92, 93, 103, 114, 175
device, 20, 23, 24, 81, 91, 93, 100, 102, 103, 108–110, 114, 117, 120–122, 127, 169, 170, 194, 199, 201, 203
  financial device, 8, 9, 24, 26, 47, 93
  market device, 92
de-vicing, 92, 93, 109, 117, 121
  de-vicing strategy/ies, 24, 102, 103, 105, 107, 109, 112, 114, 117, 121
Deville, Joe, 183

devising, 93
Dichter, Ernest, 137, 249
digitalisation, 165, 198
digital payments, 184
digital regime of identity verification, 26, 166, 169
Diners Club, 97
  Diners Club card, 105, 113
direct deposit (wages), 35, 36, 39–42, 50, 51, 86, 206. *See also* cheque accounts for wages
documentary regime of identity verification (incl. documentary identification regime), 185, 193, 202
domestication (incl. domesticate), 1, 4, 8, 9, 15, 16, 20, 23–25, 30, 62, 64, 85–87, 91, 93, 99, 100, 102, 126, 132, 133, 149, 161, 163, 181, 200–202
domestic finance, 68
domesticity, 24, 62, 64, 67, 84, 86, 87
domestic money, 1, 24, 77, 84, 87, 201. *See also* domestic finance
domestic science, 84
Domus (department store chain owned by KF), 153, 163
drive-in banks, 34
driving licence, 171, 177, 179, 180
Dun & Bradstreet, 106, 189

E
Eastern Europe, 7, 9, 206, 207
economic independence, 63, 64, 80. *See also* financial independence
economic life, 5, 8, 9, 18, 20, 30, 87, 92
economics of the home, 76
Edwards, Amy, 19, 87
effective interest rate, 110, 129
Effosse, Sabine, 63

Ehrlemark, Gunnar, 191
electronic payments, 193. *See also* online payments
Elinder, Erik, 8, 10, 18, 22, 25, 95, 112, 114, 116, 126, 130–132, 134–147
emotion(s), (incl. affection), 24, 52, 62, 66, 75, 77, 82, 87, 154, 156, 158, 162, 201
Enterprise Fund (Näringslivets fond), 17, 18
Equal Credit Opportunity Act, 63
equity investment(s), 24, 84, 203, 204
Eriksson, Nancy, 85
Erlander, Tage, 129
Eurocard, 97, 119
Eurofinas, 89, 99
Europe, 3, 7, 15, 30, 89, 91, 94, 99–101, 103, 120, 122, 167, 168, 184, 195
  European card industry, 100
  European countries, 3, 121, 207
  European societies, 205
European Union (EU), 195
Expressen, 70, 71, 115, 224, 230, 258

F
Facebook, 168, 194
facial recognition, 185, 194
family, 8, 9, 17, 24, 47, 48, 62–64, 71, 81, 82, 84–87, 109, 159, 167, 192, 193, 201, 203
  family finances, 47, 71, 81, 82, 84, 85, 201
fashion show, 61, 69, 75, 79
FBA. *See* Fredrika Bremer Association
Federation of Swedish Merchants (Köpmannaförbundet), 94, 173, 179
fees, 49, 53, 57, 74, 126, 200, 207
femininity, 24, 67, 83

feminist movement, 76. See also women's organisations
feminst banks, 63
financial actors, financial agency, 18, 63, 64, 200. See also financial subjects
financial consumer, 19, 50, 55, 56, 79, 87
financial consumerism, 47, 48, 57
financial department store (incl. department store of finance), 19, 24, 48, 53, 87
financial device. See device
financial education, 16, 17, 55, 57, 62, 80, 82, 83, 110, 111
financial educators, 170
financial freedom, 102, 110, 121
financial history, 4, 10, 132
financial identification society, 193
financial inclusion, 205
financial independence, 17, 82, 84, 88. See also economic independence, and financial self-relience
financial information system, 187, 188
financialisation, 4–7, 9, 15, 26, 31, 86, 169, 198, 204, 206
financialisation of everyday life, 5–7, 14, 19, 26, 30, 31, 56, 57, 62, 203
financialised daily life, 14, 206
financial knowledge (incl. financially knowledgeable), 76, 110, 200
financial planning, 81, 109–111, 121
device for financial planning, 24, 102, 109
financial rationality, new, 13, 111, 121, 155, 156, 159, 163, 206
unlearning of old financial rationalities, 202
financial regulation(s), 3, 7, 57, 199

financial self-reliance, 17. See also financial independence
financial subject(s), 20, 22, 23, 26, 31, 57, 200. See also financial actor, financial agency
financial surveillance, 207
financial thinking, 4, 6, 8, 15, 17, 26, 45, 48, 57, 84
financing company, 97, 99, 119
Finax, 111, 159
Folkets Hus, 61
Foucauld, Foucaldian, 5, 23, 31, 62, 92, 127
Fourcade, Marion, 57, 106, 169
France, 6, 30, 39, 107, 205, 206
Fredrika Bremer Association (FBA), 68
free consumer choice, 156, 160, 162
free enterprise, ideology of, 128, 134
Friedman, Milton, 56
functionalism, 76

G
Gates, Kelly, 185
gender, 2, 3, 10, 19, 23, 24, 58, 61–63, 83, 85, 86, 166, 200, 203
gendered, 62, 63, 82
gender equality, 83, 199
Gieryn, Thomas, 133, 140
Global Financial Database, 205
Golden Everyday (women's conferences), 61, 68–70, 73, 77–79, 82, 87, 201
Google, 168
Göteborgs Ekonomicentral, 130, 137, 139
governmentality, 5, 31, 32
government inquiry, 36, 90, 98, 119, 136, 178, 179, 188
Guseva, Alya, 206

H

Hammer, Ferenc, 8
Handelsbanken, 2, 10, 18, 21, 24, 30, 32, 34, 36, 40–43, 45, 49, 61, 64, 66–68, 72, 73, 78, 79, 83, 85–87, 94, 133, 171, 192
Hansen, Per, 132, 150
Hart, Keith, 19
Hayek, Friedrich von, 134
Healy, Kieran, 57, 106, 169
Helgesson, Claes-Fredrik, 92
Heurgren, Sven, 153
Higgs, Edward, 166
Hildebrand, Karl-Gustav, 133
Hock, Dee, 114
home economics, 76. *See also* domestic science; economics of the home
Home Research Institute, 76, 128
household
  household budget, 12, 81, 82, 201
  household economy, 62
  household expenses, 81, 85
  households' money, 5, 6, 34
housekeeping money, 24, 47, 71, 81, 83, 84
  housekeeping money-mentality, 69
housewife(s), 47, 76, 85, 200
  housewife films, 69
Housewives' Association, 70
Hungary, 8

I

IBM, 184
Ica, 204
ID card(s), 20, 58, 165, 169, 171, 173, 175, 177–186, 194, 195, 202. *See also* identity card(s); ID document(s), identity documents
ID checks, 187, 194, 202
IdentiData, AB, 184
identification, 25, 26, 57, 58, 105, 166–195, 202, 204
  identification practices, 25, 173, 176, 193, 194, 204
  shame of identification, 174
identities, 2, 5, 31, 45, 62, 113, 114, 116, 165–195, 197, 200, 203
  computerised identities, 169
  digital identities, 195
  official identities, 165, 167, 169
  paper identities, 169
identity, 2, 3, 10, 19, 20, 23, 25, 30, 51–53, 57, 58, 105, 134, 165–195, 197, 200, 202, 203
  documented identity/ies, 175
  embedded identity/ies, 175
  identity checks, 173, 175, 178, 181, 184, 187
  identity management, 166, 168, 170, 187, 195, 202
  national identity/ies, 167, 169, 172
  proof of identity, 174, 175, 184, 188, 194
  wage-earner identity/ies, 30, 31, 52
identity card(s), 171–173, 176, 177, 179, 181, 183, 184, 202. *See also* ID cards, ID, document(s)
  post offices' identity card, 171, 177
identity documents, 2, 25, 52, 165–167, 169, 171–174, 176–179, 185, 186, 224
ideological
  ideological beliefs, 135, 161–163
  ideological boundaries, 22, 25, 206
  ideological boundary work, 25
  ideological change, 25
  ideological connection, 41
  ideological reasons, 41
  ideological views, 25, 130, 149, 161
ideology, 3, 10, 17, 128, 130, 134, 150, 152, 155, 163, 201

ID-kort, AB, 176, 177, 179–181, 183–186
Ikano Bank, 193
Ikea, 94, 130, 192, 193, 204
Ikea Family card, 192, 193
inflation (incl. inflationary economy), 110, 111, 119, 127
information card, 114, 191
information system, 187, 188
insurance, 31, 68, 85, 92, 192, 200, 204
insurance companies, 16, 204
InterConto, 10, 21, 25, 95, 96, 112–115, 117, 130, 146–150, 163, 190, 192, 202
interest rates, 9, 12, 13, 41, 42, 157, 207
International Organisation for Standardisation (ISO), 181
intimacy, 1, 9, 62, 64, 67, 82, 87, 192, 201, 203
intimate relationship, 1, 2, 77, 170, 192–194, 201–204, 206
investment, 2, 3, 5, 7, 8, 12, 15, 24, 42, 43, 47, 49, 56, 57, 68, 81, 83, 135, 138, 197, 203, 204, 206
    investment culture, 13, 19, 204, 206
    popularisation of equity investment, 203
investment clubs, 203
isotope technology, isotope marking, 177

J
Japan, 205

K
Kenya, 205
Keynesian, 132, 152
KF, 89, 143, 144, 150–155, 157–160, 163. *See also* Consumer Cooperative Union (Kooperativa Förbundet)
Konsum (Konsum shops), 126, 153, 154, 158, 160, 163
Köpkort, 10, 21, 56, 58, 93, 94, 96, 99, 101–110, 112, 114–119, 130, 141, 150, 161, 190
Kreditbanken, Sveriges Kreditbank, 29, 37, 41, 54, 55, 58, 175, 182, 186, 187
Kreditregister AB, 89, 106
Kuuse, Jan, 132, 137–142, 145–149

L
labour market, 61, 64, 68
labour movement, 12, 90, 152, 157, 161, 163, 201
Larkin, Ken(neth), 146
Larsson, Lena, 75
Lauer, Josh, 106
Lazarus, Jeanne, 6, 170
Lee, Francis, 92
Lehtonen, Turo-Kimmo, 49, 200
Lettström, Fredrik, 89, 90, 235, 239, 243
Lindström, Eric, 10, 34, 49, 230
liquidity quotas, 12, 14, 33
LM Ericsson (Telefonaktiebolaget LM Ericsson), 137, 180
LO (the Swedish Trade Union Confederation), 128, 152, 164
love, 9, 62, 67, 74, 75, 80, 87
loyalty card(s), 112, 165, 192
Lundahl, Stig, 154–156
Lundberg, Willy Maria, 75, 90, 235, 238
Lyckoslanten, children's magazine, 90, 134
Lyon, David, 177

M

machine reading (of the cards), 184
magnetic stripe, 92, 181, 184
Mandell, Lewis, 97, 147, 149
Market Court (Marknadsdomstolen), 186
market devices, 92
market economy, 66, 101
market engineering, 200
marketing, 2, 6, 8, 10, 11, 16, 21, 22, 25, 34, 47–49, 53, 62, 64, 67, 73, 91, 93, 95, 99, 101, 109, 110, 112, 114, 121, 125, 130, 134, 137, 140, 147, 149, 160, 190, 191
market-liberal views, 162
market pragmatism, 157
marriage legislation (incl. matrimonial legislation), 63, 64, 68, 80
Martin, Randy, 4, 86
mass consumer mentality, 96
mass consumer society, 64, 158, 183
mass investment culture. *See* investment culture
MasterCard, 25, 94, 115, 118
Mattsson, Helena, 76
McFall, Liz, 20, 93
means of payment, 54, 58, 107–109, 121, 173, 179
memory of the state, 20, 166
micro-infrastructure
   micro-infrastructure(s) of consumer credit, 90, 91, 127
   micro-infrastructure(s) of everyday finance, 15, 23, 29, 199
   micro-infrastructure(s) of financial surveillance, 166
Ministry of Finance, 90, 149, 161, 179
Moberg, Eva, 85, 234
modern money, 102, 107, 190, 201
Mont Pélerin Society, 134
morality, moralities
   moral attitudes, 21, 149
   moralities of debt, 2, 24, 91, 122
   moral values, 3, 24, 101
   moral technologies, 19, 102, 120
mortgages, 5, 8, 14, 197, 203, 204, 206
Mrs World's Economic Affairs, 69, 70
mutual fund(s), 7, 19, 24, 49, 204

N

National Police Board, 173, 176, 178
neoliberalism, neoliberal(s), 127, 128, 134, 150
New Zealand, 205
Nilson Report, the, 148
Nilson, Spencer, 97, 147
NK, Nordiska Kompaniet (department store), 96
Nordic countries (incl. Nordic welfare regime and Nordic social democratic welfare regime), 2, 64, 67, 69. *See also* Scandinavian countries
November Revolution, 14, 161
Nygren, Elsa, 78, 79, 233

O

Obs (chain of supermarkets owned by KF), 153, 158
O'Dwyer, Rachel, 19
oikonomisation, 9
Olsen, Niklas, 128
Olsson, Kent, 132, 138, 139, 142, 247, 249, 250
Olsson, Reine, 112, 138, 249
Olsson, Ulf, 133
online payment, 107, 109, 116, 187–189
Ossandon, José, 9

Our Economy (Kursverksamheten Vår Ekonomi), 17
overdraft(s), 45, 52–54, 105, 154

P
Pantzar, Mika, 49
paper-based regime of identification, 26, 166, 167. *See also* documentary regime
Parliament, 127, 148, 160, 172, 173
passport, 167, 169, 171, 172, 177
payment cards, 115, 183, 184, 207
payment devices, 169
payroll services, 23, 29, 35, 37, 77
Pellandini-Simányi, Lena, 8
pension(s), 1, 5, 15, 34, 68, 203
people's home *(folkhemmet)*, 15, 193
personal finance advisor, 24, 72
personal identity number *(personnummer)*, 179, 186, 187
personalisation, 191, 194, 206
  personalised marketing, 114
  personalised selling, 191
personkonto, 187
Peterson, Thage G., 129
Petre, Gunnel, 18, 81–83, 234
plastic card(s), 58, 92, 93, 108, 115, 116, 119, 121, 165, 169, 170, 183, 184, 192–194, 207
plasticisation of identity, 184
plastic money, 26, 109, 181
plastic regime of identification (incl. plastic regime of identity verification), 26, 165, 170, 193, 194, 202
plastic(s), 20, 25, 26, 92, 105, 109, 113, 166, 170, 171, 180
Polaroid, 178, 184, 186
Poovey, Mary, 1, 132, 209
popular finance, 18, 62, 87

popular movement(s) (incl. social movements), 7, 12, 15, 25, 126, 155, 161, 163, 202
popular statistics, 66
population register(s), 166, 169, 177
post-communist countries *(incl.* post-socialist countries, post socialist Eastern Europe), 6, 7, 92, 206
post office(s), 171, 176, 177, 180, 186
Post Office Bank (incl. Post Office Savings Bank), 11, 30, 37, 38, 187
post-purchase saving(s), 50, 83, 156, 201
priest's certificate, 166, 167
privacy, 168, 187, 190
public relations (PR), 9, 32, 34, 66, 87
  public relations of free enterprise, 66, 87

R
Rabén & Sjögrén (publishing house), 142–145, 152
rational consumer, 152, 154, 200
rational consumption, 152
rationally calculating, 136
register-based data, 191
regulatory legislation, 13, 98
relational work, 9, 10, 20, 22, 23, 32, 45, 49, 56, 57, 62, 71, 91, 93, 101, 132, 133, 151, 154, 161, 163, 166, 193, 200, 202, 206
Reutersvärd, Maud, 73–75, 78, 230, 231
revolving credit, 94, 103, 105, 107, 109, 111, 127
right to credit, (incl. *The Right to Credit*), 130, 136, 138, 139, 141–143, 150

Riksbank (Sweden's Central Bank), 12, 21, 33, 99. *See also* Central Bank
Rikskort, 97
Robertson, Craig, 167
Rollfilm, 184–186
Rona-Tas, Akos, 207
Rothfjell, Eric, 185, 186, 261
Rule, James, 191
rural banks, 11
Rydenfelt, Sven, 134, 135, 248

S
Säljinstitutet, 135
saving after the purchase. *See* post-purchase saving
savings accounts, 13, 30, 32, 38
savings banks, 11–13, 16, 18, 30, 32, 33, 37, 38, 41, 42, 47, 50, 63, 90, 116, 117, 119, 120, 134, 135, 149, 177, 190, 204, 219, 229, 235, 243, 250, 259
savings banks' Bureau of Information (Sparfrämjandet), 134
Savings Banks' Card (*sparbankskortet*), 116, 119
Savings Banks Act of 1955, 13
savings campaigns, 33, 134, 135
savings clubs, 43, 48, 50, 56, 200
savings-loan, savings-loan account, 19, 48, 49, 77, 79, 80, 93, 201
savings propaganda, 33, 135
Scandinavian countries, 197. *See also* Nordic countries
Schengen, 195
Science, Technology and Society Studies (STS), 5, 92
Scott, James C., 169
seeing like a market, 169, 189, 190, 194
sensory regime (of identification), 167
Sewell, William, 18
shame of identification, 174
Shareholders' Association, 18, 203
shareholding, 68, 73, 83
shares, 49, 55, 79, 83, 84, 95, 128, 184, 201
SIBOL project, 187–190
Skandinaviska Banken, 21, 32, 34, 35, 40, 41, 44, 66–69, 78, 79, 82, 84, 94, 95, 175
small deposits, 13, 33, 34, 66, 199
social democracy, 150, 152, 202
social democratic, 2, 3, 15, 87, 90, 106, 129, 152, 199
Social Democratic Party, 128, 129, 135, 140, 142
Social Democrat(s), 127
social engineering, 4, 76, 128, 200
social loans, 94
social movements. *See* popular movements
social payments, 16, 34, 57, 207
social security, 2, 30, 33, 94, 171
socio-technical devices, 121
Söderström, Bruno, 137, 140
sovereign consumer, 56, 128, 137, 152–154, 162
Spain (incl. Spanish), 63
State Institute of Consumer Affairs (the Consumer Institute), 72, 75, 76, 84, 87, 128
statement of account, 109
Statistics Sweden (Statistiska Centralbyrån), 188
Stenfors, Alexis, 15
Stockholm School of Economics, 89, 90
Stockholms Enskilda Bank, 21, 119
Stockholms Konto-Ring, 94, 112
Stockholm's Savings Bank, 116
Stockholm Stock Exchange, 68
Stock Promotion Foundation (Aktiefrämjandet), 18, 203

Stolpe, Herman, 95, 96, 134, 148, 163, 235, 238
Studieförbundet Näringsliv och Samhälle, the Centre for Business and Policy Studies (SNS), 145, 149
study circles, 17, 95, 126, 131, 144, 150, 155, 163
surveillance, 167, 168, 176, 191, 194
surveillance capitalism, 168, 169, 192
Swedberg, Richard, 76
Swedish Institute for Opinion Research (SIFO), 148
Swish (payment app), 197
Systembolaget, 116, 174

T
T&E card(s), 96
tax(es), 43, 55, 64, 67, 85, 127, 203
  high taxes, 17, 81, 127, 136
  tax deduction, tax-deductible, 67, 110, 111, 156, 157
  tax planning, 17, 43
Taxpayers' Association (*Skattebetalarnas Förening*), 17, 18, 81, 83, 84, 88, 126
Taylorian time studies, 76
telephone banks, 204
thrift, 16, 47, 49–51, 57, 58, 83, 90, 96
trade union(s), 12, 35, 39–43, 53, 126, 128, 129, 131, 140, 141, 163, 193, 200, 203
Trädgårdh, Lars, 15
transactional data, 2, 190, 191, 194, 203
transactional identities, 114, 190

U
Ukraine, 205
unbanked groups, 206
United Kingdom (incl. UK), 14, 39, 77, 82, 127, 206. *See also* Britain
United States (incl. US), 7, 14, 39, 57, 62, 63, 82, 94, 96, 99, 106, 109, 117, 121, 145, 167, 183, 185, 207
universal bank card (incl. universal card), 184, 188
Upplysningscentralen (UC, The Credit Reporting Central), 189, 190
uses of history, 133

V
Vargha, Zsuzsanna, 8
Veckans affärer (weekly popular business magazine), 48, 49, 181, 184, 185
Vendor, 97, 119
Venezuela, 205
Venmo (payment app), 197
Visa, 25, 94, 95, 109, 114–117, 119, 125, 130, 146, 147, 183. *See also* BankAmericard
Vi, weekly magazine of the Consumer Cooperative Union, 151, 153, 155

W
wage earner, 9, 13, 16, 23, 26, 29, 31, 36, 37, 44, 45, 50, 51, 53, 56, 57, 128, 153, 199, 200
wage-earner fund(s), 203, 251
wage payments (incl. payment of wages), 23, 39, 41, 50, 56, 200, 206
Wage Savings Scheme (*Lönsparandet*), 43
Wallander, Jan, 40, 78, 85, 221, 232
Wallenberg (family, group), 119, 133, 158

Wallenberg, Marcus, 17, 81
weak consumer(s), 128, 154
welfare offices (*intressekontor*), 200
welfare policies, 127
welfare provisions, 199, 206
welfare reforms, 33, 94
welfare society, 4, 33, 155, 199
welfare state, 1, 3, 4, 12, 13, 16, 22, 24, 26, 30, 31, 56, 57, 62, 68, 81, 85, 87, 106, 128, 152, 153, 198–200, 205, 209
West Bank and Gaza, 205
Westerberg, Rikard, 17
White, Hayden, 139
Wisselgren, Per, 136
women, 8, 11, 17, 22, 24, 61–88, 126, 201
women's participation in the labour market, 64
working women, 47, 74
women's economic rights, 63, 64
women's organisations, 70–72
workplace(s), 15, 23, 37, 40, 41, 43–45, 48, 50, 56, 176, 200, 203
World Bank, 205

Z
Zelizer, Viviana, 9, 31, 62, 66, 82, 87, 92, 93
Zelizerian, 31, 32, 44, 50, 62, 92, 121
Zetterberg, Hans, 148, 250
Zuboff, Shoshana, 168, 169

GPSR Compliance

The European Union's (EU) General Product Safety Regulation (GPSR) is a set of rules that requires consumer products to be safe and our obligations to ensure this.

If you have any concerns about our products, you can contact us on

ProductSafety@springernature.com

In case Publisher is established outside the EU, the EU authorized representative is:

Springer Nature Customer Service Center GmbH
Europaplatz 3
69115 Heidelberg, Germany

www.ingramcontent.com/pod-product-compliance
Lightning Source LLC
Chambersburg PA
CBHW051721190825
31365CB00004B/174